工业互联网工程实践
（双语版）

Engineering Practice of Industrial Internet
(Bilingual edition)

主　编　钟文基　宁爱民　王丽磊
副主编　张存吉　刘泽康　石　巍　董其才　区倩如
参　编　劳　薇　邓丽萍　周　顺　陈前军　莫年发
　　　　张志秀　吴丽萍　陆　腾　颜　靖

北京理工大学出版社
BEIJING INSTITUTE OF TECHNOLOGY PRESS

内 容 简 介

本书以工业互联网典型工程项目为主线，以职业能力为本位，按照岗位职业能力需求，构建教材框架结构；以工作过程为线索，按照从易到难的认知组织内容结构，每个项目包含若干学习任务，关联了该项目下所要求的全部知识与技能。

本书按照"双元编写＋数字资源＋思政元素＋学生中心＋分层教学"的思路进行开发设计，具有职教特色。共6个项目18个工作任务，包括工业互联网介绍、工业互联网网络搭建、工业数据采集设备部署与连接、工业现场数据采集与测试、工业互联网安全实践等内容。

本书可作为高职高专工业互联网技术、计算机网络技术、现代通信技术、物联网技术等相关专业的课程教材，也可用于东盟国家学生来桂留学学习参考教材，还可以用于培养"中文＋职业技能"支撑"一带一路"建设的海外技术技能本土人才的参考书籍。

版权专有　侵权必究

图书在版编目（CIP）数据

工业互联网工程实践：英汉对照／钟文基，宁爱民，王丽磊主编．－－北京：北京理工大学出版社，2024.4
ISBN 978－7－5763－3904－8

Ⅰ．①工… Ⅱ．①钟…②宁…③王… Ⅲ．①互联网络－应用－工业发展－教材－英、汉 Ⅳ．①F403－39

中国国家版本馆 CIP 数据核字（2024）第 089650 号

责任编辑：陈莉华　　**文案编辑**：李海燕
责任校对：周瑞红　　**责任印制**：施胜娟

出版发行	／北京理工大学出版社有限责任公司
社　　址	／北京市丰台区四合庄路6号
邮　　编	／100070
电　　话	／（010）68914026（教材售后服务热线）
	（010）68944437（课件资源服务热线）
网　　址	／http：／／www.bitpress.com.cn
版印次	／2024年4月第1版第1次印刷
印　　刷	／河北盛世彩捷印刷有限公司
开　　本	／787 mm×1092 mm　1/16
印　　张	／22.5
字　　数	／528 千字
定　　价	／69.00元

图书出现印装质量问题，请拨打售后服务热线，负责调换

前言

工业互联网是赋能工业企业、推动工业高质量发展的重要引擎。近年来,随着我国制造业智能制造转型升级步伐不断加快,工业互联网得到了快速发展。基于工业互联网与先进制造技术的深度融合,推动我国工业体系向数字化、网络化和智能化转型,促进了智能制造的发展。

本书以工业互联网典型应用项目为基础,改革传统教材以理论知识传播为主的模式。采用项目式开发,教材内容选取上突出教学内容的实用性和实践性。坚持以岗位职业能力培养为本位,以实践应用为目的,满足职业岗位的需要。

本书是一本活页式教材,可拆解、可组合,符合日新月异的知识变化趋势,适用于个性化教学,能够结合企业需求,对行业新业态、新技术快速应对。教材以模块进阶、项目导向、任务驱动方式编写。把工业互联网的典型应用项目整合为6个工程项目18个工作任务。由浅入深,由易到难,语言简洁明快,浅显易懂,契合学生的心理特点和认知习惯。在每个工作任务创设真实的职业情境,并作为学习的主线贯穿于完成学习任务的全部过程。本书树立以学习者为中心的教学理念,落实以实训为导向的教学改革,是任务驱动教学法的细化和落实。

本书作为广西高水平院校和专业群建设的成果,校企合作"双元"开发,由具有丰富教学经验的教师和企业技术支持一线工程师共同编写。所有案例均源于企业真实项目,反映最新的工业互联网技术发展成果。本书可作为高职高专工业互联网技术、计算机网络技术、现代通信技术、物联网技术等相关专业的课程教材,也可用于东盟国家学生来桂留学学习参考教材,还可以用于培养"中文+职业技能"支撑"一带一路"建设的海外技术技能本土人才的参考书籍。

在本书的编写过程中,参考了有关资料和文献,在此向相关的作者表示衷心的感谢,由于工业互联网技术发展迅速,书中错误和不妥之处在所难免,恳请广大读者批评指正,编者电子邮箱:396860606@qq.com。

编 者

Foreword

The Industrial Internet serves as a vital engine for empowering industrial enterprises and fostering high-quality industrial development. In recent years, with the quickening shift towards intelligent manufacturing in China, the Industrial Internet has experienced swift growth. It facilitates the transformation of China's industrial system towards digitalization, networking, and intelligence, thereby advancing the development of intelligent manufacturing.

This book revolutionizes the traditional pedagogical approach, which predominantly focuses on theoretical knowledge, by adopting a project-based development model. The selection of content emphasizes practicality and applicability, aligning with the vocational ability training as the core, practical application as the goal, and meeting the requirements of specific vocational roles.

Designed as a modular, loose-leaf textbook, it allows for content to be easily reconfigured to keep pace with evolving knowledge. Suitable for personalized teaching, it can be adapted to business needs, swiftly responding to emerging industry patterns and technologies. The textbook is structured in a modular, project-oriented, and task-driven manner, integrating typical Industrial Internet application projects across six engineering projects and eighteen work tasks. The content is straightforward and accessible, aligning with students' psychological characteristics and cognitive patterns. Each work task is anchored by a real-world vocational scenario, guiding the learning process from beginning to end.

This publication is a collaborative effort between high-level institutions and professional groups in Guangxi, utilizing a school-enterprise cooperative model. It is co-authored by seasoned educators and industry engineers, with all cases sourced from actual enterprise projects, showcasing the latest advancements in Industrial Internet technology. The book is intended for use as a course textbook in higher vocational colleges and universities for disciplines such as Industrial Internet Technology, Computer Network Technology, Modern Communication Technology, and Internet of Things Technology. It is also suitable for students from ASEAN countries studying in Guangxi and as a reference for nurturing international technical and skilled personnel in the context of the "Belt and Road" initiative.

During the compilation of this book, the editors have consulted various sources and literature. I extend my heartfelt gratitude to the contributing authors. Given the rapid evolution of Industrial Internet technology, the book may contain errors or inaccuracies. Constructive feedback is welcome, and readers are encouraged to reach out to the editors at the provided email address: 396860606@qq.com.

Compiler

目录

项目 1　走进工业互联网 ·· 1

　　任务 1　认识工业互联网 ·· 1
　　任务 2　使用工业互联网平台 ·· 25

项目 2　工业互联网网络搭建 ··· 49

　　任务 3　构建小型工业互联网网络 ·· 49
　　任务 4　确定计算机所在的网络 ··· 73
　　任务 5　用路由器连接不同的网络 ·· 89
　　任务 6　部署无线工业局域网 ··· 108

项目 3　工业大数据感知与采集 ·· 133

　　任务 7　感知工业大数据 ··· 133
　　任务 8　采集传感器数据 ··· 155
　　任务 9　采集装备控制系统数据 ·· 168
　　任务 10　采集管理软件系统数据 ·· 177

项目 4　工业互联网网络传输 ··· 189

　　任务 11　工业互联网接口技术 ··· 189
　　任务 12　构建工业物联网 ··· 210
　　任务 13　传输工业大数据 ··· 231

项目 5　工业大数据集成与融合 ·· 243

　　任务 14　集成工业大数据 ··· 243
　　任务 15　融合工业大数据 ··· 260

项目 6　工业互联网安全实践 ·· 275
任务 16　认知工业互联网安全框架 ·· 275
任务 17　在网络安全等级保护 2.0 框架下保障工业控制系统安全 ·············· 297
任务 18　部署防火墙保障网络安全 ·· 313

参考文献 ··· 350

Contents

Project 1　Stepping into the World of Industrial Internet ················ 11

   Task 1　Understand Industrial Internet ·· 11
   Task 2　Using the Industrial Internet Platform ·· 35

Project 2　How to Build an Industrial Internet ·· 61

   Task 3　Build a Small-Scale Industrial Internet ······································· 61
   Task 4　Identify the Network to Which the Computer is Connected ············· 81
   Task 5　Connect Different Networks with Routers ··································· 98
   Task 6　Deploy a Wireless Industry LAN ·· 119

Project 3　Industrial Big Data Sensing and Acquisition ························· 143

   Task 7　Sensing Industrial Big Data ·· 143
   Task 8　Acquisition of Sensing Data ·· 161
   Task 9　Acquisition of Equipment Control System Data ··························· 172
   Task 10　Comprehend Acquisition Management Software System Data ········· 182

Project 4　Network Transmission of Industrial Internet ························· 199

   Task 11　Cognize the Industrial Internet Interface Technology ···················· 199
   Task 12　Construction of Industrial Internet of Things ······························ 220
   Task 13　Apprehend Transmission of Industrial Big Data ·························· 236

Project 5　Integration and Fusion of Industrial Big Data ························· 251

   Task 14　Integration of Industrial Big Data ·· 251
   Task 15　Fusion of Industrial Big Data ··· 267

Project 6 Industrial Internet Security Practices 285

Task 16 Understanding the Industrial Internet Security Framework 285

Task 17 Securing Industrial Control Systems in the Framework of Equal Assurance 2.0 304

Task 18 Deploy a Firewall to Secure Your Network 331

References 350

项目 1

走进工业互联网

任务 1　认识工业互联网

认识工业互联网

学习目标

① 了解工业互联网的概念。
② 了解工业互联网的诞生、发展及意义。
③ 了解工业互联网架构。

建议学时

2 课时

工作情境

人工智能、大数据、5G 等新一代信息技术的革命性进步,加速推动工业的智能化变革。某公司作为传统制造企业,在世界经济局势发生深刻变革的当下,为谋求业务的转型升级,公司计划通过工业互联网,构建连接人、机、物、系统的基础网络。现公司需要对员工进行培训,要求员工通过学习,掌握工业互联网技术基础,为今后业务升级提供技术储备。

知识导图

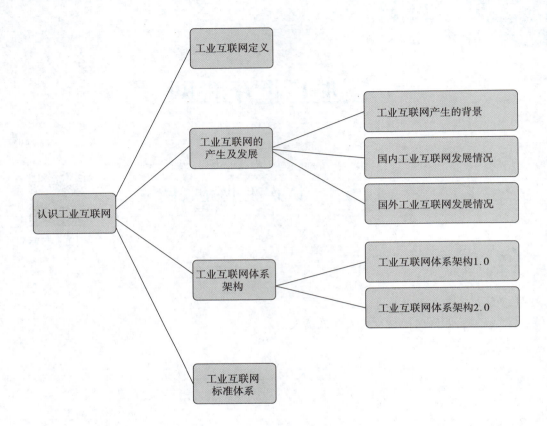

相关知识

1. 工业互联网定义

2012年11月26日,美国通用电气公司(GE)发布白皮书《工业互联网:打破智慧与机器的边界》,首次提出了工业互联网的概念。其认为工业互联网是工业革命和互联网革命的融合。

白皮书中描述工业革命的下一波浪潮是这样的:工业互联网汇集了两大革命的进步——工业革命带来的无数机器、设备组、设施和系统网络,以及互联网革命中涌现的计算、信息与通信系统方面的强大进步。这些发展汇集了三大元素,充分体现了工业互联网的精髓。一是智能机器:将世界上各种机器、设备组、设施和系统网络与先进的传感器、控制装置和软件应用程序相连接的新方式。二是高级分析:利用物理分析、预测算法、自动化,以及材料科学、电气工程及其他了解机器和更大的系统运转方式所需的重点学科的深厚的专业知识的力量。三是工作中的人:在任何时候将人相连,无论他们是在工业设施、办公室、医院中工作,还是在移动中,支持更加智能的设计、运营、维护,以及更高质量的服务和安全性。

概括来说，工业互联网是新一代信息通信技术与工业经济深度融合的新型基础设施，同时也是一种新的应用模式和工业生态。其通过对人、机、物、系统等的全面连接，构建起覆盖全产业链、全价值链的全新制造和服务体系，为工业乃至产业数字化、网络化、智能化发展提供了实现途径，是第四次工业革命的重要基石。

2. 工业互联网的产生及发展

（1）工业互联网产生的背景

传统制造模式陷入发展瓶颈，迫切需要转型升级。主要体现在四个方面：一是设计生产管理的单向驱动。工厂生产任务逐级分解，无法根据现场生产情况动态优化生产计划排产和加工参数，产品设计制造服务逐环节推进，无法及时根据制造、服务改进产品设计。二是设计生产管理间缺乏协同。刚性的装备与生产线无法根据产品设计政策而灵活调整，刚性的资源组织与生产计划无法根据产品变化而灵活调整。三是基于经验的决策。以人为核心、基于经验的决策和优化无法实现更加准确的判断。四是有限范围的资源组织。在范围方面以企业内部资源为主，无法以低成本有效整合分布于全球的优秀资源；在形式方面以采购方式为主，缺乏不同主体间高效、紧密的协作。从以上四大特征总结得出，传统制造模式的生产效率与成本控制、产品质量与产品价值的提升已接近极限，且无法应对灵活多变的市场需求。

云计算技术支撑工业云平台发展。云计算自2006年被提出至今，已从新兴技术发展成为热门技术。它的核心在于通过网络把多个成本相对较低的普通计算机服务器整合成一个具有强大计算能力的系统，并借助基础设施即服务（Infrastructure as a Service，IaaS）、平台即服务（Platform as a Service，PaaS）、软件即服务（Software as a Service，SaaS）等先进的商业模式把强大的计算能力按照用户变化的需求以可伸缩的方式分布到终端用户手中。云计算使存储和计算能力变成一种基础设施服务，人们可以根据需要购买存储和计算能力，按照实际使用付费，从而极大地降低了企业部署服务器的成本。

云计算是工业互联网核心的计算技术之一。在工业互联网平台的实际应用中，云计算呈现成本低、扩展性强和可靠性高的核心价值。随着互联网与各行业的深度融合，未来采用云平台进行计算的需求将呈爆发式增长。工业云是云计算在工业领域的应用，或者说是专门为工业提供的云计算服务。在工业云上的资源是云化工业软件。工业软件的分类决定了工业云也有相应分类，例如工业设计云、工业制造云、工业管理云、工业控制云、工业供应链云、工业标准云等。近年来，以工业云作为基础服务设施，各种工具软件和业务系统开始了上云的历程。云企业资源计划（Enterprise Resource Planning，ERP）、云供应链管理（Supply Chain Management，SCM）已经逐渐进入实用状态。

大数据技术向工业大数据方向发展。工业数据来源于工业系统中人和物的活动，从人的行动、交往到产品的设计、制造、销售、使用与回收。没有数据作为支撑的工业是不可想象的，而在前信息时代，缺乏感知技术去记录，缺乏存储手段去保存，工业数据只能靠简单的工具来操作，数据运算更是一项耗时而低效的工作。直到信息革命的到来，人类在感知技术、传输技术、平台技术和数据分析技术上的突破，使数据的价值越来越大，人们开始有意识地收集各类数据。

在我国信息产业和工业高速发展的今天，工业大数据的发展方兴未艾。工业大数据技术是在工业领域中围绕典型智能制造模式，从客户需求到销售、订单、计划、研发、设计、工艺、制造、采购、供应、库存、发货和交付、售后服务、运维、报废或回收再制造等整个产品全生命周期各个环节所产生的各类数据及相关技术和应用的总称。工业大数据以产品数据为核心，极大延伸了传统工业数据的范围，同时还包括工业大数据相关数据和应用，通过海量数据的分析，找到相关性因素，获得机器智能，解决实际问题。

人工智能技术向工业智能方向发展。人工智能自诞生以来，经历了从早期的专家系统、机器学习，到当前的深度学习等多次技术进步与规模化应用的浪潮。随着硬件计算能力、软件算法、解决方法的快速进步与不断成熟，工业生产逐渐成为人工智能的重点探索方向。通过工业大数据分析获得的工业将成为工业互联网时代工业生产力提高的主要源泉。

工业智能的本质是通用人工智能技术与工业场景、机理、知识结合，实现设计模式创新、生产智能决策、资源优化配置等创新应用。需要具备自感知、自学习、自执行、自决策、自适应的能力，以适应变化的工业环境，并完成多样化的工业任务，最终达到提升企业洞察力，提高生产效率或设备产品性能等目的。例如，工业智能可以用来预测机器的工作情况，在机器出现故障征兆时发出预警，从而可以在故障发生前排除故障因素。工业智能另外的重要应用是其分析能力。对于许多工业上的复杂问题，人们目前还无法对其构造出准确的模型。工业智能使用大数据，可以帮助人们对复杂问题进行分析，找到问题的解决方案。

（2）国内工业互联网发展情况

我国工业互联网的发展经历两个阶段。

第一个阶段是"两化融合"，即信息化与工业化融合发展阶段。两化融合是信息化和工业化的高层次的深度结合，是指以信息化带动工业化、以工业化促进信息化，走新型工业化道路。两化融合的核心就是信息化支撑，追求可持续发展模式。从历史来看，西方发达国家走了一条先工业化后信息化的发展道路，而我国是在工业化还没有完成的情况下，迎来信息化发展浪潮。传统的资源密集、劳动密集型工业体系已经难以为继。推动互联网、大数据、人工智能等新一代信息技术与传统产业融合发展，成为提升研发生产效率、创新售后服务模式、优化资源配置的有效途径。从发展趋势看，互联网自诞生之日起就体现出融合、渗透的特征，随着互联网应用领域从消费环节向制造环节的扩散，两化融合的发展历程也逐步由数字化阶段步入网络化阶段，工业互联网应运而生，智能制造成为两化深度融合的主攻方向。通过映射和具象，设备、系统、生产线、车间、工厂以及生产、管理和服务过程成为网络空间的组成部分，两化融合已经成为网络强国建设的重要推动力量。

大力推进信息化与工业化融合发展，是党中央、国务院作出的一项长期性、战略性部署。党的十五大首次提出"推进国民经济信息化"，党的十六大提出"以信息化带动工业化，以工业化促进信息化"，党的十七大正式提出"大力推进信息化与工业化融合"，党的十八大又提出"推动信息化和工业化深度融合"。

第二个阶段就是当前的工业互联网阶段。2017年11月，国务院印发了《关于深化"互联网+先进制造业"发展工业互联网的指导意见》（以下简称《意见》），提出了深化"互联网+先进制造业"相关要求，部署了未来一段时期工业互联网发展的重点领域和政策措施。《意见》明确了到2025年、2035年、21世纪中叶的发展目标，强调到2025年，基本形成具备国际竞争力的基础设施和产业体系，成为推进工业互联网创新发展的纲领。《意见》提出建设和发展工业互联网的主要任务：一是夯实网络基础，推动网络改造升级提速降费，推进标识解析体系建设；二是打造平台体系，通过分类施策、同步推进、动态调整，形成多层次、系统化的平台发展体系，提升平台运营能力；三是加强产业支撑，加大关键共性技术攻关力度，加快建立统一、综合、开放的工业互联网标准体系，提升产品与解决方案供给能力；四是促进融合应用，提升大型企业工业互联网创新和应用水平，加快中小企业工业互联网应用普及；五是完善生态体系，建设工业互联网创新中心，有效整合高校、科研院所、企业创新资源，开展工业互联网产学研协同创新，构建企业协同发展体系，形成中央地方联动、区域互补的协同发展机制；六是提升安全防护能力，建立数据安全保护体系，推动安全技术手段建设；七是推动开放合作，鼓励国内外企业跨领域、全产业链紧密协作。《意见》还部署了7项重点工程：工业互联网基础设施升级改造工程、工业互联网平台建设及推广工程、标准研制及试验验证工程、关键技术产业化工程、工业互联网集成创新应用工程、区域创新示范建设工程、安全保障能力提升工程。

（3）国外工业互联网发展情况

世界主要国家结合各自的优势和产业特色，加快了工业互联网产业布局。工业互联网成为世界主要国家推进制造业转型升级的共同选择和重要抓手。

德国围绕"工业4.0"战略推进工业互联网在智能制造领域的纵向延伸。在新一轮技术革命和产业变革中，为继续保持其在高端制造领域的全球地位，德国政府以"工业4.0"战略为核心，并将工业互联网作为"工业4.0"的关键支撑，通过研发投入、联邦支持、机构成立等多种方式，长期为相关领域的技术研发提供政策支持和资金投入，加快推动工业互联网在智能制造领域的纵向延伸，鼓励深度应用信息通信技术和信息物理系统，推进智能生产，建设智能工厂，积极抢占产业发展的制高点。

美国依托工业软件领先优势着力推动工业互联网在各产业的横向覆盖。为了在新一轮工业革命中占领先机，美国一直在用政府战略推动先进制造业发展，并将工业互联网作为先进制造的重要基础。自2006年起，美国先后出台一系列法案，对工业互联网关键技术的研发提供政策扶持和专项资金支持，确保美国先进制造业的未来竞争力。

英国为增强本国制造业对全球的吸引力，其政府致力于以智能化创新为导向重构制造业价值链，加快工业互联网布局，积极推动制造业转型升级，重振英国制造业。2022年7月，英国科技和数字经济部对前期发布的《英国数字战略》（*UK Digital Strategy*）进行更新，新增了《数字雇主的签证路线》。该战略旨在通过数字化转型建立更具包容性、竞争力和创新性的数字经济，使英国成为世界上开展和发展科技业务的最佳地点之一，提升英国在数字标准治理领域的全球领导地位，为此，英国将重点关注数字基础，创意和知识产权。数字技能和人才为数字增长畅通了融资渠道，扩大了影响力，提升了英国的国际地位，促进了6个关键领域的发展。

巴西积极对接"工业4.0"，加快工业互联网布局。巴西政府采取了一系列促进互联网和数字经济发展的政策和措施。2007年，将发展信息产业列入"加速增长计划（PAC）"，大幅降低针对信息产业的税收。2016年，发布"智慧巴西"国家统带发展计划，着力推进巴西数字基础设施建设。巴西政府积极推进数字政务发展，提高在线政府指数。

3. 工业互联网体系架构

（1）工业互联网体系架构1.0

在工业和信息化部的指导下，工业互联网产业联盟成立伊始即启动了工业互联网体系架构研究，在总结国内外发展实践的基础上，撰写了工业互联网体系架构报告（1.0版）。作为工业互联网前瞻性、系统性、战略性的顶层设计，旨在推动业界对工业互联网达成广泛共识，以体系架构为牵引，为我国工业互联网的技术创新、标准研制、试验验证、应用实践、产业生态等提供参考和引导，共同推动工业互联网的健康快速发展。

工业互联网体系架构1.0如图1.1所示，其在分析业务需求基础上，提出了工业互联网体系架构，指出网络、数据和安全是体系架构的三大核心，其中"网络"是工业系统互联和数据传输交换的支撑基础，"数据"是工业智能化的核心驱动，"安全"是网络、数据以及工业融合应用的重要前提。

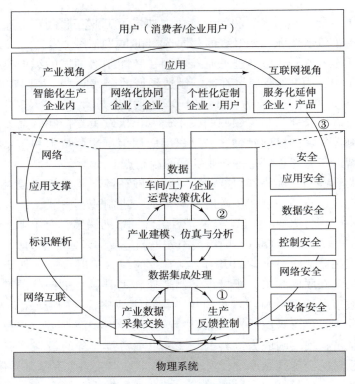

图1.1 工业互联网体系架构1.0

报告对网络、数据、安全三大体系的现状、存在问题、架构和发展趋势等进行了深度剖析。网络体系方面，提出工厂内部网络和工厂外部网络都将发生演进和变化，工厂内部网络呈现扁平化、IP化、无线化及灵活组网的发展趋势，公众网络在终端接入能力、业务能力、服务质量保障、安全性、网络柔性方面不断面临新的需求；IPv6将成为工业互联网发展的必然选择；对机器和产品进行识别的标识解析体系需要变革创新以适应工业智能化的需要。数据体系方面，工业大数据在数据体量、数据分布、数据结构、数据处理速度、数据分析置信度方面具有鲜明的特征，并需要围绕智能制造的需求开展跨层次跨环节数据整合、边缘智能处理、基于云平台的数据集成管理、深度数据分析挖掘和可视化呈现，以实现系统级的数据智能。安全体系方面，设备、网络、控制、应用和数据等不同层面将面临新的安全风险和安全挑战，设备内嵌安全、动态网络安全防御、信息安全和功能安全融合、面向工业应用的灵活安全保障能力、工业数据以及用户数据分类分级保护机制成为未来的发展方向。为有效指导企业的探索与实践，报告还给出了网络、数据、安全三大体系的实施建议。

其中"网络"是工业数据传输交换和工业互联网发展的支撑基础，"数据"是工业智能化的核心驱动，"安全"是网络与数据在工业中应用的重要保障。基于三大体系，工业互联网重点构建三大优化闭环，即面向机器设备运行优化的闭环，面向生产运营决策优化的闭环，以及面向企业协同、用户交互与产品服务优化的全产业链、全价值链的闭环，并进一步形成智能化生产、网络化协同、个性化定制、服务化延伸等四大应用模式。

我国工业互联网体系架构1.0自发布以来，有效指导我国工业互联网技术创新、标准研制、试验验证、应用实践等工作，助推我国工业互联网产业发展。

（2）工业互联网体系架构2.0

当前全球经济社会发展正面临全新挑战与机遇。一方面，上一轮科技革命的传统动能规律性减弱趋势明显，导致经济增长的内生动力不足。另一方面，以互联网、大数据、人工智能为代表的新一代信息技术发展日新月异，加速向实体经济领域渗透融合，深刻改变各行业的发展理念、生产工具与生产方式，带来生产力的又一次飞跃。在新一代信息技术与制造技术深度融合的背景下，在工业数字化、网络化、智能化转型需求的带动下，以泛在互联、全面感知、智能优化、安全稳固为特征的工业互联网应运而生。工业互联网作为全新工业生态、关键基础设施和新型应用模式，通过人、机、物的全面互联，实现全要素、全产业链、全价值链的全面连接，正在全球范围内不断颠覆传统制造模式、生产组织方式和产业形态，推动传统产业加快转型升级，新兴产业加速发展壮大。

在这一背景下，有必要对工业互联网体系架构1.0进行升级，特别是强化其在技术解决方案开发与行业应用推广的实操指导性。具体来说，一是提供一套可供企业开展实践的方法论。重点是构建一套由"业务需求–功能定义–实施部署"构成的方法论，使企业能够结合自身业务特点，明确所需要的工业互联网核心功能，并进而指导相应软硬件系统的设计、开发与部署。二是从战略层面为企业开展工业互联网实践指明方向。重点是明确企业通过工业互联网实现数字化转型的核心方向与路径，结合企业基础，确立商业战略与细分目标，充分发挥工业互联网实践价值，构建企业转型升级优势。三是结合规模化应用需求对功能架构进行升级和完善。重点是从企业工程化应用视角，参考领先企业实践经验与最新技术发展，对工业互联网功能原理进行明确与完善，形成一套实操性更强的网络、平台、安全功能体系。四是提出更易于企业应用部署的实施框架。重点是强化与现有制造系统的结合，明确各层级的工业互联网部署策略，以及所对应的具体功能、系统和部署方式，以便对企业实践提供更强参考作用。基于上述四方面考虑，工业互联网产业联盟组织研究提出了工业互联网体系架构2.0，旨在构建一套更全面、更系统、更具体的总体指导性框架，如图1.2所示。

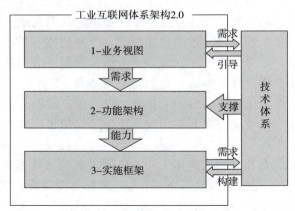

图1.2　工业互联网体系架构2.0

业务视图包括产业层、商业层、应用层、能力层四个层次。其中产业层主要定位产业整体数字化转型的宏观视角，商业层、应用层和能力层则定位企业数字化转型的微观视角。四个层次自上而下来看，实质是产业数字化转型大趋势下，企业如何把握发展机遇，实现自身业务的数字化发展并构建起关键数字化能力；自下而上来看，实际也反映了企业不断构建和强化的数字化能力将持续驱动其业务乃至整个企业的转型发展，并最终带来整个产业的数字化转型。

工业互联网的核心功能架构，是基于数据驱动的物理系统与数字空间全面互联与深度协同，以及在此过程中的智能分析与决策优化。通过网络、平台、安全三大功能体系构建，工业互联网全面打通设备资产、生产系统、管理系统和供应链条，基于数据整合与分析实现IT与OT的融合和三大体系的贯通。工业互联网以数据为核心，数据功能体系主要包含感知控制、数字模型、决策优化三个基本层次，以及一个由自下而上的信息流和自上而下的决策流构成的工业数字化应用优化闭环。

实施框架是整个体系架构2.0中的操作方案，解决"在哪做""做什么""怎么做"的问题。当前阶段工业互联网的实施以传统制造体系的层级划分为基础，适度考虑未来基于产业的协同组织，按"设备、边缘、企业、产业"四个层级开展系统建设，指导企业整体部署。设备层对应工业设备、产品的运行和维护功能，关注设备底层的监控优化、故障诊断等应用；边缘层对应车间或产线的运行维护功能，关注工艺配置、物料调度、能效管理、质量管控等应用；企业层对应企业平台、网络等关键能力，关注订单计划、绩效优化等应用；产业层对应跨企业平台、网络和安全系统，关注供应链协同、资源配置等应用。

1.0版本定义的是功能架构，2.0版本则是一个组合，涵盖功能架构、业务指南、实施框架、技术体系等部分。编制和发布工业互联网体系架构2.0，旨在进一步丰富工业互联网的理论内涵，融合工业互联网最新技术、功能、范式和流程，建立起应用实施的指导框架，以满足数字化转型的时代需求。

4. 工业互联网标准体系

工业互联网标准体系包括基础共性、网络、边缘计算、平台、安全、应用等六大部分，如图 1.3 所示。基础共性标准是其他类标准的基础支撑，网络标准是工业互联网体系的基础，平台标准是工业互联网体系的中枢，安全标准是工业互联网体系的保障，边缘计算标准是工业互联网网络和平台协同的重要支撑和关键枢纽，应用标准面向行业的具体需求，是对其他部分标准的落地细化。

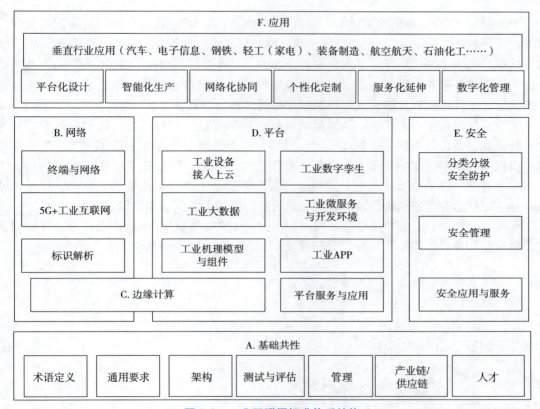

图 1.3　工业互联网标准体系结构

 **任务拓展**

中国制造 2025——从中国制造 2025 看工业互联网与国家发展战略

中国制造 2025 是我国政府提出的一项重要战略规划，旨在推动中国制造业向制造强国迈进。中国制造 2025 战略的核心目标是通过推动信息化、智能化和绿色化等手段，提升中国制造业的技术水平、质量水平和竞争力。其中，工业互联网被视为实现中国制造 2025 战略的关键支撑和重要手段之一。通过工业互联网技术与制造业的深度融合，能实现工业生产的数字化、网络化和智能化，提高制造业的整体效率和竞争力。

工业互联网在实现国家制造强国战略目标中扮演着重要角色。通过推动制造业的智能化、升级和创新，加强供应链管理和运营效率，保障数据安全和加强隐私保护，工业互联网可以提高我国制造业的竞争力和可持续发展能力，推动中国制造业向更高水平迈进。当代大学生应把所学工业互联网专业知识与国家战略紧密关联，肩负责任和使命，将爱国情怀、社会责任感和创新精神投入国家发展建设中，为建设中国制造强国贡献力量。

作业：分析调研，分析工业互联网与中国制造 2025 战略的关系，以及工业互联网对国家发展战略的重要作用，撰写报告分享启发。

Project 1

Stepping into the World of Industrial Internet

Task 1 Understand Industrial Internet

◎ Learning Objective

①Definition of Industrial Internet.
②Origin, development and significance of Industrial Internet.
③A framework for Industrial Internet.

◎ Suggested Hours

2 hours

◎ Work Situations

There is a huge revolutionary advance in new-generation information technology, which mainly includes artificial intelligence, big data and 5G. These technologies are accelerating the intelligent transformation of industry. There is a traditional manufacturing enterprise planning to build a basic network connecting people, machines, objects, and systems through the Industrial Internet, in order to pursue business transformation and upgrading then the world economic situation is undergoing profound changes. Currently, the company is going to conduct a training which requires employees to master the fundamental knowledge of Industrial Internet technology, so as to provide technical reserves for future business upgrades.

Knowledge Map

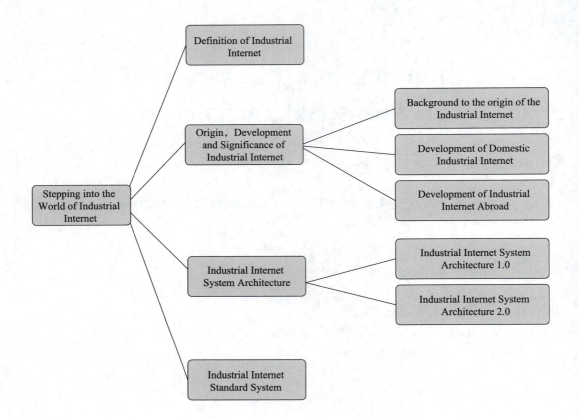

Relevant Knowledge

1. Definition of Industrial Internet

On November 26, 2012, General Electric (GE) released a white paper titled "The Industrial Internet: Breaking the Boundaries Between Intelligence and Machines", which presented the first definition of the Industrial Internet. It posits that the Industrial Internet represents the fusion of industrial revolution and internet revolution.

The white paper outlines the next wave of the industrial revolution, highlighting how the Industrial Internet amalgamates advancements from two significant revolutions. It juxtaposes the industrial revolution, characterized by myriad networks of machines, equipment sets, facilities, and systems, with the Internet revolution, marked by recent and powerful progressions in computing, information, and communication systems. These developments encapsulate three essential elements that define the essence of the Industrial Internet. Firstly, smart machines introduce novel ways of connecting the world's diverse network of machines, equipment groups, facilities, and systems through advanced sensors, controls, and software applications. Secondly, advanced analytics leverage deep expertise across key disciplines to comprehend the operations of machines and larger systems, utilizing physical analysis, predictive algorithms, automation, materials science, and electrical engineering. Thirdly, people at work emphasize the continuous connection of individuals, whether they are situated in industrial facilities, offices, hospitals, or on the move, to support intelligent design, operations, maintenance, and ensure higher quality service and safety.

In essence, the Industrial Internet represents a new infrastructure enabling the deep integration of next-generation information and communication technologies with the industrial economy, introducing a new application mode and industrial ecology. It achieves comprehensive connectivity among people, machines, systems, and other elements, establishing a new manufacturing and service system that spans the entire industrial and value chains. It serves as a pathway towards achieving digital, cyber, and intelligent development within the industry, positioning itself as a pivotal cornerstone of the fourth industrial revolution.

2. Origin, Development and Significance of Industrial Internet

(1) Background to the origin of the Industrial Internet

The traditional manufacturing model faces a development bottleneck and requires urgent transformation and upgrade. This challenge is mainly manifested in four aspects:

Firstly, the existing model relies on one-way drive design and production management, where factory production tasks are decomposed hierarchically, hindering timely adjustments to product design in response to manufacturing and service demands.

Secondly, there is a lack of synergy between design and production management, resulting in rigid equipment and production lines that cannot be flexibly adjusted according to product design policies or changes.

Thirdly, decision-making is often based on experience rather than data-driven insights, limiting the accuracy of judgments and optimizations.

Fourthly, the scope of resource organization is restricted primarily to internal enterprise resources, failing to efficiently integrate globally distributed excellent resources at low costs, leading to a lack of collaboration among different stakeholders.

These characteristics collectively impede the traditional manufacturing model's ability to enhance production efficiency, cost control, product quality, and value, making it ill-equipped to adapt to dynamic market demands.

Cloud computing technology emerges as a solution to support the development of industrial cloud platforms. Since its inception in 2006, cloud computing has evolved from an emerging to a ubiquitous technology, integrating multiple low-cost ordinary computer servers into a powerful computing system accessible via the network. Through innovative business models like Infrastructure as a Service (IaaS), Platform as a Service (PaaS), and Software as a Service (SaaS), cloud computing distributes computing power to users based on their evolving needs in a scalable manner, significantly reducing the cost of server deployment for enterprises.

Cloud computing serves as a core computing technology for the Industrial Internet, offering low cost, high scalability, and reliability in practical applications. With the increasing integration of the internet across various industries, the demand for cloud computing platforms is expected to skyrocket, propelling the growth of industrial clouds. Industrial clouds leverage cloud computing to host cloud-enabled industrial software, which spans various domains such as industrial design, manufacturing, management, control, supply chain, and standards. In recent years, numerous tools, software, and business systems have transitioned to the cloud, including Enterprise Resource Planning (ERP) and Supply Chain Management (SCM), advancing towards practical implementation.

Furthermore, big data technologies are transitioning towards industrial big data, which encompasses data generated throughout the entire product lifecycle within industrial systems. The proliferation of sensing technology and data analysis advancements has transformed industrial data into a valuable asset, driving breakthroughs in perception, transmission, platform, and analysis technologies.

In China, industrial big data is experiencing rapid development, fueling innovation and productivity improvements across the industrial sector. As for artificial intelligence (AI), its evolution is directed towards industrial intelligence, with applications spanning design innovation, intelligent decision-making, and resource allocation optimization within industrial scenarios. Industrial intelligence harnesses AI technologies to predict machine behavior, provide early warnings of malfunctions, analyze complex industrial problems, and optimize production processes. By combining general-purpose AI with industrial knowledge and mechanisms, industrial intelligence aims to enhance enterprise insights, production efficiency, and product performance in the era of the Industrial Internet.

Artificial intelligence (AI) technology is evolving towards industrial intelligence. Since its inception, AI has undergone several waves of technological advancements and widespread applications, starting from early expert systems and machine learning to the current state of deep learning. With rapid progress and continuous maturation of hardware computing power, software algorithms, and solution methods, industrial production has gradually emerged as a key exploration area for AI. The insights gleaned from industrial big data analysis are poised to become the primary driving force of productivity enhancement in the era of the Industrial Internet.

The essence of industrial intelligence lies in achieving innovative applications such as design mode innovation, intelligent decision-making in production, and optimal resource allocation. This necessitates the integration of general-purpose AI technologies with industrial scenarios, mechanisms, and knowledge, along with capabilities for self-perception, self-learning, self-execution, self-decision-making, and self-adaptation. Such capabilities enable AI systems to adapt to evolving industrial environments and perform diverse tasks effectively. The ultimate goal is to enhance enterprise insights, production efficiency, and equipment or product performance. For instance, industrial intelligence can be employed to predict machine behavior and issue early warnings when signs of malfunction arise, allowing for the preemptive elimination of failure factors. Another significant application of industrial intelligence lies in its analytical prowess. Many industrially complex problems defy accurate modeling; industrial intelligence utilizes big data to assist in analyzing these challenges and devising solutions for them.

(2) Development of Domestic Industrial Internet

The development of China's Industrial Internet has undergone two stages. The first stage, known as "integration of the two," signifies the integration and development of information technology and industrialization. This integration represents a high-level and profound merging of informatization and industrialization. Specifically, it involves utilizing information technology to propel industrialization and leveraging industrialization to advance information technology, thereby embarking on the path of new industrialization. At the core of this dual integration is the support of informatization and the pursuit of a sustainable development model. Historically, Western developed countries followed a development trajectory of industrialization followed by informatization. In contrast, China experienced a wave of informatization development before completing industrialization.

The traditional resource-intensive and labor-intensive industrial system is no longer sustainable. Hence, it is imperative to promote the integration and development of new-generation information technologies such as the Internet, big data, and artificial intelligence with traditional industries. This integration will serve as an effective means to enhance R&D and production efficiency, innovate sales and service models, and optimize resource allocation. From a developmental perspective, the Internet has epitomized integration and penetration since its inception. As Internet applications proliferate from consumption to manufacturing, the trajectory of integration of the two is transitioning from the digital stage to the networked stage. The Industrial Internet has emerged, with intelligent manufacturing becoming the primary direction of deep integration. Through mapping and visualization, equipment, systems, production lines, workshops, factories, and production, management, and service processes become integral components of cyberspace. This fusion serves as a significant impetus in China's cyber power construction. The second stage is the current phase of the Industrial Internet. The Chinese government has outlined several key tasks for the construction and development of the Industrial Internet:

Consolidate the network foundation: This involves promoting network transformation and upgrading, increasing speed, reducing charges, and advancing the construction of the marking resolution system.

Build a platform system: Establishing a multi-level and systematic platform development system and enhancing platform operation capabilities through categorized measures, simultaneous promotion, and dynamic adjustment.

Strengthen industrial support and intensify research on key common technologies: This includes accelerating the establishment of a unified, comprehensive, and open Industrial Internet standard system and enhancing the ability to supply products and solutions.

Promote integration and application: Enhancing the level of Industrial Internet innovation and application in large enterprises while accelerating the adoption of Industrial Internet applications in small and medium-sized enterprises.

Improve the ecological system and establish an Industrial Internet innovation center: This entails effectively integrating innovation resources from universities, research institutes, and enterprises to facilitate collaborative innovation in the Industrial Internet industry, academia, and research. It aims to construct a collaborative development system for enterprises and establish a mechanism for central-local linkage and regional complementarity.

Enhance security protection capabilities and establish a data security protection system: This involves promoting the construction of security technology means to safeguard data and system integrity.

Promote open cooperation: Encourage close collaboration between domestic and foreign enterprises across various fields and the entire industry chain.

(3) Development of Industrial Internet Abroad

Major countries in the world have accelerated the Industrial Internet industrial layout by combining their respective advantages and industrial characteristics. Industrial Internet has become a common choice and an important hand for major countries in the world to promote the transformation and upgrading of the manufacturing industry.

Germany is promoting the vertical extension of the Industrial Internet in the field of intelligent manufacturing around the "Industry 4.0" strategy. In the new round of technological revolution and industrial change, in order to continue to maintain its global position in the field of high-end manufacturing, the German government takes the "Industry 4.0" strategy as the core. Industrial Internet is the key support of "Industry 4.0". Through research and development investment, federal support, the establishment of institutions and other means, long-term policy support and financial investment for technology research and development in related fields. To accelerate the vertical extension of the Industrial Internet in the field of intelligent manufacturing. Encourage the in-depth application of information and communications technology and information physical systems, promote smart production, build smart factories, and actively seize the commanding heights of industrial development.

The United States, relying on its leading edge in industrial software, has endeavored to promote the horizontal coverage of Industrial Internet in various industries. In order to occupy the first opportunity in the new round of industrial revolution, the United States has been using government strategies to promote the development of advanced manufacturing. The United States will take the Industrial Internet as the important foundation of advanced manufacturing. Since 2006, the U.S. has introduced a series of bills to provide policy support and special financial support for the research and development of key technologies of Industrial Internet to ensure the future competitiveness of the U.S. advanced manufacturing industry.

In order to enhance the attractiveness of the UK manufacturing industry to the world, the UK government is committed to reconstructing the manufacturing value chain with intelligent innovation. The UK has accelerated the layout of the Industrial Internet, actively promoted the transformation and upgrading of the manufacturing industry, and revitalized the UK manufacturing industry. 2022 In July, the UK Department of Science, Technology and the Digital Economy (DSTDE) updated the UK Digital Strategy, which was published in the previous period, with the addition of a new "Visa Route for Digital Employers". The strategy aims to build a more inclusive, competitive and innovative digital economy through digital transformation. The strategy makes the UK one of the best places in the world to start and grow a tech business, and enhances the UK's position as a global leader in the governance of digital standards. To do this, the UK will focus on digital foundations, creativity and intellectual property. Digital skills and talent open up access to finance for digital growth. In doing so, it extends reach, enhances the UK's international standing and promotes growth in six key areas.

Brazil is actively connecting with "Industry 4.0" and accelerating the layout of Industrial Internet. The Brazilian government has adopted a series of policies and measures to promote the development of the Internet and digital economy. 2007, Brazil included the development of the information industry in the "Plan for Accelerated Growth (PAC)", and drastically reduced taxes on the information industry. 2016, the Brazilian government released the "Smart Brazil" national unified development plan, focusing on promoting the construction of Brazil's digital infrastructure. In 2016, the "Smart Brazil" National Unified Development Plan was released, focusing on promoting the construction of Brazil's digital infrastructure. The Brazilian government is actively promoting the development of digital government and improving the online government index.

3. Industrial Internet System Architecture

(1) Industrial Internet System Architecture 1.0

Under the guidance of the Ministry of Industry and Information Technology (MIIT), the Industrial Internet Industry Alliance has embarked on a comprehensive study concerning the architecture of the Industrial Internet since its inception. Drawing upon insights garnered from both domestic and international development practices, the study has culminated in the production of the Industrial Internet Architecture Report (Version 1.0). This report stands as a forward-thinking, systematic, and strategic top-level blueprint for the Industrial Internet. Its primary objective is to foster industry-wide consensus on the trajectory of the Industrial Internet. With the architecture serving as a guiding framework, the design not only offers valuable reference points but also provides essential guidance for the technological innovation and standard development within China's Industrial Internet landscape. Through collaborative efforts, it endeavors to propel the Industrial Internet towards healthy and rapid advancement.

Displayed in Figure 1.1, the Industrial Internet Architecture Report (Version 1.0) delineates an Industrial Internet architecture derived from a meticulous analysis of business requirements. The report underscores that the architecture's foundation rests upon three primary pillars: network, data, and security. The "network" serves as the fundamental support for interconnecting industrial systems and facilitating data transmission and exchange. Meanwhile, "data" emerges as the central catalyst for driving industrial intelligence forward. Lastly, "security" assumes paramount importance as it lays down the essential groundwork for network, data, and industrial convergence applications to thrive securely and robustly.

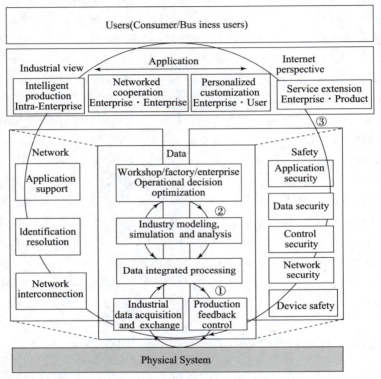

Figure 1.1　Industrial Internet Architecture 1.0

The report delves into a comprehensive analysis of the current state, challenges, architecture, and developmental trends across the three major systems: network, data, and security. In terms of the network system, the report forecasts significant evolution and transformation in both internal and external plant networks. The internal network within plants is projected to trend towards flat, IP-based, wireless, and flexible networking. Meanwhile, the public network is continually confronting fresh demands concerning terminal access capability, service quality assurance, and network flexibility, among others. The adoption of IPv6 is deemed inevitable for the Industrial Internet's progression. Moreover, it stresses the necessity for the adaptation and innovation of machine and product identification systems to meet the requisites of industrial intelligence.

Regarding the data system, industrial big data presents unique characteristics concerning volume, distribution, structure, processing speed, and analysis confidence. Consequently, there's a pressing need to undertake various cross-level and cross-link processing endeavors aligned with the imperatives of intelligent manufacturing. This entails activities such as data integration, edge intelligent processing, cloud platform-based data integration management, deep data analysis mining, and visualization presentation, ultimately culminating in system-level data intelligence.

The security system poses novel challenges and risks for equipment, networks, controls, applications, and data at various levels. Key areas of focus include device-embedded security, dynamic network security defense, and the integration of information security with functional security. Moreover, flexible security capabilities for industrial applications and the establishment of classification and grading protection mechanisms for industrial and user data represent future developmental directions. In order to effectively steer enterprises' exploration and implementation efforts, the report offers practical recommendations for the implementation of the network, data, and security systems.

The Industrial Internet places emphasis on constructing three optimization closures based on the aforementioned systems. These include the optimization closures for machine and equipment operation, production and operation decision-making, and the entire industry and value chain, oriented towards enterprise collaboration, user interaction, and product service enhancement. Additionally, it foresees the emergence of four application modes, namely intelligent production, network collaboration, personalized customization, and service extension.

Since the release of China's Industrial Internet architecture version 1.0, it has served as a guiding beacon for technological innovation, standard development, and overall industrial advancement, effectively catalyzing industrial development efforts.

(2) Industrial Internet System Architecture 2.0

Global economic and social development currently faces a set of novel challenges and opportunities. On the one hand, there's a discernible trend of gradual weakening in the traditional kinetic energy stemming from the previous round of the scientific and technological revolution. This deficiency in endogenous momentum has stunted economic growth. On the other hand, the swift evolution of new-generation information technology has hastened the infiltration and amalgamation of information technology into the real economy, fundamentally altering development paradigms, production tools, and modes of production across various industries, thereby catalyzing a new surge in productivity.

The emergence of the Industrial Internet unfolds within the context of deep integration between the new generation of information technology and manufacturing technology. Characterized by ubiquitous interconnection, comprehensive perception, intelligent optimization, security, and stability, the Industrial Internet stands as a new industrial ecosystem, pivotal infrastructure, and a fresh application model. It facilitates the comprehensive connectivity of all elements, the entire industrial chain, and the entire value chain through the seamless interconnection of people, machines, and objects. Globally, the Industrial Internet continually undermines traditional manufacturing modes, production organizations, and industrial forms, thereby expediting the transformation and upgrading of traditional industries and the rapid development and growth of emerging industries.

In summary, there's a pressing need to upgrade Architecture 1.0, particularly enhancing its practical guidance in developing technical solutions and promoting industry applications. Firstly, it necessitates furnishing enterprises with a set of methodologies for practical implementation, focusing on constructing a methodology comprising "business requirements-function definition-implementation and deployment." This empowers enterprises to delineate the core functions required from the Industrial Internet based on their unique business characteristics, thereby guiding the design, development, and deployment of corresponding hardware and software systems.

Secondly, the framework delineates strategic-level directions for enterprises to embark on Industrial Internet practices, emphasizing the clarification of core directions and pathways for achieving digital transformation. It entails formulating business strategies and segmenting objectives in tandem with the enterprise's foundation, thereby leveraging the value of Industrial Internet practices and fortifying the advantages of enterprise transformation and upgrading.

Thirdly, the architecture undergoes upgrades and enhancements tailored to meet large-scale application needs, elucidating and refining the functional principles of the Industrial Internet from the perspective of enterprise engineering applications. Drawing on the practical experience of leading enterprises and the latest technological developments, this process culminates in the formulation of a more practical network, platform, and security function system.

Fourthly, the framework proposes an implementation framework tailored to facilitate enterprise applications deployment, with a focus on bolstering integration with existing manufacturing systems. It outlines Industrial Internet deployment strategies at each level, along with corresponding specific functions, systems, and deployment methods, furnishing enterprises with a robust reference for practical implementation.

Building upon these considerations, the Industrial Internet Industry Alliance (IIA) has spearheaded research endeavors to propose the Industrial Internet Architecture 2.0. This initiative aims to craft a more comprehensive, systematic, and specific overarching guiding framework, as depicted in Figure 1.2.

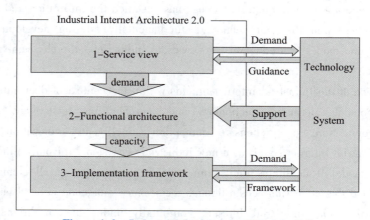

Figure 1.2　Industrial Internet Architecture 2.0

The business perspective encompasses four layers: industry, business, application, and capability. The industry layer primarily focuses on the macro view of overall industry digital transformation, whereas the business, application, and capability layers operate within the micro perspective of enterprise digital transformation. When viewed from the top down, the essence lies in how enterprises seize development opportunities, achieve digital business development, and cultivate key digital capabilities. Conversely, from bottom to top, it reflects the ongoing development of digital capabilities within enterprises, which continuously propel business transformation and development, ultimately fostering digital transformation across the entire industry.

At the heart of the Industrial Internet's core functional architecture lies data-driven comprehensive interconnection and deep collaboration between physical systems and digital space, alongside intelligent analysis and decision-making optimization. Through the construction of three major functional systems—network, platform, and security—the Industrial Internet comprehensively connects equipment assets, production systems, management systems, and supply chains. Leveraging data integration and analysis, it achieves the integration of Information Technology (IT) and Operational Technology (OT), ensuring coherence among the three systems. Central to the Industrial Internet is data, with the data function system comprising three fundamental levels: perception and control, digital modeling, and decision-making and optimization. Additionally, there exists a closed loop of industrial digital application optimization, encompassing bottom-up information flow and top-down decision flow.

The implementation framework serves as the operational blueprint for Architecture 2.0, addressing the "where to do" "what to do" and "how to do" aspects. At present, Industrial Internet implementation is based on the hierarchical division of traditional manufacturing systems, with moderate consideration given to future industry-based collaborative organization. The implementation framework guides system construction across four levels— "equipment, edge, enterprise, and industry" —and steers overall enterprise deployment.

– The equipment layer caters to industrial equipment and product operation and maintenance functions, focusing on applications such as monitoring, optimization, and fault diagnosis.

– The edge layer addresses workshop or production line operation and maintenance functions, emphasizing applications like process configuration, material scheduling, energy efficiency management, and quality control.

– The enterprise layer encompasses key capabilities such as enterprise platform and network, concentrating on applications such as order planning and performance optimization.

– The industrial layer involves cross-enterprise platforms, networks, and security systems, focusing on applications such as supply chain collaboration and resource allocation.

While version 1.0 delineates the functional architecture, version 2.0 integrates additional components, including business guidelines, implementation framework, technical systems, and more. Industrial Internet Architecture 2.0 aims to further enrich the theoretical underpinnings of the Industrial Internet, integrating the latest technologies, functions, paradigms, and processes to establish a guiding framework for application implementation, ultimately meeting the needs of the digital transformation era.

4. Industrial Internet Standard System

The Industrial Internet Standard System comprises six major components: basic commonality, network, edge computing, platform, security, and application, as depicted in Figure 1.3. The basic commonality standards serve as the foundational support for other categories of standards. Network standards constitute the bedrock of the Industrial Internet system, while platform standards act as its central pivot. Security standards ensure the robustness of the Industrial Internet system, and edge computing standards serve as crucial support and key junctions for collaboration between Industrial Internet networks and platforms. Application standards are tailored to the specific needs of industries and represent the practical implementation of other standard components.

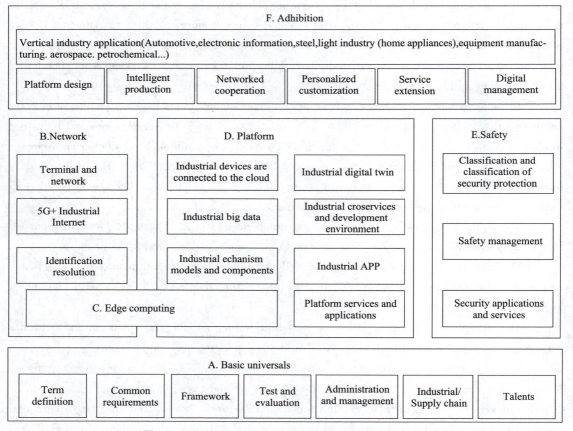

Figure 1.3　Industrial Internet Standards Architecture

 Mission Expansion

Made in China 2025 Strategy—Industrial Internet and National Development Strategy from the Version of "Made in China 2025 Strategy"

The relationship between the Industrial Internet and the Made in China 2025 strategy is intricate and fundamental to China's national development objectives. Made in China 2025 represents a pivotal strategic plan devised by the Chinese government with the overarching goal of transforming China into a global manufacturing powerhouse. At its core, this strategy aims to enhance the technological prowess, quality standards, and overall competitiveness of China's manufacturing sector by leveraging informatization, intelligence, and green technologies. Within this strategic framework, the Industrial Internet emerges as a critical enabler and indispensable tool to actualize the objectives set forth in Made in China 2025.

The Industrial Internet serves as a linchpin for realizing the strategic imperatives of Made in China 2025. By fostering deep integration of Industrial Internet technologies with traditional manufacturing processes, China can achieve digitalization, networking, and intelligence within industrial production. This integration facilitates the enhancement of efficiency and competitiveness across the manufacturing industry.

One of the primary roles of the Industrial Internet within the Made in China 2025 strategy is the optimization of supply chain management and operational efficiency. Through the utilization of data analytics, automation, and connectivity, manufacturers can streamline their supply chains, optimize production processes, and reduce costs. This leads to heightened productivity and agility, aligning with the goals of Made in China 2025 to elevate technological and quality standards within Chinese manufacturing.

Furthermore, the Industrial Internet plays a crucial role in ensuring data security and privacy protection. As manufacturing processes become increasingly reliant on digital technologies, safeguarding sensitive data and intellectual property becomes paramount. The Industrial Internet enables the implementation of robust cybersecurity measures, thereby protecting valuable assets from potential cyber threats.

Moreover, the Industrial Internet fosters innovation and technological advancement within the manufacturing sector. By integrating advanced technologies such as artificial intelligence, machine learning, and IoT into production processes, manufacturers can drive innovation, develop new products and services, and enhance competitiveness on a global scale. This aligns with the objectives of Made in China 2025 to promote technological innovation and upgrade China's industrial capabilities.

In conclusion, the Industrial Internet plays a pivotal role in advancing the objectives of the Made in China 2025 strategy by facilitating digitalization, intelligence, and sustainability within the manufacturing industry. Its integration enables China to strengthen its position as a global manufacturing leader and achieve sustainable development and growth.

Assignment: To analyze the research task, please analyze the relationship between the Industrial Internet and the Made in China 2025 strategy, as well as the significant role of the Industrial Internet in national development strategy, and write a report to share insights.

任务 2 使用工业互联网平台

使用工业
互联网平台

学习目标

①了解工业互联网平台的定义及类型。
②了解工业互联网平台的主要功能。
③了解工业互联网平台的应用场景。
④了解国内外典型工业互联网平台。

建议学时

2 课时

工作情境

公司计划推进工业互联网建设项目,以提升生产和管理效率,优化产品研发,降低运营成本。现在派你去了解关于工业互联网平台的一些信息,以便结合自身情况作出选型,使用符合业务需求的工业互联网平台,发挥平台价值。

知识导图

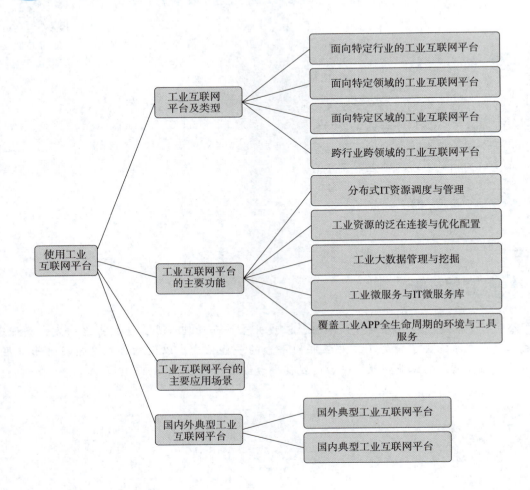

相关知识

1. 工业互联网平台及类型

工业互联网平台是面向制造业数字化、网络化、智能化需求，向下接入海量设备、自身承载工业知识与微服务，向上支撑工业 APP 开发部署的工业操作系统，是工业全要素、全产业链、全价值链全面连接和工业资源配置的中心，是支撑制造资源泛在连接、弹性供给、高效配置的载体。

工业互联网平台主要有 4 种类型：特定行业平台、特定领域平台、特定区域平台和跨行业跨领域平台。

（1）面向特定行业的工业互联网平台

面向特定行业的工业互联网平台应具备行业设备接入能力、行业软件部署能力和行业用户覆盖能力。行业设备接入能力指的是平台在特定行业具有设备规模接入能力，连接不少于一定数量特定行业工业设备或不少于一定数量特定行业工艺流程数据采集点。行业软件部署能力是指平台在特定行业具有工业知识经验的沉淀、转化与复用能力，提供不少于一定数量行业软件集成接口、特定行业机理模型、微服务组件，以及不少于一定数量特定行业工业APP。行业用户覆盖能力是指平台在特定行业具有规模化应用能力，覆盖不少于一定数量特定行业企业用户或不少于一定比例特定行业企业。

（2）面向特定领域的工业互联网平台

面向特定领域的工业互联网平台应具备特定领域平台的关键数据打通能力和关键领域优化能力。关键数据打通能力是指特定领域平台能够实现研发设计、物料采购、生产制造、运营管理、仓储物流、产品服务等产品全生命周期，供应链企业、协作企业、市场用户、外部开发者等各主体数据的打通，实现全流程的数据集成、开发、利用。关键领域优化能力是指特定领域平台能够实现在某一关键领域的应用开发与优化服务，提升关键环节生产效率与产品质量。例如协同设计、供应链管理、智能排产、设备预测性维护、产品质量智能检测、仓储与物流优化等。

（3）面向特定区域的工业互联网平台

面向特定区域的工业互联网平台应具备区域地方合作能力、区域资源协同能力和区域规模推广能力。区域地方合作能力是指平台在特定区域（工业园区或产业集聚区）落地，在该地具有注册实体，与地方政府签订合作协议，具备在地方长期开发投入、运营服务能力。区域资源协同能力是指平台具有面向特定区域产业转型升级共性需求的服务能力，能够促进区域企业信息共享与资源集聚，带动区域企业协同发展。区域规模推广能力是指平台具有特定区域企业的规模覆盖能力，为不少于一定数量特定区域企业或不低于一定比例特定区域企业提供服务。

（4）跨行业跨领域的工业互联网平台

跨行业跨领域的工业互联网平台除了具备特定行业能力、特定领域能力、特定区域能力外，还应具备跨行业、跨领域、跨区域以及平台运营、平台安全可靠等5个方面能力。

平台跨行业能力是指平台应覆盖不少于一定数量特定行业：每个行业连接不少于一定数量行业设备（离散制造业）或不少于一定数量行业工艺流程数据采集点（流程制造业），每个行业部署不少于一定数量行业机理模型、微服务组件，以及不少于一定数量行业工业APP；每个行业覆盖不少于一定数量企业用户或不少于一定比例行业企业。

平台跨领域能力是指平台应覆盖不少于一定数量特定领域：每个领域之间能够实现不同环节、不同主体的数据打通、集成与共享；每个领域具有不少于一定数量面向该领域（关键环节）的工业机理模型、微服务组件或工业APP。

平台跨区域能力是指平台应覆盖不少于一定数量特定区域：平台在全国主要区域（华北、华东、华南、华中、西北、东北）注册不低于一定数量的运营实体，负责平台在当地区域的运营推广，每个区域具有不少于一定数量的特定区域企业用户或为不低于一定比例的特定区域企业提供服务。

平台运营能力是指平台应具备独立运营能力，具有独立法人实体或完整组织架构的集团独立部门，人员不少于一定规模；平台具备开放运营能力，建立"产、学、研、用"长期合作机制，建有开发者社区，且第三方开发者占平台开发者总数不低于一定比例。

平台安全可靠能力是指工控系统安全可靠。在平台中建立工控系统安全防护机制，主动防护漏洞危害与病毒风险。在平台边缘计算或人工智能应用中关键零部件安全可靠，且平台创新开发一定数量工业机理模型、微服务组件或工业APP。

2. 工业互联网平台的主要功能

工业互联网平台已成为企业智能化转型的重要基础设施。第一，帮助企业实现智能化生产和管理。通过对生产现场"人、机、料、法、环"各类数据的全面采集和深度分析，发现导致生产瓶颈与产品缺陷的深层次原因，不断提高生产效率及产品质量。基于现场数据与企业计划资源、运营管理等数据的综合分析，实现更精准的供应链管理和财务管理，降低企业运营成本。第二，帮助企业实现生产方式和商业模式创新。企业通过平台可以实现对产品售后使用环节的数据打通，提供设备健康管理、产品增值服务等新型业务模式，实现从卖产品到卖服务的转变，实现价值提升。基于平台还可以与用户进行更加充分的交互，了解用户个性化需求，并有效组织生产资源，依靠个性化产品实现更高利润水平。第三，不同企业还可以基于平台开展信息交互，实现跨企业、跨区域、跨行业的资源和能力集聚，打造更高效的协同设计、协同制造、协同服务体系。

（1）分布式IT资源调度与管理

工业互联网平台建立IT软硬件的异构资源池，提供高效的资源调度与管理服务，通过实现IT能力平台化，降低企业信息化建设成本，加速企业数字化进程，推动核心业务向云端迁移，为运营技术和IT的融合和创新应用提供基础支撑。平台具备IT资源调度与管理服务，可以对接入平台的计算、存储、网络等云基础设施进行注册、认证、虚拟化运行维护等基础管理，结合微服务、工业APP的运行，实现IT资源的动态调节，并且可以按照实际需求提供弹性扩容、多租户的资源隔离与计量等服务。

（2）工业资源的泛在连接与优化配置

工业互联网平台通过在边缘层运用边缘处理技术，围绕"人、机、料、法、环"等方面，将分布在各地的各类工业资源接入平台，并实现识别、注册、认证等基础管理功能。另外将数据化、模型化的工业资源进行加工、组合、优化，形成模块化的制造能力，并通过对工业资源的基础管理、动态调度、优化配置等，促进制造能力的在线交易、动态配置、共享利用。

（3）工业大数据管理与挖掘

工业互联网平台应具备海量异构工业数据的汇聚共享、价值挖掘能力，支持多源海量异构数据的转换、清洗、分级存储、可视化处理等，并应提供多种分析算法和工具，支持相关方基于大数据处理形成工业机理模型、知识图谱等，提升数据利用水平，实现各参与主体知识的复用、传播、提升，形成基于数据驱动、持续迭代的工业知识体系。

（4）工业微服务与IT微服务库

工业互联网平台应支持各类微服务组件提供商，围绕"人、机、料、法、环"等方面快速构建人员技能、设备、生产资源、工业环境等一系列高度解耦、可复用的工业微服务及微组件等。支持各类微服务组件提供商结合工业微服务及微组件、IT微服务及微组件的使用情况，对它们进行持续迭代优化。同时，支持平台建设运营主体对各类微服务及微组件进行认证、注销等基础管理，并结合工业 APP 的运行需求实现微服务及微组件的快速发现、编排与调用。

（5）覆盖工业 APP 全生命周期的环境与工具服务

工业互联网平台应建立开发社区，汇聚工业、IT、通信等领域的各类开发者，并提供覆盖工业 APP 全生命周期的环境与工具，支持各类工业 APP 的开发、测试验证、虚拟仿真实施部署、运行、调度、优化，为企业转型升级提供可用、好用的工业 APP。支持开发者在多种开发工具及语言环境下，快速将其掌握的工业技术、经验、知识和最佳实践进行模型化、软件化和再封装，形成一系列工业 APP，满足行业、领域的应用要求。

从实践上看，把来自机器设备、业务系统、产品模型、生产过程以及运行环境的大量数据汇聚到平台层，并将技术、知识、经验和方法以数字化模型的形式也沉淀到工业互联网平台上，通过调用各种数字化模型与不同数据进行组合、分析、挖掘、展现，可以快速、高效、灵活地开发出各类工业 APP，提供全生命周期管理、协同研发设计、生产设备优化、产品质量检测、企业运营决策、设备预测性维护等多种多样的服务。

3. 工业互联网平台的主要应用场景

工业互联网平台主要应用于四个常见的场景。

一是应用于工业现场的生产过程优化。工业互联网平台能够有效采集和汇聚设备运行数据、工艺参数、质量检测数据、物料配送数据和进度管理数据等生产现场数据，通过数据分析和反馈，在制造工艺、生产流程质量管理、设备维护和能耗管理等具体场景中实现优化应用。其具体场景主要有制造工艺、生产流程、质量管理、设备维护和能耗管理。

制造工艺是指通过对工艺参数、设备运行等数据进行综合分析，找出生产过程中的最优参数，提升制造品质。

生产流程是指通过对生产进度、物料管理、企业管理等数据进行分析，实现提高排产进度、物料、人员等方面管理的准确性。

质量管理是指通过产品检验数据和"人、机、料、法、环"等过程数据进行关联性分析，实现在线质量检测和成品分析，降低产品不良率。

设备维护是指通过设备历史数据与实时运行数据构建"数字孪生"，及时监控设备运行状态，并实现设备预测性维护。

能耗管理是指通过现场能耗数据的采集与分析，对设备、生产线、场景能效使用进行合理规划，提升能源使用效率，实现节能减排。

二是应用于企业运营的管理决策优化。借助工业互联网平台打通生产现场数据、企业管理数据和供应链数据，提升决策效率并基于大数据挖掘分析实现管理决策优化。其具体场景主要有供应链管理、生产管控一体化和企业决策管理。

供应链管理是指通过实时跟踪现场物料消耗，结合库存情况安排供应商进行精准配货，实现零库存管理，降低成本。

生产管控一体化是指通过进行业务管理系统和生产执行系统集成，实现企业管理和现场生产的协同优化。

企业决策管理是指通过对企业内部数据的全面感知和综合分析，有效支撑企业智能决策。

三是应用于社会化生产的资源优化配置与协同。工业互联网平台可实现制造企业与外部用户需求、创新资源、生产能力的全面对接，推动设计、制造、供应和服务环节的协同优化。其具体场景主要有协同制造、制造能力交易、个性定制和产融结合。

协同制造是指通过有效集成不同设计企业、生产企业及供应链企业的业务系统，实现设计、生产的并行实施，大幅缩短产品研发设计与生产周期，降低成本。

制造能力交易是指通过对外开放空闲制造能力，实现制造能力的在线租用和利益分配。

个性定制是指通过企业与用户的无缝对接，形成满足用户需求的个性化定制方案，提升产品价值，增强用户黏性。

产融结合是指通过工业数据的汇聚分析，为金融行业提供评估支撑，为银行放贷股权投资、企业保险等金融业务提供量化依据。

四是应用于产品全生命周期的管理与服务优化。工业互联网平台可以将产品设计、生产、运行和服务数据进行全面集成，以全生命周期可追溯为基础，在设计环节实现可制造性预测，在使用环节实现健康管理，并通过生产与使用数据的反馈改进产品设计。其具体场景主要有产品溯源、产品/装备远程预测性维护、产品设计反馈优化等。

产品溯源是指通过借助标识技术记录产品生产、物流、服务等各类信息，综合形成产品档案，为全生命周期管理应用提供支撑。

产品/装备远程预测性维护是指通过将产品/装备的实时运行数据与其设计数据、制造数据、历史维护数据进行融合，提供运行决策和维护建议，实现设备故障的提前预警、远程维护等设备健康管理应用。

产品设计反馈优化是指将产品运行和用户使用行为数据反馈到设计和制造阶段，从而改进设计方案，加速创新迭代。

4. 国内外典型工业互联网平台

（1）国外典型工业互联网平台

1）通用电气公司的 Predix 平台

美国通用电气公司是世界上最大的装备与技术服务企业之一，业务范围涵盖航空、能源、医疗、交通等多个领域。Predix 是通用电气公司推出的全球第一个工业互联网大数据分析服务平台，围绕工业设备健康管理、生产效率优化、能耗管理等提供了丰富的应用场景，并提供多种应用程序的微服务市场。通用电气公司的工业互联网平台经历了一个从企业内部的资产管理平台向综合工业平台转型，由 IT 向 OT 延伸，最终发展为工业互联网平台的过程。Predix 平台的主要功能是将各类数据按照统一的标准进行规范化梳理，并提供随时调取和分析的能力。

Predix 平台结构分为 3 层：边缘连接层、基础设施层和应用服务层。其中，边缘连接层主要负责收集数据并将数据传输到云端；基础设施层主要提供全球范围的安全的云基础架构，满足日常的工业工作和监督的需求；应用服务层主要负责提供工业微服务和各种服务交互的框架，主要提供创建、测试、运行工业互联网程序的环境和微服务市场，通用电气公司基于 Predix 平台开发部署了计划和物流、互联产品、智能环境、现场人力管理、工业分析、资产绩效管理、运营优化等多类工业 APP。

2）ABB 公司的 ABB Ability 平台

ABB 是设备制造和自动化技术领域的领导厂商，拥有电力设备、工业机器人、传感器、实时控制和优化系统等广泛的产品线。ABB 于 2017 年推出了工业互联网平台 ABB Ability，探索将数字技术与其在电气自动化设备制造等领域的专业优势结合。

ABB Ability 定义为从设备、边缘计算到云服务的跨行业、一体化的数字化解决方案。简单来说，ABB Ability 平台就是"边缘计算 + 云"架构，边缘设备负责工业设备的接入对关键设备的参数、值和属性进行数据采集，由 ABB Ability 边缘计算服务进行数据的处理和展现，最上层云平台用来对工业性能的高级优化和分析。

第一种方式，通过 ABB Ability 智能传感器进行数据采集。第二种方式，对于不能通过贴附采集的工业设备，ABB Ability 也可通过对单台计算机或功能型服务器进行配置来实现对关键设备数据的采集。对服务器进行有效配置使服务器可支持 OPCUA、Modbus 等常用的工业通信协议。边缘计算通过两种数据采集方式基本解决了设备的数据采集问题。边缘计算硬件在采集数据之后可以及时地对这些数据进行分析处理，包括关键性能指标绩效、趋势和聚合等状态。

AbilityCloud 基于 MicrosoftAzure 云基础架构及其应用服务，通过数据集成管理和大数据分析，形成智能化决策与服务应用。

3）西门子的 MindSphere 平台

西门子是全球电子电气工程领域的领先企业，业务主要集中在工业、能源、基础设施及城市、医疗四大领域。西门子于 2016 年推出 MindSphere 平台，是德国"工业 4.0"平台的典型代表，主要面向广大工业企业提供预防性维护、能源数据管理等数字化服务。该平台采用基于云的开放物联网架构，可以将传感器、控制器及各种信息系统收集的工业现场设备数据，通过安全通道实时传输到云端，并在云端为企业提供大数据分析挖掘、工业 APP 开发和智能应用增值等服务。MindSphere 平台架构基于云的开放式物联网操作系统 MindSphere 平台，包括边缘连接层、开发运营层、应用服务层 3 个层级。主要包括 MindConnect、MindCloud、MindAPPs 3 个核心要素，其中 MindConnect 负责将数据传输到云平台，MindCloud 为用户提供数据分析、应用开发环境及应用开发工具，MindAPPs 为用户提供集成行业经验和数据分析结果的工业智能应用。

在对工业设备进行数据采集时，提供的 MindConnect 工具盒子，可以让设备连接入网。其中有 Nano 工具，拥有配套的网关，使连接变得容易，并且可以集成到 MES 软件上。这个工具目前是有限制条件的，要求设备支持西门子 S7 的通信协议或 OPCUA 通信协议。MindSphere 平台主要依托 Nano 这一网关型硬件产品，向上与 MindSphere 的云端进行连接，向下与西门子众多的具有以太网通信能力的硬件产品和支持通用协议的其他品牌产品进行通信，完成数据采集与传输。如果设备的通信协议比较特殊，用户可以基于 Nano 中的开源软件自行开发设备通信与数据采集程序。

MindSphere 平台向下提供数据采集 APT，既支持开放式通信标准 OPCUA，也支持西门子和第三方设备的数据连接；向上提供开发 API，方便合作伙伴和用户开发应用程序。MindSphere 平台应用开发也是基于 CloudFoundry 框架构建，即搭建完整的大数据预处理存储及分析的技术框架，融合了西门子以前在若干个领域积累的分析模型与算法，提供开放的接口，便于用户嵌入满足个性化需求的分析算法模型。

(2) 国内典型工业互联网平台

1) 航天云网 INDICS 平台

航天科工集团基于自身在制造业的雄厚实力和在工业互联网领域的先行先试经验，打造了工业互联网平台——航天云网 INDICS。航天云网 INDICS 平台是一个以云制造服务为核心，以信息互通、资源共享、能力协同、开放合作、互利共赢为理念的"互联网+智能制造"产业化创新服务平台。

航天云网 INDICS 平台总体架构包括资源层、工业物联网层、平台接入层、INDICS 云平台层、INDICS 工业应用 APP 层等 5 层。

资源层：实现产品研制全产业链资源/能力的接入，提供生产制造、试验验证、计量检测等各类资源/能力的接入，以及各类工业设备，包括机械加工、环境试验、电器互联、计量器具、仿真试验等 21 类工业设备的接入。

工业物联网层：实现各类工业设备的通信互联，支持 OPCUA、MQTT、Modbus、PROFINET 等主流工业现场通信协议的通信互联，支持工业现场总线、有线网络、无线网络的通信互联。

平台接入层：实现工厂/车间的云端接入，提供自主知识产权的 SmartoT 系列智能网关接入产品（标准系列、传感器系列、高性能系列）和 INDICS-APIS 软件接入接口，支持"云计算+边缘计算"的混合数据计算模式。

INDICS 云平台层：提供云资源基础设施管理、大数据管理和应用支撑公共服务等云服务功能。以业界主流开源 PaaS 云平台 CloudFoundry 基础架构作为底层支撑架构，有效支持工业云的能力扩展，同时自建数据中心，直接提供 PaaS 层和通用平台 IaaS 层的基础云服务。

INDICS 工业应用 APP 层：提供面向制造全产业链、基于平台开发的原生工业应用 APP，同时提供开发接口，形成基于平台的第三方应用，支持多样化、个性化的用户需求。

2) 海尔 COSMOPlat 平台

海尔 COSMOPlat 是一个以用户驱动实现大规模定制的平台，COSMOPlat 将社会资源纳入平台中，能够有效连接人、机、物，不同类型的企业可快速匹配智能制造解决方案。该平台强调用户全流程参与、零距离互联互通、打造开放共赢的新生态三大特性，用户可以全流程参与产品交互、设计、采购、制造、物流、体验和迭代升级等环节，形成了用户、企业、资源三位一体，开放共赢的有机全生态。

COSMOPlat 平台全流程共有 7 大模块，包括用户交互定制平台、精准营销平台、开放设计平台、模块化采购平台、智能生产平台、智慧物流平台、智慧服务平台。COSMOPlat 平台已打通交互定制、开放研发、数字营销、模块采购、智能生产、智慧物流、智慧服务等业务环节，通过智能化系统使用户持续、深度参与产品设计研发、生产制造物流配送、迭代升级等环节，满足用户个性化定制需求，为各方协同创造条件，帮助更多中小制造企业借助规范的平台进行转型升级。

第一层是资源层，以开发模式对全球资源，包括软件资源、服务资源、业务资源、硬件资源等进行聚集整合，打造平台资源库，为以上各层提供资源服务。

第二层是平台层，是 COSMOPlat 平台的核心技术所在，支持工业应用的快速开发、部署、运行、集成，实现工业技术的软件化，各类资源的分布式调度和最优匹配。

第三层是应用层，通过模式软件化、云化等，为企业提供具体的互联工厂应用服务，形成全流程的智能解决方案。

第四层是模式层，依托互联工厂应用服务实现模式复制和资源共享，实现跨行业的复制，通过赋能中小企业，助力中小企业提质增效，转型升级。

3）东方国信 BIOP 平台

东方国信基于软硬件相结合的端到端工业大数据解决方案，推出工业互联网平台——BIOP。东方国信 BIOP 平台架构包含采集层、传输层、IaaS 层、PaaS 层、SaaS 层 5 个部分。其中主要的是采集层、PaaS 层和 SaaS 层，采集层包含 BIOP – EG 智能网关接入设备和接口组件，支持各类数据的接入。PaaS 层集成了工业微服务、大数据分析、应用开发等功能。SaaS 层面向工业各个环节和场景，向平台内租户提供工业领域通用专用服务，以及基于大数据分析的云化、智能化工业应用及解决方案服务。

4）树根互联根云（RootCloud）平台

树根互联技术有限公司由三一重工物联网团队创建，是独立开放的工业互联网平台企业。2017 年年初，树根互联发布了根云（RootCloud）平台。根云平台主要基于三一重工在装备制造及远程运维领域的经验，由 OT 层向 IT 层延伸构建平台，重点面向设备健康管理，提供端到端工业互联网解决方案和服务。树根互联根云平台主要具备 3 方面功能。

一是智能物联。通过传感器、控制器等感知设备和物联网，采集、编译各类设备数据。

二是大数据和云计算。面向海量设备数据，提供数据清洗、数据治理、隐私安全管理等服务，以及稳定可靠的云计算能力，并依托工业经验知识图谱构建工业大数据工作台。

三是 SaaS 应用和解决方案。为企业提供端到端的解决方案和即插即用的 SaaS 应用，并为应用开发者提供开发组件，方便其快速构建工业互联网应用。

目前，根云平台能够为企业提供资产管理、智能服务、预测性维护等工业应用服务。同时基于平台开展产业链金融创新，已有 UBI 保险、维保等产品实践，服务于保险公司等金融机构，提升其风险管控和金融服务能力。

任务拓展

速度中国——从工业互联网技术的应用看中国数字经济的飞速发展

党的二十大报告中提出"加快发展数字经济,促进数字经济和实体经济深度融合"。工业互联网通过结合新一代信息技术,为数字化、网络化、智能化提供实现途径,加速了我国产业数字化进程。工业互联网是未来制造业竞争的制高点,正在推动创新模式、生产方式、组织形式和商业范式的深刻变革,推动工业链、产业链、价值链的重塑再造,必将对未来工业发展产生全方位、深层次、革命性的变革,对社会生产力、人类历史发展产生深远影响。

当今世界,新一轮科技革命和产业变革蓬勃兴起,工业互联网作为制造业与互联网深度融合的产物,已经成为新工业革命的关键支撑和智能制造的重要基石。在5G及工业互联网推动下,产业数字化将成为数字经济发展的引擎,工业互联网对数字经济的带动作用也会变得更加明显。工业互联网时代,切实提高自身的综合素质,担负起时代赋予的历史使命和社会责任,是当代大学生应有的使命感和责任感。

作业:分析调研我国工业互联网发展现状,撰写报告分享启发。

Task 2 Using the Industrial Internet Platform

 Learning Objective

①Definition and types of Industrial Internet platforms.
②Main functions of Industrial Internet platforms.
③Application scenarios of Industrial Internet platform.
④Typical Industrial Internet platforms at home and abroad.

 Suggested Hours

2 hours

 Work Situations

The company is moving forward with an Industrial Internet construction project aimed at enhancing efficiency, optimizing product development, and reducing operating costs. As part of this initiative, you have been tasked with gathering information about Industrial Internet platforms. The objective is to select equipment that aligns with the company's needs and leverage the appropriate Industrial Internet platform to maximize its value.

Knowledge Map

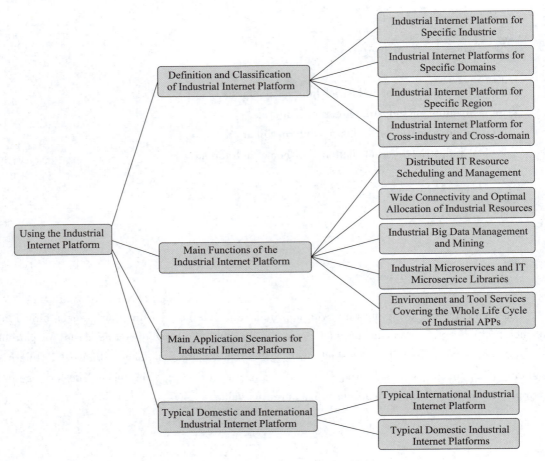

Relevant Knowledge

1. Definition and Classification of Industrial Internet Platform

The Industrial Internet platform operates as a foundational system tailored to meet the digitalization, networking, and intelligentization needs of the manufacturing industry. This platform is intricately connected to a vast array of devices and encapsulates industrial knowledge and microservices. It facilitates the development and deployment of industrial applications (APPS) upwards. Serving as the nexus for the interconnection of all facets of industry, including the entire industrial chain, value chain, and resource allocation, the Industrial Internet platform acts as a conduit supporting extensive connectivity, elastic supply, and efficient allocation of manufacturing resources.

There are four primary types of Industrial Internet platform: industry-specific platform, domain-specific platform, region-specific platform, and cross-industry and cross-domain platform.

(1) Industrial Internet Platform for Specific Industrie

Industrial Internet platforms tailored for specific industries should possess three key capabilities: industry equipment access, industry software deployment, and industry user coverage.

Industry Equipment Access Capability: This refers to the platform's capability to seamlessly integrate with industry-specific equipment. It enables the connection of a specified number of industrial equipment or data collection points relevant to the particular industry.

Industry Software Deployment Capability: This capability involves the platform's capability to aggregate, transform, and utilize industrial knowledge and expertise. It requires providing a variety of industry software integration interfaces, mechanism models, microservice components, and a selection of industrial applications (APPS) tailored to meet industry-specific requirements.

Industry User Coverage Capability: This pertains to the platform's capability in catering to users within the specific industry. It should encompass a defined number of enterprise users or a significant proportion of enterprises within the industry, ensuring widespread adoption and utilization of the platform's functionalities.

(2) Industrial Internet Platforms for Specific Domains

Domain-specific Industrial Internet platforms should possess two crucial functions: key data access and key domain optimization.

Key Data Access Capability: This capability enables the platform to facilitate the comprehensive management of product data throughout its entire lifecycle. It includes accessing data from various stakeholders involved in the lifecycle, integrating, developing, and utilizing data across different stages such as R&D, design, procurement, manufacturing, operations management, warehousing, logistics, and product services. Stakeholders may include supply chain enterprises, collaborative partners, end-users, external developers, and others.

Key Domain Optimization Capability: This capability focuses on the platform's ability to provide application development and optimization services in critical areas. The goal is to enhance production efficiency and product quality in specific domains, such as collaborative design, supply chain management, intelligent production scheduling, predictive maintenance of equipment, intelligent product quality testing, and optimization of warehousing and logistics processes.

(3) Industrial Internet Platform for Specific Region

Industrial Internet platform designed for specific regions should possess three essential capabilities: regional local cooperation, regional resource synergy, and regional scale promotion.

Regional Local Cooperation Capability: This capability entails the platform's establishment of a presence within a specific region, including registering as a local entity and forming cooperative agreements with the regional government. This ensures the platform's long-term development and provision of input and operational services tailored to the local area.

Regional Resource Synergy Function: This function facilitates information sharing and resource aggregation among enterprises operating within the region. By promoting collaboration among regional businesses, the platform drives collective development and growth within the local economy.

Regional Scale Promotion Function: This function enables the platform to extend its services to a significant number of enterprises or a notable proportion of businesses within the specified region. By catering to the needs of local enterprises on a broad scale, the platform contributes to the overall advancement and prosperity of the region.

(4) Industrial Internet Platform for Cross-industry and Cross-domain

The Industrial Internet platform for cross-industry and cross-domain applications should encompass five key capabilities: cross-industry integration, cross-domain compatibility, cross-regional coverage, platform operation, and platform security and reliability.

Platform Operation Capability: The platform should operate as an independent entity, either as a standalone legal entity or as an autonomous department within a larger organization. It should have an open operational model, fostering collaboration among industry, academia, research, and application sectors. Additionally, the platform should cultivate a developer community, with third-party developers constituting a significant portion of its user base.

Platform Security and Reliability Capability: This capability focuses on ensuring the security and reliability of the industrial control systems integrated into the platform. It involves implementing robust security measures to mitigate vulnerabilities and protect against potential cyber threats. Furthermore, the platform should prioritize the reliability of key components, particularly in edge computing and artificial intelligence applications. Additionally, the platform should innovate and develop industrial mechanism models, microservice components, and industrial applications to enhance its functionality and utility.

2. Main Functions of the Industrial Internet Platform

The Industrial Internet platform has emerged as a crucial infrastructure for driving the intelligent transformation of enterprises. Firstly, it facilitates intelligent production and management by comprehensively collecting and analyzing various types of data from production sites, including data related to "man, machine, material, method, and environment." Timely identification of root causes through data analysis helps mitigate production bottlenecks and minimize product defects. Moreover, leveraging data-driven insights enables more precise supply chain and financial management, ultimately reducing operational costs and optimizing resource utilization across various aspects such as field data and enterprise planning resources.

Secondly, the platform enables enterprises to innovate their production methods and business models. By opening up data related to post-sale product usage, enterprises can leverage the platform to offer services such as equipment health management and value-added product services, thereby transitioning from product-centric to service-centric business models and enhancing overall value proposition. Additionally, the platform fosters enhanced user engagement by understanding personalized user needs and effectively organizing production resources to deliver personalized products, thereby driving higher profitability.

Thirdly, the platform facilitates information exchange among different enterprises, enabling cross-enterprise, cross-regional, and cross-industry collaboration to aggregate resources and capabilities. This collaborative ecosystem fosters more efficient collaborative design, manufacturing, and service systems, leading to improved productivity and innovation across the industry landscape.

(1) Distributed IT Resource Scheduling and Management

The Industrial Internet platform establishes a heterogeneous resource pool encompassing IT hardware and software. This platform offers efficient resource scheduling and management services, which not only reduce the cost of enterprise information technology construction but also accelerate the digitalization process by enabling the platformization of IT capabilities. Additionally, the platform facilitates the migration of core business operations to the cloud, aiming to provide fundamental support for integrating and innovatively applying operational and IT technologies.

The IT resource scheduling and management services provided by the platform include basic management of cloud infrastructure access. Specific management tasks encompass registration, authentication, virtualization operation, and maintenance. Leveraging the operational capabilities of micro-services and industrial APPs, the platform dynamically adjusts IT resources. Moreover, it offers services such as elastic capacity extension, multi-tenant resource isolation, and metering based on actual demand.

(2) Wide Connectivity and Optimal Allocation of Industrial Resources

The Industrial Internet platform implements edge processing technology at the edge layer. It focuses on integrating various industrial resources related to "man, machine, material, law, and environment" onto the platform to achieve basic management functions such as identification, registration, and authentication. Additionally, the platform processes, integrates, and optimizes data-driven and model-driven industrial resources to develop modular manufacturing capabilities. Through these efforts, it facilitates online trading, dynamic configuration, and shared utilization of manufacturing capabilities.

(3) Industrial Big Data Management and Mining

The Industrial Internet platform should include functions for the convergence and sharing of vast heterogeneous industrial data and value extraction. It should support the conversion, cleaning, hierarchical storage, and visualization of diverse data from various sources. Additionally, the platform should offer multiple analysis algorithms and tools to facilitate the creation of industrial mechanism models, knowledge graphs, etc., based on big data processing. Its goal is to elevate the level of data utilization and achieve the reuse, dissemination, and enhancement of knowledge across all participating entities. Ultimately, this will lead to the development of a data-driven, continuously evolving industrial knowledge system.

(4) Industrial Microservices and IT Microservice Libraries

The Industrial Internet platform should facilitate various types of microservice component providers. It should enable the rapid development of a wide range of highly decoupled industrial microservices and micro-components across various domains, including personnel skills, equipment, production resources, and industrial environments. The platform should support the integration of industrial microservice components and IT microservice components, with continuous iterative optimization processes in place.

Simultaneously, the platform should support the management body in basic tasks such as authentication and deactivation of various microservices. It should integrate the operational needs of industrial applications to enable swift discovery, scheduling, and invocation of microservices.

(5) Environment and Tool Services Covering the Whole Life Cycle of Industrial APPs

The Industrial Internet platform should establish a development community, bringing together developers from various sectors including industry, IT, and communications. It should provide an environment and tools covering the entire lifecycle of industrial applications (APPs), supporting development, testing, virtual simulation, operational scheduling, and optimization of various industrial APPs.

The platform should enable developers to model, softwarize, and repackage their knowledge and expertise using a range of development tools and programming languages. This facilitates the creation of a diverse set of industrial APPs to meet the application requirements of different industries and fields.

3. Main Application Scenarios for Industrial Internet Platform

Industrial Internet platform is utilized in four common scenarios. First, it is applied to optimize the production process at industrial sites. The platform effectively collect and aggregate production site data, including equipment operation, process parameters, quality inspection, material distribution, and progress management. By analyzing this data and providing feedback, optimization applications are achieved in specific scenes such as manufacturing process, production progress, quality management, equipment maintenance, and energy consumption management.

Manufacturing process involves a comprehensive analysis of equipment operation data to identify the optimal parameters for production processes and enhance manufacturing quality.

The production process entails analyzing data related to production progress, materials management, and business operations. The platform improves accuracy in scheduling, material management, and personnel management.

Quality management involves correlating and analyzing product inspection data and process data to conduct online quality inspections and analyze finished products, thereby reducing defective rates.

Equipment maintenance involves creating "digital twins" using historical equipment data and real-time operational data to monitor equipment status promptly and achieve predictive maintenance.

Energy consumption management involves strategically planning the energy-efficient use of equipment in production scenarios by collecting and analyzing on-site energy consumption data. This approach enhances energy efficiency and facilitates energy savings and emission reductions.

Second, the platform is employed to optimize management decision-making in enterprise operations. By opening up production site data, enterprise management data, and supply chain data, decision-making efficiency is improved and management decisions are optimized through big data mining and analysis. Specific scenarios include supply chain management, production control integration, and enterprise decision-making management.

Supply chain management involves precise supplier allocation achieved through real-time tracking of on-site material consumption and inventory, ultimately leading to zero inventory management and cost reduction.

Production control integration entails integrating the business management system with the production execution system to synergistically optimize enterprise management and on-site production.

Enterprise decision management encompasses comprehensive perception and analysis of internal data, effectively supporting intelligent decision-making processes.

Third, the platform facilitates the optimal allocation of resources and collaboration in socialized production. It realizes the docking between manufacturing enterprises and external users, promoting collaborative optimization in design, manufacturing, supply, and service links. Scenarios here include collaborative manufacturing, manufacturing capacity trading, personalized customization, and industry-finance integration.

Collaborative manufacturing involves effectively integrating the business systems of different design companies, production companies, and supply chain companies, which significantly shortens the product development cycle and reduces costs.

Manufacturing capacity trading entails opening vacant manufacturing capacity to the public, enabling the online rental of manufacturing capacity and the equitable distribution of benefits.

Personalized customization involves establishing a seamless connection between the enterprise and the user, resulting in a personalized customized solution that meets the specific needs of users. This enhances the value of the product and fosters user loyalty.

The combination of industry and finance involves aggregating and analyzing industrial data to provide assessment support for the financial industry and a quantitative basis for financial operations such as bank lending.

Fourth, the platform is utilized for the management and service optimization of the entire product life cycle. By integrating product design, production, operation, and service data based on full life cycle traceability, it enables manufacturability prediction in the design segment and health management in the use segment. Specific scenarios encompass product traceability, remote predictive maintenance of products, and product design feedback optimization.

Product traceability involves recording product production, logistics, service, and other relevant information through the use of RFID technology. This comprehensive recording creates product files that support the application of full life cycle management, allowing for efficient tracking and management of products throughout their entire life cycle.

Remote predictive maintenance of products combines real-time operational data of products with their design data, manufacturing data, and historical maintenance data. This integration enables the platform to provide operational decisions and maintenance recommendations based on predictive analytics. By offering early warnings of equipment failure, this approach facilitates equipment health management applications such as remote maintenance, enhancing overall operational efficiency and reducing downtime.

Product design feedback optimization involves integrating feedback from product operation and user usage behavior data into the design and manufacturing stages. This process enables the refinement of design solutions and accelerates innovation iterations by incorporating real-world insights.

4. Typical Domestic and International Industrial Internet Platform

(1) Typical International Industrial Internet Platform

1) General Electric's Predix Platform

General Electric Company of the United States is one of the world's largest equipment and technical services companies. Its business scope covers a wide range of fields such as aviation, energy, healthcare, and transportation. Predix is the world's first Industrial Internet big data analysis service platform launched by General Electric. The platform provides rich application scenarios around industrial equipment health management, productivity optimization, and energy consumption management, among others. Additionally, the platform offers a microservices marketplace for multiple applications.

General Electric's Industrial Internet platform has evolved from an asset management platform within the enterprise to a comprehensive industrial platform. This transformation extends from IT to OT and eventually develops into an Industrial Internet platform. The main function of the Predix platform is to normalize and organize various types of data according to uniform standards. It also provides the capability for retrieval and analysis at any time.

The Predix platform is organized into three layers: the edge connectivity layer, the infrastructure layer, and the application services layer. The Edge Connectivity Layer is responsible for collecting and transferring data to the cloud, while the Infrastructure Layer provides a global cloud infrastructure to meet the needs of daily industrial work and supervision. The application service layer primarily offers industrial microservices and a framework for various service interactions. It includes services such as creating, testing, running environments, and a microservice marketplace. General Electric has developed multiple types of industrial apps based on the Predix platform, including connected products, intelligent environments, on-site manpower management, industrial analytics, asset performance management, and operations optimization.

2) ABB's ABB Ability Platform

ABB is a leader in equipment manufacturing and automation technology, with a wide range of product lines including power equipment, industrial robots, sensors, and real-time control and optimization systems. In 2017, ABB launched its Industrial Internet platform, ABB Ability, aiming to combine digital technologies with its specialized strengths.

ABB Ability is characterized as a cross-industry, integrated digitalization solution spanning from devices and edge computing to cloud services. Essentially, the ABB Ability platform adopts an "edge computing + cloud" architecture. Edge devices are tasked with accessing industrial equipment and collecting data on key equipment parameters, values, and attributes, while ABB Ability edge computing services process and present this data. The top-layer cloud platform is utilized for advanced optimization and analysis of industrial performance.

Data collection through ABB Ability begins with smart sensors. For industrial equipment that cannot be directly accessed by sensors, ABB Ability can be configured to capture data from key equipment via a single PC or functional server. Proper configuration of the server enables support for commonly used industrial communication protocols such as OPCUA and Modbus. Edge computing resolves the data collection challenge through two methods: hardware analysis and processing of collected data in a timely manner, addressing key performance indicators, performance trends, and aggregation.

AbilityCloud relies on Microsoft Azure cloud infrastructure and its application services to integrate and manage data, facilitating big data analysis and forming intelligent decision-making applications.

3) Siemens' MindSphere Platform

Siemens is a global leader in electrical and electronic engineering, focusing primarily on four major fields: industry, energy, urban infrastructure, and healthcare. In 2016, Siemens launched the MindSphere platform, which stands as a typical representative of Germany's "Industry 4.0" platform. This platform offers digital services for industrial companies, including preventive maintenance and energy data management.

MindSphere adopts a cloud-based open IoT architecture, transmitting real-time data from industrial field equipment to the cloud through a secure channel. Enterprises benefit from services such as big data mining, industrial app development, and value-added intelligent applications in the cloud. The data includes information collected by sensors, controllers, and various information systems. The architecture of the MindSphere platform consists of three layers: the edge connection layer, development and operation layer, and application service layer.

The platform comprises three core elements: MindConnect, MindCloud, and MindApps. MindConnect facilitates data transfer to the cloud platform, while MindCloud offers users data analysis and an application development environment with tools. MindApps are industrial intelligence applications providing integrated industry experience and data analysis results.

The MindConnect toolbox enables device connection to the network for data collection on industrial equipment. The MindSphere platform primarily relies on Nano, a gateway-type hardware product, connecting to the MindSphere cloud above and communicating with various Siemens hardware products and other brands supporting common protocols below. For devices with special communication protocols, users can develop their own device communication and data acquisition programs using open-source software in Nano.

The MindSphere platform supports data acquisition APT and both the open communication standard OPC UA and data connectivity between Siemens and third-party devices. It provides development APIs for partners and users to create applications, built on the Cloud Foundry framework. This framework establishes a comprehensive technical framework for big data preprocessing, storage, and analysis, integrating Siemens' analysis models and algorithms from various fields. Additionally, the platform offers open interfaces for users to embed their own customized analytical models and algorithms.

(2) Typical Domestic Industrial Internet Platforms

1) AeroCloud INDICS Platform

Aisino Group has developed an Industrial Internet platform named Aisino Cloud INDICS, leveraging its robust manufacturing industry expertise and pioneering experience in the Industrial Internet domain. Aisino Cloud INDICS revolves around cloud manufacturing services, embodying principles of information interoperability, resource sharing, capacity synergy, open cooperation, and mutual benefit. It serves as an "Internet + Intelligent Manufacturing" industrialization innovation service platform.

The overarching architecture of Aisino Cloud INDICS consists of five layers: the resource layer, industrial IoT layer, platform access layer, INDICS cloud platform layer, and INDICS industrial application APP layer.

Resource Layer: Realize the access of resources in the whole industry chain of product development. This layer enables access to various resources such as manufacturing, testing, verification, and measurement. Additionally, it provides access to diverse industrial equipment, including mechanical processing, environmental testing, electrical interconnection, measuring instruments, and simulation tests.

Industrial Internet of Things Layer: Realize the communication interoperability among various industrial equipment. This layer supports communication protocols such as OPC UA, MQTT, Modbus, PROFINET, and other mainstream industrial field communication protocols. It also facilitates communication across industrial field buses, wired networks, and wireless networks.

Platform Access Layer: Realize the cloud access for factories and workshops. This layer offers access to SmartoT series intelligent gateway access products with independent intellectual property rights and INDICS-APIS software. Its interface supports a hybrid data computing mode combining "cloud computing + edge computing."

INDICS Cloud Platform Layer: Provide cloud service functionalities such as cloud resource infrastructure management, big data management, and application support public services. Leveraging the Cloud Foundry infrastructure, an industry-standard open-source PaaS cloud platform, this layer effectively enhances industrial cloud capabilities. Additionally, it establishes its data center to directly offer fundamental cloud services for the PaaS layer and the IaaS layer of the universal platform.

INDICS Industrial Application APP Layer: Provide native industrial application APPs for the whole manufacturing industry chain and platform-based development. It also offers development interfaces to foster third-party applications based on the platform, thus supporting diverse and personalized user needs.

2) Haier COSMOPlat Platform

Haier COSMOPlat is a platform driven by user needs, aiming to achieve mass customization by incorporating social resources. It effectively connects people, machines, and things, enabling different enterprises to swiftly access intelligent manufacturing solutions. The platform emphasizes three main characteristics: user participation throughout the entire process, zero-distance interconnection, and the establishment of an open, new ecology. Users can engage in various stages of product interaction, design, procurement, manufacturing, logistics, experience, and iterative upgrading, fostering a trinity of users, enterprises, and resources within an open organic ecosystem.

The COSMOPlat platform comprises seven modules covering the entire process: a user customization platform, an accurate marketing platform, an open design platform, a modular procurement platform, an intelligent production platform, an intelligent logistics platform, and an intelligent service platform. It has opened up business links such as interactive customization, open R&D, digital marketing, modular procurement, intelligent production, intelligent logistics, and intelligent services. The intelligent system enables continuous and deep user participation in product design, development, and iteration, meeting personalized customization needs and facilitating collaboration among all parties. Ultimately, it aids more small and medium-sized manufacturing enterprises in transforming and upgrading through a standardized platform.

The platform architecture consists of four layers:

Resource Layer: Gathers and integrates global resources including software, service, business, and hardware resources, establishing a platform resource base and providing resource services for the upper layers.

Platform Layer: The core technology of COSMOPlat platform, supporting rapid development, deployment, operation, and integration of industrial applications. It enables software-based industrial technology, distributed scheduling, and optimal resource matching.

Application Layer: Provides specific connected factory application services for enterprises through software and cloud-based solutions, offering comprehensive intelligent solutions for the entire process.

Model Layer: Utilizes connected factory application services to achieve model replication and resource sharing, facilitating cross-industry replication and empowering SMEs to improve quality, efficiency, and transformation through standardization.

3) Orient State BIOP Platform

Orient-GX launched the Industrial Internet platform BIOP, based on an end-to-end industrial big data solution combining hardware and software.

The BIOP platform architecture comprises five parts: collection layer, transmission layer, IaaS layer, PaaS layer, and SaaS layer. Key components include BIOP-EG Smart Gateway access devices in the collection layer, industrial microservices, big data analysis, and application development in the PaaS layer, and cloud-based, intelligent industrial applications and solution services based on big data analysis in the SaaS layer, catering to various industry aspects and scenarios.

4) TreeRoots Internet RootCloud Platform

TreeRoots Internet Technology Co. was established by the IoT team from Trinity Heavy Industries, positioning itself as an independent and open Industrial Internet platform enterprise. In early 2017, Shugen Internet introduced the RootCloud platform. RootCloud primarily draws on San Heavy Industry's expertise in equipment manufacturing and remote operation and maintenance, extending from the OT layer to the IT layer. The platform focuses on equipment health management, offering end-to-end Industrial Internet solutions and services. The TreeRoots Internet RootCloud platform encompasses three key functionalities.

Firstly, intelligent IoT enables the collection and compilation of various equipment data through sensing devices like sensors, controllers, and the Internet of Things.

Secondly, big data and cloud computing address the challenges posed by massive equipment data by providing services such as data cleaning, data governance, privacy security management, and reliable cloud computing capabilities. Leveraging industrial experience knowledge graphs, the technology establishes an industrial big data workbench.

Thirdly, SaaS applications and solutions offer end-to-end solutions and plug-and-play SaaS applications for enterprises. The technology equips application developers with development components to facilitate the rapid construction of Industrial Internet applications.

Presently, the RootCloud platform delivers industrial application services including asset management, intelligent services, and predictive maintenance to enterprises. Moreover, based on the platform, it carries out financial innovation in the industrial chain, and has UBI insurance, maintenance and other product practices. It collaborates with financial institutions like insurance companies to enhance their risk control and financial service capabilities.

 **Mission Expansion**

Speed China—The Rapid Development of China's Digital Economy from the Application of Industrial Internet Technology

The Chinese Government's report proposes "accelerating the development of the digital economy and promoting the deep integration of the digital economy with the real economy," emphasizing the fusion of the Industrial Internet and new generation information technology. The Industrial Internet serves as a catalyst for digitalization, networking, and intelligence, hastening the digital transformation of China's industries. It represents the pinnacle of future manufacturing competition, driving profound changes in innovation models, production methods, organizational structures, and business paradigms. Concurrently, it fosters the reshaping and reengineering of industrial chains, supply chains, and value chains, promising comprehensive, profound, and revolutionary changes in future industrial development. As a result, it will profoundly impact social productivity and the trajectory of human history.

In today's world, a new wave of scientific and industrial advancements is burgeoning, with the Industrial Internet emerging as a product of the deep integration of manufacturing and the Internet. It stands as a linchpin of the new industrial revolution and a vital cornerstone of intelligent manufacturing.

Driven by the advancements in 5G technology and the Industrial Internet, industrial digitization is poised to become the engine propelling the development of the digital economy. The catalytic role of the Industrial Internet in driving the digital economy forward will become increasingly apparent. In the era of the Industrial Internet, it is imperative for contemporary college students to embrace a sense of mission and responsibility to effectively enhance their comprehensive capabilities.

Assignment: Analyze and research the current state of Industrial Internet development in China. Write reports to share insights.

项目 2

工业互联网网络搭建

任务 3　构建小型工业互联网网络

构建小型工业互联网

学习目标

①理解交换机和路由器在网络中的作用。
②理解交换机的基本工作原理。
③掌握使用以太网交换机实现多台计算机的互联。

建议学时

2 课时

工作情境

用一根交叉双绞线将两台计算机或者工业设备相互连接在一起，就能搭建一个简单的工业互联网网络。在这个最简单的网络中，只有两台主机之间能相互访问，如图 2.1 所示。

图 2.1　两个节点的网络

但是工业环境中一般都是几台设备甚至几十台设备需要联网，那么如何把这几十台工业设备连接在一起，组建一个工业互联网网络呢？一般人会直观地想到这样一个全互联型的拓扑，如图 2.2 所示。

这样的拓扑非常复杂，而且成本很高。因为这种联网方式需要每台工业设备（计算机）安装多块网卡，才有足够的接口连接到其他的工业设备（计算机）中。而且，全世界几亿台工业设备（计算机），通过这样的方式显然无法实现互联。

使用星形拓扑结构或者拓展星形拓扑结构可以很好地解决这个问题。

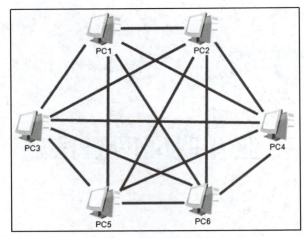

图 2.2 全互联型拓扑

知识导图

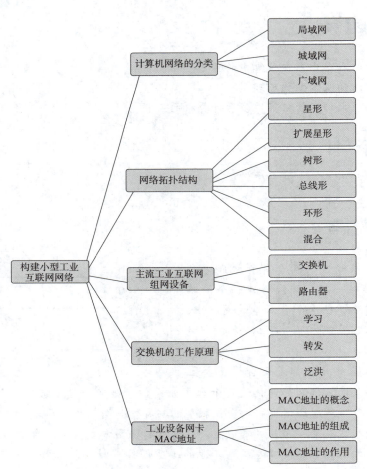

相关知识

1. 计算机网络的分类

计算机网络按覆盖的范围大小来分类，可以分为以下三类：

（1）局域网（Local Area Network，LAN）

局域网指在某一地理区域内由计算机、服务器以及各种网络设备组成的网络。局域网的覆盖范围一般是方圆几千米以内。典型的局域网有一个厂区的工业互联网络、一家公司的办公网络、一个网吧的网络、一个家庭网络等。

（2）城域网（Metropolitan Area Network，MAN）

城域网指在一个城市范围内所建立的计算机通信网络。典型的城域网有宽带城域网、教育城域网、市级或省级电子政务专网等。

（3）广域网（Wide Area Network，WAN）

广域网通常覆盖很大的地理范围，从几十千米到几千千米。它能连接多个城市甚至国家，并能提供远距离通信，形成国际性的大型网络。典型的广域网有 Internet（因特网）。

2. 网络拓扑结构

网络拓扑结构是指用传输媒体互连各种设备的物理布局，就是用什么方式把网络中的计算机等设备连接起来。常见的网络拓扑结构有星形、扩展星形、树形、总线形、环形、混合等结构。

（1）星形

星形网络拓扑结构的是以中央节点为中心，与各个节点相互连接组成。如果站点之间需要传输数据，首先传输到中央节点，再通过中央节点转发给相应节点。星形网络拓扑拓扑结构的网络搭建简单、可扩展性好，容易添加和删除节点，故障排除简单，是局域网组网的主流拓扑，如图 2.3 所示。

（2）扩展星形

一个中心节点（例如：以太网交换机）的接口是有限的，满足不了更多用户接入，需要将交换机互联，以拓展出更多接口，供更多用户的接入需求。在扩展星形网络拓扑中，额外的以太网交换机与其他星形拓扑互联，如图 2.4 所示。

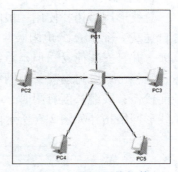

图 2.3 星形网络拓扑

（3）树形

树形网络拓扑结构是网络节点呈树状排列，形状像一棵倒置的树，顶端是树根，树根以下带多个分支，每个分支还可再带子分支，树根接收各站点发送的数据，如图 2.5 所示。树形网络拓扑节点扩展简单快捷，容易管理和维护，一个节点的故障不会影响网络的其余部分，在园区网中经常被使用。

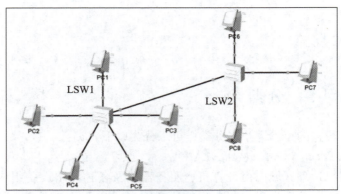

图 2.4 扩展星形网络拓扑

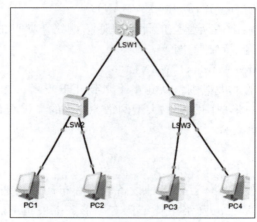

图 2.5 树形网络拓扑

(4) 总线形

总线形网络拓扑使用一根电缆连接所有的节点，电缆充当整个网络的主干，并在两端各自挂载一个 50Ω 的电阻吸收电磁信号。总线形网络拓扑不需要中心节点设备，因此价格低廉，并且安装简易。但是总线形网络拓扑存在诸多缺点，例如：链路上一台设备发生故障，则整个系统将崩溃；当网络流量较大或节点过多时，很容易在网络中产生冲突，网络性能较低；线缆长度有限时，不利于网络扩展。因此，在现代工业网络组网中，使用较少。总线形网络拓扑如图 2.6 所示。

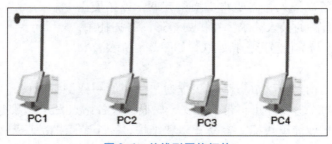

图 2.6 总线形网络拓扑

（5）环形

环形网络拓扑中每台设备都连接到另一台设备，最后一个节点与第一个节点组合在一起，形成一个闭环，如图2.7所示。环形网络拓扑中使用令牌将信息从一台计算机传递到另一台计算机，所有消息都以相同的方向通过环，安装和配置简单，添加或删除环内设备较为方便。但环形网络是单向流量，单环中断可能会导致整个网络中断，故障排除非常困难，在局域网中也较为少见。

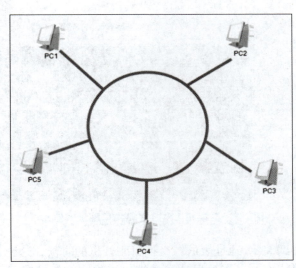

图2.7 环形网络拓扑

（6）混合

混合网络拓扑使用任何两种或多种网络拓扑结构的组合，以这种方式得到的网络呈现不同标准的拓扑结构，如图2.8所示。

3. 主流工业互联网组网设备

工业互联网的主流组网拓扑是星形网络拓扑结构，星形网络拓扑结构的中心节点主要由交换机担当。因此，在工业互联网组网中，最常见的网络设备是交换机。

交换机的功能是连接工业设备、计算机、服务器、网络打印机、网络摄像头、IP电话等终端设备，并实现与其他交换机、无线接入点、路由器、网络防火墙等网络设备的互联，从而构建局域网络，实现所有设备之间的通信。随着交换技术的不断发展，交换机的价格不断下降，交换到终端已是大势所趋。

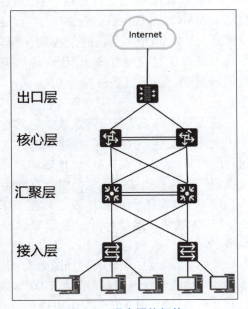

图2.8 混合网络拓扑

4. 交换机的工作原理

交换机的功能主要有学习、转发、过滤等。交换机有个 MAC 地址表，MAC 地址记录了每个终端的 MAC 地址和对应的端口关系，当交换机接收到数据时，就会根据 MAC 地址表来决定数据该从交换机的哪个端口转发出去，如图 2.9 所示。

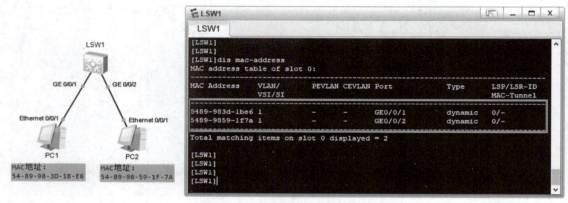

图 2.9 交换机 LSW1 的 MAC 地址表信息

交换机是如何学习到 MAC 地址表的？交换机刚开机的时候，这个 MAC 地址表是空的，但交换机有很好的学习能力。当有数据从某个端口流进交换机的时候，会自动读取数据包中发送方的 MAC 地址，建立该 MAC 地址和接收到该数据端口一一对应的映射关系，并将其写入 MAC 地址表中。经过多次学习，就会学习到一个较为完整的 MAC 地址表。需要注意的是，MAC 地址表是临时生成的，在交换机断电后会丢失，并且有过期老化的时间。当某个端口长时间没有该 MAC 地址的流量流入时，该 MAC 地址和端口的映射也会因为过期被删除。也可以通过命令 undo mac – address 在不断电的状态下清空交换机的 MAC 地址表。

那么交换机又是如何转发数据包的？当需要转发数据包时，交换机将数据包中的目的 MAC 地址同已建立的 MAC 地址表进行比较，以决定由哪个端口进行转发；如果数据包中的目的 MAC 地址不在 MAC 地址表中，则向所有端口转发，这一过程称为泛洪。如果交换机收到广播帧和组播帧，也会向所有的端口转发。

以如图 2.9 所示的 PC1 发送数据给 PC2 为例进行解析。PC1 把数据发到交换机 LSW1 后，LSW1 就像快递员一样，去读取数据帧上接收方 MAC 地址（目的 MAC 地址），如图 2.10 所示。

然后去查 MAC 地址表，如图 2.11 所示。

发现接收方接入的端口号是 GE0/0/2，同时，接收方跟自己同属 VLAN1，于是将发送给 PC2 的数据从 GE0/0/2 发出去。

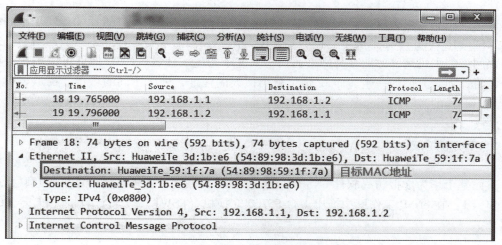

图 2.10 PC1 发送 PC2 的数据包

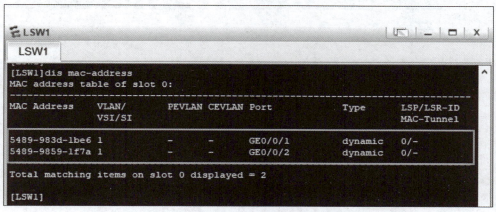

图 2.11 交换机 LSW1 的 MAC 地址表信息

5. 工业设备网卡 MAC 地址

MAC 是 Media Access Control 的简称，MAC 地址直译为介质访问控制位址，也称为物理地址（Physical Address），是由网络设备制造商生产时烧录在硬件内部的 EPROM（Erasable Programmable Read Only Memory）芯片上的一个参数，这个参数代表着主机在网络中的唯一标识。

MAC 地址的长度为 48 位（6 个字节），通常表示为 12 个 16 进制数，例如 00 - 16 - EA - AE - 3C - 40 就是一个 MAC 地址。其中，前 6 位 16 进制数 00 - 16 - EA 代表网络硬件制造商的编号，它由 IEEE（电气与电子工程师协会）分配，而后 6 位 16 进制数 AE - 3C - 40 代表该制造商所制造的某个网络产品（如网卡）的系列号。只要不更改自己的 MAC 地址，MAC 地址在世界上就是唯一的。形象地说，MAC 地址就如同身份证上的身份证号码，具有唯一性。

如果不用非常规手段去修改它，那么 MAC 地址是固定的，不会随着设备处于不同的网络而发生变化。与 MAC 地址不一样的是，IP 地址则会随着设备迁移到不同的网络，必须要获得该网络的主机地址才能参与网络通信。从这个角度去比较，MAC 地址可以类比成身份证号，将伴随着人们的一生；而 IP 地址就类似人的住址，处于不同的城市，街道名称和门牌号是不一样的。

6. 课堂实践

下面基于华为虚拟仿真软件 eNSP 组建一个小型局域网，实现多台计算机的互联互通。

步骤1：在 eNSP 工作区中拖出 1 台 S5700 交换机（LSW1）、4 台计算机（PC1~PC4），如图 2.12 所示。

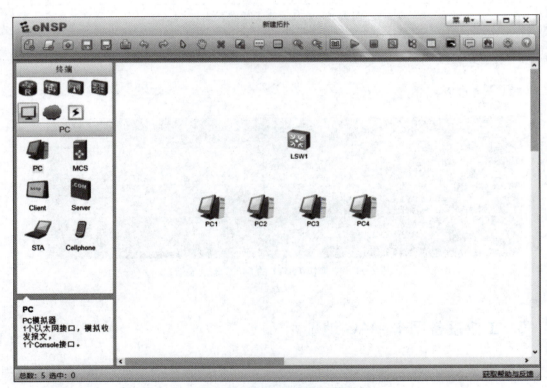

图 2.12　拖出交换机和计算机

步骤2：用线缆将计算机（工业网络设备）连接到交换机，如图 2.13 所示。

步骤3：按表 2.1 所示为 4 台计算机（工业网络设备）配置 IP 地址（子网掩码使用默认值）。

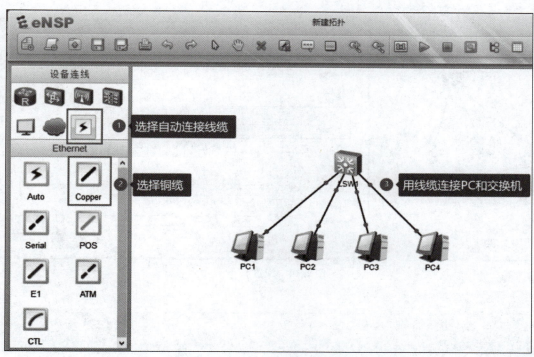

图 2.13 用线缆将计算机(工业网络设备)连接到交换机

表 2.1 IP 地址分配表

主机名	IP 地址	子网掩码
PC1	192.168.1.1	255.255.255.0
PC2	192.168.1.2	255.255.255.0
PC3	192.168.1.3	255.255.255.0
PC4	192.168.1.4	255.255.255.0

设置 PC1 的 IP 地址,如图 2.14 所示。
用同样的方法配置其他三台计算机(工业网络设备)的 IP 地址。
步骤 4:开启设备,测试。
单击"开启设备"按钮,启动所有设备,从 PC1 主机 ping PC2,结果如图 2.15 所示。
从其他主机相互 ping,结果也是通的。

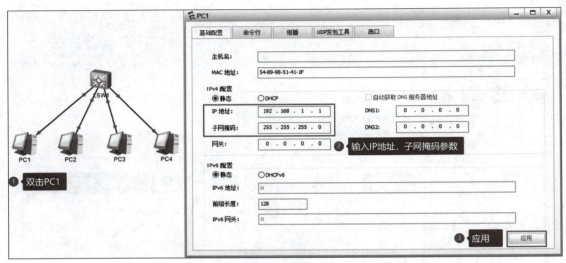

图 2.14 配置 IP 地址

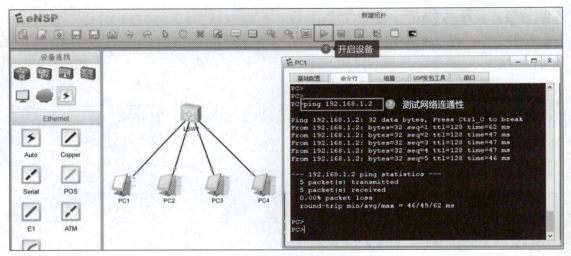

图 2.15 ping 测试结果

 任务拓展

团队协作筑就高效桥梁——小型局域网的打造与实践

一个完整的网络工程项目实施,需要与团队成员合作,进行需求分析、方案设计、实施建设等工作。这要求项目团队人员具备良好的组织与协作能力,能够有效地与他人合作、沟通和协调,达成共识并共同完成任务。

小型局域网络的部署,为团队协作创造了更好的条件。团队精神已经成为职业发展中最重要的软技能之一,在学习和工作中培养正确的集体观念显得尤为重要。团队协作建立在团队的基础上,发挥团队精神、互补互助以达到团队最大工作效率。对于团队成员来说,不仅要有个人能力,更需要有在不同的位置上各尽所能,与其他成员协调合作的能力。当代大学生在工作中要学会有效沟通、分工合作,同时,在工程实践中应注重学思结合、知行合一,培养善于发现问题、解决问题的实践能力。

作业:随着国家技术水平的提升,华为等一大批国产网络设备越来越多地用在局域网中,请参照本任务,使用国产网络设备组建小型办公局域网,实现不同工业网络设备之间的相互通信。

Project 2

How to Build an Industrial Internet

Task 3 Build a Small-Scale Industrial Internet

◉ Learning Objective

①Understand the role of switches and routers in the network.
②Understand the basic principles of switches.
③Master the use of Ethernet switches to achieve interconnection of multiple computers.

◉ Suggested Hours

2 hours

◉ Work Situations

A simple industrial network can be built by connecting two computers or industrial equipment to each other with a crossover twisted pair cable. In this basic network setup, only two hosts can access each other, as depicted in Figure 2.1.

Figure 2.1 A Network of Two Nodes

In industrial environments, multiple devices, often dozens, need to be networked together. How to connect these industrial equipment to form an industrial network? Typically, people might intuitively consider a fully interconnected topology, as depicted in Figure 2.2.

The complexity and costliness of such a topology stem from the need for multiple network cards to be installed in each industrial device (computer) to provide enough interfaces for connections to other industrial devices (computers). Additionally, with hundreds of millions of industrial devices (computers) worldwide, fully interconnecting them in this manner is clearly impractical.

Employing a star topology or expanding upon it can present a viable solution to this challenge.

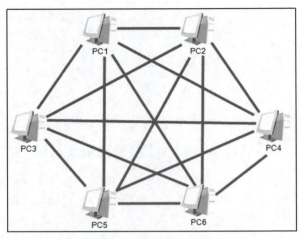

Figure 2.2　Fully Interconnected Topology

Knowledge Map

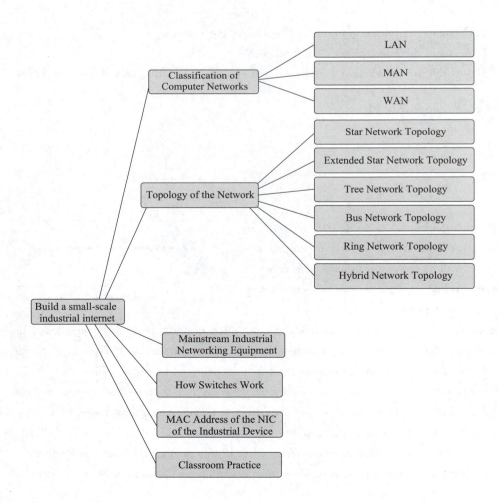

Project 2　How to Build an Industrial Internet

Relevant Knowledge

1. Classification of Computer Networks

Computer networks are classified based on the size of their coverage and can be categorized into the following three types:

(1) Local Area Network (LAN)

A LAN is a network consisting of computers, servers, and various network devices within a specific geographic area. Typically, the coverage area of a LAN spans a few kilometers. Examples of LANs include Industrial Internet in factories, office networks in companies, networks in Internet cafes, home networks, etc.

(2) Metropolitan Area Network (MAN)

A MAN refers to a computer communications network established within a city. Typical MANs include broadband MANs, educational MANs, and municipal or provincial e-government networks.

(3) Wide Area Network (WAN)

A WAN covers large geographical areas, ranging from tens to thousands of kilometers. They can connect multiple cities or countries and provide long-distance communications to form large international networks. The Internet is a typical example of a WAN.

2. Topology of the Network

Network topology refers to the physical layout of interconnected devices with transmission media, i.e., the method of connecting computers and other devices in the network. Common network topologies include star, extended star, tree, ring, bus, mesh, hybrid, and other structures.

(1) Star Network Topology

A star-structured network consists of a central node serving as the hub, interconnected with individual nodes. Data transmission between nodes occurs via the central hub. Star network topology is simple to build, scalable, allow for easy addition and removal of nodes, and are straightforward to troubleshoot. They are the predominant topology for LAN networking, as depicted in Figure 2.3.

(2) Extended Star Network Topology

In an Extended star network topology, the central node (e.g., an Ethernet switch) has a finite number of interfaces,

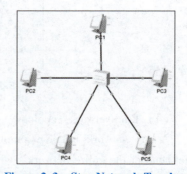

Figure 2.3　Star Network Topology

which may not be adequate for expanding user access requirements. To address this limitation, switches must be interconnected to accommodate additional interfaces for increased user access demands. In an extended star topology, additional Ethernet switches are interconnected with other star topologies, as depicted in Figure 2.4.

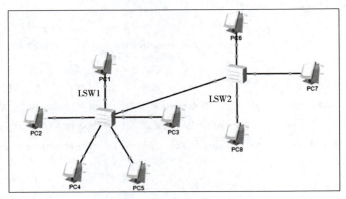

Figure 2.4 Extended Star Network Topology

(3) Tree Network Topology

The tree network topology is structured like an inverted tree, with a root at the top, multiple branches below the root, and sub-branches extending from each branch. Data is transmitted from each site to the root node. This arrangement is depicted in Figure 2.5. Tree network topology nodes are straightforward to expand, manage, and maintain, making them a popular choice for campus networks. Additionally, if a node fails, it typically does not impact the rest of the network.

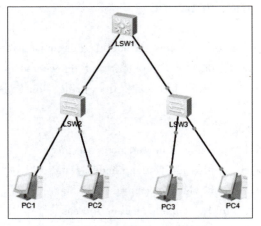

Figure 2.5 Tree Network Topology

(4) Bus Network Topology

A bus network topology employs a single cable to interconnect all nodes, serving as the backbone of the entire network, with a 50Ω resistor installed at each end to absorb electromagnetic signals. Bus topologies do not necessitate a central node device, making them cost-effective and easy to deploy. However, there are several drawbacks to the bus topology. For instance, if a device fails on the link, the entire system will collapse. Moreover, when network traffic is heavy or there are too many nodes, conflicts can easily arise, resulting in low network performance. Additionally, the cable length is limited, which hinders network extension. Consequently, bus topologies are less commonly utilized in modern industrial network configurations. See Figure 2.6 for reference.

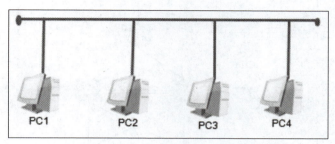

Figure 2.6　Bus Network Topology

(5) Ring Network Topology

In a ring network topology, each device is connected to another device, forming a closed ring where the last node is connected to the first node, as depicted in Figure 2.7. Ring network topology utilizes tokens to transmit information from one computer to another, and all messages circulate through the ring in the same direction, simplifying installation, configuration, and the addition or removal of devices from the ring. However, ring-type networks feature unidirectional traffic, and a single ring outage can lead to the entire network going down, resulting in challenging troubleshooting and making them less common in LANs.

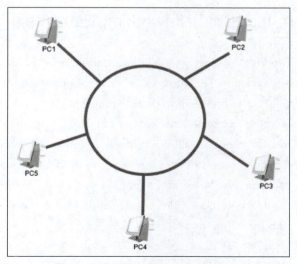

Figure 2.7　Ring Network Topology

(6) Hybrid Network Topology

The hybrid network topology combines two or more network topologies in any configuration, resulting in networks that exhibit various standard topologies, as depicted in Figure 2.8.

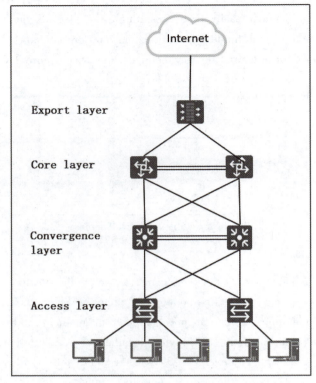

Figure 2.8　Hybrid Network Topology

3. Mainstream Industrial Networking Equipment

The mainstream networking topology in the Industrial Internet is the star network topology, where the central node is typically occupied by a switch. Consequently, in Industrial Internet networking, switches are the most prevalent network equipment.

Switches serve the purpose of connecting various industrial equipment, computers, servers, network printers, webcams, IP phones, and other terminal devices. They facilitate interconnections with other switches, wireless access points, routers, network firewalls, and other network equipment, thereby establishing a local area network to enable communication between all devices. As switching technology advances, the prices of switches are decreasing, and transitioning to terminals has become the prevailing trend.

4. How Switches Work

Switches operate primarily through functions such as learning, forwarding, and filtering. They maintain a MAC address table that records the MAC addresses of each terminal along with their corresponding port relationships. When the switch receives data, it utilizes the MAC address table to determine the appropriate port through which the data should be forwarded, as depicted in Figure 2.9.

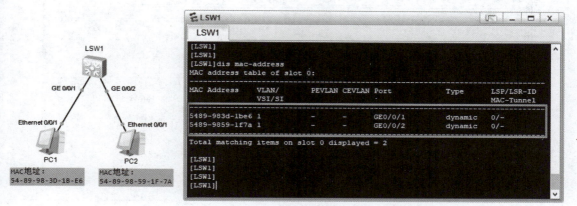

Figure 2.9   MAC Address Table Information for LSW1

The switch learns the MAC address table through a process called MAC address learning. Initially, when the switch is powered on, the MAC address table is empty. However, as data flows into the switch from various ports, it automatically reads the sender's MAC address from the incoming packets. The switch then establishes a one-to-one mapping relationship between this MAC address and the port from which the data was received, and writes it into the MAC address table. Over time, as data continues to flow through the switch, this process repeats, resulting in a more comprehensive MAC address table. It's important to note that the MAC address table is temporary and will be lost when the switch is powered off. Additionally, it has an expiration aging time. If there is no incoming traffic on a port associated with a specific MAC address for an extended period, the mapping between that MAC address and port will be removed from the table due to expiration. The switch's MAC address table can also be cleared without powering down using the command "undo mac-address."

Regarding packet forwarding, when a data frame needs to be forwarded, the switch compares the destination MAC address in the frame with the entries in the MAC address table to determine which port to forward it to. If the destination MAC address is found in the MAC address table, the switch forwards the frame only to the corresponding port. However, if the destination MAC address in the packet is not found in the MAC address table, the switch forwards the frame to all ports, a process known as flooding. Additionally, if the switch receives broadcast and multicast frames, it forwards them to all ports.

To illustrate this process, consider the example of PC1 sending data to PC2 in Figure 2.9. After PC1 sends the data to switch LSW1, LSW1 reads the destination MAC address on the data frame and forwards it accordingly, acting like a courier, as depicted in Figure 2.10.

Then query the MAC address table, as depicted in Figure 2.11.

Upon investigation, it is determined that the receiver accessed port number GE0/0/2, and

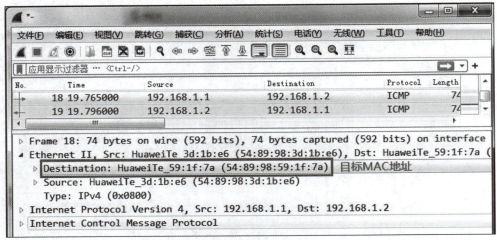

Figure 2.10　Data frame sent from PC1 to PC2

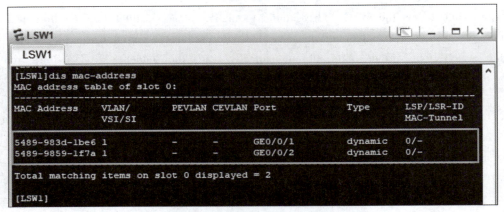

Figure 2.11　MAC address table information for LSW1

simultaneously, the receiver belongs to the same VLAN 1 as itself. Therefore, the data sent to PC2 is transmitted from port GE0/0/2.

5. MAC Address of the NIC of the Industrial Device

A MAC, short for Media Access Control, and MAC address also known as a Physical address, is a parameter embedded into the EPROM (Erasable Programmable Read Only Memory) chip within the hardware during production by the network equipment manufacturer. It serves as the unique identification of the host within the network.

A MAC address comprises 48 bits (6 bytes) and is commonly represented as 12 hexadecimal numbers. For instance, 00 – 16 – EA – AE – 3C – 40 is an example of a MAC address. The initial 6 hexadecimal digits (00 – 16 – EA) denote the network hardware manufacturer's number, assigned by the IEEE (Institute of Electrical and Electronics Engineers), while the subsequent 6 hexadecimal digits (AE - 3C - 40) represent the serial number of a specific network product (e. g. , a network card) manufactured by that company. MAC addresses are globally unique unless intentionally altered. Metaphorically, the MAC address is as unique as the ID number on an ID card.

If no unconventional methods are employed to modify it, the MAC address remains fixed and does not change as the device connects to different networks. In contrast, the IP address migrates with the device to different networks and requires obtaining the host address of that network to engage in network communications. From this perspective, a MAC address can be likened to an ID number, which remains with the individual for life, while an IP address resembles a person's address, which changes when moving to a different city, and the street name and house number differ.

6. Classroom Practice

The following instructions are based on Huawei's virtual simulation software eNSP for creating a small LAN and establishing interconnections between multiple computers.

Step 1: Drag one S5700 switch (LSW1) and four computers (PC1 ~ PC4) onto the eNSP workspace, as depicted in Figure 2.12.

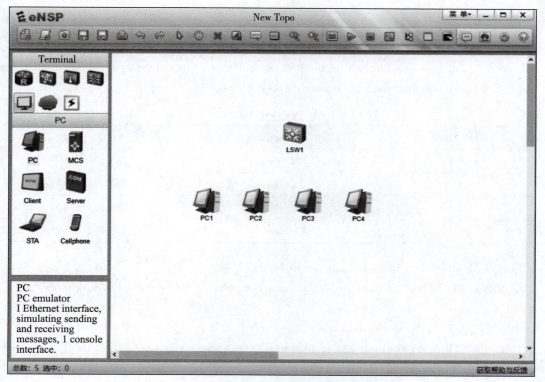

Figure 2.12 Drag Out Switches and Computers

Step 2: Connect the computer (industrial network device) to the switch with a cable, as depicted in Figure 2.13.

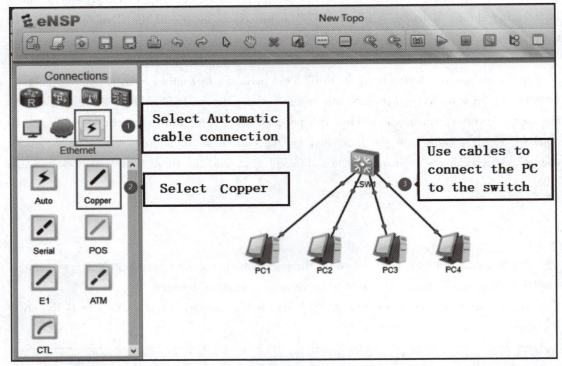

Figure 2.13 Connect the Computer (Industrial Network Device) to the Switch with a Cable

Step 3: Configure IP addresses for the four computers (industrial network devices) according to Table 2.1 (use default values for subnet masks).

Table 2.1 IP Address Assignment Table

Host Name	IP Address	Subnet Mask
PC1	192.168.1.1	255.255.255.0
PC2	192.168.1.2	255.255.255.0
PC3	192.168.1.3	255.255.255.0
PC4	192.168.1.4	255.255.255.0

Set the IP address of PC1. As depicted in Figure 2.14.

Configure the IP addresses of the other three computers (industrial network devices) in the same way.

Step 4: Turn on the device and test.

Click the "Turn on Device" button to start all the devices and ping PC2 from PC1 host. The result is depicted in Figure 2.15.

Pinging each other from other hosts results in a successful response.

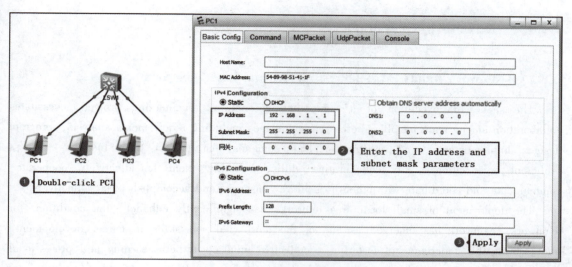

Figure 2.14   Configuring IP Address

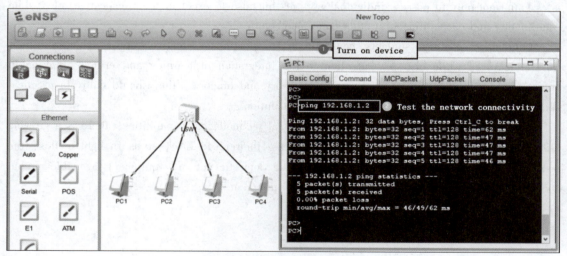

Figure 2.15   Ping Test Results

Mission Expansion

Teamwork Builds Efficiency—Building and Practicing Small-Scale LANs

The successful execution of a comprehensive network engineering project necessitates collaboration among team members across various stages including requirements analysis, program design, implementation and construction. This demands that project team members possess proficient organizational and collaborative skills, enabling them to effectively cooperate, communicate and coordinate with others to achieve consensus and accomplish tasks collectively.

The deployment of small local area networks has significantly enhanced the conditions for teamwork. Teamwork has emerged as one of the most vital soft skills in career development, underscoring the importance of fostering a collective mindset in both learning and professional endeavors. Effective teamwork is predicated on the foundation of cohesive teamwork, fostering team spirit, complementarity, and mutual assistance to maximize team efficiency. For team members, it is essential not only to possess individual abilities but also to excel in their respective roles while coordinating and cooperating with other team members.

Contemporary college students should strive to communicate effectively and collaborate in their work endeavors, while also pay attention to the integration of learning and critical thinking in engineering practice. Emphasizing the unity of theory and practice, they should cultivate practical skills geared toward problem identification and resolution.

Assignment: With the advancement of national technological capabilities, there is a growing utilization of domestic network equipment, such as Huawei, in LAN setups. In light of this, the task involves establishing a small office LAN using domestic network equipment to enable mutual communication among various industrial network equipment.

任务 4　确定计算机所在的网络

确定计算机所在网络

学习目标

①理解子网掩码的作用。
②掌握计算一台主机所在网络的网络地址、广播地址和可用的主机地址范围的方法。

建议学时

2 课时

工作情境

在配置 IP 地址的时候，用鼠标单击子网掩码文本框，子网掩码就会自动出现。
子网掩码重要吗？在 Windows 系统做一个测试：删除网卡的子网掩码参数，然后单击"确定"按钮，提示如图 2.16 所示。

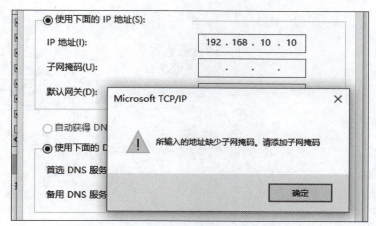

图 2.16　删除子网掩码后的提示信息

出现的警告信息告诉我们，必须添加子网掩码，否则无法设置 IP 地址。显然，对于 IP 地址而言，子网掩码是必需的。
那么，子网掩码到底是什么？有什么用？为什么如此重要？

知识导图

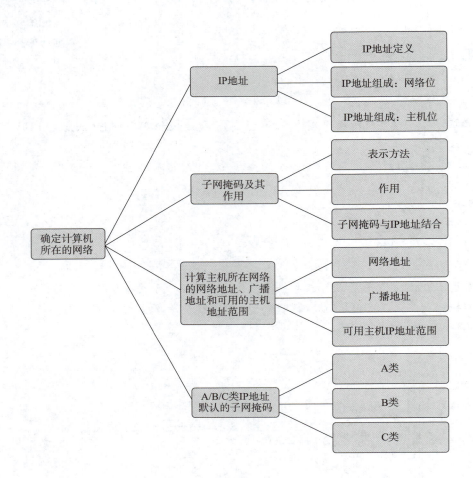

相关知识

1. IP 地址

IP 地址是主机在网络中的一个标识，用来标识网络中计算机（工业设备）的身份，每台计算机有唯一的编号。根据协议版本分为 IPv4 地址和 IPv6 地址，这里讨论的是 IPv4 地址。IPv4 地址由 32 位二进制组成，一般将其用 3 个点号分成 4 段，并将这 4 段数字分别转换成十进制来表达，以提高可读性，如图 2.17 所示。

IP 地址由网络位和主机位两部分组成。网络位部分标记的是该 IP 地址所在网络的编号，主机位部分是拥有该 IP 地址的主机在网络里的编号。可以把互联网类比成一个城市或更大的区域，那么一个小网络可以类比成一条街，网络位部分就是这条街的编号，而主机

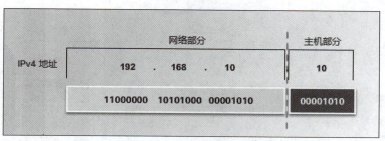

图 2.17　IPv4 地址的十进制和二进制表达方式

位部分就是这条街上每个单位的门牌号。网络设备是通过识别 IP 地址的网络位部分找到目标网络,然后在这个网络内找到目标主机。就像快递员根据地址上的街道名称找到接收方所在的街道,然后通过门牌号在这条街上找到他的具体位置一样。

互联网中的每个网络的网络号必须是唯一的,同一网络中的主机号也必须是唯一的,不能重复,否则会导致冲突,进而影响数据通信。

2. 子网掩码及其作用

子网掩码和 IP 地址本身的表示方法一样,也是采用点分十进制表示法。它用来指明一个 IP 地址的哪些部分是主机所在的网络地址以及哪些部分是主机地址。

子网掩码用于标识 IPv4 地址的网络部分/主机部分,本质上是一个 1 位序列后接 0 位序列的序列。

从以上信息可以归纳出子网掩码的两个特点:

①子网掩码跟 IP 地址一样,也是由 32 位的二进制组成的,但是 1 和 0 必须是连续的,不能交叉,如图 2.18 所示。

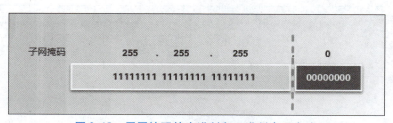

图 2.18　子网掩码的十进制和二进制表示方法

子网掩码还有另外一种很常用的更便捷的表达方式,那就是用二进制的子网掩码中"1"的个数来表示。如图 2.18 所示,子网掩码 255.255.255.0 的二进制表达有 24 个"1",则该子网掩码可以表示成"/24"的方式。因为便捷,所以用得最多的其实就是这种方式。

②子网掩码跟 IP 地址一起使用,以便区分在 32 位的 IP 地址中,哪些是网络位部分,哪些是主机位部分。

如图 2.19 所示,子网掩码"1"所对应的就是 IP 地址的网络位部分,"0"所对应的就是 IP 地址的主机位部分。

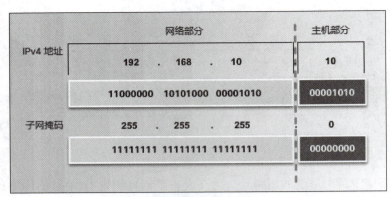

图 2.19　子网掩码和 IP 地址的对应关系

需要注意的是，子网掩码本身并不包含 IP 地址的网络信息，而只是负责告诉主机：你那串 32 位的二进制 IP 地址，哪些位是网络位，哪些位是主机位。如果没有子网掩码，主机就无法知道自己的网络位是哪些，主机位是哪些。而网络位是一个网络的编号，如果无法明确，主机的身份也就不明确，因为不知道自己所处的是哪个网络，导致无法发送数据。就像一个人如果不知道自己在哪里就无法发快递一样，别人也不知道如何寄快递给他。

3. 计算主机所在网络的网络地址、广播地址和可用的主机地址范围

知道了 IP 地址及其子网掩码，就可以明确主机所在的网络。方法很简单，就是把 IP 地址和子网掩码分别转换成二进制表达，然后进行逻辑"与"（AND）运算。

二进制的逻辑"与"运算如表 2.2 所示。

表 2.2　二进制的逻辑"与"运算

逻辑变量	逻辑运算符	逻辑变量	结果
1	AND	1	1
0	AND	1	0
0	AND	0	0
1	AND	0	0
注：逻辑运算中的 AND 运算，可以用算数运算的"乘法"去类比，其运算结果一样。			

子网掩码用来确定一个 IP 地址的网络位部分和主机位部分，同时，确定了该 IP 地址属于哪一个逻辑网络。互联网中的计算机分布在不同的逻辑网络中，但是不管是哪个逻辑网络中的计算机，必须要遵守网络的通信规则才能实现互联网中不同计算机之间的相互通信。

4. A/B/C 类 IP 地址默认的子网掩码

最初设计互联网络时，为了便于寻址以及层次化构造网络，每个 IP 地址包括两个标识

码(ID),即网络ID和主机ID。同一个物理网络上的所有主机都使用同一个网络ID,网络上的一个主机(包括网络上工业设备、计算机、服务器等)有一个主机ID与其对应。Internet委员会定义了5种IP地址类型以适应不同容量的网络,即A~E类。

其中A、B、C 3类由Internet NIC在全球范围内统一分配,D、E类为特殊地址。A、B、C 3类IP地址默认子网掩码如表2.3所示。

表2.3 A、B、C 3类IP地址默认子网掩码

类别	IP地址范围	单个网段最大主机数	私有IP地址范围
A	1.0.0.1 ~ 127.255.255.254	16777214	10.0.0.0 ~ 10.255.255.255
B	128.0.0.1 ~ 191.255.255.254	65534	172.16.0.0 ~ 172.31.255.255
C	192.0.0.1 ~ 223.255.255.254	254	192.168.0.0 ~ 192.168.255.255

在给计算机配置IP地址的时候,系统会自动分配一个默认的子网掩码,它是根据如表2.4所示的A、B、C 3类IP地址默认子网掩码来确定的。

表2.4 A、B、C 3类IP地址默认子网掩码

网络类型	默认子网掩码	掩码长度
A	255.0.0.0	/8
B	255.255.0.0	/16
C	255.255.255.0	/24

5. 课堂实践

下面通过一个案例掌握计算一台主机所在网络的网络地址、广播地址和可用的IP地址范围的方法。

案例:一台主机的IP地址为192.168.10.10,子网掩码为255.255.255.0,计算出该主机所在网络的网络地址、广播地址和可用的IP地址的范围。

步骤1:将十进制的IP地址、子网掩码转换成二进制的表达方式,如表2.5所示。

表2.5 IP地址、子网掩码的十进制和二进制对应关系

IP地址	192	168	10	10
子网掩码	255	255	255	0
二进制IP地址	11000000	10101000	00001010	00001010
二进制子网掩码	11111111	11111111	11111111	00000000

步骤2:将IP地址和子网掩码进行逻辑"与"运算,得到该主机所在网络的网络地址,如表2.6所示。

表 2.6 二进制 IP 地址和二进制子网掩码进行逻辑"与"运算

二进制 IP 地址	11000000	10101000	00001010	00001010
逻辑运算	AND			
二进制子网掩码	11111111	11111111	11111111	00000000
结果	11000000	10101000	00001010	00000000

所以，IP 地址为 192.168.10.10/24 的主机所在网络的网络地址是 11000000.10101000.00001010.00000000/24，这是一个主机位为全"0"的地址。"0"是二进制数中最小的数字。因此，网络地址就是网络中最小的地址。将网络地址转换成十进制，增加可读性，得到 192.168.10.0/24。网络地址是一个网络的编号，是网络在互联网中唯一的标记。

注意：表达一个 IP 地址的时候，一定要附带子网掩码，否则，更改 IP 地址就没有意义。

步骤 3：将网络地址主机位部分的每一个二进制位全部换成"1"，就得到该主机所在网络的广播地址，如图 2.20 所示。

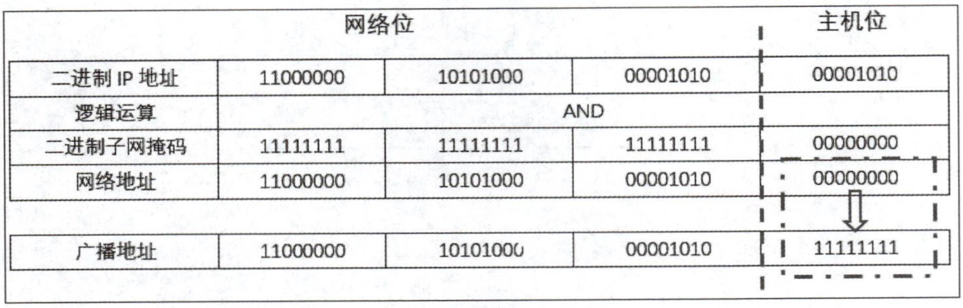

图 2.20 广播地址计算过程

广播地址的主机位全为"1"。"1"是二进制数中最大的数字，因此，广播地址就是该网络中最大的地址。将广播地址转换成十进制，以增加其可读性，得到 192.168.10.255/24。

步骤 4：确定可以分配给主机使用的 IP 地址。

通过以上步骤的计算，得出 IP 地址为 192.168.10.10/24 的主机所在网络的网络地址和广播地址如表 2.7 所示。

表 2.7 网络地址和广播地址

地址类型	值	备注
网络地址	192.168.10.0/24	该主机所在网络中的最小 IP 地址
广播地址	192.168.10.255/24	该主机所在网络中的最大 IP 地址

知道了最小 IP 地址和最大 IP 地址，就可以得出一个范围，如图 2.21 所示。

该网络中可用的主机地址就应该为 0~255。但是，192.168.10.0/24 已经被当作网络地址使用，192.168.10.255/24 已经被当作广播地址使用，所以剩下的 192.168.10.1 ~

图 2.21 IP 地址坐标区间图

192.168.10.254 可以被分配给主机使用,这就是该网络中实际可用的主机地址。需要注意的是,192.168.10.0/24 和 192.168.10.255/24 不能再被分配给主机使用。

 任务拓展

IP 地址——连接世界的数字通行证

　　IP 地址是互联网通信中用于标识设备的一组数字，可以看作设备在网络上的"住址"。在组建小型局域网的过程中，IP 地址的规划和管理是非常重要的一环，也涉及用户隐私的保护。同学们需要了解 IP 地址的分类和分配方式，合理规划和管理 IP 地址资源，确保网络的正常运行和信息的安全传输，同时，也要认识到网络通信的基础和风险，提高网络安全意识，培养个人信息保护的能力。此外，也要正确使用网络资源，遵守网络道德规范，促进网络环境的健康和秩序发展。

　　作业：在小组内展开讨论和合作，通过实践项目的设计与实施，深入理解 IP 地址在数字化时代的重要性，并思考数字化技术应用的社会责任。

Task 4　Identify the Network to Which the Computer is Connected

◎ Learning Objective

①Understand the role of subnet masks.
②Understand how to calculate the network address, broadcast address, and range of available host addresses for the network in which a host is located.

◎ Suggested Hours

2 hours

◎ Work Situations

When configuring the IP address, clicking the Subnet Mask text box with the mouse will automatically populate the subnet mask.

Is the subnet mask important? Let's conduct a test in Windows: Delete the subnet mask parameter of the network card and then click the "Confirm" button as depicted in Figure 2.16.

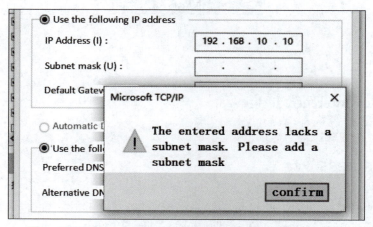

Figure 2.16　Prompt Message After Deleting a Subnet Mask

The warning message indicates that the subnet mask must be added, or else the IP address cannot be configured. Clearly, a subnet mask is essential for defining an IP address.

Now, what precisely is a subnet mask, and what function does it serve? Why is it considered crucial?

Knowledge Map

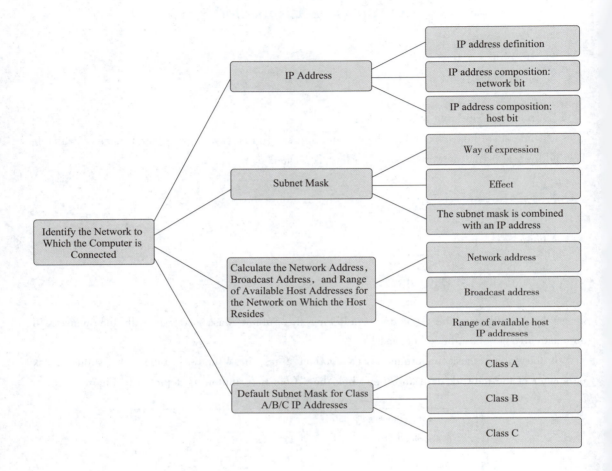

Relevant Knowledge

1. IP Address

An IP address serves as an identifier for a host within a network, uniquely identifying each computer or industrial equipment connected to the network. IP addresses are categorized into IPv4 and IPv6 addresses based on the protocol version. In this discussion, we focus on IPv4 addresses. IPv4 addresses are represented as 32-bit binary numbers, typically divided into four segments separated by dots. These four segments are then converted into decimal numbers for better readability, as depicted in Figure 2.17.

An IP address is composed of two components: the network bits and the host bits. The network

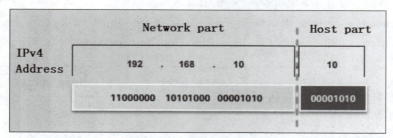

Figure 2.17 Decimal and Binary Representation of IPv4 Addresses

bits designate the network to which the IP address belongs, while the host bits specify the individual host within that network. To illustrate, consider the internet as a city or a larger geographical area, where a small network can be likened to a street. The network bits serve as the street number by identifying the specific network, while the host bits function as the door numbers of each unit on the street, pinpointing individual hosts within the network. When a network device receives an IP address, it uses the network bits to locate the target network and then locates the specific host within that network. This process is akin to a courier identifying the street based on the street name in the address and then locating the exact location on that street using the door number.

Each network in the Internet must have a unique network number, and the host numbers within the same network must also be unique and non-duplicative. Failure to ensure uniqueness can lead to conflicts, disrupting data communication.

2. Subnet Mask

The Subnet mask, akin to the IP address itself, is represented in dotted decimal notation and serves to distinguish the network address from the host address within an IP address.

The subnet mask aids in identifying the network portion and host portion of an IPv4 address, essentially comprising a sequence of 1 bit followed by 0 bit.

From the information provided, two key characteristics of subnet masks can be deduced:

①A subnet mask, like an IP address, comprises 32 bits of binary. However, the 1 and 0 must be consecutive and cannot be interspersed, as depicted in Figure 2.18. Another common and convenient representation of subnet masks is using the count of "1" bit, such as "/24" to denote a Subnet mask of 255.255.255.0, as depicted in Figure 2.18.

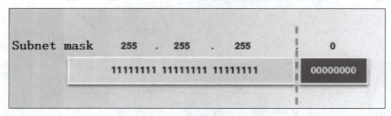

Figure 2.18 Decimal and Binary Representations of Subnet Mask

②Subnet Mask works in conjunction with IP address to distinguish the network bit portion from the host bit portion of a 32 – bit IP address. Each "1" in the subnet mask corresponds to a network bit in the IP address, while each "0" designates a host bit, as depicted in Figure 2.19.

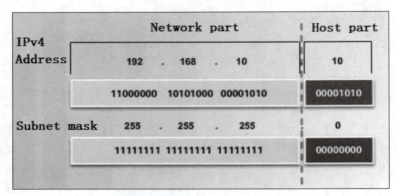

Figure 2.19 Correspondence Between Subnet Mask and IP Address

It should be noted that the subnet mask itself does not contain network information about the IP address, but is only responsible for telling the host which bits are network bits and which bits are host bits of your 32 – bit binary IP address. Without the subnet mask, hosts would be unable to discern their network bits, leading to ambiguity in their network identity. This lack of clarity hampers data transmission, as hosts cannot determine their network affiliation, analogous to a person being unaware of their location and unable to receive deliveries. Subnet masks are essential for enabling hosts to identify their network and participate effectively in data communication.

3. Calculate the Network Address, Broadcast Address, and Range of Available Host Addresses for the Network on Which the Host Resides

Once you have the IP address and its corresponding subnet mask, you can determine the specific network to which the host belongs. This process involves converting both the IP address and subnet mask to binary notation and then performing a logical "AND" operation between the two.

Refer to Table 2.2 for guidance on binary logical "AND" operations.

Table 2.2 Binary Logical "And" Arithmetic

Logical variable	Logical operator	Logic variable	Result
1	AND	1	1
0	AND	1	0
0	AND	0	0
1	AND	0	0

Note: The logical operation AND operation, can be used in arithmetic operations "multiplication" to the analogy, the result of the operation is the same.

The subnet mask plays a crucial role in delineating the network bit portion and host bit portion of an IP address. Simultaneously, it determines the logical network to which the IP address belongs. Computers across the Internet are organized into various logical networks. Irrespective of the specific logical network to which they are assigned, comply with the network's communication protocols is essential for facilitating communication among computers within the Internet.

4. Default Subnet Mask for Class A/B/C IP Addresses

When the Internet was initially designed, each IP address consisted of two identifiers: a network ID and a host ID. This structure facilitates efficient addressing and the hierarchical organization of the network. All hosts within the same physical network shared the same network ID, while each individual host, including industrial equipment, computers, servers, etc., on the network, was assigned a unique host ID. The Internet Engineering Task Force (IETF) defines five types of IP addresses to accommodate networks of varying capacities, denoted as Classes A through E.

Classes A, B, and C (as depicted in Table 2.3) are globally allocated by the Internet Assigned Numbers Authority (IANA), while Classes D and E are reserved for specific purposes.

Table 2.3 Default Subnet Mask for Each Type of IP Address

Category	IP address range	Maximum number of hosts in a CIDR block	Private IP address range
A	1.0.0.1 ~ 127.255.255.254	16 777 214	10.0.0.0 ~ 10.255.255.255
B	128.0.0.1 – 191.255.255.254	65 534	172.16.0.0 ~ 172.31.255.255
C	192.0.0.1 ~ 223.255.255.254	254	192.168.0.0 – 192.168.255.255

When configuring an IP address for a computer, the system automatically assigns a default subnet mask. It determines this default subnet mask based on Table 2.4.

Table 2.4 Default Subnet Mask for Each Type of IP Address

Type of network	Default subnet mask	Mask length
A	255.0.0.0	/8
B	255.255.0.0	/16
C	255.255.255.0	/24

5. Classroom Practice

Here is a case study to understand the method of calculating the network address, broadcast address, and available IP address range of the network where a host is located.

Example: Suppose a host has an IP address of 192.168.10.10 and a subnet mask of

255.255.255.0. We need to calculate the network address, broadcast address, and range of available host addresses for the network in which the host is located.

Step 1: Convert the decimal IP address and subnet mask to a binary expression, see Table 2.5.

Table 2.5 Decimal and Binary Correspondence of IP Addresses, Subnet Masks

IP Address	192	168	10	10
Subnet mask	255	255	255	0
Binary IP address	11000000	10101000	00001010	00001010
Binary subnet mask	11111111	11111111	11111111	00000000

Step 2: Logically "sum" the IP address and subnet mask to get the address of the network where the host is located, see Table 2.6.

Table 2.6 Logical "and" Tables for Binary IP Addresses and Binary Subnet Masks

Binary IP address	11000000	10101000	00001010	00001010
logical operation	AND			
Binary subnet mask	11111111	11111111	11111111	00000000
result	11000000	10101000	00001010	00000000

The network address of the host with IP address 192.168.10.10/24 is 11000000.10101000.00001010.00000000/24, representing an address with all "0" host bits. In binary notation, "0" is the smallest value. Therefore, the network address is the smallest address within the network. Converting the network address to decimal format enhances readability, resulting in 192.168.10.0/24. The network address serves as a unique identifier for the network on the Internet.

Note: When representing an IP address, it must be accompanied by a subnet mask; otherwise, altering the IP address is meaningless.

Step 3: Replace every binary bit in the host bit portion of the network address with a "1" in its entirety to get the broadcast address of the network where the host is located, as depicted in Figure 2.20.

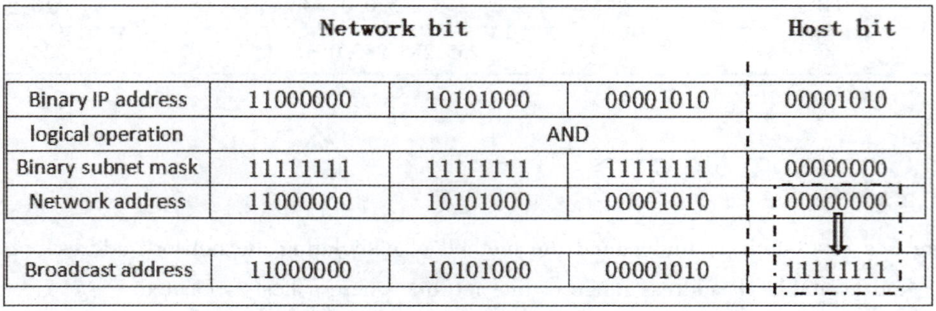

	Network bit			Host bit
Binary IP address	11000000	10101000	00001010	00001010
logical operation	AND			
Binary subnet mask	11111111	11111111	11111111	00000000
Network address	11000000	10101000	00001010	00000000
Broadcast address	11000000	10101000	00001010	11111111

Figure 2.20 The Process of Broadcast Address Calculation

The host bits of a broadcast address are all set to "1." In binary notation, "1" represents the largest value, making the broadcast address the highest address within the network. Converting the broadcast address to decimal format enhances readability, yielding 192.168.10.255/24.

Step 4: Determine the IP addresses available for assignment to hosts.

The calculations conducted in the preceding steps yield the network address and broadcast address of the network where the host with the IP address 192.168.10.10/24 is situated, as depicted in Table 2.7.

Table 2.7 Network Address and Broadcast Address Tables

Address type	Value	Remark
Network address	192.168.10.0/24	Minimum IP address of the network where the host resides
Broadcast address	192.168.10.255/24	Maximum IP address of the network where the host resides

Understand the minimum and maximum IP addresses and derive a range, as depicted in Figure 2.21.

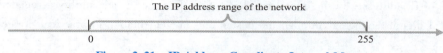

Figure 2.21 IP Address Coordinate Interval Map

The available host addresses within that network range from 192.168.10.1 to 192.168.10.254. However, addresses 192.168.10.0/24 and 192.168.10.255/24 have already been allocated for the network address and broadcast address, respectively. Therefore, these addresses cannot be assigned to hosts. Thus, the range from 192.168.10.1 to 192.168.10.254 comprises the actual available host addresses within the network.

Mission Expansion

IP Address—A Digital Passport to The World

An IP address serves as a unique identifier for devices in Internet communications, akin to their "address" on the network. During the setup of a small LAN, meticulous planning and management of IP addresses are crucial aspects, also encompassing the safeguarding of user privacy. Students must grasp the classification and allocation of IP addresses, engaging in rational planning and resource management to ensure smooth network operations and secure information transmission. Simultaneously, they should comprehend the foundation and risks of network communication, heightening awareness of network security, and fostering the ability to protect personal information. Moreover, responsible utilization of network resources and adherence to network ethics are imperative to foster a healthy and orderly network environment.

Assignment: Engage in group discussions and collaboration to delve deeper into the significance of IP addresses in the digital era. Reflect on the social responsibility associated with the application of digital technology through the design and implementation of practical projects.

任务5 用路由器连接不同的网络

用路由器连接
不同的网络

学习目标

①理解路由器的作用及其工作原理。
②掌握路由器的配置,实现不同网络之间的通信。

建议学时

2 课时

工作情境

交换机只能转发相同网络的数据,不能转发不同网络之间的数据。要转发不同网络之间的数据,需要借助三层网络设备,比如路由器和三层交换机等。

路由器是连接两个或多个网络的硬件设备,在网络间起网关的作用,工业互联网数据从一个网络传输到另一个网络中,需要通过路由器的路由功能进行处理。

那么应该如何配置路由器实现不同网络之间的通信呢?

知识导图

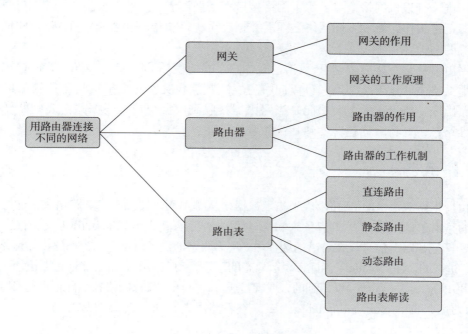

相关知识

1. 网关

顾名思义，网关是一个网络连接到另一个网络的"关口"，是网络的关卡。网关的作用就是帮助不同网络之间实现互联互通，一般用作网络的入口点和出口点。从一个房间走到另一个房间，必然要经过一扇门，同样，从一个网络向另一个网络发送信息，也必须经过一道"关口"，这道关口就是网关。

如图 2.22 所示，数据要从网络 A 发到网络 B，数据先从网络 A 的网关进入，再由网络 A 的网关转发给网络 B 的网关（如果网络 A 和网络 B 是邻接网络），最后从网络 B 的网关出来，转发给网络 B 内的接收方。

根据不同的分类标准，网关有很多种，它可以将两个使用不同传输协议的网络连

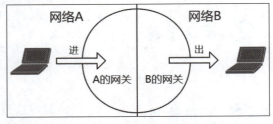

图 2.22 网关示意图

接在一起，对两个网段中使用不同传输协议的数据进行互相的翻译转换。其也可以充当 TCP/IP 网络的关卡，当工业网络设备（计算机）要把数据包从一个网络发往另外的网络时，需要把数据转发给网关，再由网关处理后转发出去。

2. 路由器

路由器是连接两个或多个网络的硬件设备，在网络中起到网关的作用。路由器相当于一台计算机，有很多网络接口，每个网络接口都需要配置一个 IP 地址才可以参与通信。要让路由器正常工作，转发不同网络之间的数据，至少需要给路由器接口配置 IP 地址，以充当计算机的网关。

当路由器从某个接口收到 IP 数据包时，它会确定使用哪个接口来将该数据包转发到目的地。那么路由器是怎么知道它可以向哪里发送数据包呢？它会根据自己所在的网络来创建一个路由表。路由表的主要功能是当路由器接收到数据包后，根据路由表判断转发数据包的最佳路径，并将数据包转发到其目的地。

3. 路由表

路由器根据缓存中的 IP 路由表来决定数据该从哪个端口转发出去。路由表中包含去往已知网络的路由条目列表，这些信息来自直连网络、静态路由、动态路由协议。直连网络用"Direct"标记，路由信息就在自己的缓存中，不需要别的设备发给它；静态路由是网络管理员手动配置进去的，用"Static"标记，表示静态的意思；动态路由是路由器通过路由协议（RIP、OSPF、BGP 等）跟"邻居"学习到的，或者是通过"邻居"发来的信息，自己算出来的。

可以通过 display ip routing-table 命令来查看路由表，如图 2.23 所示。

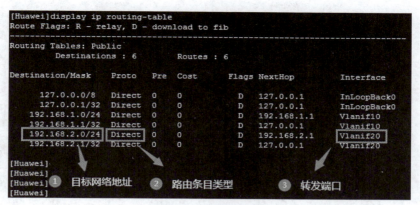

图 2.23　查看路由表

这个路由表中记录了什么信息呢？这里解读其中一个路由条目。第一个字段是网络号（192.168.2.0/24）；第二个字段"Direct"表示这是一个直连网络，也就是说这个网络是直接连在这台设备上的；最后一个字段表示发往 192.168.2.0/24 网络的数据要从 Vlanif20 接口转发出去。

跟交换机一样，路由器将数据包转发出去以后，就完成任务了。它不会去管接收方是否会接收到，甚至不知道接收方是否真的存在。只要路由条目里写的应该从哪个端口转发出去，它就严格按照路由表中路由条目的要求去转发。

与交换机转发数据包不一样的是，当路由器去查询路由表时，如果查不到目的网络的路由条目，则会把这个数据包丢弃。

4. 课堂实践

通过使用路由器连接两个不同的网络，实现不同网络的互联互通。如图 2.24 所示，路由器 AR1 的 GE0/0/0 接口就是网络 A 的网关，负责网络 A 与其他网络的数据流量转发；GE0/0/1 接口就是网络 B 的网关，负责网络 B 与其他网络的数据流量转发。

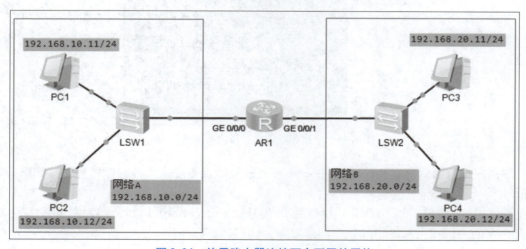

图 2.24　使用路由器连接两个不同的网络

步骤 1：用一根 CTL 线缆（设备配置线缆）将管理计算机 PC5 的 RS232 接口连接到路由器的 Console 接口，如图 2.25 所示。

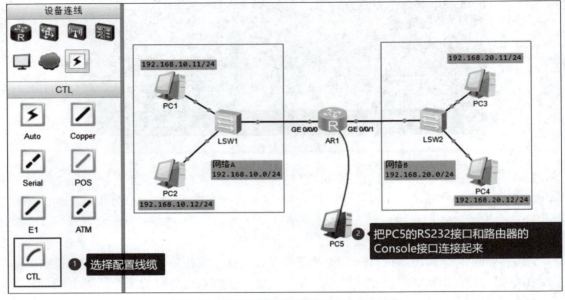

图 2.25　管理计算机连接设备 Console 接口

步骤 2：启动管理计算机 PC5，通过超级终端软件登录到路由器的控制台界面，如图 2.26 所示。

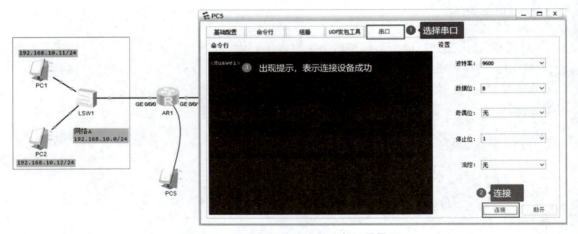

图 2.26　通过超级终端登录设备配置界面

注：在华为虚拟仿真软件 eNSP 中，也可直接双击设备登录设备的配置界面，如图 2.27 所示。

步骤 3：配置路由器 GE0/0/0 接口的 IP 地址为 192.168.10.1/24，作为网络 A 的网关，为网络 A 的主机提供跨网络的数据转发服务。代码如下：

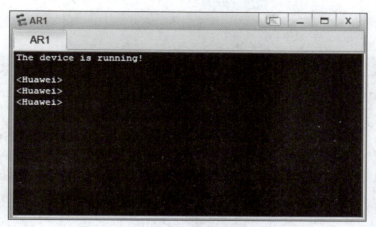

图 2.27　通过双击设备登录设备配置界面

　　＜Huawei＞sys　　//进入特权模式
　　[Huawei]interface G0/0/0　　　//进入端口 G0/0/0
　　[Huawei-GigabitEthernet0/0/0]ip address 192.168.10.1 24　　//配置端口 IP 地址
　　[Huawei-GigabitEthernet0/0/0]quit　　//退出当前端口

步骤 4：配置路由器 GE0/0/1 的接口的 IP 地址为 192.168.20.1/24，作为网络 B 的网关，为网络 B 的主机提供跨网络的数据转发服务。代码如下：

　　＜Huawei＞sys　　//进入特权模式
　　[Huawei]interface G0/0/1　　　//进入端口 GE0/0/1
　　[Huawei-GigabitEthernet0/0/1]ip address 192.168.20.1 24　　//配置端口 IP 地址
　　[Huawei-GigabitEthernet0/0/1]quit　　//退出当前端口

步骤 5：测试 PC 与网关的连通性。

先测试主机是否可以 ping 通自己的网关，从主机 PC1 ping 路由器的 GE0/0/0 接口的地址（192.168.10.1），结果如图 2.28 所示。

从主机 PC3 ping 路由器的 GE0/0/1 接口的地址（192.168.20.1），结果如图 2.29 所示。

显然，网络 A 和网络 B 的主机都可以跟自己的网关通信，如图 2.30 所示。

步骤 6：为主机配置网关参数。

如图 2.31 所示，在配置 IP 地址的界面，为主机 PC1 配置网关信息，告诉主机 PC1 它的网关是 192.168.10.1，如果有数据要发到其他网络，请把数据发给它。

用同样的方法配置其他主机的网关。注意：网络 B 的网关是 192.168.20.1。

最后，从主机 PC1 去 ping 主机 PC3，测试一下不同网络之间的通信是否正常，结果如图 2.32 所示。

PC1 和 PC3 能正常通信，说明成功实现了跨网络的数据传输。

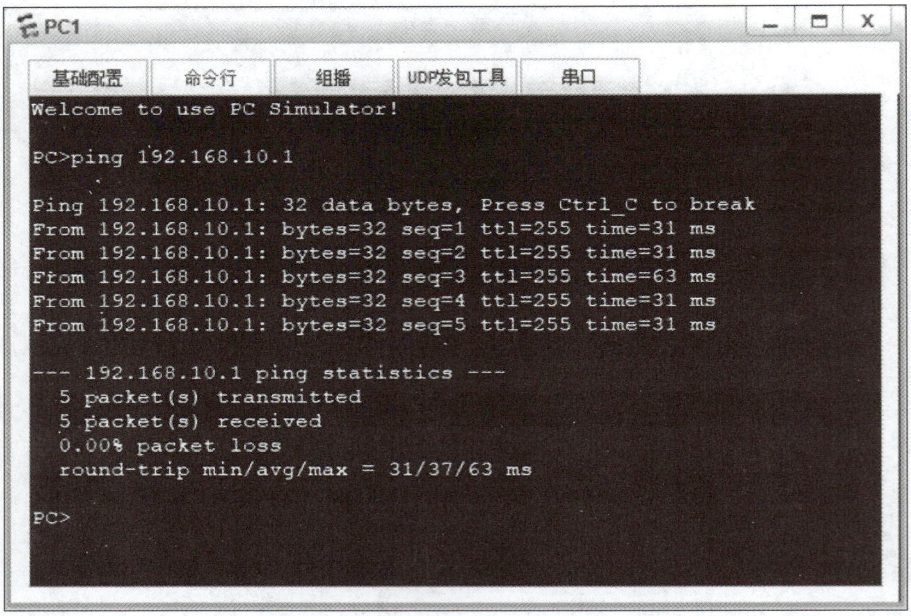

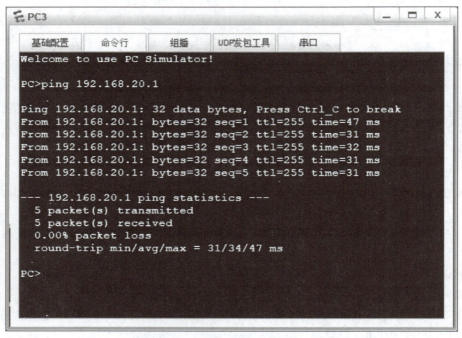

图 2.28　从主机 PC1 ping 路由器的 GE0/0/0 接口的结果

图 2.29　从主机 PC3 ping 路由器的 GE0/0/1 接口的结果

项目 2　工业互联网网络搭建

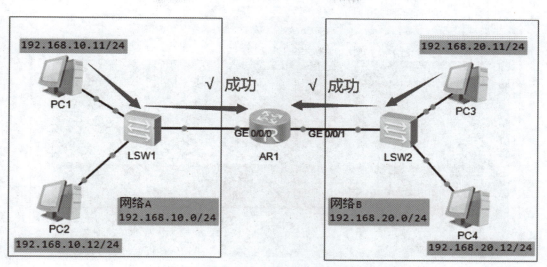

图 2.30　网络内主机和自己网关通信示意图

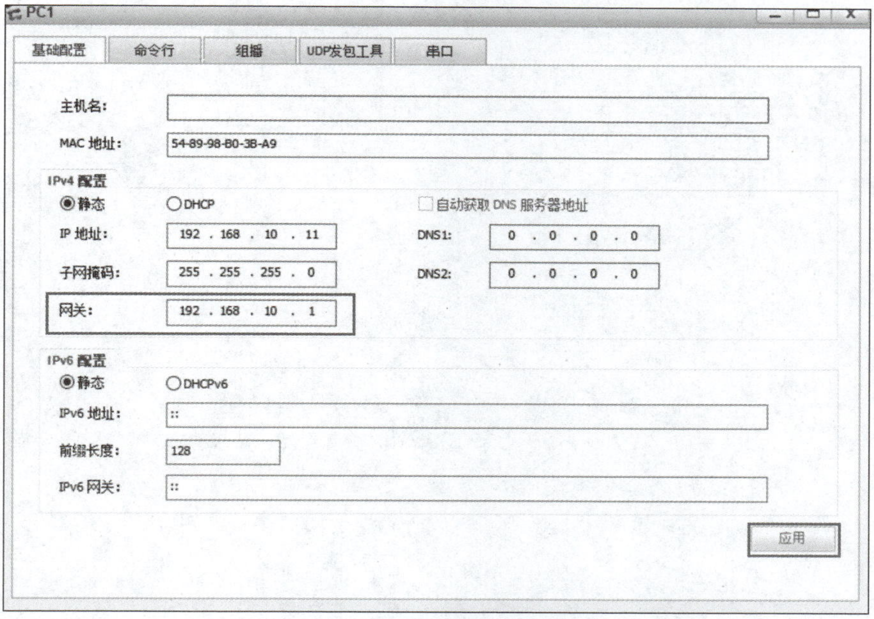

图 2.31　为主机 PC1 配置网关

图 2.32　从主机 PC1 ping 主机 PC3 结果

 **任务拓展**

路由技术——网络通信的核心

在信息化时代,网络通信已经成为人们日常生活和工作中不可或缺的一部分,而路由技术作为网络通信的核心技术,对于构建高效可靠的网络基础设施至关重要。一方面,路由技术可以实现数据的安全传输,确保信息在传输过程中不被非法获取或篡改,通过使用加密算法、访问控制和认证机制,路由技术可以保护敏感信息的机密性,防止国家机密和个人隐私受到侵害。另一方面,路由技术可以对网络流量进行管理和控制,确保网络资源的合理分配和使用,通过实施流量监测、负载均衡和优先级设置等策略,可以提高网络的稳定性和性能,防止网络拥塞和资源滥用,保障国家重要的网络应用和服务的正常运行。

大学生应具备安全风险管控及隐患排查治理的能力,通过合理应用和配置路由技术,保护国家重要信息的机密性、防御网络攻击、提高网络稳定性和应急响应能力,确保国家网络的安全运行,维护国家安全和社会稳定。

作业:路由技术作为网络通信的核心技术之一,对社会的发展和个人的生活产生了深远的影响。请分组探讨路由技术的发展历程、社会影响和责任。

Task 5 Connect Different Networks with Routers

Learning Objective

①Understand the role of a router and how it works.
②Master the configuration of routers to enable communication between different networks.

Suggested Hours

2 hours

Work Situations

Switches can only forward data within the same network and cannot forward data between different networks. To enable data forwarding between different networks, Layer 3 network devices are required, such as routers and Layer 3 switches.

A router is a hardware device that connects two or more networks and acts as a gateway between them. In the context of the industrial Internet, data transmission between networks necessitates processing through the routing function of the router.

Now, the question arises: How should one configure the router to facilitate communication between different networks?

Knowledge Map

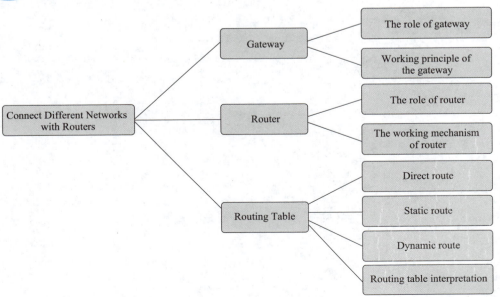

Relevant Knowledge

1. Gateway

As its name implies, a gateway serves as a "gateway" that connects one network to another, serving as an entry and exit point for network traffic. Its primary role is to facilitate interconnection between different networks. Just as one must pass through a door to move from one room to another, sending information from one network to another requires passing through a "gateway".

As depicted in Figure 2.22, data intended for transmission from network A to network B first enters network A through the gateway and is then forwarded by the gateway from network A to network B (if they are neighboring networks). Finally, the data exits network B through its gateway and is forwarded to the intended recipient within network B.

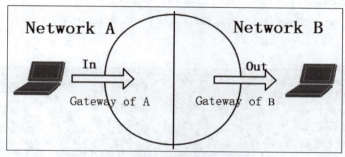

Figure 2.22 Gateway Diagram

Gateways come in various types based on different categorization criteria. They can connect two networks that use different transmission protocols, translating and converting data between the two networks segments as necessary. Additionally, gateways can function as a gateway to a TCP/IP network. When an industrial network device (such as a computer) wishes to transmit a packet of data from one network to another, it must send the data to the gateway, which will then process and forward it accordingly.

2. Router

A router is a hardware device that connects two or more networks and serves as a gateway within a network. Essentially, a router functions as a computer with multiple network interfaces, each requiring configuration with an IP address before engaging in communication. To facilitate proper operation and data forwarding between different networks, the router must be configured with at least one IP address for each interface, enabling it to act as a gateway for network communication.

When a router receives an IP packet from an interface, it assesses which interface to utilize for forwarding the packet to its destination. This decision-making process is facilitated by the router's routing table, which is generated based on the networks it is connected to. The primary function of the routing table is to guide the router in determining the optimal path for forwarding packets to their respective destinations.

3. Routing Table

The router determines the port for data forwarding based on its IP routing table stored in its cache. This table comprises route entries to known networks, derived from directly connected networks, static routes, and dynamic routing protocols. The direct connection network is marked as "Direct", and the routing information is stored locally and doesn't require transmission from another device. Static route, labeled as "Static" is manually configured by network administrators. Dynamic route is learned by the router through routing protocols (such as RIP, OSPF, BGP), exchanged with neighbors, and calculated independently.

You can view the routing table with the display ip routing-table command, as depicted in Figure 2.23.

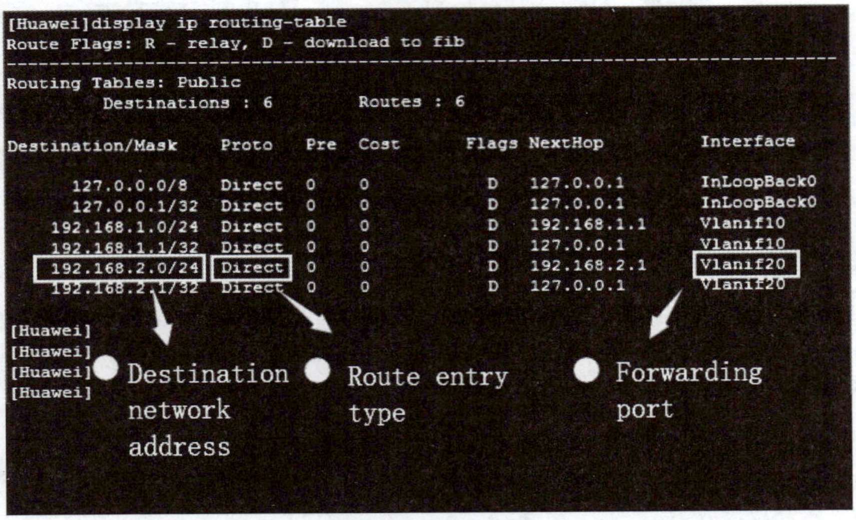

Figure 2.23 Routing Table of MS0

What information is stored in this routing table entry? Here is an explanation of one of the routing entries. The first field represents the network number (192.168.2.0/24). The second field, labeled "Direct," signifies that this entry denotes a directly connected network, indicating that the network is directly linked to this device. The final field specifies that data intended for the 192.168.2.0/24 network should be forwarded through the Vlanif20 interface.

Similar to a switch, a router executes its function when forwarding a packet. It does not concern itself with whether the recipient will receive the packet or if the recipient actually exists. As long as the routing entry specifies the port for forwarding, the router adheres strictly to the routing entry in the routing table.

In contrast to a switch that forwards data frames, a router consults the routing table and discards the packet if it cannot locate a routing entry for the destination network.

4. Classroom Practice

Using a router to connect different networks facilitates the interconnection of these networks. For instance, in Figure 2.24, the GE0/0/0 interface of router AR1 serves as the gateway for network A, forwarding data traffic between network A and other networks. Similarly, the GE0/0/1 interface acts as the gateway for network B, facilitating data traffic exchange between network B and other networks.

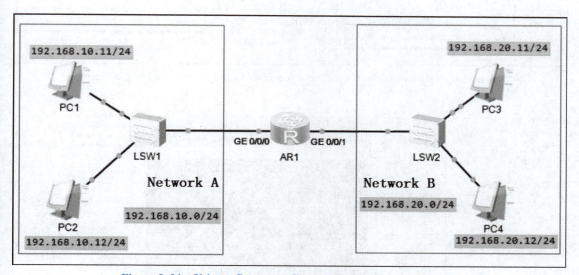

Figure 2.24 Using a Router to Connect Two Different Networks

Step 1: Connect the RS232 interface of the management computer PC5 to the Console interface of the router with a CTL cable (device configuration cable), as depicted in Figure 2.25.

Step 2: Start the management computer PC5 and log in the Console interface of the router through the Hyper Terminal software, as depicted in Figure 2.26.

Note: In Huawei Virtual Simulation Software eNSP, you can also directly double-click the device to log in to the configuration interface of the device, as depicted in Figure 2.27.

Step 3: Configure the IP address of the GE0/0/0 interface of the router as 192.168.10.1/24 to serve as the gateway for Network A and facilitate data forwarding services across the network for the hosts on Network A.

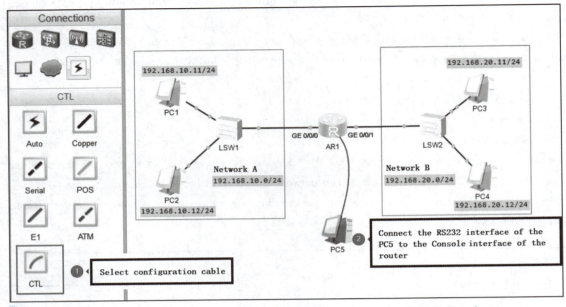

Figure 2.25 Manage the Computer Connection to the Device Console Interface

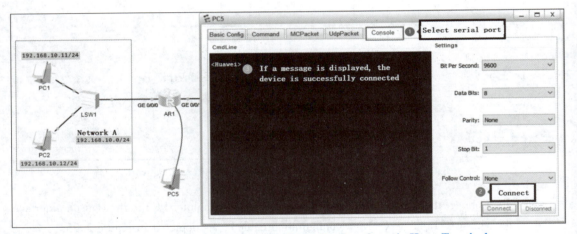

Figure 2.26 Login to the Device Configuration Interface via HyperTerminal

```
<Huawei>sys    //Access to Privileged Mode
[Huawei]interface G0/0/0    //Enter port G0/0/0
[Huawei-GigabitEthernet0/0/0]ip address 192.168.10.1 24    //Configure
the port IP address
[Huawei-GigabitEthernet0/0/0]quit    //Exit the current port
```

Step 4: Configure the IP address of the interface of router GE0/0/1 as 192.168.20.1/24 to serve as the gateway for Network B and facilitate data forwarding services across the network for the hosts on Network B.

Project 2 How to Build an Industrial Internet

Figure 2.27 Log in to the Device Configuration Screen by Double-clicking on the Device

```
<Huawei>sys    //Access to Privileged Mode
[Huawei]interface G0/0/1    //Enter port GE0/0/1
[Huawei-GigabitEthernet0/0/1]ip address 192.168.20.1 24   //Configure the port IP address
[Huawei-GigabitEthernet0/0/1]quit   //Exit the current port
```

Step 5: Test the connectivity between the PC and the gateway.

First, test whether the host can ping through its own gateway by pinging the address of the router's GE0/0/0 interface (192.168.10.1) from the host PC1, and the result as depicted in Figure 2.28.

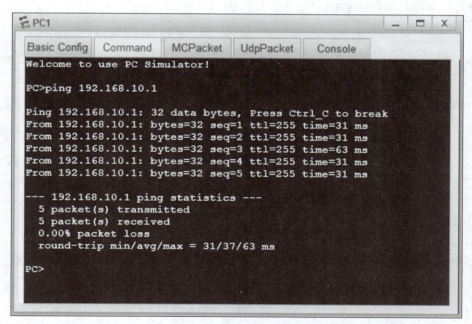

Figure 2.28 Results of Pinging the Router's GE0/0/0 Interface from Host PC1

From host PC3 ping the address of the router's GE0/0/1 interface (192.168.20.1), the result as depicted in Figure 2.29.

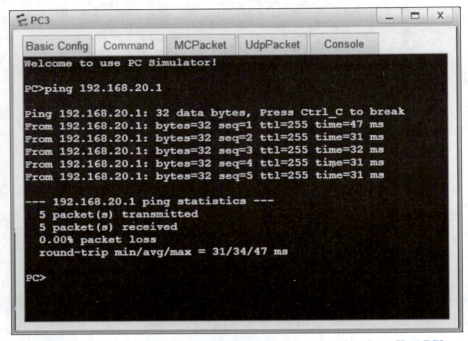

Figure 2.29　Results of Pinging the Router's GE0/0/1 Interface from Host PC3

Obviously, hosts on both Network A and Network B can communicate with their own gateways, as depicted in Figure 2.30.

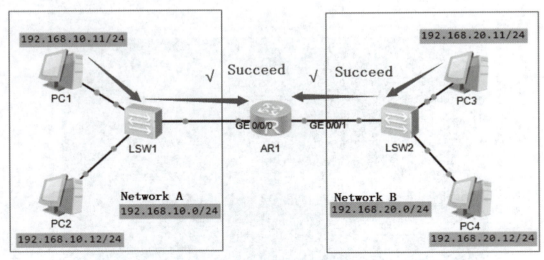

Figure 2.30　Schematic Diagram of Communication Between Hosts in the Network and Their Own Gateway

Step 6: Configure gateway parameters for the host.

In the "Configure IP Address" screen, as depicted in Figure 2.31, set up gateway information for host PC1. Specify to host PC1 that its gateway is 192.168.10.1. Instruct PC1 to route any data intended for other networks through this gateway.

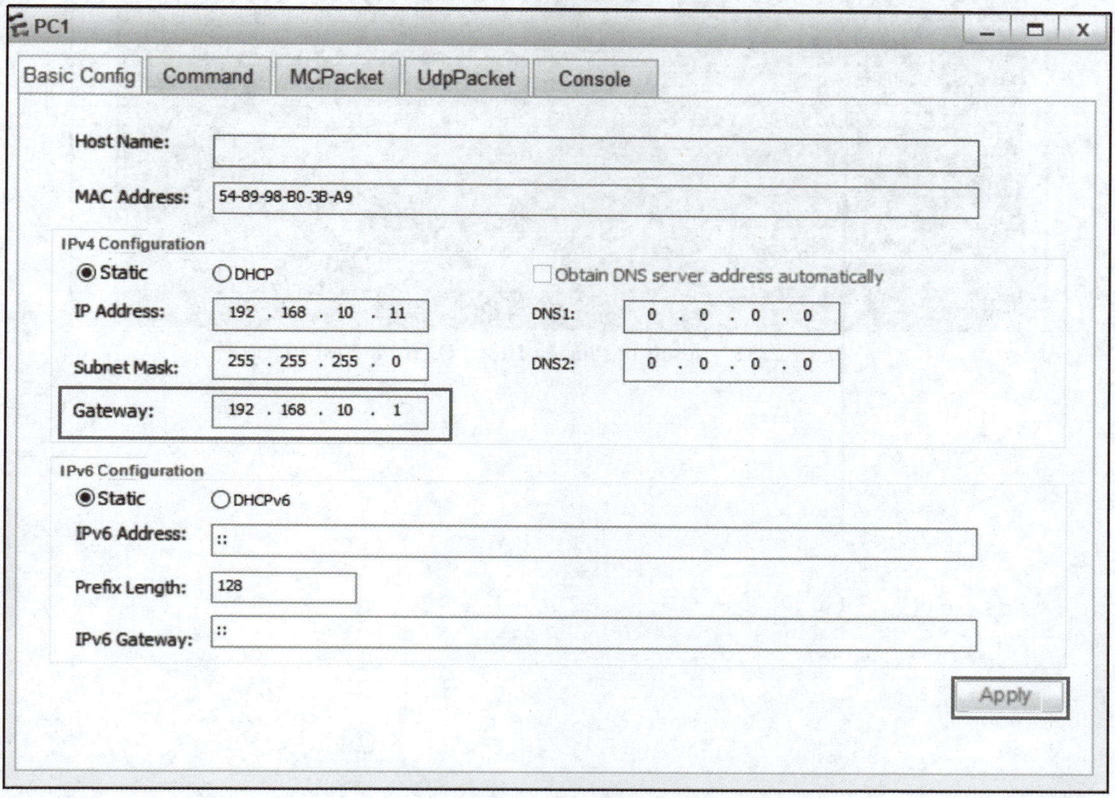

Figure 2.31 Configure a Gateway for Host PC1

Configure the gateways of the other hosts in the same way. Note: Network B's gateway is 192.168.20.1.

Finally, proceed to ping host PC2 from host PC1 to verify if communication between different networks is functioning properly. The test results as depicted in Figure 2.32.

PC1 and PC3 can communicate seamlessly, indicating successful data transfer across networks.

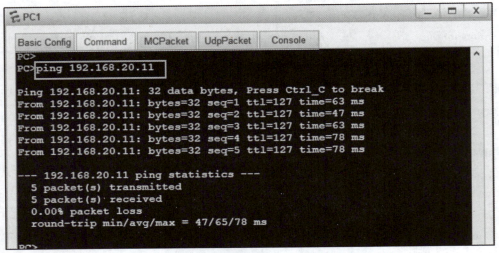

Figure 2.32 Result of Pinging Host PC3 from Host PC1

 Mission Expansion

Routing Technology—The Core of Network Communication

In the era of digitalization, network communication has become an integral part of people's daily lives and work routines. Routing technology stands as a cornerstone in network communication, playing a pivotal role in establishing an efficient and dependable network infrastructure. On one front, routing technology facilitates secure data transmission, ensuring that information remains inaccessible and unaltered during the transfer process. Through encryption algorithms, access control, and authentication mechanisms, routing technology upholds the confidentiality of sensitive data, safeguarding against breaches of state secrets and personal privacy. On the other hand, routing technology governs and regulates network traffic to ensure the judicious allocation and utilization of network resources. By implementing strategies such as traffic monitoring, load balancing, and priority assignment, it enhances network stability and performance, mitigating network congestion and resource mismanagement. In turn, this ensures the uninterrupted operation of critical national network applications and services.

College students should possess the competency to manage security risks and address potential vulnerabilities effectively. By employing routing technology through prudent application and configuration, they can safeguard the confidentiality of vital national information, fortify defenses against network assaults, enhance network stability and emergency response capabilities, thus guaranteeing the secure operation of the national network and preserving national security and social stability.

Assignment: Routing technology, as a core component of network communication, has significantly influenced societal development and individuals' lives. Please examine routing technology's historical evolution, its social ramifications, and the responsibilities it entails within your groups.

任务6 部署无线工业局域网

部署无线工业互联网

学习目标

①理解无线局域网的工作原理。
②掌握无线路由器的配置,为移动用户提供网络访问服务。

建议学时

2 课时

工作情境

移动互联网的快速发展,移动终端呈现爆炸式增长,极大地推动了无线网络的快速发展。无线网络由于其便捷性和灵活性,具有传输速率快、传输质量高、误码率低等优势,可以在工业环境中将小范围内的工业设备、计算机、终端和各类信息设备互相连通,给工业网络的前期组建、中期维护和后期拓展都带来了极大的便利。

知识导图

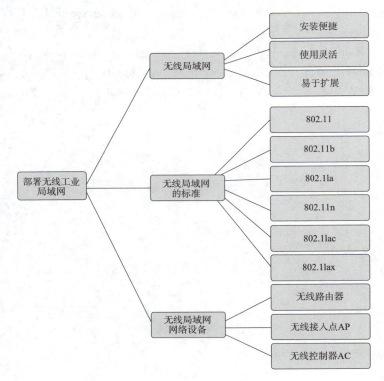

相关知识

1. 无线局域网

无线局域网也就是平常人们所说的 WLAN,它由一个无线路由设备在一定区域内发射无线电波组成,是近年来一项新兴的网络技术。无线局域网使用射频技术,利用电磁波在空气中传输网络信号,不需要使用网络缆线,取代了由传统双绞线组建的局域网,更方便快捷。

与有线局域网相比较,无线局域网具备以下优点:

(1) 安装便捷

一般的网络建设施工周期较长,对周边环境影响最大的就是网络综合布线工程。有线网络在施工过程中,往往要破墙掘地、架管穿线,而无线局域网最大的优势就是免去或减少了网络布线的工作量。一般只要安装一个或多个接入点无线网络设备,就可建立覆盖整个建筑或地区的局域网络。

(2) 使用灵活

由于有线网络缺少灵活性,要求在网络规划时尽可能地考虑未来发展的需要,这就导致要预设大量利用率较低的信息点。一旦网络发展超出了设计规划,又要花费较多费用进行网络改造。而无线局域网可以避免或减少以上情况的发生,对于无线局域网而言,在无线网的信号覆盖区域内任何一个位置都可以接入网络。与有线局域网相比,无线局域网的应用范围更加广泛,而且开发运营成本低、时间短、投资回报快、易扩展、受自然环境地形及灾害影响小、组网灵活快捷。

(3) 易于扩展

无线局域网有多种配置方式,能够根据需要灵活选择。这样,无线局域网就能胜任从只有几个用户的小型局域网到有上千用户的大型网络,并且能够提供"漫游"等有线网络无法提供的服务。

2. 无线局域网的标准

无线局域网第一个版本 IEEE 802.11 发表于 1997 年,其中定义了介质访问接入控制层和物理层。物理层定义了工作在 2.4 GHz 的 ISM 频段上的两种无线调频方式和一种红外传输的方式,总数据传输速率设计为 2Mbit/s。经过几十年的发展,无线局域网技术已经广泛应用在商务区、大学、机场及其他需要无线网的公共区域。

通常情况下,很多人认为 WLAN 就是 WiFi。需要说明的是,它们不是同一个概念。WLAN 的标准叫 IEEE 802.11,WiFi 只是 IEEE 802.11 标准的一种实现,只是对于普通用户来说,WiFi 使用得最普遍。基于 IEEE 802.11 标准的产品除了 WiFi 外,还有无线千兆 (Wireless Gigabit, WiGig) 联盟。WiGig 联盟于 2013 年 1 月 4 日并入 WiFi 联盟。

目前为止,WiFi 已发展到第六代,如表 2.8 所示。

表2.8 WiFi 发展世代表

世代	年份	依据的标准	工作频段	最高速率
第一代	1997	IEEE 802.11 原始标准	2.4 GHz	2 Mbit/s
第二代	1999	IEEE 802.11b	2.4 GHz	11 Mbit/s
第三代	1999	IEEE 802.11a	5 GHz	54 Mbit/s
第四代	2009	IEEE 802.11n	2.4 GHz 和 5 GHz	600 Mbit/s
第五代	2013	IEEE 802.11ac	5 GHz	6.9 Gbit/s
第六代	2019	IEEE 802.11ax	2.4 GHz 和 5 GHz	9.6 Gbit/s

3. 无线局域网网络设备

与有线网络相同，无线网络也需要网络设备充当中心节点。但与有线网络不同的是，在无线网络中使用到的设备主要是无线路由器和无线 AP。其中，无线路由器主要应用于小型无线网络，而无线 AP 则可应用于大中型无线网络中。

（1）无线路由器

无线路由器是无线 AP 与宽带路由器的结合，借助于无线路由器，可实现家庭或小型网络的无线互联和 Internet 连接共享。

无线路由器除可用于无线网络连接外，还拥有 4 个以上以太网口，用于直接连接传统的计算机或工业网络设备，也可以用于连接交换机，为更多的计算机提供 Internet 连接共享。

（2）无线接入点 AP

无线接入点也称为无线 AP（Access Point），其作用类似于以太网中的集线设备，用于为无线终端设备（如便携式计算机、无线打印机、无线摄像头等）提供无线网络接入。通常情况下，大部分 AP 最多可以支持多达 30 台计算机的接入，有些大吞吐量的 AP 甚至可以接入 50~80 台计算机，但为了保证无线 AP 的性能，建议数量以不超过 20 台为宜。在大规模的工业互联网络中，无线 AP 需要结合无线控制器（AC）使用。

AP 分为"瘦"AP 和"胖"AP。"瘦"AP 相当于有线网络中的交换机，在无线局域网中不停地接收和传送数据，"瘦"AP 本身并不能进行配置，需要一台无线控制器（AC）进行集中控制管理配置。"胖"AP 除无线接入功能外，还具备 WAN、LAN 两个接口，支持地址转换（NAT）功能，功能跟无线路由器类似。

（3）无线控制器 AC

无线控制器（AC）是一种网络设备，用来集中控制局域网内所有的无线 AP，也称为 AP"管家"。无线控制器 AC 是在大规模无线覆盖中使用的，通过集中管理所有的 AP，使所有的 AP 能协同工作，提供漫游、信号自动切换等功能。

4. 课堂实践

下面通过一个案例来一起学习无线工业局域网的部署。无线网络由于组网灵活、安装便捷、易于扩展的特点，在工业互联网领域越来越受到大家的欢迎。利用华为虚拟仿真软件 eNSP 组建一个全新的无线互联网络，更好地服务工业互联网。

步骤1：在网络中部署无线 AC、AP，拓扑如图 2.33 所示。

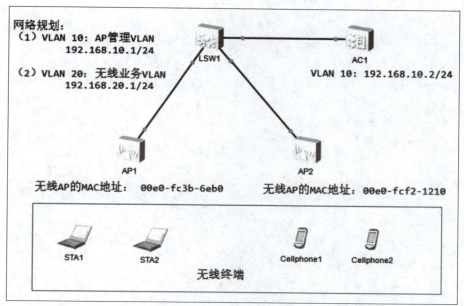

图 2.33　部署无线 AC 和 AP

步骤 2：开启设备，配置交换机 LSW1。
划分 VLAN，代码如下：

```
<Huawei>sys                          //进入特权模式
Enter system view,return user view with Ctrl+Z.
[Huawei]vlan batch 10 20             //划分 VLAN10,20
Info:This operation may take a few seconds.Please wait for a moment...done.
[Huawei]
```

给 VLAN 配置 IP 地址，代码如下：

```
[Huawei]int vlan 10                              //进入 VLAN10
[Huawei-Vlanif10]ip address 192.168.10.1 24      //配置 IP 地址
[Huawei-Vlanif10]quit                            //退出
[Huawei]int vlan 20                              //进入 VLAN10
[Huawei-Vlanif20]ip address 192.168.20.1 24      //配置 IP 地址
[Huawei-Vlanif20]quit                            //退出
```

配置 DHCP，代码如下：

```
[Huawei]dhcp enable                  //启用 DHCP 服务
Info:The operation may take a few seconds.Please wait for a moment.done
[Huawei]ip pool vlan10               //创建地址池 VLAN10,该地址池分配给
                                       无线 AP
```

111

```
Info:It's successful to create an IP address pool.
[Huawei-ip-pool-vlan10]network 192.168.10.0 mask 24    //分配网络号
                                                        和掩码
[Huawei-ip-pool-vlan10]gateway-list 192.168.10.1       //分配网关
[Huawei-ip-pool-vlan10]option 43 sub-option 3 ascii 192.168.10.2
//指定无线控制器 AC 地址
[Huawei-ip-pool-vlan10]quit                             //退出
[Huawei]
[Huawei]ip pool vlan20                                  //创建地址池 VLAN10,该地址池
                                                        分配给无线用户
Info:It's successful to create an IP address pool.
[Huawei-ip-pool-vlan20]network 192.168.20.0 mask 24    //分配网络号
                                                        和掩码
[Huawei-ip-pool-vlan20]gateway-list 192.168.20.1       //分配网关
[Huawei-ip-pool-vlan20]dns-list 114.114.114.114        //分配 DNS
[Huawei-ip-pool-vlan20]quit                             //退出
[Huawei]int vlan 10                                     //进入 VLAN10*/
[Huawei-Vlanif10]dhcp select global                     /* 该 VLAN 用户从
刚创从刚创建的地址池获取地址*/
[Huawei-Vlanif10]quit                                   //退出
[Huawei]int vlan 20      //进入 VLAN20
[Huawei-Vlanif20]dhcp select global    //VLAN 用户从创建的地址池中获
取地址
[Huawei-Vlanif20]quit     //退出
```

配置干道协议,代码如下:

```
[Huawei]port-group group-member g0/0/1 tog0/0/3        //进入端口组 G0/0
                                                        /1 到 G0/0/3
[Huawei-port-group]port link-type trunk                //端口组所有端口设
                                                        置为干道 Trunk
[Huawei-GigabitEthernet0/0/1]port link-type trunk
[Huawei-GigabitEthernet0/0/2]port link-type trunk
[Huawei-GigabitEthernet0/0/3]port link-type trunk
[Huawei-port-group]port trunk allow-pass vlan 10 20   //允许通过的
                                                        VLAN 是 10 和
                                                        20
[Huawei-GigabitEthernet0/0/1]port trunk allow-pass vlan 10 20
[Huawei-GigabitEthernet0/0/2]port trunk allow-pass vlan 10 20
[Huawei-GigabitEthernet0/0/3]port trunk allow-pass vlan 10 20
```

```
[Huawei-port-group]port trunk pvid vlan 10            //端口组所有端
                                                        口的 PVID 是
                                                        10
[Huawei-GigabitEthernet0/0/1]port trunk pvid vlan 10
[Huawei-GigabitEthernet0/0/2]port trunk pvid vlan 10
[Huawei-GigabitEthernet0/0/3]port trunk pvid vlan 10
[Huawei-port-group]quit
[Huawei]
```

注:PVID,端口默认的 VLAN ID 号,用来标识端口接收到的未标记的帧。

步骤3:配置无线控制器 AC。

划分 VLAN 并且给 VLAN 配置地址,代码如下:

```
<AC6605>sys                                             //进入特权模式
Enter system view,return user view with Ctrl+Z.
[AC6605]vlan batch 10 20                                //划分 VLAN10,20
Info: This operation may take a few seconds. Please wait for a moment..done.
[AC6605]
[AC6605]int vlan 10                                     //进入 VLAN10
[AC6605-Vlanif10]ip address 192.168.10.224              //配置 IP 地址
[AC6605-Vlanif10]quit                                   //退出
```

配置干道协议,代码如下:

```
[AC6605]int G0/0/1                                      //进入端口 G0/0/1
[AC6605-GigabitEthernet0/0/1]port link-type trunk       //端口的类
                                                         型设置为
                                                         干
                                                         道 Trunk
[AC6605-GigabitEthernet0/0/1]port trunk allow-pass vlan 10 20
//允许 VLAN10,20 通过干道
[AC6605-GigabitEthernet0/0/1]port trunk pvid vlan 10    //干道 PVID 是
                                                         VLAN10
[AC6605-GigabitEthernet0/0/1]quit
```

配置 AP 认证模式,代码如下:

```
[AC6605]wlan                                            //进入无线配置模式
[AC6605-wlan-view]ap auth-mode mac-auth                 //无线 AP 认证是基
于 MAC
[AC6605-wlan-view]quit
```

绑定无线 AP,代码如下:

```
[AC6605]capwap source interface vlan 10      //配置AC建立CAPWAP隧道使用
的接口,作为AC的源接口,用于AC和AP间建立CAPWAP隧道通信。
[AC6605]wlan                                 //进入无线配置模式
[AC6605-wlan-view]ap-id1 ap-mac 00e0-fc38-40a0    //绑定第一个
AP的MAC
[AC6605-wlan-ap-1]ap-name ap1                //命名为AP1
[AC6605-wlan-ap-1]quit                       //退出
[AC6605-wlan-view]ap-id2 ap-mac 00e0-fc87-2400    //绑定第二个
AP的MAC
[AC6605-wlan-ap-2]ap-name ap2                //命名为AP2
[AC6605-wlan-ap-2]quit                       //退出
[AC6605-wlan-view]quit                       //退出
[AC6605]display ap all                       //查看AP是否上线了
Info:This operation may take a few seconds. Please wait for a moment.
done.
Total AP information:
nor:normal[2]
--------------------------------------------------------------------
ID MAC Name Group IP Type State STA Uptime
--------------------------------------------------------------------
1 00e0-fc38-40a0 ap1 default 192.168.10.254 AP2050    nor  02M:50S
2 00e0-fc87-2400 ap2 default 192.168.10.253 AP2050DN nor 03M:3S
--------------------------------------------------- -Total:2
[AC6605]
当状态是nor的时候,表示AP已经上线了。
```

配置无线信号模板:无线信号模板需要配置:信号模板、安全模板、调用模板。代码如下:

```
[AC6005]wlan                                 //进入无线配置模式
[AC6005-wlan-view]ssid-profile   name   aa   //创建一个ssid
模板,名称是aa
[AC6005-wlan-ssid-prof-aa]ssid GYHLW         //广播出来的ssid
是GYHLW
Info:This operation may take a few seconds,please wait. done.
[AC6005-wlan-ssid-prof-aa]quit               //退出
[AC6005-wlan-view]
[AC6005-wlan-view]security-profile name bb   //创建一个安全模板,
名称是bb
```

[AC6005-wlan-sec-prof-bb]security wpa2 psk pass-phrase Aa123456   //aes 密码是 Aa123456
[AC6005-wlan-sec-prof-bb]quit
[AC6005-wlan-view]

[AC6005-wlan-view]vap-profile name cc   //创建调用模板,名称是 cc
[AC6005-wlan-vap-prof-cc]ssid-profile aa   /*调用 ssid 模板 aa 的参数*/
Info:This operation may take a few seconds,please wait. done.
[AC6005-wlan-vap-prof-cc]security-profile   bb//调用安全模板 bb 的参数
Info:This operation may take a few seconds,please wait. done.
[AC6005-wlan-vap-prof-cc]service-vlan vlan-id 20   //指定业务无线用户的业务 VLAN 是 20
Info:This operation may take a few seconds,please wait. done.
[AC6005-wlan-vap-prof-cc]quit   //退出
[AC6005-wlan-view]

发射无线信号,代码如下:

[AC6005]wlan   //进入无线配置模式
[AC6605-wlan-view]ap-group name default   //进入默认 AP 组 default,默认情况下,所有的 AP 都在默认组 default 中
[AC6605-wlan-ap-group-default]vap-profile cc wlan 1 radio all
//按调用模板 cc 的配置要求,发射无线信号

发射无线信号后,效果如图 2.34 所示。

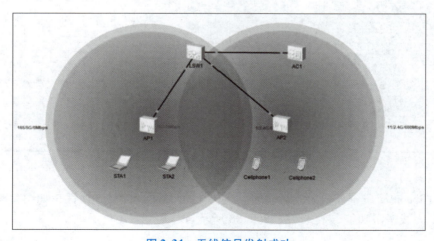

图 2.34 无线信号发射成功

步骤 4:测试无线信号连接情况。

①把无线终端连上无线信号，如图 2.35 所示。

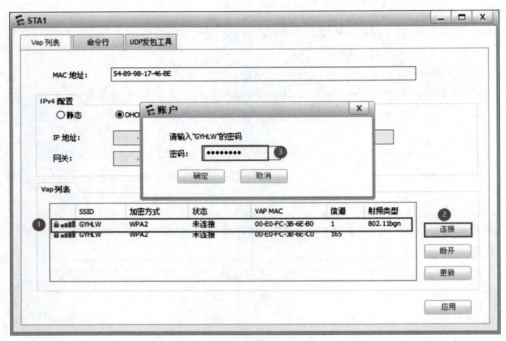

图 2.35　把无线终端连上无线信号

②终端连上无线信号效果，如图 2.36 所示。

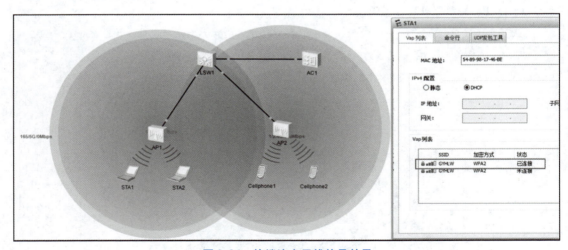

图 2.36　终端连上无线信号效果

③通过 ipconfig 命令查看无线终端的 IP 地址，并且测试网络连通性，如图 2.37 所示。
④测试无线漫游功能，效果图如图 2.38 所示。

项目 2　工业互联网网络搭建

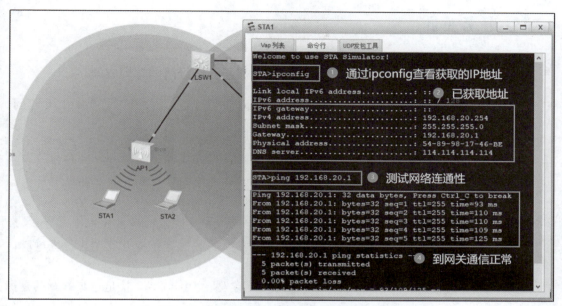

图 2.37　无线终端获取地址和测试网络连通性

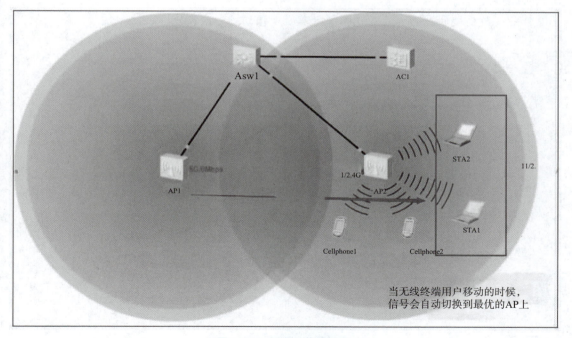

图 2.38　无线漫游效果图

任务拓展

中国互联网 30 周年礼赞——科技发展与网络经济的辉煌成就

自 1994 年中国正式接入国际互联网以来，中国互联网已进入发展的第 30 年。30 年间，中国互联网在科技创新方面取得了举世瞩目的成果，从最初的电子邮件、新闻网站，到如今的社交媒体、电商平台，中国的互联网产业不断创新发展，为人民群众提供了更加便捷、丰富的信息服务。特别是近年来，中国政府大力支持科技创新，快速推进数字基础设施建设，鼓励企业加大研发投入，推动产学研用紧密结合，为中国互联网产业的快速发展奠定了坚实基础，千行百业实现"触网"，新业态、新模式不断涌现，数字经济成为推动经济增长的重要引擎。工业互联网呈现出较快发展态势，工业互联网标识解析体系覆盖 31 个省（区、市），具有一定影响力的工业互联网平台超过 240 家，国家工业互联网大数据中心体系基本建成。

短短 30 年，中国的互联网技术和产业从一无所有发展为引领者。长足进步的背后是国家的高度重视、对自主创新理念的秉承和坚持。作为青年学生，要坚定四个自信，从自身做起，勤于学习、刻苦钻研，为实现科技强国的建设和中华民族的伟大复兴贡献自己的力量。

作业：分析调研我国工业互联网平台发展现状，撰写报告分享启发。

Task 6　Deploy a Wireless Industry LAN

Learning Objective

①Understand how a wireless LAN works.
②Master the configuration of wireless router and provide network access services for mobile users.

Suggested Hours

2 hours

Working Context

The swift advancement of mobile internet and the explosive proliferation of mobile devices have significantly propelled the rapid extension of wireless networks. Thanks to their convenience and flexibility, wireless networks offer numerous advantages such as high transmission rates, superior transmission quality, and low Bit Error Rate (BER). They enable the interconnection of industrial equipment, computers, terminals, and various information devices within a confined area in industrial environments, greatly facilitating the pre-establishment, mid-term maintenance, and post-extension phases of industrial networks.

Knowledge Map

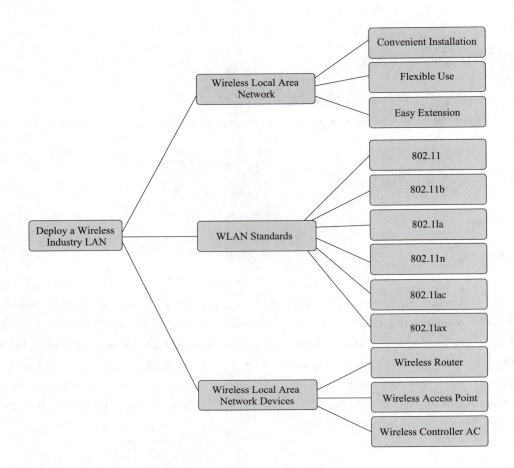

Related Knowledge

1. Wireless Local Area Network

Wireless LAN, commonly referred to as WLAN, comprises a wireless routing device that emits radio waves within a designated area and represents a burgeoning network technology in recent times. WLAN utilizes radio frequency technology, employing electromagnetic waves to transmit network signals through the air, thereby eliminating the necessity for network cables like traditional twisted pairs of copper wires, thus forming a local area network in a more convenient and rapid manner.

In comparison to wired LAN, WLAN boasts the following advantages:

(1) Convenient Installation

In general network construction, the network cabling construction project typically entails the longest construction period and has the most significant impact on the surrounding environment. Wired network construction often involves breaking walls, digging, and threading pipes. The primary advantage of WLAN is its ability to eliminate or reduce the workload associated with network wiring. Typically, installing one or more access points of wireless network equipment is sufficient to establish a local area network covering an entire building or area.

(2) Flexible Use

Due to the limited flexibility of wired networks, network planning often requires consideration of future development needs, leading to the pre-installation of numerous information points with low utilization rates. When network development surpasses the initial design, additional expenses are incurred for network transformation. WLANs can help circumvent or alleviate such scenarios. With WLANs, any location within the signal coverage area can access the network. In comparison to wired LANs, WLANs offer broader applications, lower development and operational costs, quicker deployment, faster return on investment, easy scalability, reduced susceptibility to natural environment, terrain, and disaster impacts, as well as flexible and rapid network organization.

(3) Easy Extension

WLAN offers a variety of configuration methods that can be flexibly selected according to requirements. This versatility enables WLANs to accommodate small LANs with just a few users or large networks with thousands of users. Additionally, WLANs can provide features like "roaming" that are unavailable in wired networks.

2. WLAN Standards

The first version of WLAN, IEEE 802.11, was published in 1997, defining both the medium access control layer and the physical layer. The physical layer outlined two wireless FM modes and one infrared transmission mode operating in the ISM band at 2.4 GHz, with a total data rate designed for 2 Mbit/s. Over decades of development, WLAN technology has found widespread application in business districts, universities, airports, and other public areas necessitating wireless networks.

While many individuals commonly equate WLAN with WiFi, it's essential to differentiate between the two concepts. WLAN refers to the standard defined by IEEE 802.11, whereas WiFi represents a specific implementation of the IEEE 802.11 standard. For the average user, WiFi is the most prevalent usage. Alongside WiFi, products based on the IEEE 802.11 standard include the Wireless Gigabit (WiGig) Alliance, which merged into the WiFi Alliance on January 4, 2013.

So far, WiFi has developed to the sixth generation, as depicted in Table 2.8.

Table 2.8 WiFi development world representative

For generations	Year	The basis of the standard	Work frequency band	Top speed
First generation	1997	IEEE 802.11 original standard	2.4 GHz	2 Mbit/s
second generation	1999	IEEE 802.11b	2.4 GHz	11 Mbit/s
Third generation	1999	IEEE 802.11a	5 GHz	54 Mbit/s
Fourth generation	2009	IEEE 802.11n	2.4 GHz and 5 GHz	600 Mbit/s
Fifth generation	2013	IEEE 802.11ac	5 GHz	6.9 Gbit/s
Sixth generation	2019	IEEE 802.11ax	2.4 GHz and 5 GHz	9.6 Gbit/s

3. Wireless Local Area Network Devices

Similar to wired networks, wireless networks also require network equipment to serve as central nodes. However, unlike wired networks, wireless networks predominantly utilize wireless routers and wireless Access Points (APs). Wireless routers are primarily employed in small wireless networks, whereas wireless APs are suitable for medium and large wireless networks.

(1) Wireless Router

A wireless router is a hybrid device that combines the functions of a wireless Access Point (AP) and a broadband router. With a wireless router, users can achieve wireless interconnection within a household or small network and share internet connections.

In addition to wireless network connectivity, a wireless router typically includes more than four Ethernet ports for direct connections to traditional computers or industrial network equipment. Moreover, it can be connected to a switch to facilitate internet connection sharing for multiple computers.

(2) Wireless Access Point

A Wireless Access Point (AP), also known simply as a wireless AP, serves a role akin to that of a hub device in Ethernet networks, providing wireless network access to wireless terminal equipment such as laptops, wireless printers, and wireless cameras. Most APs can support up to 30 computer connections, with some high-throughput APs accommodating between 50 to 80 computers. However, to ensure optimal performance, it's advisable to limit connections to around 20. In large-scale industrial networking, wireless APs are typically used in conjunction with a Wireless Controller (AC).

APs are categorized into "thin" APs and "fat" APs. "Thin" APs operate similarly to switches in wired networks, continuously transmitting and receiving data within the WLAN. They lack built-in configuration options and require a wireless controller for centralized control and management. On the other hand, "fat" APs not only provide wireless access but also feature WAN and LAN interfaces, supporting Network Address Translation (NAT) functionality akin to that of wireless routers.

(3) Wireless Controller AC

Wireless controller (AC) is a network device, used to centrally control all the wireless AP in the LAN, also known as AP "housekeeper". Wireless controller AC is used in large-scale wireless coverage, through centralized management of all the AP, so that all the AP can work together to provide roaming, automatic signal switching and other functions.

4. Classroom Practice

A Wireless Controller (AC) is a network device employed to centrally manage all wireless Access Points (APs) within a Local Area Network (LAN), often referred to as the AP "housekeeper". In large-scale wireless coverage scenarios, the Wireless Controller AC facilitates centralized management of all APs, enabling them to collaborate in providing features such as roaming and automatic signal switching.

Step 1: Deploy the wireless AC and AP in the network, and the topology is depicted in Figure 2.33.

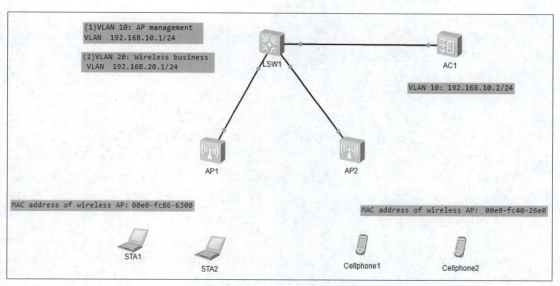

Figure 2.33 Deploy the Wireless AC and AP

Step 2: Access the device and configure the LSW 1 switch.
partition VLAN, the code is as follows:

```
<Huawei>sys                    //go into privilege mode
Enter system view, return user view with Ctrl + Z.
[Huawei]vlan batch 10 20       //division VLAN10,20
```

Info: This operation may take a few seconds. Please wait for a moment... done.
[Huawei]

Configure the IP address for the VLAN, the code is as follows:

[Huawei]int vlan 10   into the VLAN10
[Huawei - Vlanif10] ip address 192.168.10.1 24   //Configure the IP address
[Huawei - Vlanif10]quit   //exit
[Huawei]int vlan 20   //into the VLAN10
[Huawei - Vlanif20] ip address 192.168.20.1 24   //Configure the IP address
[Huawei - Vlanif20]quit   //exit

Configure DHCP, the code is as follows:

[Huawei]dhcp enable   //Enable the DHCP service
Info: The operation may take a few seconds. Please wait for a moment. done.
[Huawei] ip pool vlan10   //Create address pool VLAN10, change address pool is assigned to wireless AP
Info: It's successful to create an IP address pool.
[Huawei - ip - pool - vlan10] network 192.168.10.0 mask 24   //Assign the network number and the mask
[Huawei - ip - pool - vlan10] gateway - list 192.168.10.1   //distribution gateway
[Huawei - ip - pool - vlan10]option 43 sub - option 3 ascii 192.168.10.2
    //Specify the AC address of the wireless controller
[Huawei - ip - pool - vlan10]quit   //exit
[Huawei]
[Huawei] ip pool vlan20   //Create address pool VLAN10, change address pool is assigned to the wireless user
Info: It's successful to create an IP address pool.
[Huawei - ip - pool - vlan20] network 192.168.20.0 mask 24   //Assign the network number and the mask
[Huawei - ip - pool - vlan20] gateway - list 192.168.20.1   //distribution gateway
[Huawei - ip - pool - vlan20] dns - list 114.114.114.114   //assigned DNS
[Huawei - ip - pool - vlan20]quit   //exit

```
[Huawei]int vlan 10        //goes into the VLAN10 port
[Huawei - Vlanif10]dhcp select global     //The VLAN user gets the address from the address pool you just created
[Huawei -Vlanif10]quit     //exit
[Huawei]int vlan 20        //goes into the VLAN20 port
[Huawei - Vlanif20]dhcp select global     //The VLAN user gets the address from the address pool you just created
[Huawei -Vlanif20]quit     //exit
```

Configure the trunk road protocol, the code is as follows:

```
[Huawei]port - group group - member g0 /0 /1 tog 0 /0 /3     //Access port group G 0 /0 /1 to G0 /0 /3
[Huawei -port -group]port link - type trunk     //port group all ports are set to the trunk road T runk
[Huawei -GigabitEthernet0/0/1]port link - type trunk
[Huawei -GigabitEthernet0/0/2]port link - type trunk
[Huawei -GigabitEthernet0/0/3]port link - type trunk
[Huawei -port -group]port trunk allow -pass vlan 10 20     //allowed VLAN is 10 and 20
[Huawei -GigabitEthernet0/0/1]port trunk allow -pass vlan 10 20
[Huawei -GigabitEthernet0/0/2]port trunk allow -pass vlan 10 20
[Huawei -GigabitEthernet0/0/3]port trunk allow -pass vlan 10 20
[Huawei -port -group]The PVID for all ports in the port trunk pvid vlan 10     //port group is 10
[Huawei -GigabitEthernet0/0/1]port trunk pvid vlan 10
[Huawei -GigabitEthernet0/0/2]port trunk pvid vlan 10
[Huawei -GigabitEthernet0/0/3]port trunk pvid vlan 10
[Huawei -port -group]quit
[Huawei]
```

Note: PVID, the default VLAN ID number of the port, identifies the unmarked frames received by the port.

Step 3: Configure the wireless controller AC.

Divide the VLAN and configure the address for the VLAN, the code is as follows:

```
<AC6605 >sys                    //go into privilege mode
Enter system view,return user view with Ctrl + Z.
[AC6605]vlan batch 10 20        //division VLAN10,20
Info:This operation may take a few seconds.Please wait for a moment...done.
```

```
[AC6605]
[AC6605]int vlan 10                          //into the VLAN10
[AC6605-Vlanif10]ip address 192.168.10.2 24           //Configure the
IP address
[AC6605-Vlanif10]quit   //exit
```

Configure the trunk road protocol, the code is as follows:

```
[AC6605]int G0/0/1   //entry port G 0/0/1
[AC6605-GigabitEthernet0/0/1]port link-type trunk   //port is set to the arterial road Trunk
[AC6605-GigabitEthernet0/0/1]port trunk allow-pass vlan 10 20   //allows VLAN10,20 to pass through the arterial road
[AC6605-GigabitEthernet0/0/1]port trunk pvid vlan 10   //trunk road PVID is the VLAN10
[AC6605-GigabitEthernet0/0/1]quit
```

Configure the AP authentication mode, the code is as follows:

```
[AC6605]wlan   //Enter the wireless configuration mode
[AC6605-wlan-view]ap auth-mode mac-auth   //Wireless AP certification is based on MAC certification
[AC6605-wlan-view]quit
```

Bind the wireless AP, the code is as follows:

```
[AC6605]capwap source interface vlan 10   //Configuring the interface used by AC for establishing CAPWAP tunnel serves as the source interface of AC for establishing CAPWAP tunnel communication between AC and AP.
[AC6605]wlan                 //Enter the wireless configuration mode
[AC6605-wlan-view]ap-id 1 ap-mac 00e0-fc38-40a0   //binds the MAC of the first AP
[AC6605-wlan-ap-1]ap-name ap1                //named a p1
[AC6605-wlan-ap-1]quit                       //exit
[AC6605-wlan-view]ap-id 2 ap-mac 00e0-fc87-2400   //binds the MAC of the second AP
[AC6605-wlan-ap-2]ap-name ap2                //named a p2
[AC6605-wlan-ap-2]quit                       //exit
[AC6605-wlan-view]quit                       //exit
[AC6605]display ap all                       //Check if the AP is online
```

```
    Info: This operation may take a few seconds. Please wait for a
moment. done.
    Total AP information:
    nor:normal    [2]
    ------------------------------------------------
    ID  MAC       Name Group  IP       Type   State STA Uptime
    ------------------------------------------------
    1   00e0 - fc38 - 40a0 ap1 default 192.168.10.254 AP2050DN nor   0
2M:50S
    2   00e0 - fc87 - 2400 ap2 default 192.168.10.253 AP2050DN nor   0
3M:3S
    ------------------------------------------ Total:2
    [AC6605]
    The AP is indicated when the state is a nor It's online
```

Configure the wireless signal template. Wireless template configuration needs to configure: signal template, security template, call template, the code is as follows:

```
    [AC6005]wlan           //Enter the wireless configuration mode
    [AC6005 - wlan - view] ssid - profile name aa      //Create a ssid
template with the name of aa
    [AC6005 - wlan - ssid - prof - aa]ssid GYHLW   //the broadcast out of the
ssid is the GYHLW
    Info:This operation may take a few seconds,please wait. done.
    [AC6005 - wlan - ssid - pro of - aa]quit       //exit
    [AC6005 - wlan - view]

    [AC6005 - wlan - view]security - profile name bb      //Create a security
template,the name is bb
    [AC6005 - wlan - sec - prof - bb] security wpa2 psk pass - phrase
Aa123456 //aes code is the Aa123456
    [AC6005 - wlan - sec - prof - bb]quit
    [AC6005 - wlan - view]


    [AC6005 - wlan - view] vap - profile name cc          //Create call
template with name cc
    [AC6005 - wlan - vap - prof - cc]ssid - profile aa       //call the ssid
template aa
    Info:This operation may take a few seconds,please wait. done.
```

[AC6005-wlan-vap-prof-cc]security-profile bb   //to call the parameters of the safe template bb
    Info:This operation may take a few seconds,please wait. done.
[AC6005-wlan-vap-pro-cc]service-vlan vlan-id 20   //The VLAN for service wireless user's service is 20
    Info:This operation may take a few seconds,please wait. done.
[AC6005-wlan-vap-prof-cc]quick   //exit
[AC6005-wlan-view]

Send wireless signals, the code is as follows:

[AC6005]wlan   //Enter the wireless configuration mode
[AC6605-wlan-view]ap-group name default   //into the default AP group d efault,by default,all AP are in the default group d efault
[AC6605-wlan-ap-group-default]vap-profile cc wlan 1 radio all
//to transmit wireless signals according to the configuration requirements of the call template cc

After transmitting the wireless signal, the effect is depicted in Figure 2.34.

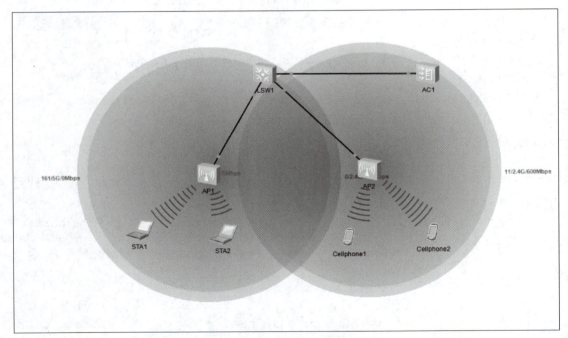

Figure 2.34   The Wireless Signal is Transmitted Successfully

Step 4: Test the wireless signal connection condition.
①Connect the wireless terminal to the wireless signal, as depicted in Figure 2.35
②The wireless signal effect is connected to the terminal, as depicted in Figure 2.36.

128

Project 2 How to Build an Industrial Internet

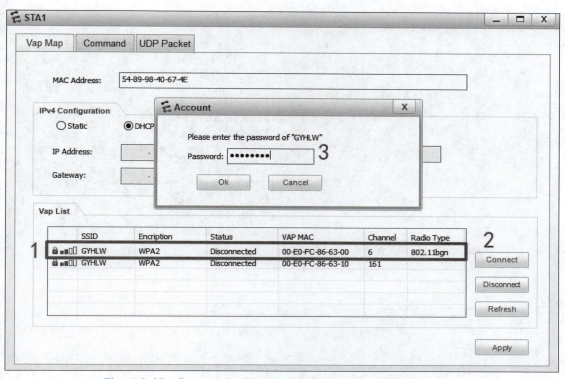

Figure 2.35 Connect the Wireless Terminals to the Wireless Signals

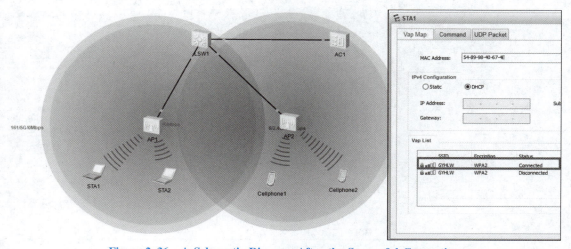

Figure 2.36 A Schematic Diagram After the Successful Connection

③View the IP address of the wireless terminal using the ipconfig command and test network connectivity. The results are depicted in Figure 2.37.

④Test the wireless roaming function, and the results are depicted in Figure 2.38.

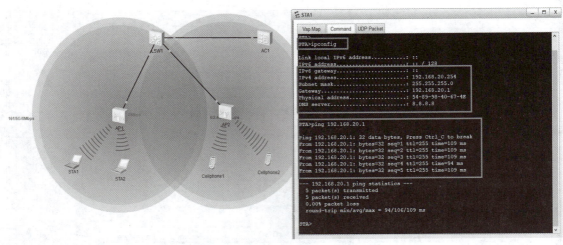

Figure 2.37　Screenshot of Wireless Terminal Access to Address and Test Network Connectivity

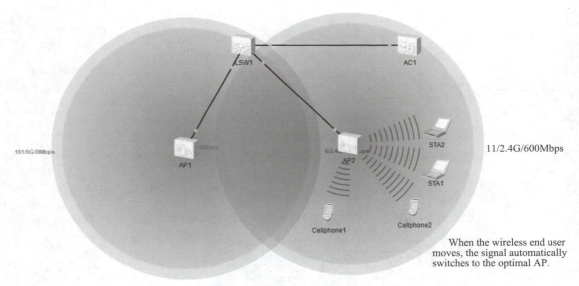

Figure 2.38　Wireless Roaming Renderings

Mission Expansion

China's Internet 30th Anniversary Salute—Splendid Achievements in Technological Development and Network Economy

Since 1994, when China formally accessed the Internet, the Internet in China has entered its 30th year of development. In the past 30 years, China's Internet has made remarkable achievements in science and technology innovation, from the initial e-mail and news websites to the current social media and e-commerce platforms. From the initial e-mail and news websites to social media and e-commerce platforms, China's Internet industry has continued to innovate and develop, providing more convenient and rich information services for the people, the Internet industry in China has continued to innovate and develop, providing the people with more convenient and rich information services. Especially in recent years, the Chinese government has strongly supported scientific and technological innovation, rapidly pushed forward the construction of digital infrastructure, and encouraged enterprises to increase research and development. Construction of digital infrastructure, encouraging enterprises to increase investment in R&D, and promoting the close integration of industry, academia, research and utilization, which has laid a solid foundation for the rapid development of China's Internet industry.

The Chinese government has laid a solid foundation for the rapid development of China's Internet industry, which has led to the realization of "touching the Internet" by thousands of industries, the emergence of new forms and modes of business, and the digital economy becoming an important engine for economic growth. The digital economy has become an important engine for economic growth. Industrial Internet has shown rapid development, with the industrial Internet identification and resolution system covering 31 provinces (autonomous regions and municipalities), there are more than 240 influential industrial Internet platforms, and the national industrial Internet big data center system has basically been built. The national industrial Internet big data center system has been basically built.

In a short span of 30 years, China's Internet technology and industry has developed from nothing to a leader. Behind the great progress is the country's great attention to the concept of independent innovation and adherence to it. As a young student, we should be firm in the four self-confidence, start from ourselves, study hard, and learn from others. Starting from ourselves, we should study diligently, study hard, and contribute to the realization of the construction of a strong scientific and technological country and the great rejuvenation of the Chinese nation.

Assignment:

①Analyze and research China's industrialization.

②Analyze and research the development status of China's industrial Internet platform, and write a report to share the inspiration.

项目 3

工业大数据感知与采集

任务 7　感知工业大数据

感知工业大数据

学习目标

①掌握制造资源标识解析技术。
②掌握工业大数据传感技术。
③掌握制造资源定位技术。
④理解群智感知技术。

建议学时

2 课时

工作情境

工业大数据的发展与数据感知技术密不可分,数据感知为工业数据分析提供源源不断的数据资源,是工业数据技术的基石,其效率、准确度和鲁棒性直接影响到后续数据处理与分析业务的效果。充分了解工业大数据感知技术,为后续数据采集、传输、处理及分析打下坚实基础。

知识导图

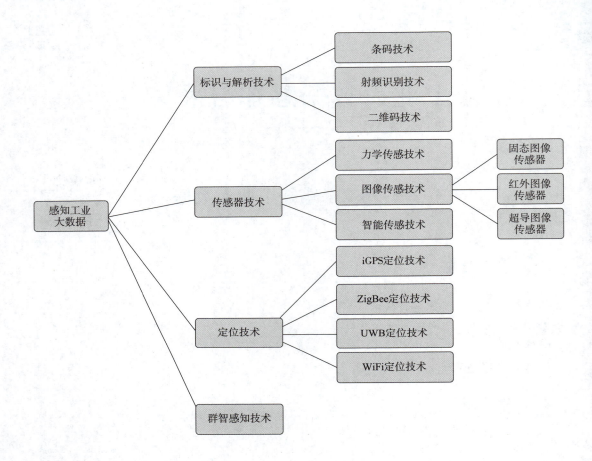

相关知识

数据感知技术是一种通过物理、化学或生物效应感知目标的状态、特征和方式等信息，并按照一定的规律将其转换成可利用信号，用以表征目标特征信息的信息获取技术。工业数据感知的核心技术体系包括标识与解析技术、传感器技术、定位技术等。以智能车间的数据感知为例，标识与解析技术表明了工件等物料的身份编码，传感器技术感知工件的加工表面质量、形位误差等数据，定位技术可以感知工件物流数据。近年来，随着智能AGV、智能手持终端等智能移动设备的广泛普及，群智感知技术通过设备在移动过程中完成大范围的感知任务，受到了大量关注，逐渐成为一种新的数据感知手段。

1. 标识与解析技术

在数字化的工业系统中，标识指设备、物料、工装、夹具等资源的"身份证"号码；

标识的解析,就是利用所建立的标识,对设备、物料、工装、夹具等资源进行唯一性的定位和信息查询。常见的标识解析技术包括条码技术、射频识别技术(Radio Frequency Identification,RFID)、二维码技术等。

(1)条码技术

条码是将线条与空白按照一定的编码规则组合起来的符号,用以代表一定的字母、数字等资料,如图3.1所示。最早的条码标识通过条码的宽度和数量来标识数据,通过扫描条码进行不同色条不同宽度的识别,进而可以获取到条码上的信息。条码技术主要由扫描阅读、光电转换和译码输出到计算机三大部分组成。这种技术的最大优点是速度快、错误率低、可靠性高、性价比高,但损污后可读性差。

图3.1 条码

在工业领域中通常应用于仓库管理和生产管理。将条码技术与信息处理技术结合,实施条码化的仓库管理,可确保库存量的准确性,保证必要的库存水平及仓库中物料的移动与进货、发货协调一致,减少库存积压。在汽车等现代化、大规模的生产行业中,条码技术不仅应用于生产过程控制和生产效率统计等领域,而且具有对成品终身质量跟踪等功能,可保证数据的实时和准确。

在进行解析的时候,是用条码阅读机(即条码扫描器,又称条码扫描枪或条码阅读器)扫描,得到一组反射光信号,此信号经光电转换后变为一组与线条、空白相对应的电子信号,经解码后还原为相应的文字或数字,再传入计算机。目前也能通过手机拍照方式对照片进行识别来获取条码中的数据。

(2)射频识别技术

射频识别技术是一种非接触的自动识别技术。其基本原理是利用射频信号和空间耦合(电感或电磁耦合)传输特性实现识读器与标签间的数据传输。射频识别系统一般由三个部分组成,如图3.2所示,即标签、识读器和天线,部分功率要求不高的RFID设备把识读器和天线集成在一起统一称作识读器。在应用中,射频电子标签粘附在被识别的物品上,当

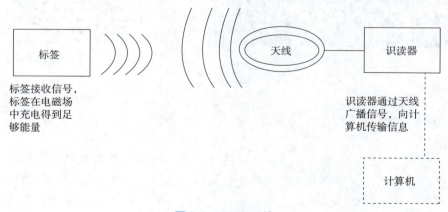

图3.2 RFID系统

该物品移动至识读器驱动的天线工作范围内时，识读器可以无接触地把物品所携带的标签中的数据读取出来，从而实现物品的无线识别。可读写的 RFID 设备还可以通过识读器把附着在物品上的标签中的数据写入标签，从而完整地实现产品的标记与识别。

在工业生产中，利用 RFID 技术可以实时对生产计划执行过程进行监控及可视化管理，增强生产计划与调度的时效性，大大降低工作中的人为失误。可以通过工位读写器、电子托盘、RFID 标签挂件等产品，实现可视化的生产过程监控平台，从毛坯到成品进行全程跟踪，记录产品的自动报工、各产品/批次的完工数量、工件的当前工序、各工序的执行设备和操作工人、各工序的实时状态等，为计划调度、线边物料管理、现场物流、质量追溯提供原证数据，也为企业开展价值工程活动提供依据。基于 RFID 技术形成产品溯源追踪系统，可大大提高公司产品的信誉度，建立一个完善的质量体系。

（3）二维码技术

二维码可以分为行排式二维码和矩阵式二维码。行排式二维码由多行一维码堆叠在一起构成，但与一维码的排列规则不完全相同；矩阵式二维码是深色方块与浅色方块组成的矩阵，通常呈正方形，在矩阵中深色块和浅色块分别表示二进制中的 1 和 0。

行排式二维码（见图 3.3）又称堆积式或层排式二维码。其形态类似一维码，编码原理与一维码的编码原理类似，可以用相同的设备对其进行扫描识读。由于行排式二维码的容量更大，所以校验功能有所增强，但不具有纠错功能。行排式二维码中具有代表性的是 PDF417 码。

矩阵式二维码（见图 3.4）以矩阵的形式组成，每一个模块的长与宽相同，模块与整个符号通常都以正方形的形态出现。矩阵式二维码是一种图形符号自动识别处理码制，通常都有纠错功能。具有代表性的矩阵式二维码有 Data Matrix 码、Code One 码、Quick Response 码、汉信码。

图 3.3 行排式二维码

图 3.4 矩阵式二维码

2. 传感器技术

传感器技术是数据感知的核心技术，是数据处理与分析的源头和基础。智能传感技术在普通传感的基础上，利用微处理器对相关数据执行运算、分析等操作，从而使传感器更好地与外部环境交互以更快、更好地获取设备需要的信息。在大数据时代，传感器技术的应用已经渗透到了仓储供应、生产加工、能源保障、环境控制、楼宇办公、安全保卫等各个方面。

(1) 力学传感技术

力传感器（Force Sensor）是应用力学传感技术，将力的量值转换为相关电信号的器件。力是引起物体运动状态变化的直接原因。力传感器包括力、力矩、振动、转速、加速度、质量、流量、硬度和真空度等传感器。按照用途来分，力传感器又可分为力、称重（衡器）和压力传感器。按照工作原理来分，力传感器又可分为电阻式（应变式、压阻式和电位器式）、电感式（压磁式）、电容式、磁电式（霍尔式）、压电式、表面声波（Surface Acoustic Wave，SAW）、光纤、薄膜（连续膜）力传感器等。

(2) 图像传感技术

图像传感技术是在光电技术基础上发展起来的，利用光电器件的光电转换功能，将其感光面上的光信号转换为与光信号成对应比例关系的电信号"图像"的一门技术，该技术将光学图像转换成一维时序信号，其关键器件是图像传感器。

①固态图像传感器。

固态图像传感器利用光敏元件的光电转换功能将投射到光敏单元上的光学图像转换成电信号"图像"，即将光强的空间分布转换为与光强成比例的电荷包空间分布，然后利用移位寄存器功能将这些电荷包在时钟脉冲控制下实现读取与输出，形成一系列幅值不等的时钟脉冲序列，完成光图像的电转换。固态图像传感器一般包括光敏单元和电荷寄存器两个主要部分。根据光敏元件的排列形式不同，固态图像传感器可分为线型和面型两种。根据所用的敏感器件不同，又可分为CCD、MOS线型传感器以及CCD、CID、MOS阵列式面型传感器等。

②红外图像传感器。

遥感技术多应用于 5~10 μm 的红外波段，现有的基于MOS器件的图像传感器和CCD图像传感器均无法直接工作于这一波段，因此，需要研究专门的红外图像传感技术及器件来实现红外波段的图像探测与采集。目前，红外CCD图像传感器有集成（单片）式和混合式两种。集成式红外CCD固态图像传感器是在一块衬底上同时集成光敏元件和电荷转移部件而构成的，整个片体要进行冷却。混合式红外CCD图像传感器的感光单元与电荷转移部件相分离，工作时，红外光敏单元处于冷却状态，而 Si – CCD 的电荷转移部件工作于室温条件。

③超导图像传感器。

超导图像传感器包括超导红外传感器、超导可见光传感器、超导微波传感器、超导磁场传感器等。超导传感器的最大特点是噪声很小，其噪声电平小到接近量子效应的极限，因此，超导传感器具有极高的灵敏度。超导图像使用时，还要配以准光学结构组成的测量系统。来自电磁喇叭的被测波图像，通常用光学透镜聚光，然后在传感器上成像。因此，在水平和垂直方向上微动传感器总是能够探测空间的图像。这种测量系统适用于毫米波段。

(3) 智能传感技术

智能传感器是具有信息处理功能的传感器。智能传感器带有微处理机，具有采集、处理、交换信息的能力，是传感器集成化与微处理机相结合的产物。与一般传感器相比，智能传感器有三个优点：通过软件技术可实现高精度的信息采集，而且成本低；具有一定的编程自动化能力；功能多样化。

现有的智能传感器保留了传统传感器中数据获取的功能，通过无线网络实现数据交互。而得益于人工智能技术的发展，海量的数据得以有发挥的空间，通过模糊逻辑、自动知识收集、神经网络、遗传算法、基于案例推理和环境智能对传感器进行优化，给予用户相关建议并协助其完成任务。

鉴于智能传感器在灵活性、可重新配置能力和可靠性方面的优势，配备了智能传感器的设备与系统在越来越多的任务中表现出超越人类的性能。智能传感器因而广泛应用于装配、建筑建模、环境工程、健康监控、机器人、遥控作业等领域。

3. 定位技术

在以智能车间为代表的工业系统中，工件资源、人员信息与位置是自动控制、系统调度等系统运行优化业务所必需的基础信息。定位技术是指利用无线通信和传感器来感知当前资源位置的技术，是车间常用的感知技术之一。本节重点介绍 iGPS、ZigBee 定位、超宽带定位、WiFi 定位等主流技术。

（1）iGPS 定位技术

iGPS 又称室内 GPS 技术，它是一种三维测量技术，其借鉴了 GPS 定位系统的三角测量原理，通过在空间建立三维坐标系，并采用红外激光定位的方法计算空间待测点的详细三维坐标值。iGPS 具有高精度、高可靠性和高效率等优点，主要用于解决大尺寸空间的测量与定位问题。iGPS 技术为大尺寸的精密测量提供了全新的思路。在 iGPS 技术之前，很难对飞机整机、轮船船身等大尺寸物体进行精密的测量。iGPS 技术可以很方便地解决这一难题，同时具有相当高的测量精度，在 39 m 的测量区域内其测量精度可以高达 0.25 mm。此外，iGPS 系统可以通过建立一个大尺寸的空间坐标系，实现坐标测量、精确定位和监控装配等。

iGPS 系统主要包括三个部分：发射器、接收器和控制系统。发射器分布在测量空间的不同位置，发出一束线性激光脉冲信号和两束扇形激光平面信号；接收器又称 3D 靶镜，即能采集激光信号的传感器，位于待测点处，负责接收发射器发出的激光信号，并根据发射器投射来的激光时间特征参数计算待测点的角度和位置，将其转换为数字脉冲信号并通过 ZigBee 无线网络传输给控制系统；控制系统负责数字脉冲信号的分析处理工作，通过解码，并根据各发射器的相对位置和位置关系计算出各待测点的空间三维坐标。

（2）ZigBee 定位技术

ZigBee 定位由若干个待定位的盲节点和一个已知位置的参考节点与网关形成组网，每个微小的盲节点之间相互协调通信以实现全部定位。其优点在于成本低、功耗低，但 ZigBee 的信号传输容易受到多径效应和移动的影响，而且定位精度取决于信道物理品质、信号源密度、环境和算法的准确性，定位软件的成本较高。

ZigBee 在工业场景中常用于厂内人员定位，采用新导智能的无线室内人员实时定位系统能够实现精确定位、实时跟踪、历史轨迹回放、区域准入、移动考勤、安保巡检等功能，定位最高精度可达 3 m。ZigBee 的应用可以对企业员工以及进出工厂的临时人员进行有效管理，从而提高工厂人员的管理效率。

(3) 超宽带定位技术

超宽带 (Ultra Wide Band, UWB) 定位技术, 它是一种无载波通信技术, 利用纳秒级的非正弦波窄脉冲传输数据, 因此, 其所占的频谱范围很宽。UWB 定位采用宽带脉冲通信技术, 具备极强的抗干扰能力, 使定位误差减小。该技术的出现填补了高精度定位领域的空白, 它具有对信道衰落不敏感、发射信号功率谱密度低、截获能力低、系统复杂度低、能提供厘米级的定位精度等优点, 但实施成本相对较高, 主要用于重要产品和资产的定位跟踪。

(4) WiFi 定位技术

WiFi 定位的原理和基站定位相似, 每一个无线接入点 (AP) 都有一个全球唯一的媒体存取控制地址 (MAC), 同时无线 AP 在通常情况下不会移动。目标设备在开启 WiFi 的情况下, 即可扫描并收集周围的 AP 信号, 无论是否加密, 是否已连接, 甚至信号强度不足以显示在无线信号列表中, 都可以获取到 AP 广播出来的 MAC 地址。设备将这些能够标识 AP 的数据发送到位置服务器, 服务器检索出每一个 AP 的地理位置, 并结合每个信号的强弱程度, 计算出设备的地理位置并返回到用户设备。

目前 WiFi 定位技术有两种, 一种是根据移动设备和 3 个无线网络接入点的无线信号强度, 通过差分算法来比较精准地对移动设备进行三角定位；另一种是事先记录巨量的确定位置点的信号强度, 通过用新加入的设备的信号强度对比拥有巨量数据的数据库来确定位置。在工业生产中, WiFi 定位在厂区巡查、移动作业和参观引导方面有相关应用。

4. 群智感知技术

群智感知是指通过人们已有的移动设备形成交互式的、参与式的感知网络, 并将感知任务发布给网络中的个体或群体来完成, 从而帮助专业人员或公众收集数据、分析信息和共享知识。

群智感知主要涉及两个关键因素, 即用户与数据, 可以提供高质量的感知与计算服务。根据关注因素不同, 可将群智感知划分为移动群智感知和稀疏群智感知。其中, 移动群智感知主要关注用户, 强调利用移动用户的广泛存在性、灵活移动性和机会连接性来执行感知任务; 而稀疏群智感知则更加关注数据, 通过挖掘和利用已感知数据的时空关联, 来推断未感知区域的数据。

移动群智感知的典型架构如图 3.5 所示, 主要划分为应用层、网络层和感知层。应用层主要处理任务发起者自身需求及网络层获得的数据, 应用层向所有用户发布任务, 移动用户携带着智能设备执行任务并上传数据至网络层, 以向任务发起者提供感知与计算服务。

如图 3.6 所示, 典型的稀疏群智感知系统通常由少量的参与用户利用其随身携带的智能设备采集其所在区域的感知数据; 接下来, 通过挖掘和利用已采集感知数据中存在的时空关联, 推断其他未感知区域的数据。以这种方式, 稀疏群智感知系统可以大幅减少需要感知的区域数量, 从而减少感知消耗; 同时, 利用感知数据的时空关联, 可以由稀疏的感知数据准确地推断完整感知地图, 为大规模且细粒度的感知任务提供一个更为实际的感知范例。

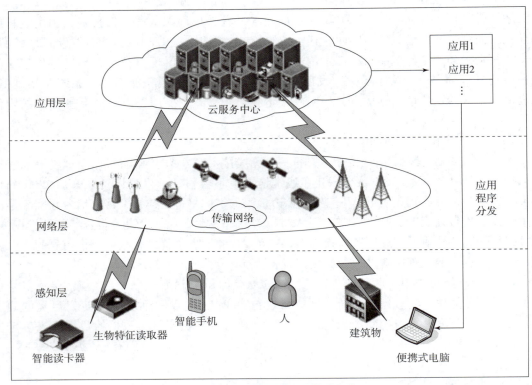

图 3.5　移动群智感知的典型架构

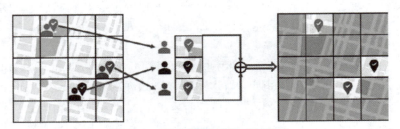

图 3.6　典型的稀疏群智感知系统

车联网是物联网和移动互联网在交通运输领域应用后的衍生概念，它借助新一代通信与信息处理技术，实现车与人、车、路、服务平台的全方位网络连接与智能信息交换，如图 3.7 所示。车联网可以提升汽车智能化水平，是实现自动驾驶、智能交通和智慧城市的重要途径。车辆通过车联网进行群智协作，可以改善单辆车感知精度、感知范围、通信能力、计算能力和存储能力方面的局限性。通过利用车与车、车与云端、车与边缘协作来提高车联网中"车–网–环境"感知与信息服务的质量，同时降低对车联网中感知与通信资源的开销。

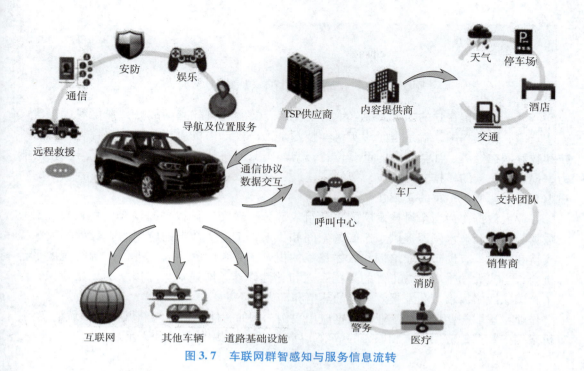

图 3.7　车联网群智感知与服务信息流转

任务拓展

科教兴国——加快建设国家战略人才力量

习近平总书记在党的二十大报告中鲜明提出,要实施科教兴国战略,强化现代化建设人才支撑。科教兴国,就是全面落实科学技术是第一生产力的思想,坚持教育为本,把科技和教育摆在经济、社会发展的重要位置,增强国家的科技实力及向现实生产力转化的能力,提高全民族的科技文化素质,把经济建设转移到依靠科技进步和提高劳动者素质的轨道上来,加速实现国家的繁荣强盛。

工业大数据作为当今科技发展的重要组成部分,对实现科教兴国具有重要意义。工业大数据为科研和技术发展提供了广阔的空间和机遇,工业大数据的应用为教育教学改革提供支持和指导,有助于产业培训和人才培养的提升。党和国家为人才提供广阔的发展平台和机会,当代大学生应树立正确的爱国观念和党性修养,增强对党和国家的忠诚意识,深入了解国家战略需求,激发报效国家的热情和动力。

作业:选取一些典型的工业大数据应用案例,例如智能制造、智慧城市等领域的案例,分析案例中数据的应用方式和取得的成效,同时总结案例中的经验和不足之处。

Project 3

Industrial Big Data Sensing and Acquisition

Task 7　Sensing Industrial Big Data

 Learning Objective

①Master Manufacturing Resource Identification Resolution technology.
②Master industrial big data sensing technology.
③Master Manufacturing resource location technology.
④Understand Swarm Intelligence Perception technology.

 Suggested Hours

2 hours

 Work Situations

　　The advancement of industrial big data is closely intertwined with data perception technology, which supplies a continuous stream of data resources for industrial data analysis, serving as the bedrock of industrial data technology. The efficiency, accuracy, and robustness of data perception directly influence the effectiveness of subsequent data processing and analysis operations. A comprehensive understanding of industrial big data perception technology lays a solid foundation for subsequent data acquisition, transmission, processing, and analysis.

Knowledge Map

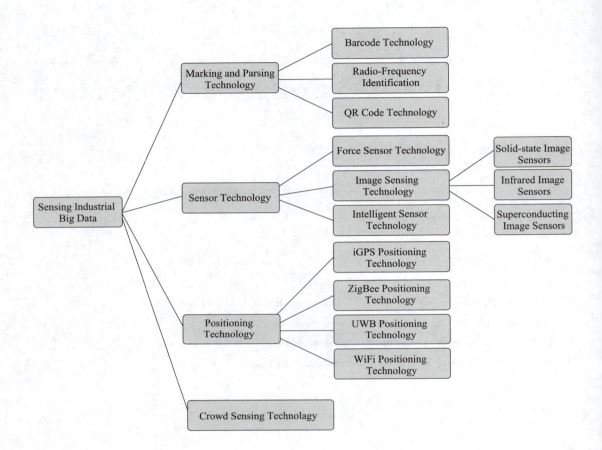

Relevant Knowledge

Data perception technology is a form of information acquisition that captures the state, characteristics, and mode information of a target through physical, chemical, or biological effects, converting them into usable signals according to specific laws. These signals are then used to characterize the features of the target. The core technological system of industrial data sensing includes marking and parsing technology, localization technology, and sensing technology, among others. For instance, in the context of intelligent workshops, coding and marking technology is employed to indicate the identity code of workpieces and other materials, localization technology is utilized to sense workpiece logistics data, and intelligent sensing technology captures data related to the processing surface quality of workpieces, as well as shape and positional errors. In recent years, with the widespread adoption of intelligent mobile devices such as intelligent AGVs and handheld terminals, crowd sensing technology has garnered significant attention. This technology accomplishes a wide array of sensing tasks through devices while in motion, gradually emerging as a new method of data sensing.

1. Marking and Parsing Technology

In a digital industrial system, identification involves assigning a unique identifier to equipment, materials, tooling, fixtures, and other resources, often akin to an "identity card" number. Identification analysis involves utilizing established identification methods to pinpoint the location and retrieve relevant information about these resources. Common technologies used for marking and resolution include barcode technology, Radio Frequency Identification technology (RFID), and two-dimensional code technology. These methods help ensure the uniqueness of each resource and facilitate efficient information retrieval.

(1) Barcode Technology

Barcode is a symbol that combines lines and blanks according to certain coding rules to represent certain letters, numbers, and other information, as depicted in Figure 3.1. The earliest barcode identification was based on the width and number of bars to identify the data. Scanning barcodes involves identifying different colors and widths of bars, which in turn provide access to the information

Figure 3.1 Barcodes

encoded in the barcode. Barcode technology mainly consists of three main parts: scanning and reading, photoelectric conversion, and decoding output to the computer. The biggest advantage of this technology is its speed, low error rate, high reliability, and cost-effectiveness. However, it suffers from poor readability after damage.

In the industrial field, barcode technology is usually applied to warehouse management and production management. By combining barcode technology with information processing technology, barcode warehouse management can ensure the accuracy of inventory and the coordination of incoming shipments to reduce inventory backlog. In the automobile and other modernized, large-scale production industries, barcode technology is not only applied to production process control and production efficiency statistics but also to functions such as lifelong quality tracking of finished products, ensuring real-time and accurate data. During analysis, a barcode reader (i.e., barcode scanner, also known as a barcode scanner gun or barcode reader) scans and receives a set of reflected light signals. These signals are converted into electronic signals corresponding to lines and blanks through photoelectric conversion, decoded into corresponding text or digital information, and then transmitted to the computer. Currently, data in barcodes can also be obtained through methods such as taking pictures with a cell phone for photo identification.

(2) Radio-Frequency Identification

Radio Frequency Identification technology (RFID) is a non-contact automatic identification technology. Its basic principle involves using radio frequency signals and spatial coupling (inductance or electromagnetic coupling) to transmit data between a reader and a label. The RFID system generally comprises three parts, as depicted in Figure 3.2: the electronic label, the reader, and the antenna. In cases where power requirements are not high, RFID equipment integrates the reader and the antenna together uniformly, referred to as the reader. In practice, radio frequency electronic tags are affixed to the items to be identified. When these items move into the operating range of the reader-driven antenna, the reader can contactlessly read the data stored in the tags, enabling wireless identification of the items. Read-write RFID devices can also write required data into the tag attached to the article, facilitating product marking and identification.

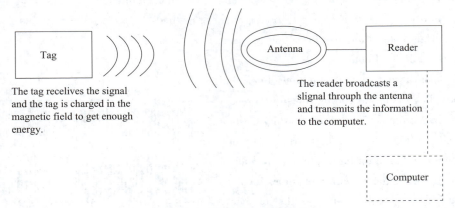

Figure 3.2   RFID System

In industrial production, RFID technology enables real-time monitoring and visualization management of production plans, enhancing the timeliness of production planning and scheduling while significantly reducing human errors. By utilizing workstations, electronic pallets, RFID tag pendants, and other products, we can achieve visualization of the production process monitoring platform, tracking the entire process from raw materials to finished products. This includes automatically recording completed products/batches, the current process of workpieces, equipment and operators involved in each process, and real-time status updates for each process. This data serves as evidence for planning and scheduling, line material management, on-site logistics, and quality control. Establishing a product traceability tracking system based on RFID technology can greatly enhance the credibility of a company's products and establish a robust quality system.

(3) QR Code Technology

QR codes can be categorized into row-row QR codes and matrix QR codes. Row-row QR codes consist of multiple rows of one-dimensional codes stacked together, although the arrangement rules may not be exactly the same as those for one-dimensional codes. Matrix QR codes, on the other hand, are composed of a matrix of dark and light-colored squares, typically arranged in a square pattern. Within the matrix, dark and light-colored blocks represent binary 1 and 0, respectively.

Row-row QR codes are also known as stacked or layered QR codes. Their form is similar to one-dimensional codes, and their coding principle resembles that of one-dimensional codes. They can be scanned and read by the same equipment. Although row-type two-dimensional codes have a larger capacity than one-dimensional codes, they lack error correction functionality. A representative row-type two-dimensional code is the PDF417 code, as depicted in Figure 3.3.

Matrix QR codes are composed in a matrix format where each module has the same length and width. The modules and the entire symbol are typically arranged in a square pattern. Matrix QR codes are a type of graphic symbol automatic identification processing code system and usually include error correction functionality. Representative matrix 2D codes include Data Matrix code, Code One code, Quick Response code, and Hanxin code, as depicted in Figure 3.4.

Figure 3.3 Rows and Rows of QR Codes

Figure 3.4 Matrix QR Code

2. Sensor Technology

Sensor technology is the core technology for data perception, serving as the source and foundation for data processing and analysis. Intelligent sensing technology builds upon ordinary sensing by leveraging microprocessors to perform operations on relevant data, enabling analysis and other functions. This allows sensors to interact more effectively with the external environment, facilitating faster and better access to the information required by equipment. In the era of big data, the application of sensor technology has permeated various domains including warehousing and supply, production and processing, energy security, environmental control, building and office management, as well as safety and security.

(1) Force Sensor Technology

Force sensors are devices that convert the quantitative value of a force into a relevant electrical signal. Force is the direct cause of changes in the state of motion of an object. Force sensors encompass various types, including force, torque, vibration, speed, acceleration, mass, flow, hardness, and vacuum sensors. Force sensors can be categorized based on their use into force sensors, weighing (scale) sensors, and pressure sensors. They can also be classified based on their operating principle, including resistive (such as strain, piezoresistive, and potentiometer types), inductive (like piezomagnetic), capacitive, magnetoelectric (such as Hall-type), piezoelectric, surface acoustic wave (SAW), fiber optic, and thin-film (continuous film) force sensors.

(2) Image Sensing Technology

Image sensing technology is developed based on photoelectric technology, utilizing photoelectric devices to convert optical signals into corresponding electrical signals. This technology converts the light-sensitive surface's optical signal into an electrical signal "image" with a proportional relationship. It then converts this "image" into a one-dimensional time series of signals, with the key device being the image sensor.

①Solid-state Image Sensors.

Solid-state image sensors utilize photosensitive components for photoelectric conversion. They project the optical image onto the photosensitive unit, converting the spatial distribution of light intensity into a spatial distribution of charge packets proportional to the light's intensity. These charge packets are controlled by clock pulses through a shift register function to achieve readout and output, forming a series of clock pulse sequences of equal amplitude to complete the electrical conversion of the light image. Solid-state image sensors typically consist of two main parts: the photosensitive unit and the charge register. Depending on the arrangement of photosensitive elements, solid-state image sensors can be classified into line and area types. Depending on the sensitive devices used, they can also be divided into CCD, MOS line sensors, and CCD, CID, MOS array type surface sensors, etc.

②Infrared Image Sensors.

Remote sensing technology is commonly applied to the infrared band of $5 \sim 10 \mu m$. Existing MOS device-based image sensors and CCD image sensors cannot directly operate in this band. Therefore, specialized infrared image sensing technology and devices are needed to achieve image detection and acquisition in the infrared band. Currently, there are two types of infrared CCD image sensors: integrated (monolithic) and hybrid. Integrated infrared CCD solid-state image sensors integrate photosensitive components and charge transfer components on a substrate, requiring the entire chip to be cooled. In hybrid infrared CCD image sensors, the photoreceptor unit and charge transfer components are separate. During operation, the infrared photosensitive unit is cooled, while the charge transfer components of the Si-CCD work at room temperature.

③Superconducting Image Sensors.

Superconducting image sensors encompass superconducting infrared sensors, superconducting visible light sensors, superconducting microwave sensors, and superconducting magnetic field sensors. The most significant characteristic of superconducting sensors is their very low noise level, which is close to the limit of quantum effects, resulting in extremely high sensitivity. Superconducting images are typically used with a measurement system consisting of a quasi-optical structure. The image of the measured wave from the electromagnetic Raman is usually concentrated with an optical lens and then imaged on the sensor. Thus, the micro motion sensor can detect the image of the space both horizontally and vertically. This measurement system is suitable for millimeter wavelengths.

(3) Intelligent Sensor Technology

Intelligent sensors are sensors endowed with information processing capabilities. These sensors incorporate a microprocessor for the collection, processing, and exchange of information, constituting a fusion of sensor technology and microprocessor integration. Compared to conventional sensors, intelligent sensors offer three key advantages: they enable high-precision information acquisition at low cost through software technology, possess a certain level of programming automation capabilities, and exhibit functional diversity.

Existing intelligent sensors maintain the fundamental data acquisition functions of traditional sensors, with data interaction facilitated through wireless networks. The advancement of artificial intelligence technology has provided opportunities to leverage vast amounts of data, enabling sensor optimization through techniques such as fuzzy logic, automatic knowledge collection, neural networks, genetic algorithms, case-based reasoning, and ambient intelligence. These approaches offer users relevant advice and assistance in completing tasks.

With their inherent flexibility, reconfigurability, and reliability, intelligent sensors-equipped devices and systems have demonstrated superior performance compared to humans in an increasing array of tasks. Consequently, intelligent sensors find application across diverse fields such as assembly, building modeling, environmental engineering, health monitoring, robotics, and remote-control operations.

3. Positioning Technology

In industrial systems exemplified by intelligent workshops, essential information for automatic control, system scheduling, and optimization operations includes workpiece resources, personnel information, and location data. Positioning technology involves utilizing wireless communication and sensors to ascertain the current location of resources, making it one of the commonly employed sensing technologies in workshops. This section will focus on mainstream technologies such as iGPS, ZigBee positioning, UWB positioning, and WiFi positioning.

(1) iGPS Positioning Technology

iGPS, also known as indoor GPS technology, is a three-dimensional measurement technology that leverages the triangulation principle of GPS positioning systems. It calculates detailed three-dimensional coordinate values of points in space by establishing a three-dimensional coordinate system and employing infrared laser positioning. iGPS offers high accuracy, reliability, and efficiency, primarily addressing measurement and positioning challenges in large-scale spaces. This technology introduces a novel approach to precision measurement of large objects. Prior to iGPS, precision measurements on large-scale objects such as entire aircraft and ship hulls were challenging. iGPS technology easily resolves this issue with high measurement accuracy, achieving up to 0.25 mm accuracy in a measurement area of 39 m. Additionally, the iGPS system enables coordinate measurement by establishing a large-scale spatial coordinate system and precise positioning and assembly monitoring.

The iGPS system comprises three main components: the transmitter, the receiver, and the control system. Transmitters are positioned at various locations in the measurement space, emitting linear laser pulse signals and two fan-shaped laser plane signals. The receiver, also known as the 3D target mirror, is situated at the point to be measured. It collects laser signals emitted by the transmitters, calculates the angle and position of the point to be measured based on the laser time characteristic parameters projected by the transmitters, and converts them into digital pulse signals. These signals are then transmitted to the control system via the ZigBee wireless network. The control system analyzes and processes the digital pulse signals, decodes them, and calculates the spatial 3D coordinates of the points to be measured based on the relative positions of the transmitters and their positional relationships.

(2) ZigBee Positioning Technology

ZigBee positioning comprises several blind nodes to be located, a reference node with a known location, and a gateway, forming a group network. Each tiny blind node coordinates communication with one another to achieve positioning. Its advantages include low cost and low power consumption. However, ZigBee signal transmission is susceptible to multipath effects and movement, and positioning accuracy depends on the physical quality of the channel, signal source density, environment, algorithm accuracy, and the high cost of positioning software.

ZigBee is commonly employed in industrial scenarios for personnel localization in factories. The wireless indoor personnel real-time positioning system by New Guide Intelligence enables precise positioning, real-time tracking, historical track playback, area access control, mobile attendance, security patrol, and other functions. It offers positioning accuracy of up to 3 meters. ZigBee applications effectively manage enterprise employees and temporary personnel entering and leaving the factory, thereby enhancing factory personnel management efficiency.

(3) UWB Positioning Technology

UWB (Ultra Wide Band) is a carrierless communication technology that utilizes nanosecond non-sinusoidal narrow pulses to transmit data, thereby occupying a wide spectral range. UWB positioning adopts broadband pulse communication technology, which offers robust anti-interference capabilities and reduces positioning errors. The emergence of this technology fills a gap in the field of high-precision positioning. It boasts advantages such as insensitivity to channel fading, low power spectral density of transmitted signals, low interception capability, low system complexity, and the ability to provide centimeter-level positioning accuracy. However, the implementation cost is relatively high, making it primarily suitable for the positioning and tracking of critical products and assets.

(4) WiFi Positioning Technology

The principle of WiFi positioning is akin to base station positioning. Each wireless Access Point (AP) possesses a globally unique Media Access Control (MAC) address, and under normal circumstances, wireless APs remain stationary. When WiFi is enabled, the target device scans and collects surrounding AP signals, regardless of encryption status, connection status, or signal strength. Even if the signal strength is insufficient to display in the wireless signal list, the device can obtain the MAC address broadcast by the AP. The device then sends the data identifying the APs to a location server. The server retrieves the geographic location of each AP and, based on the signal strength of each, calculates the geographic location of the device, returning it to the user's device.

Currently, there are two WiFi positioning technologies. One triangulates mobile devices more accurately using differential algorithms and the wireless signal strength of the mobile devices and three wireless network access points. The other records the signal strength of a vast number of predetermined location points in advance, determining location by comparing the signal strength of newly joined devices with the extensive database. In industrial production, WiFi positioning finds applications in plant inspections, mobile operations, and tour guidance.

4. Crowd Sensing Technology

Crowd sensing refers to the establishment of interactive and participatory sensing networks through mobile devices that individuals already possess. Sensing tasks are then distributed to individuals or groups within the network to complete, aiding professionals or the public in data collection, information analysis, and knowledge sharing.

Crowd sensing primarily involves two key factors: users and data, enabling the provision of high-quality sensing and computing services. Depending on the focus, crowd sensing can be categorized into mobile crowd sensing and sparse crowd sensing. Mobile crowd sensing primarily centers on users, leveraging their widespread presence, flexible mobility, and opportunistic connectivity to execute sensing tasks. Sparse crowd sensing places greater emphasis on data, mining and exploiting spatio-temporal correlations of sensed data to infer information in unperceived areas.

The typical architecture of mobile crowd sensing, as depicted in Figure 3.5, comprises three main layers: the application layer, the network layer, and the perception layer. The application

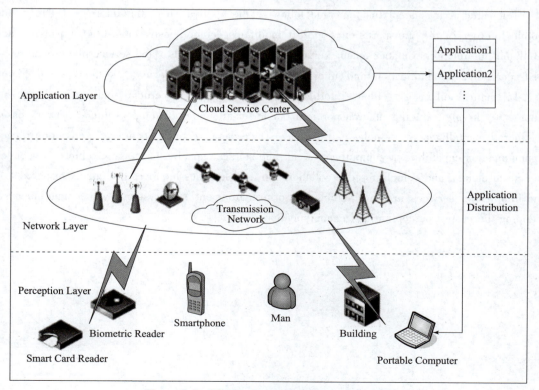

Figure 3.5 Mobile Crowd Sensing Architecture

layer manages task initiator requirements and data obtained from the network layer. It releases tasks to all users, who then utilize smart devices to execute tasks and upload data to the network layer, providing the task initiator with sensing and computing services.

As depicted in Figure 3.6, a typical sparse crowd sensing system typically involves a small number of participating users who utilize their portable smart devices to collect sensory data within their respective areas. Subsequently, spatial and temporal correlations within the collected sensory data are mined and utilized to infer data in other unperceived areas. This approach significantly reduces the areas requiring sensing, thereby decreasing sensing consumption. Additionally, by leveraging the spatial and temporal correlations of the sensing data, a complete sensing map can be accurately deduced from sparse sensing data, offering a practical sensing paradigm for large-scale and fine-grained sensing tasks.

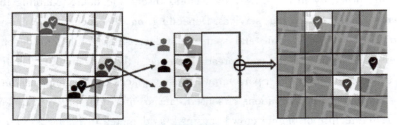

Figure 3.6 Schematic of Sparse Crowd Sensing

Telematics is a concept that emerged following the application of the Internet of Things and mobile Internet in the transportation sector. It facilitates comprehensive network connectivity and intelligent information exchange among vehicles, individuals, roads, and service platforms through next-generation communication and information processing technologies, as depicted in Figure 3.7. Telematics enhances vehicle intelligence and represents a crucial pathway to realizing automated driving, intelligent transportation, and smart cities. Through vehicle network-based collaborative intelligence, vehicles can enhance single-car perception accuracy, perception range, communication capabilities, computing power, and storage capacity. Leveraging vehicle-to-vehicle, vehicle-to-cloud, and vehicle-to-edge collaboration in Telematics improves the quality of perception and information services in the "vehicle-network-environment" ecosystem, while simultaneously reducing the cost of perception and communication resources.

Project 3　Industrial Big Data Sensing and Acquisition

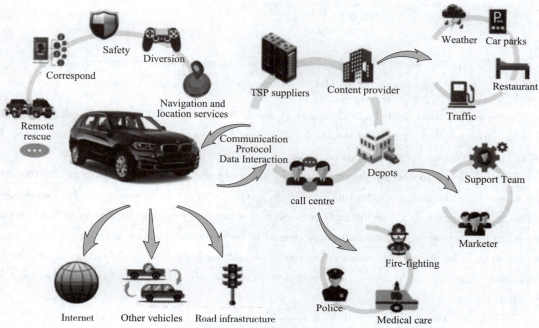

Figure 3.7　Telematics Crowd Sensing and Service Information Flow

Mission Expansion

Revitalizing the country through science and education—Accelerating the building of a strategic national human resource force

In the report of the 20th Party Congress, General Secretary Xi Jinping clearly put forward the need to implement the strategy of developing the country through science and education, and to strengthen the support for modernization.

Talent support. To develop the country through science and education is to fully realize the idea that science and technology is the first productive force, to insist on education as the foundation, and to place science and technology and education at the forefront of economic and social development. Technology and education are placed in an important position in economic and social development, to enhance the country's scientific and technological strength and its ability to be transformed into real productivity, and to improve the scientific and technological development of the whole nation.

To enhance the scientific and technological strength of the country and its ability to be transformed into real productive forces, it is also important to shift the economic construction to the track of relying on scientific and technological progress and improving the quality of workers, so as to accelerate the realization of national prosperity.

As an important part of today's scientific and technological development, industrial big data is of great significance for realizing the development of the country through science and education.

Industrial big data provides a broad space and opportunity for scientific research and technological development, and the application of industrial big data provides support and guidance for the reform of education and teaching, and contributes to the development of science and education.

The application of industrial big data provides support and guidance for education reform and helps to improve industrial training and talent cultivation. The Party and the country provide a broad development platform and opportunities for talents.

Contemporary college students should establish correct patriotic concepts and party spirit, enhance the sense of loyalty to the party and the country, and deeply understand the strategic needs of the country.

They should enhance their sense of loyalty to the Party and the country, understand the strategic needs of the country, and inspire their enthusiasm and motivation to serve the country.

Assignment:

①Select some typical industrial big data application cases, such as intelligent manufacturing, smart cities and other fields, and analyze the data application methods and the application of data in the cases.

②Analyze the way of data application and the results achieved in the cases, and summarize the experiences and shortcomings in the cases.

任务8　采集传感器数据

采集传感数据

学习目标

①理解工业现场传感器感知数据类型。
②掌握RFID系统原理及数据格式。
③理解基于RFID数据的订单与生产进度跟踪。

建议学时

2课时

工作情境

工业现场传感器的类型和数量众多，比如加装在设备、产品、工具上的传感器，其目的是监测设备、产品、工具的实时状态信息（振动、温度、磨损量、尺寸偏移量、能耗等）；又如加装在移动物体上的识别跟踪装置，用于监测移动物体（工具、物流设施、在制品、人）的位置信息；再如生产环境传感器，用于监测温度、湿度、灰尘、电磁等；还有用于实时视频和图像获取的监控设施等。这类数据是典型的时序数据，由于采集频率较高，数据规模通常非常大，但价值密度异常低。

知识导图

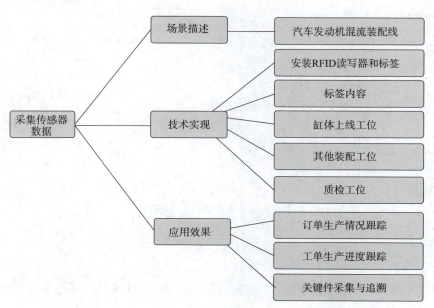

相关知识

1. 场景描述

汽车发动机混流装配线可同时组装多种型号的发动机。如图 3.8 所示，一条完整的装配线由缸体分装线、缸盖分装线、活塞连杆分装线及合装线组成，共有多达上百个工位。各装配线铺设有辊轮，由 PLC 控制，发动机放置在有特定支架的托盘上，托盘通过线体的辊轮带动传输，发动机的整个装配过程都在托盘上进行。当承载发动机的托盘在生产线上流转时，由于发动机型号不同，生产线控制系统需要让托盘在不同的工位停留，并且根据 BOM 结构的要求装配不同的零部件。因此，如何自动识别发动机的订单和型号成为生产跟踪和装配防错的关键。

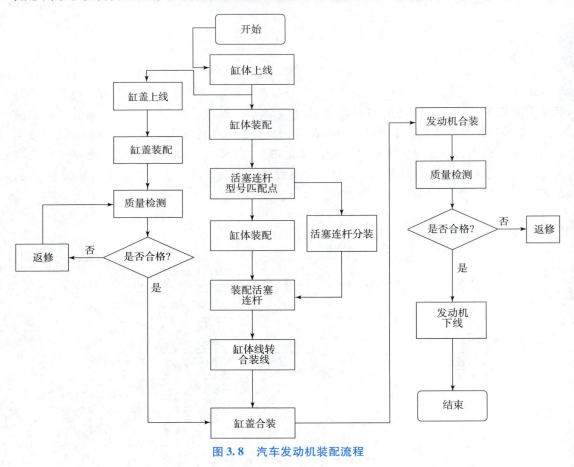

图 3.8 汽车发动机装配流程

2. 技术实现

如图 3.9 所示，在装配线的每个工位安装固定的 RFID 读写器，并在发动机托盘底下安上 RFID 标签，当托盘到达某工位光电传感器处时，光电传感器检测到发动机托盘到达，通知 RFID 读写器读取 RFID 标签，获取发动机 ID 等信息，各工位的 PC 终端根据该 ID 调用并显示相应的装配工艺指导文档。待该工序完成报工后，托盘离开光电传感器处，光电传感器即可检测到发动机离开，通知 RFID 读写器往 RFID 标签中写入新的信息。

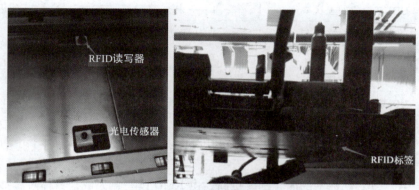

图 3.9 安装 RFID 读写器和标签

RFID 标签存储的内容如表 3.1 所示，含托盘信息、产品信息和加工信息。其中，托盘信息包括托盘号、托盘区域号和标签数据初始化状态，托盘信息在产品上线前已提前写入并初始化；产品信息包括订单号、发动机 ID 号、产品型号、缸体型号、缸盖型号和活塞连杆型号，产品信息在缸体上线工位写入，实现托盘和发动机的信息关联；加工信息包括总合格状态、最后加工工位、各工位加工状态和合格状态等，加工信息在每个工位逐步写入。

表 3.1 RFID 标签存储的内容

内容分组	存储内容	字节长	释义
托盘信息	托盘号	2	每个 RFID 标签对应一个托盘，示例：0001
	托盘区域号	1	1——缸体分装线，2——缸盖分装线，3——活连分装线，4——合装线
	标签数据初始化状态	1	0——未初始化，1——已初始化。产品上线设为 1，下线设为 0
产品信息	订单号	9	一个生产订单对应一个订单号，示例：EE0100098
	发动机 ID 号	8	每台发动机都刻有唯一的 ID 号，与工单号一一对应，示例：E4039415
	产品型号	13	示例：JND412D167-42
	缸体型号	13	与产品型号一致，示例：JND412D167-42
	缸盖型号	13	与产品型号一致，示例：JND412D167-42
	活塞连杆型号	13	与产品型号一致，示例：JND412D167-42

续表

内容分组	存储内容	字节长	释义
加工信息	总合格状态	1	1——未加工，2——合格，3——不合格
	最后加工工位	5	示例：OP010
	OP010 工位加工状态	1	1——未加工，2——已加工，3——下线返修
	OP010 工位合格状态	1	1——未加工，2——合格，3——不合格
	OP020 工位加工状态	1	—
	OP020 工位合格状态	1	—
	OP030 工位加工状态	1	—
	OP030 工位合格状态	1	—
	……	1	后续工位同上

在各个工位，RFID 标签的内容都要更新，由 RFID 读写器完成，具体过程如下：

①缸体上线工位。该工位是在制品跟踪的开始，需完成产品信息的绑定和写入。当缸体托盘到达时，首先初始化托盘 RFID 标签数据：清除原来的产品信息，初始化加工信息，保留托盘信息。缸体上线后，通过扫描条码，获取缸体的机加工 ID 号。MES 系统根据生产订单分配发动机 ID 号，并与机加工 ID 号绑定，然后将发动机产品信息和加工信息写入 RFID 标签。

②其他装配工位。根据产品型号展示装配工艺指导文档和采集发动机组装的零件信息，并验证零件型号是否匹配。当线体 PLC 检测到有托盘到达时，RFID 读写器读取托盘标签数据，MES 终端显示产品信息，并展示相应产品型号的工艺指导文档。工人装配前先扫描零件条码，MES 检测零件型号与产品型号是否匹配。若不匹配，则提示需更换零件，工人无法完成报工操作；若匹配，则允许完成报工，并更新 RFID 标签内的加工信息，将当前工位改为"已加工"状态，将当前工位的合格状态改为"合格"，将最后加工工位改为当前工位。

③质检工位。质检工位的质检设备将检测结果上传给车间数据采集系统，系统发送相应的写入指令给 RFID 读写器，对 RFID 标签的数据进行更新。除了更新最后加工工位外，若发动机质量检测合格，将当前工位合格状态和总合格状态设为"合格"，并将当前工位状态设为"已加工"，在制品流入下一道工序；若检测不合格，则当前工位合格状态和总合格状态设为"不合格"，并将当前工位状态设为"下线返修"，线体 PLC 控制回转台将不合格在制品下线返修，返修完成后重新上线，再次进行质量检测，直到在制品检测合格。

3. 应用效果

RFID 应用环境搭建好后，MES 系统可对发动机在制品进行跟踪，具体包括对订单生产情况的跟踪、工单生产进度的跟踪、发动机装配的关键件数据采集与追溯等。

（1）订单生产情况跟踪

通过检测各在制品在各工位的到达和离开信号，数据采集系统可以统计各订单生产情况。订单包括若干个工单,每个工单对应一台发动机产品。系统可统计每个订单的开工工单个数、完工工单个数、冻结工单个数、报废工单个数等。系统也可以记录各订单的开工时间、结束时间等整体信息。

(2) 工单生产进度跟踪

一个订单可分解为若干个工单,系统也可以跟踪每个工单的具体生产进度,可以查询到各工单目前所在工位、生产状态、生产进度等信息。其中,尾号为"0030"的工单共有197道工序,目前完成97道,当前工位为"A7270",目前处于开工状态。系统也记录了每个工单经过各工序的完工时间、合格状态等信息。

(3) 关键件采集与追溯

对于发动机装配的关键零部件,工人在装配前必须先使用扫码枪扫描关键件条码,并由数据采集系统将其与发动机进行型号匹配,只有型号匹配的关键件才能进行装配。系统通过读取 RFID 标签内的产品信息可获取发动机 ID 和型号,并与装配的关键件进行验证和绑定。它主要包括关键件条码、物料编码、物料名称,以及绑定的发动机 ID 号(批次号)、工单号、产品编码、产品名称等信息。通过关键件与发动机绑定,可实现质量追溯。一旦某台发动机出现质量问题,它所装配的关键件都可查询,并进一步找到责任供应商和问题批次。

 任务拓展

传感器技术——推动可持续发展和智慧生活的引擎

传感器始于工业生产领域，经过了长达数十年的不断突破和创新，现今已经得到广泛的应用。传感器技术应用在光伏新能源领域中，能提高光伏新能源系统的效率、可靠性和维护管理能力，帮助光伏发电领域实现更加可持续和清洁的能源转换；应用在智能制造领域中，能实现设备监测、故障预测和生产优化，提高生产效率、降低成本、改善产品质量和实现可持续发展；应用在智慧生活领域中，能使智慧生活领域更加智能化、便捷化和个性化，为人们提供更好的生活品质和体验。传感器技术的科技创新推动了社会经济的发展，改善了人民的生活品质，对社会的影响和贡献巨大。

党的二十大强调科技创新是国家发展的战略支撑和核心竞争力，新时代的大学生是国家未来科技创新的主力军和接班人，应当深刻理解和践行党的二十大关于科技创新的要求，应当深入理解党的二十大的精神，增强科技创新意识，培养创新能力，关注国家科技创新战略，积极参与科技创新实践，为实现国家科技强国的目标贡献自己的力量。

作业：小组讨论，分享对传感器的认识和理解，探讨传感器技术在不同领域的应用前景和挑战，鼓励同学们关注相关技术的发展动态和行业趋势。

Task 8 Acquisition of Sensing Data

Learning Objective

①Understand the types of data sensed by industrial field sensors.
②Understand knowledge of RFID system principles and data formats.
③Understand order and production progress tracking based on RFID data.

Suggested Hours

2 hours

Work Situations

There exists a wide array of industrial field sensors, including those installed on equipment, products, and tools to monitor real-time status information (such as vibration, temperature, wear and tear, dimensional deviation, and energy consumption). Additionally, identification and tracking devices are installed on moving objects to monitor their location information (such as tools, logistic facilities, work-in-progress items, and people). Production environment sensors are used to monitor parameters like temperature, humidity, dust, and electromagnetism. Surveillance facilities are also employed for real-time video and image acquisition. This type of data is typically in the form of time-series data. Due to the high frequency of acquisition, the data size is usually large, but the value density is relatively low.

Knowledge Map

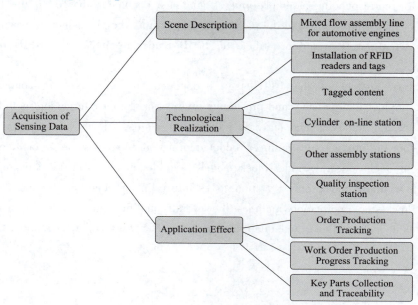

Relevant Knowledge

1. Scene Description

An automobile engine mixed-flow assembly line is capable of assembling multiple types of engines simultaneously. As depicted in Figure 3.8, a complete assembly line comprises a cylinder block sub-assembly line, a cylinder head sub-assembly line, a piston connecting rod sub-assembly line, and a combined assembly line, totaling up to hundreds of stations. Each assembly line is equipped with rollers controlled by PLC (Programmable Logic Controller). Engines are placed on pallets with specific supports, which are then propelled by the rollers along the assembly line. The entire engine assembly process takes place on these pallets. As the pallet carrying the engine progresses along the production line, the line control system, in response to different engine models, must allow the pallet to pause at various stations to assemble different parts according to the Bill of Materials (BOM) structure requirements. Thus, efficient management of this process becomes crucial for production tracking and preventing assembly errors.

2. Technological Realization

As depicted in Figure 3.9, a fixed RFID reader is installed at each station along the assembly line, with RFID tags positioned beneath the engine tray. When the tray reaches the photoelectric sensor at a station, the sensor detects its arrival and signals the RFID reader to read the RFID tags, retrieving the engine ID and other relevant information. The PC terminals at each station then access and display the corresponding assembly process guidance documents based on the ID. Once the assembly process is completed, and the pallet moves away from the photoelectric sensor, indicating the engine's departure, the sensor notifies the RFID reader to update the RFID tag with new information.

The storage content of the RFID tag is depicted in Table 3.1, encompassing pallet information, product information, and processing information. Pallet information includes the pallet number, pallet area number, and tag data initialization status, all of which are pre-written and initialized before the product goes online. Product information comprises the order number, engine ID number, product model, cylinder block model, cylinder head model, and piston rod model, written at the cylinder block online station to establish linkage between the pallet and engine information. Processing information includes the overall qualification status, the last processing station, status at each station, and qualification status. This information is gradually recorded at each station.

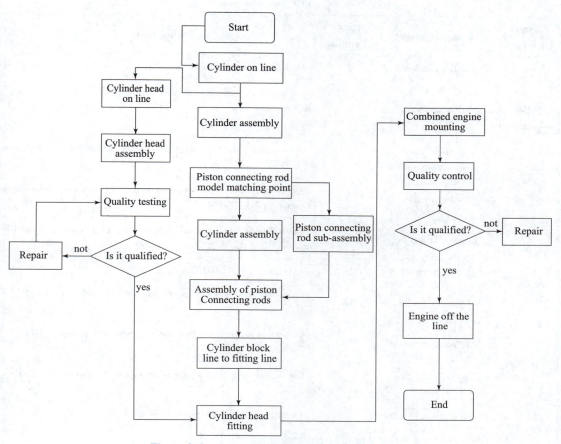

Figure 3.8 Automobile Engine Assembly Process

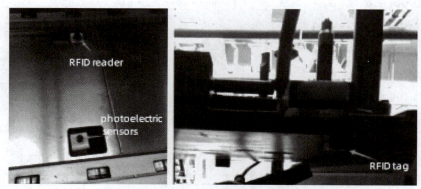

Figure 3.9 Installation of RFID Readers and Tags

Table 3.1 RFID Tag Storage Content

Content Grouping	Storage Content	Byte Length	Paraphrase
Pallet Information	Pallet number	2	Each RFID tag corresponds to one tray, example: 0001
	Pallet area code	1	1—a cylinder block sub-assembly line. 2—a cylinder head sub-assembly line, 3—a live link sub-assembly line, 4—a combined assembly line
	Label data information state	1	0—uninitialized, 1—initialized. Product on line set to 1 off line set to 0
Product Information	Order number	9	One production order corresponds to one order number, example: EE0 100098
	Engine ID number	8	Each engine is engraved with a unique D number, which corresponds to the work order number, example: E4039415
	Product model	13	Example: JND412D167－42
	Cylinder model	13	Consistent with product model number, example: JND4120167－42
	Cylinder head model	13	Consistent with product model number, example: JND412D167－42
	Piston connecting rod model	13	Consistent with product model number, example: JND412D167－42
Processing Information	Total qualified status	1	1—unprocessed, 2—pass, 3—fail
	Final processing station	5	Example: OP010
	OP010 machining status	1	1—unprocessed, 2—processed, 3—under the line repair
	OP010 qualified status	1	1—unprocessed, 2—pass, 3—fail
	OP020 machining status	1	—
	OP020 qualified status	1	—
	OP030 machining status	1	—
	OP030 qualified status	1	—
	……	1	The follow-up stations are the same as above

At each station, the content of the RFID tag is updated through the following process:

① Cylinder Online Station: This station marks the initiation of product tracking and necessitates the completion of product information binding and writing. Upon the arrival of the cylinder pallet, the pallet RFID tag data is initialized, clearing the previous product information while preserving the pallet information. Subsequently, the cylinder's machining ID number is obtained by scanning its barcode. The Manufacturing Execution System (MES) assigns an engine ID number based on the production order and binds it with the machining ID number. Then, the engine product information and machining information are written into the RFID tag.

②Other Assembly Stations: The assembly process instruction document is displayed, and engine assembled part information is collected based on the product model. The system verifies whether the part model matches the product model. Upon detecting the arrival of a pallet, the line Programmable Logic Controller (PLC) activates the RFID reader to read the pallet label data. The MES terminal displays the product information and shows the corresponding process instruction document based on the product model. Workers scan the part barcode before assembly, and MES verifies whether the part model matches the product model. If a match is confirmed, the worker completes the work report operation, updating the processing information in the RFID tag, marking the current workstation as "processed", setting the qualified status of the current workstation to "Qualified", and designating the last processing station as the current station. If a mismatch occurs, the system prompts the need to replace the parts, preventing the workers from completing the work report operation.

③Quality Inspection Station: The quality inspection equipment at this station uploads data to the workshop data acquisition system. The system then sends appropriate write instructions to the RFID reader to update the RFID tag data. In addition to updating the last processing station, if the engine passes the quality inspection, the qualified status of the current station and the total qualified status are set to "qualified", and the current station status is updated to "processed", allowing the work in progress to flow into the next process. If the inspection results are unsatisfactory, the qualified status of the current station and the total qualified status are set to "unqualified". The current workstation status is updated to "offline repair", and the line PLC controls the rotary table to move the defective in-process products offline for repair. Once the repair is completed, the products are returned online for quality testing again until they pass inspection.

3. Application Effect

After establishing the RFID application environment, the Manufacturing Execution System (MES) can track the engine in-process, specifically including order production tracking, work order production progress tracking, and key parts collection and traceability.

(1) Order Production Tracking

By detecting the arrival and departure signals of each work-in-progress at each station, the data acquisition system can monitor the production status of each order. Each order consists of several work orders, with each work order corresponding to one engine product. The system tracks the number of started, completed, frozen, and scrapped work units of each order. Additionally, it records the start time, end time, and other overall information of each order.

(2) Work Order Production Progress Tracking

Each order can be further divided into multiple work orders, and the system can track the specific production progress of each work order. You can query the current location, production status, and progress of each work order. For instance, work order "0030" comprises a total of 197 processes, with 97 completed so far, and the current workstation is "A7270". The system also records the completion time and qualification status of each work order after each process.

(3) Key Parts Collection and Traceability

During engine assembly, workers must scan the barcode of key parts using a code scanning gun before assembly. The data acquisition system then matches the scanned barcode with the engine model number. Only key parts with matching model numbers are allowed for assembly. By reading the product information stored within the RFID tag, the system obtains the engine ID and model number, verifying and binding them with the assembled key parts. The system contains the information of barcode, material code, material name, as well as the bound engine ID number (batch number), work order number, product code, and product name. Quality traceability is achieved by binding key parts to the engine. In case of any quality issues with an engine, the key parts it is assembled with can be queried, facilitating identification of the responsible supplier and problematic batch.

Mission Expansion

Sensor Technology—The Engine for Sustainable and Smart Living

To achieve the interconnectedness of manufacturing elements such as people, machines, and things in the industrial field, it is crucial to utilize various types of sensors for real-time perception of these elements, collecting state data of manufacturing resources, and integrating and fusing data. Therefore, the level of sensor development determines the type of data collection and real-time monitoring capabilities. However, China's independent innovation ability in sensor technology still has significant room for improvement. I encourage students to diligently study scientific and cultural knowledge and aspire to contribute to the advancement of China's sensor technology in the future.

Assignment: Search the internet to understand the current situation in the field of sensors in our country, and analyze the lack of development, especially in the field of industrial sensors. How do you think our country should improve the technical level of industrial sensors?

任务 9 采集装备控制系统数据

采集装备控制
系统数据

学习目标

①掌握数控机床控制系统的状态数据。
②掌握状态数据的含义。
③理解数控机床控制系统数据的应用。

建议学时

2 课时

工作情境

数控机床是机械加工车间最重要的制造设备，其健康状态对车间生产效率和产品质量有关键性的影响。因此，实现数控机床的状态数据采集与可视化监控是大多数制造企业的典型应用场景。同时，基于对所采集数据的分析，实现健康状态评估和预测性维护也是目前国内外广泛关注的热点。

知识导图

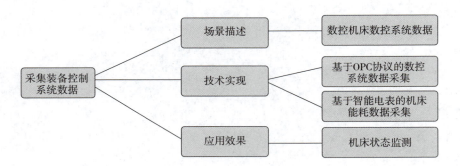

相关知识

1. 场景描述

数控机床的数控系统中记录了大量状态数据，比如开机时间、关机时间、报警状态、报警号、报警信息、设备状态、程序号、加工时间、产量、进给量、进给倍率、主轴转速、主轴倍率、主轴负载、各轴负载、当前刀具号等。数控系统的类型非常多,常见的包括西门子 840D/810D 系列、FANUC 系统、Heidenhain 系统、MAZAK640、三菱 M70 系列、华中数控等,其数据采集方式各有差异。

2. 技术实现

下面以某机床公司的大型双龙门铣床为例,介绍数据采集的实现过程。该机床采用西门子 840D 数控系统。

(1) 基于 OPC 协议的数控系统数据采集

西门子 840D 数控系统是一种开放式的数控系统,具有 OPC 服务器接口,可以通过 OPC 技术实现数控系统内部数据的采集。数据采集软件建立 OPC 客户端,通过标准的 OPC 接口访问 OPC 服务器,完成数据交互。西门子 840D 数控系统包含 3 大类数控(NC)变量,分别为静态变量、动态变量及 PLC 变量。这 3 种变量均可通过 OPC 规范的接口函数,以统一的方式进行访问。3 大类数据变量共计 12 000 多个,通过对变量文件的分析及筛选,最终确定主轴转速、进给量、刀具坐标、各主轴电流等对设备状态监控及状态评估较为重要的数据,共计 20 个左右变量。NC 变量存储于数据块中,数据块将不同的区域分配给 NC 变量。各个区域分配的变量详细情况如表 3.2 所示。有 3 种变量:由一行构成的 NC 变量;由多行构成的 NC 变量;由多行多列构成的 NC 变量。

表 3.2 NC 区域分配

区域	NC 变量
NC(N)	含有适用于整个数控系统的所有变量,例如系统数据(Y)、保护区(PA)、G 功能组(YNCFL)等
BAG(B)	含有适用于运行方式组的所有变量,例如状态数据(S)
通道(C)	含有适用于各个通道的所有变量,例如系统数据(Y)、保护区(PA)、全局状态数据(S)等
刀具(T)	含有适用于机床上刀具的所有变量,例如刀具补偿数据(TO)、通用刀具数据(TD)、刀具监控数据(TS)等。每个刀具区域 T 分配给一个通道
轴(A)	包含了适用于每根进给轴或主轴的机床数据和设定数据
进给驱动/主驱动(V/H)	包含了适用于每个驱动的机床数据或作为服务参数的机床数据

访问 NC 变量时,须在地址中对相关信息进行说明。对于单行 NC 变量,在地址中提供区域、数据块和 C 变量名称;对于多行变量,提供区域和区块号、数据块、NC 变量名称以及行号。以下列出了一些变量的读取示例:

操作模式:/Bag/State/opMode;

程序状态:/Channel/State/AcProg;

主轴转速:/Nck/Spindle/actSpeed [u1, 7];

主轴负载：/Nck/Spindle/driveLoad［ul, 7］；

轴向进给实际值：/Channel/MachineAxis/actFeedRate［ul, 3］。

以轴向进给实际值为例进行说明：C［.］为区域，actFeedRate 为变量名，ul 为通道号，3 为行号。

数据采集软件安装了组态软件和 OPC 客户端驱动，OPC 客户端驱动通过变量文件实现从数控机床 OPC 服务器中读取变量数据，组态软件将所读取的数据实时存入数据服务器中进行管理，从而实现 840D 数控系统内部数据的整体采集过程。

（2）基于智能电表的机床能耗数据采集

如图 3.10 所示，智能电表是机床能耗数据的采集终端，安装在机床电柜里，通过 RS485 总线终端，智能电表外接互感器可获取机床的电压、频率、功率、电流等各项能耗参数。通过 RS485 串口转网口通信模块进行协议转换，实现能耗数据的无线传输。组态软件安装以太网驱动，使用 TCP/IP 协议来实现和通信模块的连接，并监听端口，读取对应电表的实时能耗数据，然后通过批量数据库连接功能将数据存入数据库中。

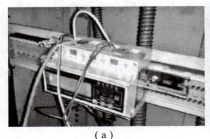 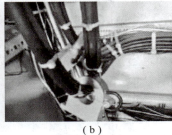 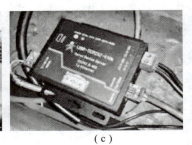

(a)   (b)   (c)

图 3.10　智能电表及安装位置
（a）智能电表；（b）互感器；（c）串口转网口

3. 应用效果

基于上述数据采集技术的实现，开发了机床状态监控系统，实现了数据接入、数据存储、数据可视化展示、数据分析等功能。对各数控机床当前的主轴、进给轴、当前操作模式、能耗、机床特定位置的状态（振动、温度）等进行实时监控。机床总体状态监控页面每隔 1~5 s 刷新数据，实时监控所有设备状态，包含主轴信息、生产信息、设备信息、能耗信息等详情，特别是各个主轴的转速、负载、电流，进给轴的负载、速度、电流，机床的电流、能耗等情况。并且通过传感器接入的机床特定位置的振动、温度、位移等数据也在监控界面中进行显示，一旦数值超标，将自动报警。

 **任务拓展**

精益求精——精确可靠采集装备控制系统数据

采集装备控制系统数据是指通过传感器和其他设备收集和记录与装备控制系统相关的信息和数据。这些数据可以包括设备运行状态、传感器测量值、控制信号等。采集装备控制系统数据可以用于监测和分析设备性能，进行故障诊断和预测，优化设备运行和维护管理，提高生产效率和质量。通过精确、可靠地采集和利用装备控制系统数据，可以实现对生产过程的实时监控和精细化管理，提高生产效率和产品质量，降低成本和能源消耗，推动工业智能化和可持续发展。

在数据的采集中要有精益求精的工匠精神，任何数据的误差都会导致信息的不准确或失真，进而影响后续的分析和决策。精益求精的工匠精神要求我们在数据采集过程中注重细节，严格控制每个环节的准确性和可靠性，确保数据的真实性和完整性。只有这样，我们才能基于可靠的数据进行准确的分析和判断，做出正确的决策和行动，推动工作和项目的顺利进行。因此，在数据采集中，精益求精的工匠精神是非常重要的。

作业：通过网络查询我国智能装备发展的现状，谈谈自己对工匠精神的理解。

Task 9 Acquisition of Equipment Control System Data

Learning Objective

①Master the status data of CNC machine control systems.
②Understand the meaning of status data.
③Understand the application of CNC machine control system data.

Suggested Hours

2 hours

Work Situations

CNC machine tools are pivotal manufacturing equipment in machining shops, profoundly influencing shop productivity and product quality. Therefore, implementing condition data acquisition and visual monitoring for CNC machine tools is a typical scenario for most manufacturing enterprises. Additionally, the analysis of collected data is crucial for achieving health state assessment and predictive maintenance, garnering significant attention both domestically and internationally.

Knowledge Map

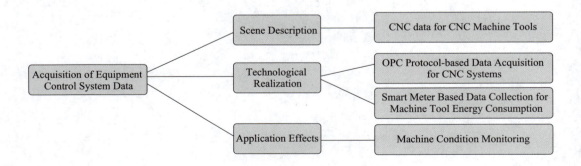

Project 3 Industrial Big Data Sensing and Acquisition

Relevant Knowledge

1. Scene Description

A large amount of status data is recorded in the CNC system of CNC machine tools, such as power-on time, power-off time, alarm status, alarm number, alarm message, equipment status, program number, machining time, output, feed, feed multiplier, spindle speed, spindle multiplier, spindle load, load of each axis, and current tool number. There are many types of CNC systems, common ones include Siemens 840D/810D series, FANUC system, Heidenhain system, MAZAK640, Mitsubishi M70 series, Huazhong CNC, etc., and their data acquisition methods are different.

2. Technological Realization

The following is an example of a large double gantry milling machine from a machine tool company, illustrating the process of data acquisition. The machine tool utilizes a Siemens 840D CNC system.

(1) OPC Protocol-based Data Acquisition for CNC Systems

The Siemens 840D CNC system is an open CNC system featuring an OPC server interface, enabling data acquisition within the CNC system through OPC technology. The data acquisition software establishes an OPC client and accesses the OPC server via the standard OPC interface to facilitate data interaction. Within the Siemens 840D CNC system, three major types of numerical control (NC) variables exist: static variables, dynamic variables, and PLC variables. These variables can be accessed uniformly through the interface function of the OPC specification. Among the 12,000 variables across these three categories, approximately 20 variables are identified as crucial for equipment status monitoring and condition assessment, including spindle speed, feed rate, tool coordinates, and spindle current. NC variables are stored in a data block, with each data block assigning different areas to NC variables. Further details regarding the variables assigned to each area are depicted in Table 3.2, encompassing three types of variables: single-row NC variables, multi-row NC variables, and multi-row and column NC variables.

Table 3.2 NC Regional Distribution

Region	NC Variables
NC (N)	Contains all variables that apply to the entire CNC system, e.g. system data (Y) protected area (PA) G function group (YNCFL), etc.
BAG (B)	Contains all variables applicable to the run mode group, e.g. status data (S)

续表

Region	NC Variables
Channel (C)	Contains all variables applicable to each channel. Examples include system data (Y), protected area (PA), global status data (S), etc.
Tool (T)	Contains all the variables applicable to the tool on the machine, such as tool compensation data (TO), common tool data (TD), tool monitoring data (TS), etc. Each tool area T is assigned to a channel
Shaft (A)	Contains machine data and setup data for each feed axis or spindle.
Feed drive/ Main drive (V/H)	Contains machine data applicable to each drive or as a service parameter

When accessing NC variables, the relevant information shall be described in the address. For single-line NC variables, provide the area, data block, and C variable name in the address; for multi-line variables, provide the area and block number, data block, NC variable name, and line number. The following lists some examples of variable reads:

Operation mode: /Bag/State/opMode;

Program status: /Channel/State/AcProg;

Spindle speed: /Nck/Spindle/actSpeed [ul, 7];

Spindle load: /Nck/Spindle/driveLoad [ul, 7];

Actual value of axial feed: /Channel/MachineAxis/actFeedRate [ul, 3].

An example illustrating the axial feed actual value is as follows: C [.] represents the region, actFeedRate is the variable name, ul indicates the channel number, and 3 denotes the row number.

The data acquisition software includes configuration software and OPC client driver. The OPC client driver reads variable data from the OPC server of the CNC machine tool via the variable file, while the configuration software stores the read data in real time within the data server for management. This facilitates the comprehensive data acquisition process within the 840D CNC system.

(2) Smart Meter Based Data Collection for Machine Tool Energy Consumption

As depicted in Figure 3.10, the smart meter serves as the collection terminal for machine tool energy consumption data, typically installed within the electrical cabinet of the machine tool. Connected via the RS485 bus terminal, the smart meter utilizes an external transformer to gather various energy consumption parameters such as voltage, frequency, power, and current. Employing an R485 serial port to network port communication module for protocol conversion, wireless transmission of energy consumption data is enabled. The configuration software includes an Ethernet driver, leveraging the TCP/IP protocol to establish communication with the communication module. It listens to the designated port, reading real-time energy consumption data from the corresponding meter and subsequently storing this data into the database via batch database connection functionality.

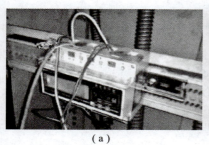 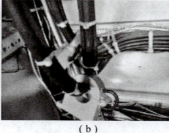 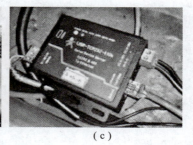

(a)　　　　　　　　　　　　(b)　　　　　　　　　　　　(c)

Figure 3.10　Gantry Milling Machine Data Acquisition
(a) Smart Meters; (b) Transformers; (c) Serial-to-network Interface

3. Application Effects

Based on the implementation of the aforementioned data acquisition technology, a machine tool status monitoring system has been developed. This system facilitates data access, storage, visualization and display, as well as data analysis. Real-time monitoring of various parameters such as spindle status, feed axis status, current operation mode, energy consumption, and specific machine positions (vibration, temperature) is enabled for each CNC machine tool. The overall status monitoring page, which refreshes data every 1 to 5 seconds to provide real-time equipment status monitoring. This includes detailed information on spindle status, production details, equipment status, energy consumption, and more. Notably, the rotational speed, load, and current of each spindle, as well as the load, speed, and current of the feed axes, and the current energy consumption of the machine tool are monitored. Additionally, specific machine tool locations' data such as vibration, temperature, displacement, and others collected through sensors are displayed in the monitoring interface. Automatic alarms are generated if the values exceed predefined limits.

Mission Expansion

Keep Improving—Accrate and Reliable Collection of Equipment Control System Data

Equipment is pivotal for production and processing implementation, with CNC machine tools significantly impacting machining product quality through their precision and capability. Monitoring and maintaining CNC system status data throughout the machine tool life cycle are essential. While China possesses considerable potential for improving independent intellectual property rights regarding CNC machine tool precision and intelligence, there remains ample room for enhancement. It's incumbent upon younger generations to shoulder the responsibility for the intelligent advancement of CNC equipment.

Assignment: Through online research, summarize the current state of China's intelligent equipment development, analyze the shortcomings of China's CNC machine tools, and outline future development directions.

任务 10　采集管理软件系统数据

采集管理软件
系统数据

学习目标

①掌握 OPC XML 接口规范。
②掌握 OPC XML 数据采集流程。
③理解管理软件系统数据的应用。

建议学时

2 课时

工作情境

制造设备运行参数数据的采集对实时性要求较高，企业可开发专门的设备运行参数自动采集模块采集设备信号数据，也可开发特定软件与设备通信并获取数据。但由于企业的生产设备多种多样，各设备生产厂家的设备通信协议不一样，而且很多不对外公开，企业开发成本高，工作量大。

知识导图

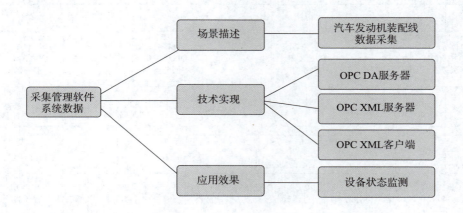

相关知识

1. 场景描述

针对不同类型设备，相对而言，基于 OPC 标准的数据采集技术效率更高，成本更低，特别是 OPC XML 技术。OPC XML – DA 规范是第一个 OPC XML 接口规范，定义了所支持的数据类型、数据结构、调用方法，并对底层传输协议、错误处理、发现机制、互操作性等进行了规定，它与 OPC DA 支持相同的数据类型。OPC XML – DA 规范根据 SOAP 协议将生产信息进行 XML 描述，并封装成 Web 服务，再通过 HTTP 协议在局域网或广域网上传输，将生产信息或控制信息传递给 OPC XML – DA 客户端或服务器。这样可实现 OPC 数据在异构网络和不同操作平台上的共享，有效解决底层生产控制系统和上层信息系统的信息集成问题。因此本任务采用 OPC XML 技术采集制造设备运行参数数据。

2. 技术实现

如图 3.11 所示是基于 OPC XML 的汽车发动机装配线数据采集方案硬件构成图，主要由 OPC DA 服务器、OPC XML 服务器、OPC XML 客户端构成，各硬件通过以太网分层连接。

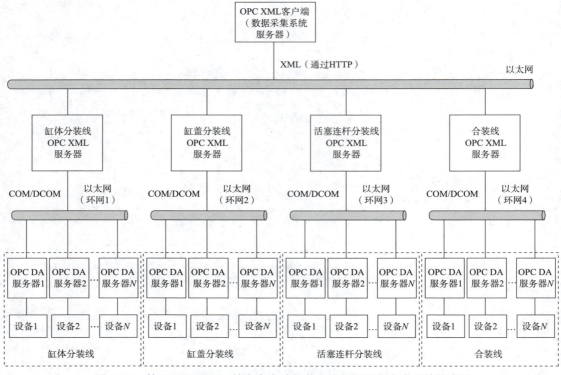

图 3.11 基于 OPC XML 的汽车发动机装配线数据采集方案硬件构成图

(1) OPC DA 服务器

OPC DA 服务器与线体设备是一对一的关系，每台设备都需安装 OPC DA 服务器。生产设备一般由工控机和 PLC 设备两部分组成，OPC DA 服务器安装在工控机上；而装配线线体根据线体工位数量不同，可以统一由一台工控机控制，也可以由多台工控机分区控制，每台工控机都需安装 OPC DA 服务器。OPC DA 服务器采集到数据后，将数据推送给 OPC XML 服务器。

(2) OPC XML 服务器

OPC XML 服务器安装于各线体的上线点或下线点终端上，与 OPC DA 服务器在同一环网内。OPC XML 服务器由 OPC DA 客户端、数据管理模块、数据库和 Web 服务接口构成。OPC DA 客户端负责从 OPC DA 服务器获取数据，数据管理模块负责对数据进行转换、保存、解析、封装等，数据库用于缓存现场数据，Web 服务接口负责向 OPC XML 客户端提供 Web 服务。

(3) OPC XML 客户端

OPC XML 客户端即数据采集系统服务器，可通过 HTTP 的方式向 OPC XML 服务器提出获取数据的请求，并将接收的数据存入后台数据库进行集中管理。

基于 OPC XML 的汽车发动机装配线数据采集流程如图 3.12 所示。PLC 设备采集相关数据，并将数据存入指定寄存器；OPC DA 服务器通过现场设备驱动程序从寄存器中读取数据并放入数据缓冲区；当 OPC XML 客户端向 OPC XML 服务器请求获取数据时，OPC XML 服务器的数据管理模块解析请求数据，并传递给 OPC DA 客户端；OPC DA 客户端再向 OPC DA 服务器请求获取数据；OPC DA 服务器接收到请求后返回相关数据；OPC XML 服务器接收到返回数据后再返回给 OPC XML 客户端；OPC XML 客户端收到返回数据后存入数据库，供其他应用模块使用。其中，各客户端对服务器的访问采用异步方式，单独为每个服务器的访问分配一个线程，这样可以同时连接多个服务器，减少等待时间。

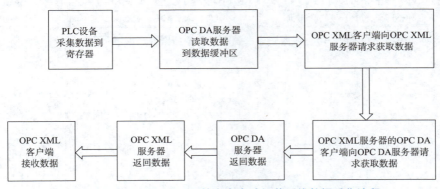

图 3.12 基于 OPC XML 的汽车发动机装配线数据采集流程

3. 应用效果

要实现生产设备的状态监控，首先需为生产线每台设备安装 OPC DA 服务器。工厂采用的 OPC DA 服务器为 Kepware KepServerEX v5。由于 OPC DA 服务器可同时采集多台设备的数据，为节省成本，距离较近的几台生产设备可共用一个服务器。其中，内装线安装了3个服务器，缸盖分装线安装了1个，外装线安装了4个。活塞连杆分装线的生产设备由内装线的服务器采集。

OPC XML应用环境搭建好后，数据采集系统作为OPC XML客户端，将OPC XML服务器采集的设备状态数据存入后台数据库，并在页面上进行状态显示，同时可将各设备的运行状态展示到车间的LED大屏上，也可以将设备的统计数据显示到电视大屏上，方便用户进行实时监控。如图3.13所示为数据采集系统设备状态数据报表展示页面，车间所有采集到的设备状态数据都在该页面进行集中显示和查询。该页面可显示生产设备、采集项、采集值、采集时间等内容，其中采集值为“true”表示对应项（设备状态）已发生，采集值为“false”表示对应采集项未发生。

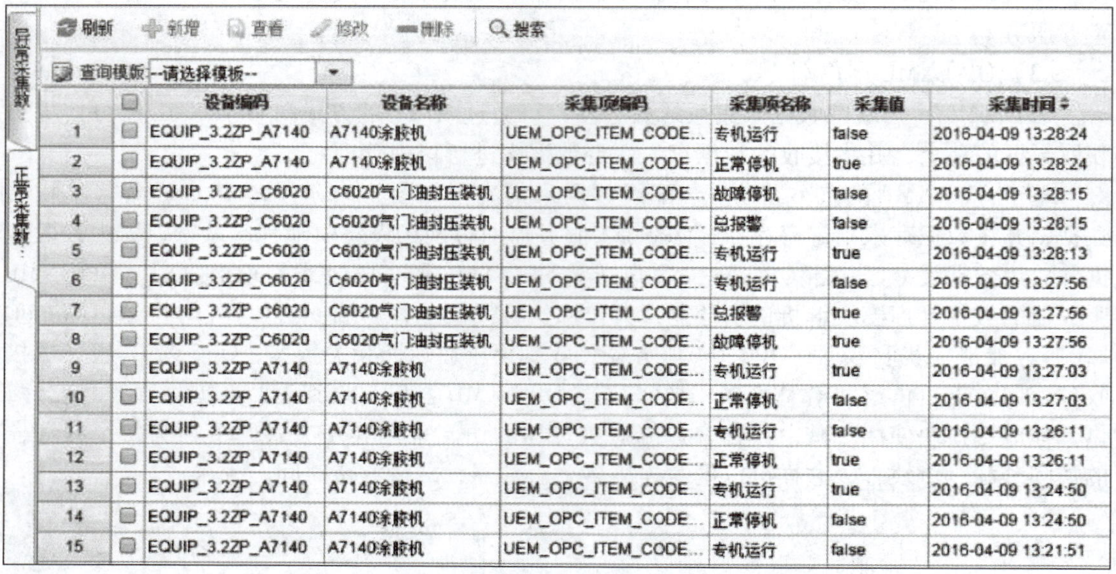

	设备编码	设备名称	采集项编码	采集项名称	采集值	采集时间
1	EQUIP_3.2ZP_A7140	A7140涂胶机	UEM_OPC_ITEM_CODE...	专机运行	false	2016-04-09 13:28:24
2	EQUIP_3.2ZP_A7140	A7140涂胶机	UEM_OPC_ITEM_CODE...	正常停机	true	2016-04-09 13:28:24
3	EQUIP_3.2ZP_C6020	C6020气门油封压装机	UEM_OPC_ITEM_CODE...	故障停机	false	2016-04-09 13:28:15
4	EQUIP_3.2ZP_C6020	C6020气门油封压装机	UEM_OPC_ITEM_CODE...	总报警	false	2016-04-09 13:28:15
5	EQUIP_3.2ZP_C6020	C6020气门油封压装机	UEM_OPC_ITEM_CODE...	专机运行	true	2016-04-09 13:28:13
6	EQUIP_3.2ZP_C6020	C6020气门油封压装机	UEM_OPC_ITEM_CODE...	专机运行	false	2016-04-09 13:27:56
7	EQUIP_3.2ZP_C6020	C6020气门油封压装机	UEM_OPC_ITEM_CODE...	总报警	true	2016-04-09 13:27:56
8	EQUIP_3.2ZP_C6020	C6020气门油封压装机	UEM_OPC_ITEM_CODE...	故障停机	true	2016-04-09 13:27:56
9	EQUIP_3.2ZP_A7140	A7140涂胶机	UEM_OPC_ITEM_CODE...	专机运行	true	2016-04-09 13:27:03
10	EQUIP_3.2ZP_A7140	A7140涂胶机	UEM_OPC_ITEM_CODE...	正常停机	false	2016-04-09 13:27:03
11	EQUIP_3.2ZP_A7140	A7140涂胶机	UEM_OPC_ITEM_CODE...	专机运行	false	2016-04-09 13:26:11
12	EQUIP_3.2ZP_A7140	A7140涂胶机	UEM_OPC_ITEM_CODE...	正常停机	true	2016-04-09 13:26:11
13	EQUIP_3.2ZP_A7140	A7140涂胶机	UEM_OPC_ITEM_CODE...	专机运行	true	2016-04-09 13:24:50
14	EQUIP_3.2ZP_A7140	A7140涂胶机	UEM_OPC_ITEM_CODE...	正常停机	false	2016-04-09 13:24:50
15	EQUIP_3.2ZP_A7140	A7140涂胶机	UEM_OPC_ITEM_CODE...	专机运行	false	2016-04-09 13:21:51

图3.13　数据采集系统设备状态数据报表展示页面

任务拓展

严谨态度与责任意识——数据采集中的科学精神和职业操守

采集管理软件系统数据是指通过特定的软件系统收集、记录和管理与采集过程相关的数据。这些数据可以包括采集设备的状态信息、采集参数和采集结果等。采集管理软件系统数据可以帮助实现对采集过程的监控和控制，提高数据采集的效率和准确性。通过对采集管理软件系统数据的分析和处理，可以获得有关采集过程的关键指标和统计信息，为决策和优化提供依据。

在数据采集过程中要有严谨的工作态度和责任意识，注重数据的准确性、完整性和一致性。同时，注重数据的准确性、完整性和一致性也符合社会主义核心价值观中的科学精神和诚信原则，大学生要树立良好的道德观念和职业操守。

作业：以数据采集系统数据的重要性为主题，撰写一篇体会，指出采集管理软件系统数据的重要性以及培养良好道德观念和职业操守的意义。

Task 10 Comprehend Acquisition Management Software System Data

Learning Objective

①Master the OPC XML interface specification.
②Master the OPC XML data capture process.
③Application of data from learning management software systems.

Suggested Hours

2 hours

Work Situations

Acquiring real-time data on manufacturing equipment operating parameters is essential for enterprises. They can develop a specialized module to automatically collect equipment signal data. Additionally, specific software can be developed to communicate with the equipment and retrieve the necessary data. However, the enterprise faces challenges because its production equipment is diverse. Each equipment manufacturer may use different communication protocols, many of which are not publicly available. As a result, the development cost for enterprises is high, and the workload is substantial.

Knowledge Map

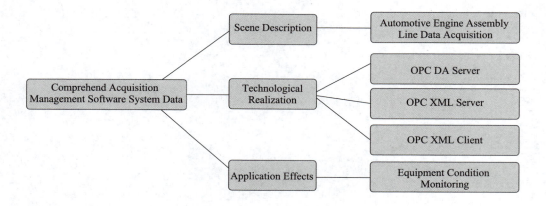

Relevant Knowledge

1. Scene Description

For different types of equipment, relatively speaking, the data collection technology based on OPC standard is more efficient and less costly, especially OPC XMI technology. The OPC XML – DA specification is the initial OPC XML interface specification. It defines supported data types, data structures, calling methods, and specifies the underlying transmission protocol, error handling, discovery mechanism, interoperability, etc. It is the same with the OPC DA supports the same data types. The OPC XML – DA specification XML describes production information using the SOAP protocol. It encapsulates this information into a Web service. This service is then transmitted over a LAN or WAN using the HTTP protocol. The purpose is to deliver production or control information to the OPC XML – DA client or server. This approach enables sharing of OPC data across heterogeneous networks and diverse operating platforms. It effectively addresses the challenge of integrating information between the underlying production control system and the upper information system. Therefore, this section adopts OPC XML technology to collect manufacturing equipment operation parameter data.

2. Technological Realization

Figure 3.11 depicts the hardware composition diagram of the automotive engine assembly line data acquisition solution based on OPC XML. It mainly includes an OPC DA server, an OPC XML server, and an OPC XML client. Each hardware component is connected hierarchically via Ethernet.

(1) OPC DA Server

OPC DA server and line equipment have a one-to-one relationship, meaning each device needs to have an OPC DA server installed. The production equipment typically comprises two parts: the ICM and PLC equipment. The OPC DA server is installed on the ICM. The assembly line can be controlled uniformly by one ICM or divided into multiple ICMs based on the number of line stations. Each ICM requires the installation of an OPC DA server. The OPC DA server collects the data and then pushes it to the OPC XML server.

(2) OPC XML Server

The OPC XML server is installed on the terminal of each line body, either at the up-line point or down-line point, and is in the same ring network as the OPC DA server. It comprises several components, including the OPC DA client, the data management module, the database, and the Web service interface. The OPC DA client retrieves data from the OPC DA server. The data management module handles tasks such as conversion, preservation, parsing, and encapsulation.

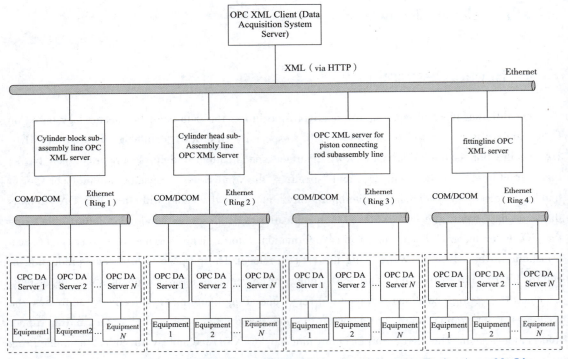

Figure 3. 11　OPC XML – Based Data Acquisition Solution for Automotive Engine Assembly Line

The database stores field data for caching purposes, while the Web service interface provides web services to the OPC DA server.

(3) OPC XML Client

The OPC XML client, which serves as the server of the data acquisition system, can request data acquisition from the OPC XML server via HTTP. It then stores the received data into the background database for centralized management.

The OPC XML – based data acquisition process for an automotive engine assembly line is depicted in Figure 3. 12. Here's how it works:

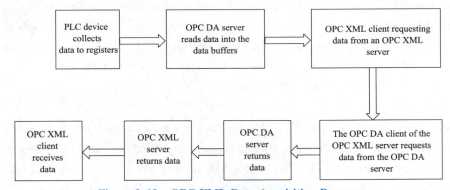

Figure 3. 12　OPC XML Data Acquisition Process

The PLC device collects relevant data and stores it in a designated register.

The OPC DA server reads the data from the register and transfers it to the data buffer via the field device driver.

When the OPC XML client requests data from the OPC XML server, the Data Management Module of the OPC XML Server parses the requested data and forwards it to the OPC DA client.

The OPC DA client then sends a request to the OPC DA server to obtain the data.

The OPC DA server receives the request and returns the relevant data.

The OPC XML server receives the returned data and delivers it to the OPC XML client.

Finally, the OPC XML client receives the data and stores it in the database for use by other application modules.

In this scenario, each client's access to the servers is asynchronous. A separate thread is allocated to each server access, allowing simultaneous connection to multiple servers and reducing waiting time.

3. Application Effects

To implement production equipment status monitoring, each piece of equipment on the production line needs to have an OPC DA server installed. In our plant, we utilize the Kepware KepServerEX v5 as the OPC DA server. Since one OPC DA server can collect data from multiple devices simultaneously, to reduce costs, we can have several production devices in close proximity share the same server. For instance, within the internal assembly line, three servers are installed, one in the cylinder head sub-assembly line, and four in the external assembly line. The production equipment of the piston connecting rod sub-assembly line is collected by the server of the internal assembly line.

Once the OPC XML application environment is established, the data collection system, acting as an OPC XML client, stores equipment status data gathered by the OPC XML server in the backend database. It then presents this status on a webpage. Simultaneously, it can display the operational status of each equipment on the LED screen in the workshop. Furthermore, it can showcase equipment statistical data on the TV screen, facilitating real-time monitoring for users. Figure 3.13 depicts the data collection system's equipment status data report display page, where all the equipment status data collected in the workshop are centrally displayed and queried. The page can exhibit various contents such as production equipment, collection items, collection value, and collection time. In this context, a "true" collection value indicates that the corresponding item (equipment status) has occurred, while a "false" collection value signifies that the corresponding collection item has not occurred.

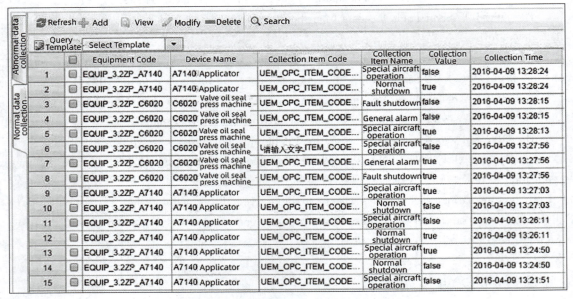

Figure 3. 13   Device Status Data Display

 **Mission Expansion**

Rigorous Attitude and Sense of Responsibility—
Scientific Spirit and Professional Ethics in Data Collection

Collecting and managing software system data refers to the collection, recording, and management of data related to the collection process through specific software systems. These data can include the status information of the collection device, collection parameters, and collection results. The data collection management software system can help monitor and control the collection process, improve the efficiency and accuracy of data collection. By analyzing and processing data from the collection management software system, key indicators and statistical information related to the collection process can be obtained, providing a basis for decision-making and optimization.

In the process of data collection, there should be a rigorous work attitude and a sense of responsibility, emphasizing the accuracy, completeness, and consistency of data. At the same time, emphasizing the accuracy, completeness, and consistency of data is also in line with the scientific spirit and integrity principles of socialist core values. College students should establish good moral concepts and professional ethics.

Assignment: With the theme of the importance of data collection system data, write an experience that points out the importance of collecting and managing software system data, as well as the significance of cultivating good moral concepts and professional ethics.

项目 4

工业互联网网络传输

任务 11　工业互联网接口技术

认知工业互联网
接口技术

学习目标

①理解 PLCopen 接口规范。
②掌握 OPC UA 架构。
③理解 MTConnect 标准。
④理解 MQTT 协议。

建议学时

2 课时

工作情境

车间内的装备一般来自不同的厂商，搭载不同控制系统，不同系统之间采用不同的数据类型和格式，导致了设备系统间的异构性。异构设备之间信息的类型、格式和语义方面的差异对设备间的数据交换和通信造成障碍，并产生"信息孤岛"。

知识导图

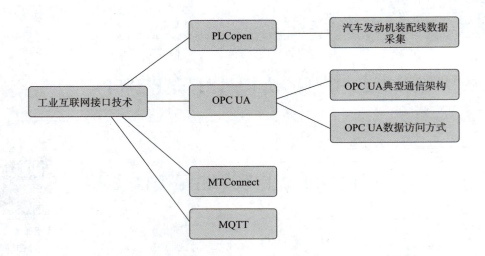

相关知识

解决数字化车间内的"信息孤岛"问题，实现设备间的互联互通和互操作，是实现智能制造的重要基础，具有严格规范的标准化信息模型则是解决这一问题的关键。PLCopen 和 OPC 正在开展合作，定义一组功能块，将 IEC 61131-3 工业控制编程全球标准映射到 OPC UA 信息通信模式。OPC UA 协议是一种跨平台的、具有更高的安全性和可靠性的通信协议，可以满足制造车间与企业之间信息的高度联通及互操作需求。MTConnect 标准有助于联网制造设备数据的标准化收集。消息队列遥测传输（Message Queuing Telemetry Transport，MQTT）是一种支持在各方之间异步通信的消息协议。

1. PLCopen

PLC 的软硬件集成技术以 PLCopen 国际组织为先导，一直在为满足工业 4.0 和智能制造日益清晰的要求作准备。如图 4.1 所示显示了 PLCopen 历年来所开发的各种规范（运动控制、安全控制、OPC UA 通信、XML 等）在工业 4.0 参考架构模型（Reference Architecture Model Industrie 4.0，RAMI4.0）相应制造环境的软硬件功能层级维度及其层级中的位置。

对于将物理实体资产经过数字化的途径映射为相关资产的产品描述（数据性能）的标准化过程，一种可行的方法是按照国际标准化组织制定的国际标准 ISO 29002-5，即《工业自动化系统和集成特征数据交换》的第五部分"标识方法"，利用分类产品描述的软件包 eCl@ss Version9.1，用 URI 和 URL 进行唯一资源标识和唯一资源定位。ISO 29002-5 规定了唯一标识管理项的数据元素和语法。

如图 4.2 所示描述的就是这种统一的格式。标识符是 URL，为每一种资产提供唯一的

项目4　工业互联网网络传输

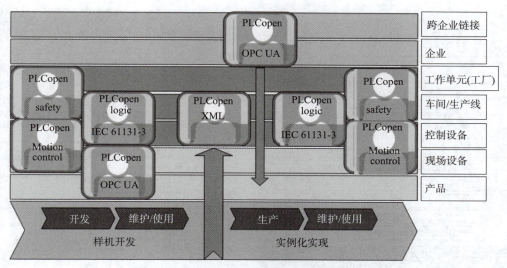

图 4.1　PLCopen 各规范在 RAMI4.0 中的位置

识别符,并与该资产对应的信息空间对应。该标识符既参照该资产的物理分类,又可链接该资产的信息空间,而信息空间的虚拟描述完全建立在其物理特性和相关数据之上。

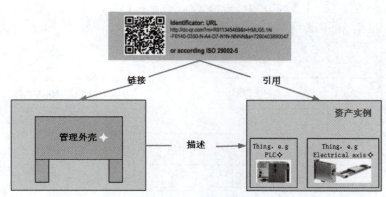

图 4.2　利用 URL 唯一标识工业 4.0 基本单元

如图 4.3 所示给出了许多标准作为信息空间中产品信息纵向集成领域/子模型的样板。

2. OPC UA

OPC 是自动化行业及其他行业用于数据安全交换时的一种主流互操作性标准,是由行业供应商、终端用户和软件开发者共同制定的一系列规范。它独立于平台,并确保来自多个厂商的设备之间信息的无缝传输,目的是把 PLC 特定的协议(如 Modbus,Profibus 等)抽象成为标准化的接口,作为"中间人"的角色把其通用的"读写"要求转换成具体的设备协议,以便 HMI/SCADA 系统可以对接。我们所熟知的 OPC 规范一般是指经典 OPC。

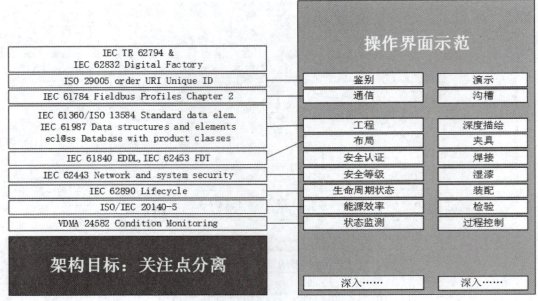

图 4.3 信息空间的领域/子模型的样板标准

如图 4.4 所示是经典 OPC 规范的组成概览,包括三个主要 OPC 规范:数据访问(Data Access,DA)、报警和事件(Alarms and Events,A&E)、历史数据访问(History Data Access,HDA)。

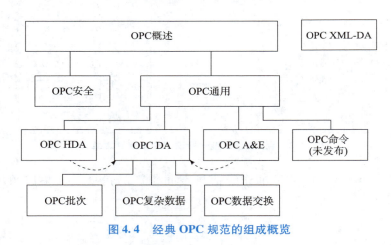

图 4.4 经典 OPC 规范的组成概览

2008 年,OPC 基金会发布了 OPC 统一架构(OPC Unified Architecture,OPC UA),这是一个独立于平台的面向服务的架构,集成了现有 OPC 规范的所有功能,并且兼容经典 OPC 规范。为满足工控领域以服务为导向的需求,OPC UA 协议把不同规范定义的信息模型重新归类设计成一系列服务集的形式供用户使用,实现了广泛互联。OPC UA 规范架构是一套集信息模型定义、服务集与通信标准为一体的标准化技术框架,共分为 13 部分技术规范。相比于经典 OPC 规范,OPC UA 具有更加安全的通信性能、标准安全的信息模型、统一的访问方式、开发具有高度的可靠性和冗余性并且实现了跨平台。

(1) OPC UA 典型通信架构

OPC UA 采用一种典型的客户端/服务器架构,如图 4.5 所示。服务器端把各制造资源的数据封装在一个统一的地址空间内,使得客户端可以以统一的方式去访问服务器。客户端通过自身的接口与客户端通信栈交互,客户端通信栈再把消息传达给服务器通信栈,服务器调用相应的服务集如节点管理服务集、监视服务集等对服务器端通信栈传入的请求进行分析处理,对网状结构的地址空间进行相应查询、操作,最后将结果传递回客户端。

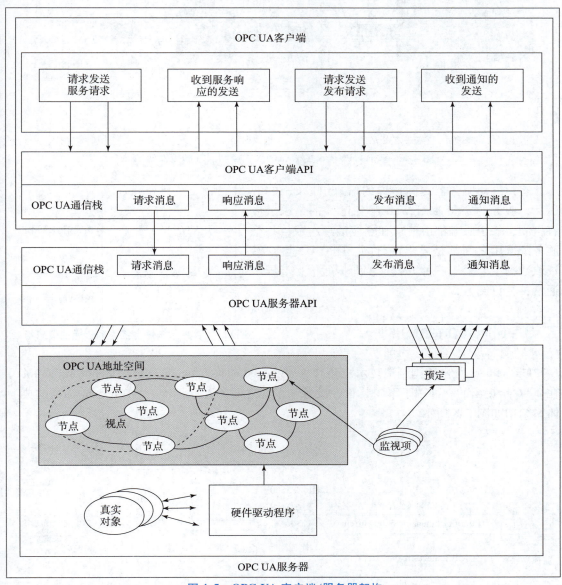

图 4.5 OPC UA 客户端/服务器架构

(2) OPC UA 数据访问方式

OPC UA 服务定义的是应用程序级的数据通信。服务以方法的形式提供给 OPC UA 客户端使用，用于访问 OPC UA 服务器提供的信息模型的数据。如图 4.6 所示是一种基于 OPC UA 的分布嵌入式控制器数据传输架构。

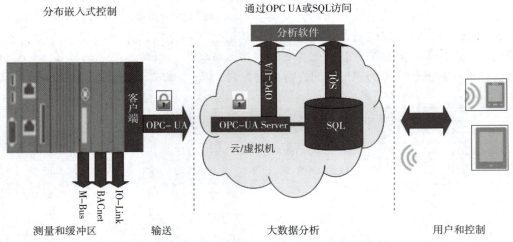

图 4.6　基于 OPC UA 的分布嵌入式控制器数据传输架构

客户端与服务器之间传递的信息组成如图 4.7 所示，服务的定义使用 Web 服务已知的请求、应答机制，每个服务都由请求和响应消息组成，每个服务的调用之间都是异步进行的。OPC UA 客户端读取数据主要采用三种方式：①同步通信；②异步通信；③订阅方式。

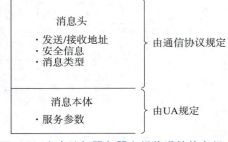

图 4.7　客户端与服务器之间传递的信息组成

3. MTConnect

MTConnect 是由美国制造技术协会（the Association for Manufacturing Technology，AMT）在 2006 年提出的一种用于不同装置、设备和系统之间的互联标准。MTConnect 标准的典型体系结构如图 4.8 所示。

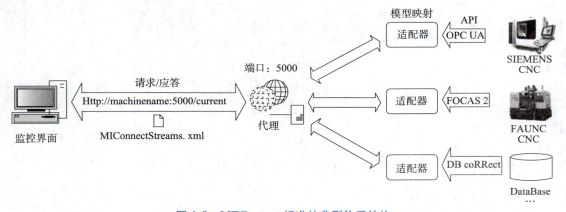

图 4.8　MTConnect 标准的典型体系结构

针对复杂系统的信息建模，往往会涉及模型的集成，模型内不同信息既要彼此独立有时又会因为功能需求进行耦合。面向对象建模机制具有很好的封装性和拓展性，非常适合制造信息的建模，而 MTConnect 就引入了面向对象机制来描述信息间关系。

如图 4.9 所示是数控机床的 MTConnect 信息模型。数控机床作为一个设备由轴组件、控制器组件和系统组件三部分组成。其中，控制器组件包含机床此时正在使用的刀具的索引，用于关联查询机床本体以外的刀具资产的详细信息。

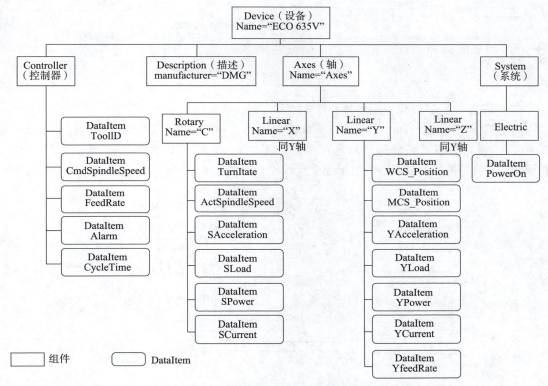

图 4.9　数控机床的 MTConnect 信息模型

4. MQTT

MQTT 是一种支持在各方之间异步通信的消息协议。异步消息协议在空间和时间上将消息发送者与接收者分离，因此可以在不可靠的网络环境中进行扩展。虽然叫做消息队列遥测传输，但它与消息队列毫无关系，而是使用了一个发布和订阅的模型，最初是为了在卫星之类的物体上使用。

（1）发布和订阅模型

发布和订阅模型如图 4.10 所示，通常也被称为 pub-sub 模式，是 MQTT 的核心，除了基于同一个消息代理的发布者和订阅者之外，还有一些其他节点围绕着该消息代理呈星形拓扑分布。

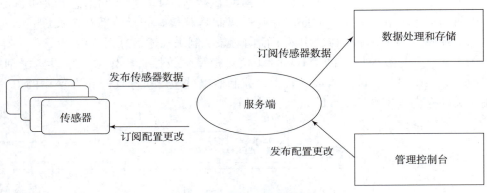

图 4.10 发布和订阅模型

（2）服务质量等级和应用场景

为了满足不同的工业应用场景，MQTT 支持三种不同级别的服务质量（Quality of Service，QoS）为不同场景提供消息可靠性：①级别 0：至多 1 次；②级别 1：至少 1 次；③级别 2：恰好 1 次。MQTT 中的服务质量水平划分如图 4.11 所示。

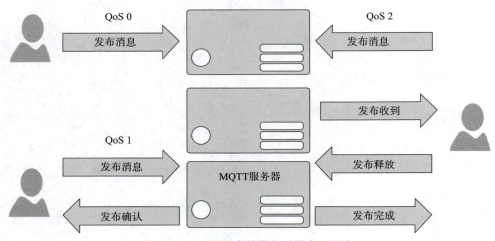

图 4.11 MQTT 中的服务质量水平划分

运用 MQTT 协议，设备可以很方便地连接到互联网云服务，管理设备并处理数据，最后应用到各种业务场景，如质量监测、工艺优化、远程运维、预防性维护等，如图 4.12 所示。

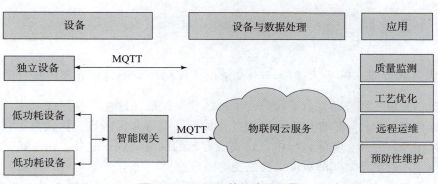

图 4.12　MQTT 协议应用场景

任务拓展

青年人才需要解决的重大挑战——设备系统异构性与信息标准规范统一的困境

工业现场的设备系统通常由不同厂商生产的设备组成，这些设备可能采用不同的通信协议和数据格式。这种异构性使设备之间的互操作性变得非常困难，导致数字化车间的推广成本变得很高，并且在实际运行中很难实现有效的网络集成。此外，由于缺乏统一的信息标准规范，不同设备之间的数据交换也变得困难。

在数字化制造的发展过程中，实现数字化车间的网络化智能化协同是一个重要目标。然而，由于设备系统的异构性和信息标准规范的缺乏，这一目标面临很大的挑战。设备和机器之间缺乏统一的通信协议和数据格式使它们无法直接进行数据交换和共享。这就需要青年人才在解决这些问题上发挥重要作用。党的二十大报告提出，必须坚持科技是第一生产力、人才是第一资源、创新是第一动力，深入实施科教兴国战略、人才强国战略、创新驱动发展战略，开辟发展新领域新赛道，不断塑造发展新动能新优势。人才是富国之本、兴邦大计，青年大学生要立志成才，为国家的发展贡献力量。

作业：为推进国家制造强国战略，针对异构设备的互联互通，你是否有好的方法来解决？请描述一下你的设想。

Project 4

Network Transmission of Industrial Internet

Task 11   Cognize the Industrial Internet Interface Technology

 Learning Objective

①Understand the PLCopen interface specification.
②Master the OPC UA architecture.
③Understand the MTConnect standard.
④Understand the MQTT protocol.

 Suggested Hours

2 hours

Work Situations

The equipment in the workshop generally originates from various manufacturers and is outfitted with diverse control systems. Varied data types and formats are utilized across these systems, resulting in heterogeneity among device systems. Discrepancies in information type, format, and semantics among heterogeneous equipment hinder data exchange and communication between devices, thus creating "information silos".

Knowledge Map

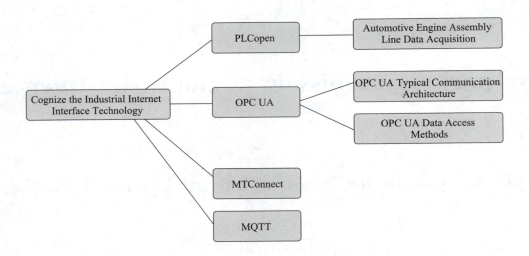

Relevant Knowledge

Addressing the challenge of "information silos" within the digital workshop and achieving interconnection and interoperability among equipment constitute a crucial foundation for realizing intelligent manufacturing. Robustly standardized information models serve as the cornerstone in tackling this issue. PLCopen and OPC are collaborating to define a suite of function blocks that align the IEC 61131-3 global standard for industrial control programming with the OPC UA information communication model. The OPC UA protocol stands as a cross-platform communication protocol characterized by enhanced security and reliability, meeting the demand for extensive connectivity and interoperability of information between the manufacturing floor and the enterprise. The MTConnect standard aids in standardizing the collection of data for Industrial Internet-enabled manufacturing equipment. Message Queue Telemetry Transport (MQTT) is a messaging protocol supporting asynchronous communication between parties.

1. PLCopen

Led by the international organization PLCopen, PLC hardware and software integration technology has been gearing up to meet the increasingly defined demands of Industry 4.0 and intelligent manufacturing. Figure 4.1 depicts the placement of various specifications developed by PLCopen over the years (such as motion control, safety control, OPC UA communication, XML, etc.) within the software and hardware functional hierarchy dimensions and corresponding manufacturing environment hierarchy of the Industry 4.0 Reference Architecture Model (RAMI4.0).

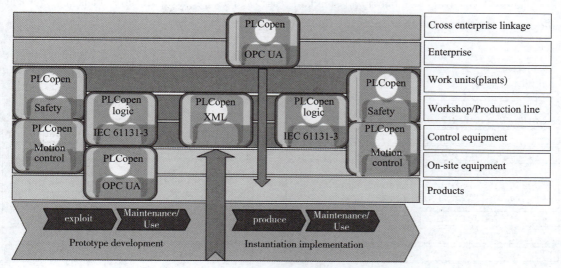

Figure 4.1 Location of PLCopen Specifications in RAMI 4.0

In the standardization process of mapping physical entity assets through a digital pathway to a product description (data performance) of the associated asset, one feasible method is to adhere to the international standard ISO 29002 – 5. This standard is the fifth part of the "Identification Methods" within "Industrial Automation Systems and Integrated Feature Data Exchange," developed by the International Organization for Standardization. Utilizing software packages for categorizing product descriptions, such as eCl@ss Version 9.1, and employing URI and URL for unique resource identification and localization are recommended practices. ISO 29002 – 5 specifies the data elements and syntax for uniquely identifying management items.

Figure 4.2 depicts this unified format, where an identifier, represented as a URL, furnishes a unique identifier for each asset and corresponds to the information space associated with that asset. This identifier not only references the asset's physical classification but also links to the asset's information space—a virtual description that solely relies on its physical characteristics and associated data.

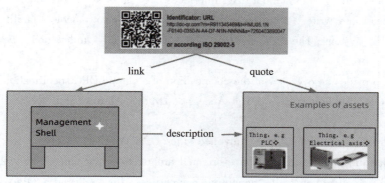

Figure 4.2 Using URL to Uniquely Identify Industry 4.0 Basic Units

Figure 4.3 gives a number of standards as samples of domain/sub-models for vertical integration of product information in the information space.

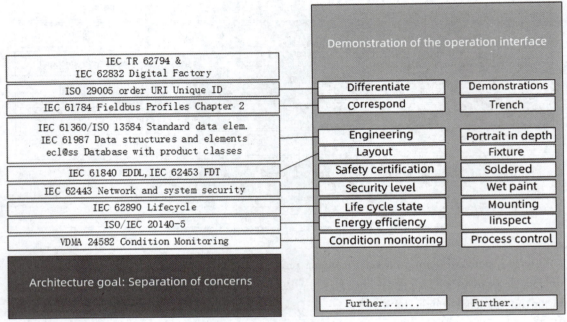

Figure 4.3 Sample Criteria for Domain/Submodel of Information Space

2. OPC UA

OPC (OLE for Process Control) stands as a mainstream interoperability standard extensively employed in the automation industry and various other sectors for secure data exchange. It comprises a series of specifications collaboratively developed by industry suppliers, end users, and software developers. Independent of the platform, OPC ensures seamless transmission of information among devices from diverse vendors. Its primary objective is to abstract PLC-specific protocols (such as Modbus, Profibus, etc.) into standardized interfaces. Acting as a "middleman," OPC translates its universal "read and write" requirements into specific device protocols, facilitating interfacing with HMI/SCADA systems. The OPC specification, as commonly understood, typically refers to classic OPC.

Figure 4.4 provides an overview of the composition of a classic OPC specification, encompassing three primary OPC specifications: Data Access (DA), Alarms and Events (A&E), and Historical Data Access (HDA).

In 2008, the OPC Foundation unveiled the OPC Unified Architecture (OPC UA), introducing a platform-independent, service-oriented architecture that consolidates all functionalities of existing OPC specifications while remaining compatible with the classic OPC specification. To cater to the service-oriented requirements of the industrial control domain, the OPC UA protocol

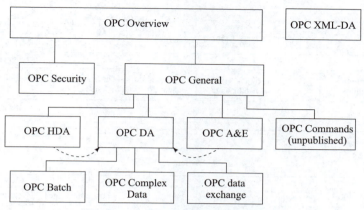

Figure 4.4 Classical OPC Specification

restructures and organizes the information models outlined in different specifications into a series of service sets, enabling a broad spectrum of interconnections. The OPC UA specification architecture constitutes a standardized technical framework encompassing information model definitions, service sets, and communication standards, divided into 13 parts of technical specifications. In comparison to the classic OPC specification, OPC UA provides enhanced communication security, standardized and secure information models, unified access, development with high reliability and redundancy, and cross-platform compatibility.

(1) Typical Communication Architecture for OPC UA

OPC UA adopts a typical client/server architecture, as depicted in Figure 4.5. On the server side, each manufacturing resource's data is encapsulated within a unified address space, enabling clients to access the server uniformly. The client interacts with its own interface to access the client communication stack. Subsequently, the client communication stack forwards the message to the server communication stack. The server then invokes the appropriate service set, such as the node management service set and monitoring service set, to analyze and process incoming requests from the server-side communication stack. It executes corresponding queries and operations on the mesh structure's address space and ultimately returns the results to the client.

(2) OPC UA Data Access Method

OPC UA services define data communication at the application level, presenting themselves as methods available for OPC UA clients to access data from the information model provided by the OPC UA server. Figure 4.6 depicts a distributed embedded controller data transmission architecture based on OPC UA.

The composition of the information transmitted between the client and the server is depicted in Figure 4.7. The definition of a service adopts the familiar request and response mechanisms of web services. Each service comprises request and response messages, and calls to each service are asynchronous. The OPC UA client retrieves data through three primary methods: ①synchronous communication; ②asynchronous communication; ③subscription method.

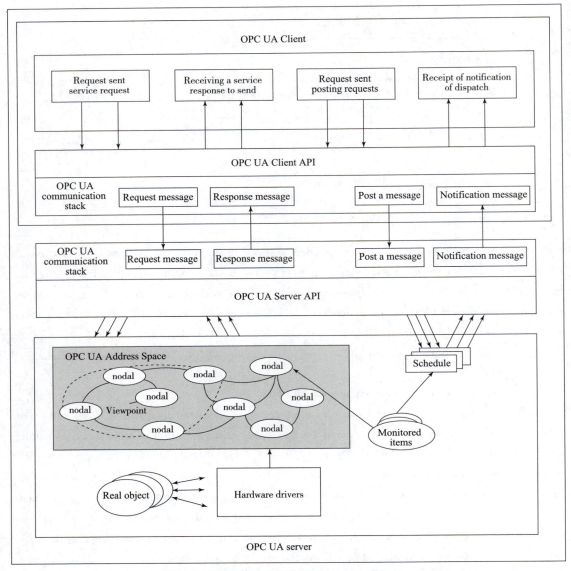

Figure 4.5　OPC UA Client/Server Architecture

3. MTConnect

MTConnect is an interconnection standard introduced by the American Society for Manufacturing Technology (AMT) in 2006, aiming to connect various devices, equipment, and systems. The architecture is depicted in Figure 4.8.

Information modeling for complex systems often involves model integration, where different pieces of information within the model are both independent and sometimes coupled due to functional requirements. Object-oriented modeling offers good encapsulation and extensibility,

Project 4 Network Transmission of Industrial Internet

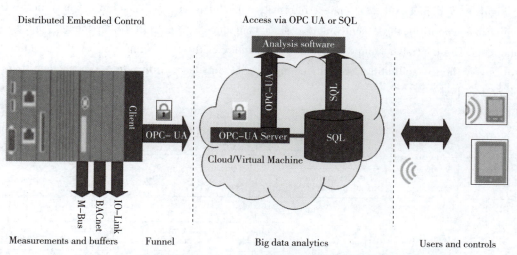

Figure 4.6 Distributed Embedded Controller Data Transfer Based on OPC UA

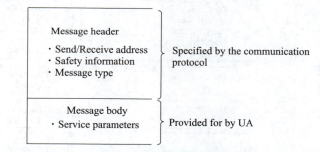

Figure 4.7 Composition of Interaction Messages Between Client and Server

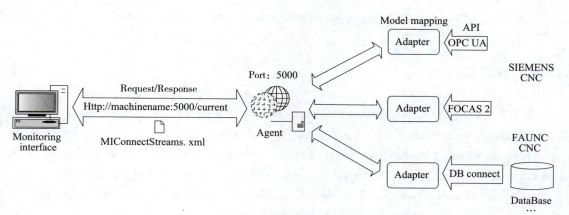

Figure 4.8 Typical Architecture of the MTConnect Standard

making it well-suited for modeling manufacturing information. MTConnect incorporates object-oriented mechanisms for describing relationships between information.

205

Figure 4.9 depicts the MTConnect information model for a CNC machining machine. A CNC machine tool comprises three components: shaft components, controller components, and system components. The controller component includes an index of the tool being used by the machine tool at any given time, facilitating associative querying of details regarding tool assets other than the machine tool body.

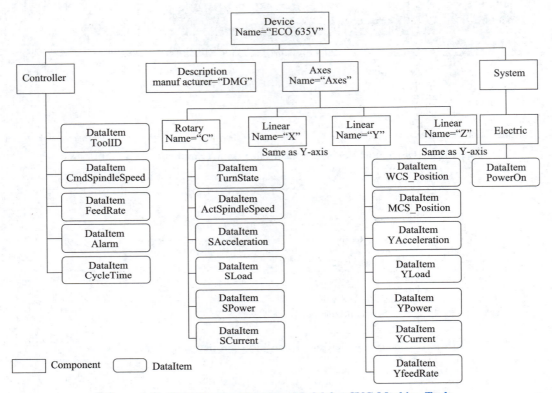

Figure 4.9　Data Storage Structure Model for CNC Machine Tools

4. MQTT

MQTT (Message Queuing Telemetry Transport) is a messaging protocol designed to facilitate asynchronous communication between parties. This asynchronous messaging protocol effectively decouples the message sender from the receiver in both space and time, enabling scalability in unreliable network environments. Despite its name, Message Queue Telemetry Transport has no direct association with message queues. Instead, it employs a publish-and-subscribe model initially intended for applications such as satellite communication.

(1) Publish and Subscribe Model

Publish/subscribe, also known as the pub/sub pattern, forms the core of MQTT. Alongside publishers and subscribers connected to the same message broker, there are also other nodes distributed in a star-shaped topology around the message broker, as depicted in Figure 4.10.

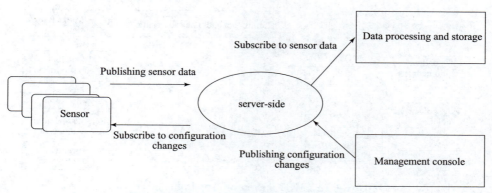

Figure 4. 10   Publishing Subscription Model

(2) Quality of Service Levels and Application Scenarios

To accommodate various industrial application scenarios, MQTT supports three different levels of Quality of Service (QoS) to ensure message reliability: ①Level 0: up to 1 time; ②Level 1: at least 1 time; ③Level 2: exactly 1 time, as depicted in Figure 4. 11.

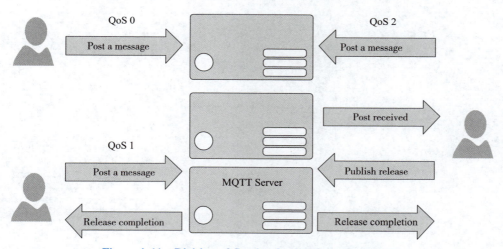

Figure 4. 11   Division of Service Quality Levels in MQTT

By utilizing the MQTT protocol, devices can seamlessly connect to Internet cloud services, manage devices, and process data. Ultimately, MQTT finds applications across diverse business scenarios such as quality monitoring, process optimization, remote operation and maintenance, preventive maintenance, and more, as depicted in Figure 4. 12.

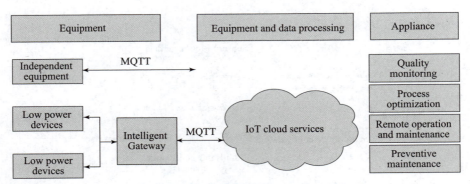

Figure 4.12 MQTT Protocol Application Scenario

 Mission Expansion

The Major Challenge That Young Talents Need to Solve—The Dilemma of Heterogeneity of Equipment Systems and the Unification of Information Standards

The absence of unified information standards and specifications, compounded by the heterogeneity of industrial field equipment systems, has resulted in high promotion costs for digital workshops. In practical operation, achieving effective network integration proves challenging, impeding the realization of networked and intelligent collaboration within digital workshops and constraining the transition from digital manufacturing to intelligent manufacturing. The interoperability among various equipment and machine protocols has emerged as a significant challenge to be addressed by future talents in the field.

Assignment: To support the national strategy of manufacturing prowess, could you propose an effective method or articulate your vision for achieving the interconnection of heterogeneous devices?

任务 12　构建工业物联网

构建工业物联网

学习目标

①掌握工业物联网体系架构。
②理解工业物联网关键技术。
③理解工业物联网应用。

建议学时

2 课时

工作情境

工业物联网环境下,生产系统关键环节、关键资源的状态信息可被实时、精准、全面的感知,使生产管理者能够更为准确地了解生产系统的实时运行状态。但是,如何利用所获取的实时信息、针对所了解的实时状态,通过智能决策帮助生产管理者对生产系统进行高质量的精益化运作管控,受到学术界和工业界的普遍关注。

项目4 工业互联网网络传输

知识导图

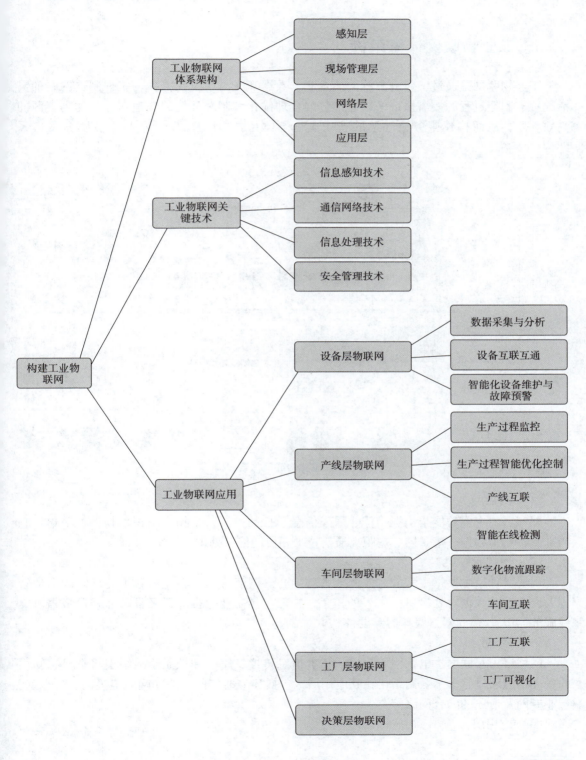

相关知识

1. 工业物联网体系架构

工业物联网是通过工业资源的网络互联、数据互通与系统互操作，实现制造原料的灵活配置、制造过程的按需执行、制造工艺的合理优化和制造环境的快速适应，达到资源的高效利用，从而构建服务驱动型的新工业生态体系。如图 4.13 所示是工业物联网体系架构。

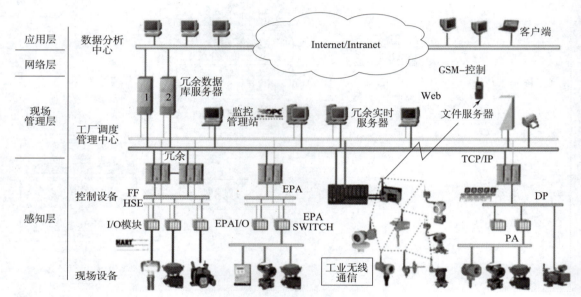

图 4.13 工业物联网体系架构

（1）感知层

感知层的主要功能是识别物体、采集信息和自动控制，是物联网识别物体、采集信息的来源；它由数据采集子层、短距离通信技术和协同信息处理子层组成。

（2）现场管理层

现场管理层主要指工厂的本地调度管理中心。调度管理中心充当着工业系统的本地管理者以及工业数据对外接口提供者的角色，一般包括工业数据库服务器、监控服务器、文件服务器以及 Web 网络服务器等设备。

（3）网络层

网络层由互联网、电信网等组成，负责信息传递、路由和控制。网络层将来自感知层的各类信息通过基础承载网络传输到应用层，包括移动通信网、互联网、卫星网、广电网、行业专网及形成的融合网络等。

（4）应用层

应用层实现所感知信息的应用服务，包括信息处理、海量数据存储、数据挖掘与分析、人工智能等技术。

2. 工业物联网关键技术

（1）信息感知技术

信息感知为物联网应用提供了信息来源，是工业物联网应用的基础，包括：①数据收集；②数据清洗；③数据压缩；④数据聚集；⑤数据融合。

（2）通信网络技术

网络是物联网信息传递和服务支撑的基础设施，通过泛在的互联功能，实现感知信息高可靠性、高安全性传送。

①接入与组网：物联网的网络技术涵盖泛在接入和骨干传输等多个层面的内容。

②通信与频管：物联网需要综合各种有线及无线通信技术，其中近距离无线通信技术将是物联网的研究重点。工业以太网、工业现场总线、工业无线网络是目前工业通信领域的三大主流技术。

（3）信息处理技术

海量感知信息的计算与处理是物联网的核心支撑。信息处理技术是对采集到的数据进行数据解析、格式转换、元数据提取、初步清洗等预处理工作，再按照不同的数据类型与数据使用特点选择分布式文件系统、关系数据库、对象存储系统、时序数据库等不同的数据管理引擎实现数据的分区选择、落地存储、编目与索引等操作。

（4）安全管理技术

工业物联网系统与许多其他物联网行业的区别是，在工业物联网系统中，一般会涉及许多工业生产设备，这些设备系统响应的实时性要求高，无论感知数据的传输还是控制指令的发放都需要在很短的时间内完成，这就给安全防护技术的实施带来了挑战。工业物联网系统的入侵攻击目标一般不是被入侵的主机系统。因为无论破坏主机系统还是从主机系统获取信息，都达不到攻击工业设施的目的。攻击者一般会通过入侵的主机系统非法控制该主机系统所能控制的受控设备，这些受控设备有些可能根本不具有智能判断能力，如PLC设备。

3. 工业物联网应用

智能工厂整体业务模型自底向上包括设备层、集成层、核心业务层、透视层，如图4.14所示。设备层是基础，包括生产加工、物料配送、质量监测等设备；集成层主要指系统集成和数据集成，系统包括ERP、目标管理（Management By Objectives，MBO）、MES、统计过程控制（Statistical Process Control，SPC）、BC（模块控制）、物料控制系统（Material Control System，MCS）等，数据集成包括虚拟产品、虚拟产线、虚拟设计、虚拟制造等来源数据；核心业务层主要包括生产管控、质量管控、物流管控、计划管控；透视层包括设备可视化、工序可视化、车间可视化、工厂可视化、企业可视化。

（1）设备层物联网

①数据采集与分析。

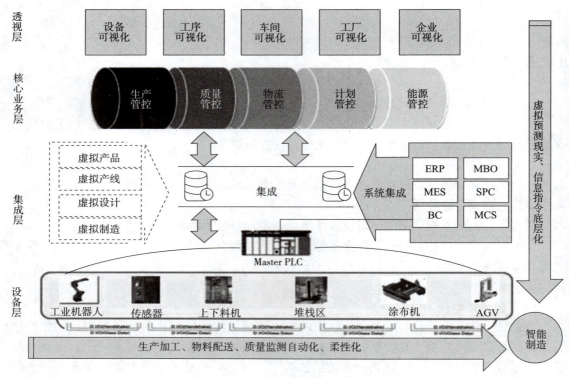

图 4.14 智能工厂整体业务模型

通过物联网技术，实时采集物料信息，由物流管控系统对其进行处理和分析，实现对物料的高效调度，降低物流成本。并在此基础上对物料在生产过程中使用的数量和质量进行准确的统计分析，从而得出不同物料的最佳使用数量，生产管理系统通过与 ERP 系统进行对接与数据共享，即可为物料的采购计划提供科学依据。

② 设备互联互通。

智能化的生产设备需要主动地感知生产环境的变化，主动采取相应控制策略进行自我调整、自我学习，实现生产过程的稳定运行；将相关的信息通过工业数据总线或物联网及时、准确、完整地传递到其他设备和系统，不但要实现单个设备的智能化，而且要实现整套生产工艺设备的互联互通，确保整个生产工艺过程处于优化运行状态，降低物料和能源的消耗，提高产品的质量；具有强大的自诊断能力，在实现有效的设备资产管理的同时，能够借助大数据分析，实现生产设备的预测性维护，降低非计划停机的可能性。

③ 智能化设备维护与故障预警。

智能化设备维护与故障预警系统包括：通信控制器、驱动控制、设备上位机、报警灯、报警看板、邮件、短信。设备 I/O 板连接上下游设备，实现整条线的连接，设备的 PLC 与整条线的 PLC 进行连接，实时监控设备状态。设备的运行状态、报警信息、产品信息都可实施上报系统。设备上人机界面便于对设备的单机操作，设备的 PC 单元用于记录设备的运行状态，并与服务器连接，实施上报生产数据，便于追溯跟踪。

（2）产线层物联网

① 生产过程监控。

根据事先约定的编码及读码原则为每种/每件/每框产品生产二维码。每种/每件/每框产品有唯一一个 ID，此 ID 使产品可一直追溯到客户端；可将 VCR 装置安装于每条产线上，用于读取产品二维码以便识别产品信息；每台读码器要有可识别的 ID，用于工作状态的监控；实时将数据上报给 MES。生产过程监控技术架构体系如图 4.15 所示。

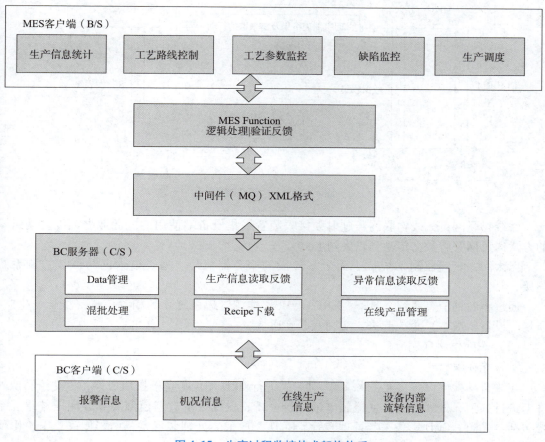

图 4.15　生产过程监控技术架构体系

② 生产过程智能优化控制。

SPC 的作用在于通过收集制造过程中的检验数据，依据统计原理建立制程管制程序及方法，以改善制程能力及提高产品质量、良率。

SPC 系统架构如图 4.16 所示，主要是通过 SPC 系统实时传递数据，通过互联网实现了数据收集、实时控制、异常处理、报表生成、统计分析与查询，且在同一页面可以监控一个控制特性的过程状态、数据表和不同的控制图表。

③ 产线互联。

通过如下方式进行产线互联：

光纤网：光纤网是设备和设备之间连接的网络，通过可编程控制器（PLC）在设备之间传输信号；

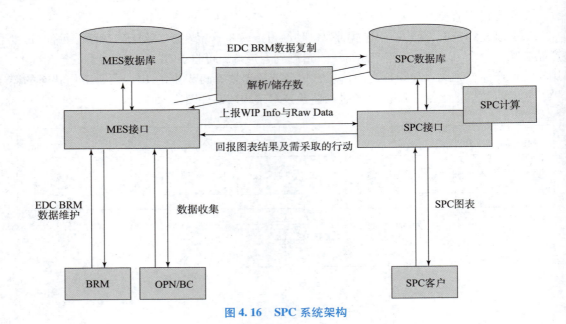

图 4.16 SPC 系统架构

无线物联网：无线物联网通过射频接收装置采集设备端使用的能源数据，以自动组网的方式通过网关将数据传输到以太网上；

以太网：车间控制系统位于无尘室外面的服务器机房，通过以太网与产线控制系统连接；

通过将各种信息系统（MES、ERP、QMS、能源管理系统）的相关信息（能耗、生产、质量、设备、成本）集成起来，实现互联互通。

(3) 车间层物联网

①智能在线检测。

在线自动检测设备（见图 4.17）对产品进行 CCD 图像传感器摄取成像，提交给影像处理卡进行处理，处理后交由主控制电脑进行分析，根据设定数据模型演算并输出结果。系统包括：光源、CCD 影像采集处理装置。CCD 影像采集处理装置主要由影像采集卡、影像处理器、主电脑、PLC 控制运输系统和输出装置组成。

②数字化物流跟踪。

车间物料跟踪系统包括仓库管理过程监控、物料状态监控、配送作业监控、运输工具监控以及线边库存监控。通过物联网技术实现对物料和物料运输工具的实时定位、追踪与监控，获取物料和运输工具的状态和位置等信息，并可以通过对这些信息的分析实现对物料的高效调度。其功能包括车间物流的自动化和物料需求分析。

③车间互联。

智能制造的首要任务是信息的处理与优化，车间内各层网络的互联互通则是其基础与前提。无论是工业云还是工业大数都需要车间工厂的互联互通和数据采集与交互来支持。可以通过无线物联网和互联网，车间层管理系统与企业层管理系统连接起来，实现车间互联。在建立各业务领域的信息化基础平台的基础上（如 MES，APS，ERP，QMS，EMS）实现各种资源的互联互通。

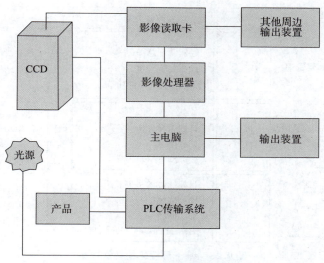

图 4.17 在线自动检测设备

（4）工厂层物联网

①工厂互联。

工厂互联是顺应全球新工业革命以及互联网时代的潮流，对大规模生产转型和大规模定制的创新性探索，是互联网转型的重要组成部分。与传统工厂不同，互联工厂实现了与用户相连，目标是从"产销分离"到"产销合一"，满足用户无缝化、透明化、可视化的最佳体验。通过建立起互联工厂体系，打造互联工厂的引领样板，可实时、同步响应企业全球用户需求，并快速交付智慧化、个性化的方案。

②工厂可视化。

建立工厂可视化系统，可实时追踪生产现场的生产运转情况、品质信息、能源消耗量等数据，通过在信息系统灵活运用生产现场的可视化信息，可大大提高工厂的效率和生产率。可视化内容包括：整个工厂车间的整体可视化，每个设备产线的运转状况，是否有报错信息，是否在正常的运转；当今有多少异常设备（工序）的可视化，如有报错信息实时可以在画面进行确认；各工序间是否存在待加工品积压滞留；哪台设备加工效率更高，没有使用的设备是否仍在运转；整个工厂的目前能源消耗，生产订单数量以及完成率。

（5）决策层物联网

决策可视化的内容包括：①工厂的销售状况，订单执行状况；②整体的能耗状况；③工厂整体的库存状况以及库存周转率；④工厂整体的设备管理效率的各项 KPI；⑤工厂整体的各项成本，财务 KPI；⑥工厂整体的环境状况等。如图 4.18 所示是基于可视化的智能决策。

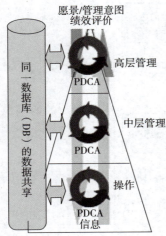

图 4.18　基于可视化的智能决策

任务拓展

从跟随到引领——中国移动通信的逆袭之路

5G（第五代移动通信技术）是具有高速率、低时延和大连接特点的新一代宽带移动通信技术，5G 技术在工业物联网的构建中起着非常重要的作用。中国移动通信技术经历了"1G 空白，2G 跟随，3G 突破，4G 并跑，5G 引领"的跨越式发展，走出了一条逆袭之路。在移动通信技术的发展历程中，中国起步较晚，最初的 1G 时代中国处于相对滞后的状态，但随着技术的进步和政策的支持，中国逐渐迎头赶上。2G 时代，中国移动通信技术开始跟随国际先进水平，引入了 GSM 技术，建设了全国性的 2G 网络，实现了移动通信的普及和商业化运营。3G 时代，中国移动通信技术实现了突破，引入了 WCDMA 和 CDMA2000 等 3G 技术标准，建设了全国范围的 3G 网络，实现了语音和数据业务的快速发展。4G 时代，中国移动通信技术实现了与国际先进水平的并跑，采用了 LTE 技术标准，建设了全国性的 4G 网络，实现了高速数据传输和多媒体业务的大规模应用。而在 5G 时代，中国移动通信技术走在了世界的前列，率先实现了商用部署，并在技术创新、标准制定、网络建设等方面取得了重要突破。

党的二十大提出了新时代中国特色社会主义思想，强调创新驱动发展和建设创新型国家的重要性，以及推动经济高质量发展和构建现代化经济体系的目标。在移动通信技术的发展中，中国走出了一条逆袭之路，正是因为党的二十大精神的指导和推动。中国移动通信技术企业积极响应党的号召，加大科技创新力度，不断推动技术突破和产业升级。中国移动通信技术的快速发展，不仅改变了人们的通信方式和生活方式，也推动了数字经济的发展和社会的进步。

作业：通过网络查询资料，掌握中国 5G 的发展历程和现状。

Task 12 Construction of Industrial Internet of Things

Learning Objective

①Master the IIoT system architecture.
②Understand the key technologies of IIoT.
③Understand the IIoT applications.

Suggested Hours

2 hours

Work Situations

Under the IIoT environment, critical information about key links and production system resources can be accurately and comprehensively sensed in real time. This capability empowers production managers to gain a more precise understanding of the real-time operational status of the production system. However, the challenge lies in effectively leveraging the real-time information, aligning it with the understood status, and supporting production managers in achieving high-quality, lean operation and intelligent control of production systems. This topic has garnered significant attention from both academia and industry.

Knowledge Map

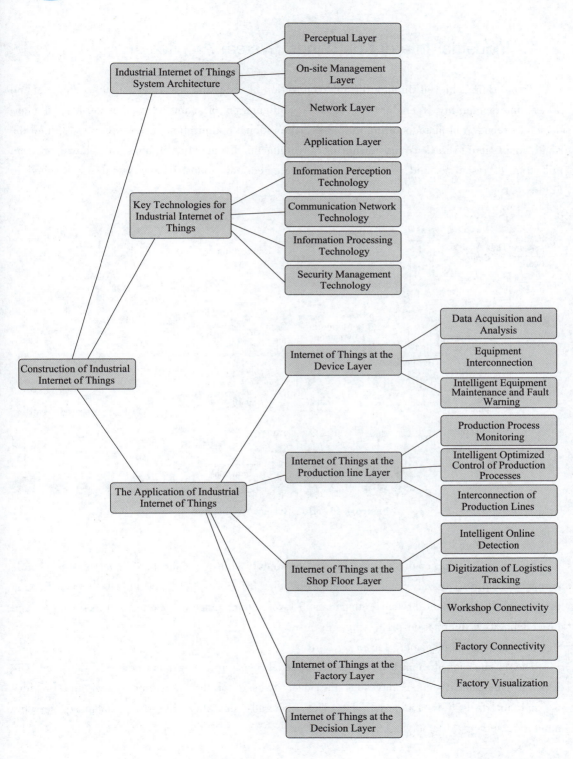

Relevant Knowledge

1. Industrial Internet of Things System Architecture

The IIoT is achieved through the interconnection of industrial resources, data exchange, and system interoperability. It enables the flexible configuration of manufacturing materials, the on-demand execution of manufacturing processes, the rational optimization of these processes, and the rapid adaptation to various manufacturing environments. Ultimately, it aims to achieve efficient utilization of resources and to build a service-oriented new industrial ecosystem. As depicted in Figure 4.13.

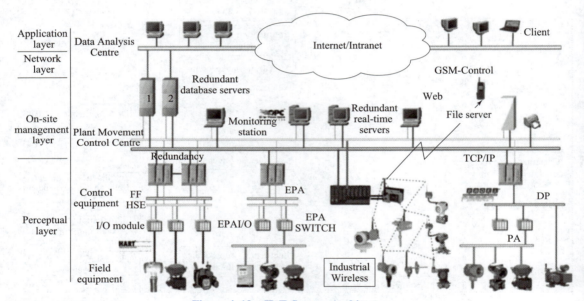

Figure 4.13 IIoT System Architecture

(1) Perceptual Layer

The main function of the sensing layer is to identify objects, collect information, and enable automatic control. This layer is the source of the IoT for identifying objects and collecting information. It consists of the data collection sub-layer, short-range communication technology, and the collaborative information processing sub-layer.

(2) On-site Management Layer

The on-site management layer refers to the local dispatch management center of the plant. The dispatch management center serves as the local manager of the industrial system and provides external interfaces for industrial data. This generally includes industrial database servers, monitoring servers, file servers, and web servers.

Project 4 Network Transmission of Industrial Internet

(3) Network Layer

The network layer consists of the Internet, telecommunication networks, etc., and is responsible for information transmission, routing, and control. It transmits various types of information from the sensing layer to the application layer through the basic bearer network, including mobile communication networks, the Internet, satellite networks, broadcasting networks, industry-specific networks, and the formation of converged networks.

(4) Application Layer

The application layer realizes the application services of the perceived information, including information processing, massive data storage, data mining and analysis, and the integration of artificial intelligence technologies.

2. Key Technologies for Industrial Internet of Things

(1) Information Perception Technology

Information perception provides the information source for IoT applications and is the basis for IIoT applications, including: ①data collection; ②data cleaning; ③data compression; ④data aggregation; ⑤data fusion.

(2) Communication Network Technology

The network is the infrastructure for IoT information delivery and service support, enabling high reliability and high-security transmission of sensory information through its ubiquitous interconnection functions.

①Access and Networking: Networking technologies for the IoT cover multiple dimensions, such as ubiquitous access and backbone transmission.

②Communication and Frequency Management: The IoT requires a combination of various wired and wireless communication technologies, with close-range wireless communication technology being a research focus. Industrial Ethernet, industrial fieldbus, and industrial wireless networks are the three mainstream technologies in the field of industrial communication at present.

(3) Information Processing Technology

The calculation and processing of massive sensory information is the core support of the IoT. Information processing technology involves collecting data for data parsing, format conversion, metadata extraction, preliminary cleaning, and other processing work. Then, based on different data types and the data use characteristics of distributed file systems, relational databases, object storage systems, time series databases, and other data management engines, it achieves data partition selection, landing storage, cataloging, and indexing operations.

(4) Security Management Technology

The difference between IIoT systems and many other IoT industries is that in IIoT systems, many industrial production equipment are generally involved. These device systems require high real-time response, and both the transmission of perception data and the issuance of control instructions need to be completed in a very short time, which poses challenges to the implementation of security protection technology. The target of intrusion attacks on IIoT systems is generally not the invaded host system. This is because neither destroying the host system nor obtaining information from the host system achieves the purpose of attacking an industrial facility. The attacker will generally illegally control the controlled devices that the host system can control through the invaded host system, and some of these controlled devices may not have intelligent judgement at all, such as PLC devices.

3. The Application of Industrial Internet of Things

The overall business model of a smart factory includes the equipment layer, integration layer, core business layer, and perspective layer from the bottom up, as depicted in Figure 4.14. The equipment layer is the foundation, including production and processing, material distribution quality inspection and other equipment; the integration layer mainly refers to system integration and data integration; the system includes ERP, MBO (target management), MES, SPC (statistical process control), BC (module control), MCS (material control system), etc.; data integration includes virtual products, virtual production lines, virtual design, virtual manufacturing and other source data; the core business layer mainly includes production control, quality control, logistics control, planning and control; The perspective layer includes equipment visualization, process visualization, workshop visualization, factory visualization, and enterprise visualization.

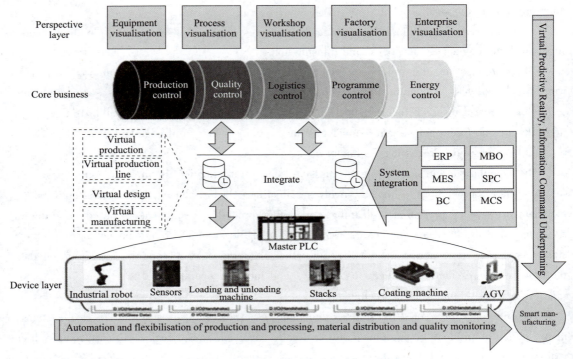

Figure 4.14　Smart Factory Based on IIoT

(1) Internet of Things at the Device Layer

①Data Acquisition and Analysis.

By IoT technology, real-time collection of material information is achieved. The logistics control system processes and analyzes this information to efficiently schedule materials and reduce logistics costs. On this basis, accurate statistical analysis is conducted on the quantity and quality of materials used in the production process to determine the optimal usage quantity of different materials. The production management system can provide a scientific basis for material procurement planning by integrating with the ERP system and sharing data.

②Equipment Interconnection.

Intelligent production equipment needs to proactively perceive changes in the production environment and take the initiative to implement the appropriate control strategies for self-adjustment and self-learning, thereby achieving stable operation of the production process. This equipment will transmit related information in a timely, accurate, and complete manner to other equipment and systems via the industrial data bus or IoT. It not only realizes the intelligence of individual equipment but also the interconnection of the entire production process equipment. This ensures that the entire production process operates in an optimized state, reduces the consumption of materials and energy, and improves product quality. The equipment has strong self-diagnostic capabilities and can facilitate predictive maintenance with the help of big data analysis, reducing the likelihood of unplanned downtime and enabling effective management of equipment assets.

③Intelligent Equipment Maintenance and Fault Warning.

The intelligent equipment maintenance and fault warning system includes a communication controller, drive control, equipment upper computer, alarm light, alarm watch board, email, and SMS. The equipment's I/O board connects upstream and downstream equipment to achieve line interconnection, and the equipment's PLC connects with the line's PLC to monitor the equipment's status in real time. The equipment's operating status, alarm information, and product information can be reported to the system. The human-machine interface on the equipment facilitates standalone operation, and the equipment's PC unit is used to record its operating status and connect with the server to report production data for easy tracking and tracing.

(2) Internet of Things at the Production line Layer

①Production Process Monitoring.

A QR code is produced for each type/piece/frame of a product according to a previously agreed-upon coding and reading principle. Each type/piece/frame has a unique ID, which represents the product at all times, all the way back to the client. A VCR device can be installed on each production line to read the QR code and identify the product information. Each code reader should have an identifiable ID for work status monitoring. The data is reported to the MES in real time. The technical architecture of the whole production process monitoring system is depicted in Figure 4.15.

②Intelligent Optimized Control of Production Processes.

The role of SPC (Statistical Process Control) is to collect inspection data during the

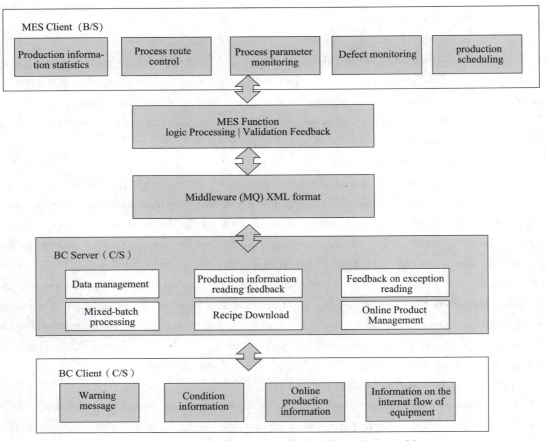

Figure 4.15　Production Process Monitoring Technology Architecture

manufacturing process and establish process control procedures and methods based on statistical principles in order to improve process capability, enhance product quality, and increase yield.

The SPC system architecture, as depicted in Figure 4.16, mainly operates by transferring data in real time through the Internet to achieve data collection, real-time control, exception processing, report generation, statistical analysis, and query. On the same page, you can monitor the process status of a control characteristic, data tables, and different control charts.

③Interconnection of Production Lines.

Production lines are interconnected through the following methods: a fiber optic network, which is a network that connects devices and transmits signals between devices through a programmable controller; wireless IoTs (Internet of Things), which collect data on the energy used at the device end via radio frequency receivers and transmit the data to the Ethernet via the Gateway in an automated networking mode; and Ethernet, where the workshop control system is located in the server room outside the cleanroom and is connected to the production line control system through Ethernet. Interconnection is achieved by integrating relevant information (energy consumption, production, quality, equipment, cost) from various information systems (MES,

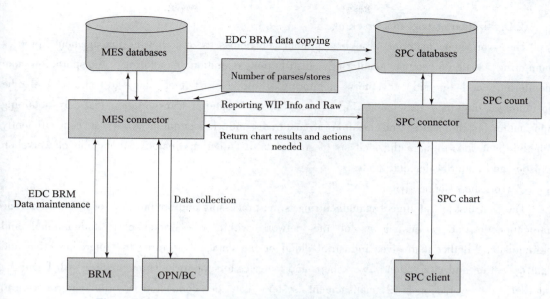

Figure 4.16 Production Process Monitoring Technology Architecture

ERP, QMS, energy management system).

(3) Internet of Things at the Shop Floor Layer

①Intelligent Online Detection.

On-line automatic inspection equipment (AOI), as depicted in Figure 4.17, captures images using a product CCD image sensor and processes them through an image processing card. After processing, the images are sent to the main control computer for analysis according to a set data model algorithm, and the results are then output. The system includes: a light source, a CCD image acquisition and processing device, which mainly consists of an image acquisition card, an image processor, a main computer, a PLC-controlled transport system, and an output device.

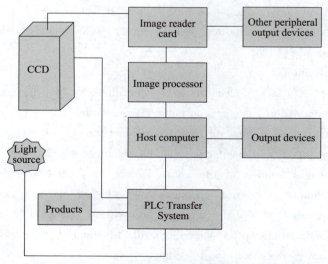

Figure 4.17 Hardware Structure of In-line Inspection Machine AOI

②Digitization of Logistics Tracking.

The workshop material tracking system encompasses warehouse management process monitoring, material status monitoring, distribution operation monitoring, transportation tool monitoring, and line-side inventory monitoring. It utilizes IoT technology to achieve real-time positioning, tracking, and monitoring of materials and material transportation tools. By obtaining information on the status and location of materials and transportation tools, it can efficiently schedule materials through the analysis of such data. Its functions include automation of workshop logistics and material demand analysis.

③Workshop Connectivity.

The first task of intelligent manufacturing is the processing and optimization of information. The interconnection of various layers of the network within the workshop is foundational and prerequisite. Whether it involves industrial cloud or big data, it requires the interconnection and data collection and interaction of workshops and factories to support it. Through wireless IoT and the Internet, the workshop-level management system can be connected to the enterprise-level management system to achieve workshop interconnection. The interconnection of various resources can be realized based on the establishment of information technology infrastructure in various business domains (such as MES, APS, ERP, QMS, EMS).

(4) Internet of Things at the Factory Layer

①Factory Connectivity.

A connected factory represents an innovative exploration from mass production to mass customization, aligning with the trends of the new global industrial revolution and the Internet era. It is an important component of Internet transformation. Unlike traditional factories, connected factories are integrated with user interfaces, aiming to transition from a "separation of production and marketing" to an "integration of production and marketing." The goal is to provide users with the best experience in terms of seamlessness, transparency, and visibility. By establishing a connected factory system and creating a leading connected factory model, it can respond to the needs of global users in real time and synchronously, and quickly deliver intelligent and personalized solutions.

②Factory Visualization.

The establishment of a factory visualization system allows for real-time tracking of production operations, quality information, energy consumption, and other data at the production site. By flexibly applying visualization information from the production site within the information system, the efficiency and productivity of the factory can be significantly improved. Visualization content includes: the overall visualization of the entire factory floor, the operational status of each equipment line, including any error messages and whether it is operating normally; the visualization of the number of abnormal equipment (processes) operating at present, such as real-time error message confirmations on the screen; the identification of any backlog in the processing of products between processes; assessment of which equipment is more efficient in processing and whether unused equipment is still operating; and the current energy consumption, production order quantity, and completion rate for the entire factory.

(5) Internet of Things at the Decision Layer

The content of decision visualization includes: ①The sales status and order execution status of the factory; ②The overall energy consumption status; ③The overall inventory status of the factory and the inventory turnover rate; ④The overall equipment management efficiency of the factory in terms of KPIs (Key Performance Indicators); ⑤The overall cost of the factory and the financial KPIs; ⑥The overall environmental conditions of the factory. As depicted in Figure 4. 18.

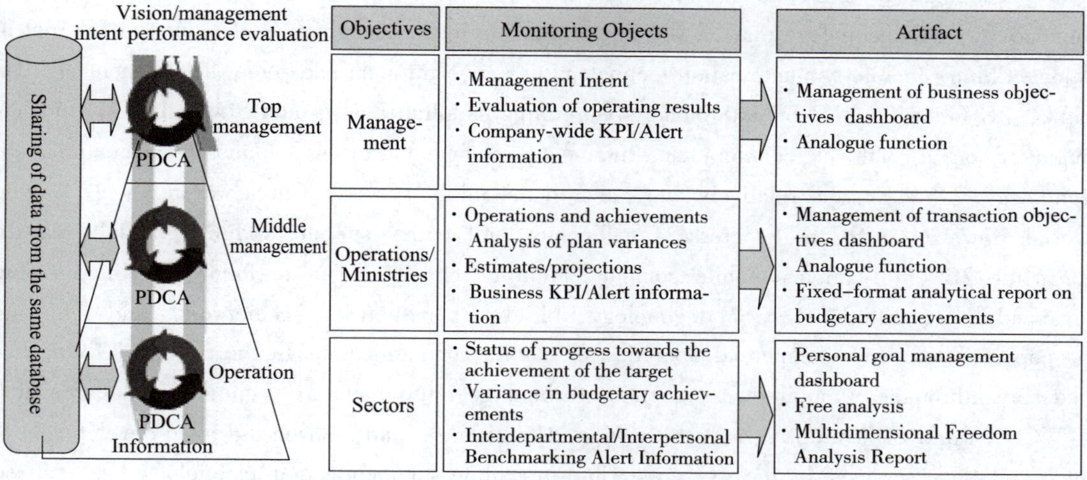
Vision/management intent performance evaluation
Sharing of data from the same database
Top management
PDCA
Middle management
PDCA
Operation
PDCA
Information
Objectives
Monitoring Objects
Artifact
Manage-ment
· Management Intent
· Evaluation of operating results
· Company-wide KPI/Alert information
· Management of business objectives dashboard
· Analogue function
Operations/ Ministries
· Operations and achievements
· Analysis of plan variances
· Estimates/projections
· Business KPI/Alert information
· Management of transaction objectives dashboard
· Analogue function
· Fixed-format analytical report on budgetary achievements
Sectors
· Status of progress towards the achievement of the target
· Variance in budgetary achievements
· Interdepartmental/Interpersonal Benchmarking Alert Information
· Personal goal management dashboard
· Free analysis
· Multidimensional Freedom Analysis Report

Figure 4. 18 Intelligent Decision Making Based on Visualization

Mission Expansion

From Following to Leading—The Counterattack Path of China Mobile Communications

5G (the fifth generation mobile communication technology) is a new generation of broadband mobile communication technology characterized by high speed, low latency, and massive connectivity. 5G technology plays a very important role in the construction of industrial Internet of Things. China's mobile communication technology has gone through a leapfrog development of "1G blank, 2G following, 3G breakthrough, 4G running simultaneously, and 5G leading", and has embarked on a path of counterattack. In the development process of mobile communication technology, China started relatively late, and in the initial 1G era, China was relatively lagging behind. However, with the progress of technology and policy support, China gradually caught up. In the 2G era, China's mobile communication technology began to follow the international advanced level, introducing GSM technology, building a nationwide 2G network, and achieving the popularization and commercial operation of mobile communication. In the 3G era, China has made breakthroughs in mobile communication technology, introduced 3G technology standards such as WCDMA and CDMA2000, built nationwide 3G networks, and realized the rapid development of voice and data services. In the 4G era, China's mobile communication technology has realized parallelism with the international advanced level, adopted LTE technology standard, built a nationwide 4G network, and realized high-speed data transmission and large-scale application of multimedia services. In the era of 5G, China's mobile communication technology has taken the lead in the world, achieving commercial deployment and making important breakthroughs in technological innovation, standard formulation, network construction, and other aspects.

The 20th National Congress of the Communist Party of China proposed the socialist ideology with Chinese characteristics for a new era, emphasizing the importance of innovation driven development and building an innovative country, as well as the goal of promoting high-quality economic development and building a modern economic system. In the development of mobile communication technology, China has embarked on a path of counterattack, precisely because of the guidance and promotion of the spirit of the 20th National Congress of the Communist Party of China. Chinese mobile communication technology enterprises actively respond to the call of the Party, increase their efforts in scientific and technological innovation, and continuously promote technological breakthroughs and industrial upgrading. The rapid development of China's mobile communication technology has not only changed people's communication and lifestyle, but also promoted the development of the digital economy and social progress.

Assignment: By searching for information online, grasp the development history and current situation of 5G in China.

任务 13　传输工业大数据

传输工业大数据

学习目标

①掌握工业现场总线通信技术。
②理解工业以太网通信技术。
③理解工业现场无线网络通信技术。

建议学时

2 课时

工作情境

在工业互联网中，通信系统的主要作用是将信息安全可靠地传送到目的地。由于工业互联网具有异构性的特点，就使得工业互联网所采用的通信方式和通信系统也具有异构性和复杂性。

知识导图

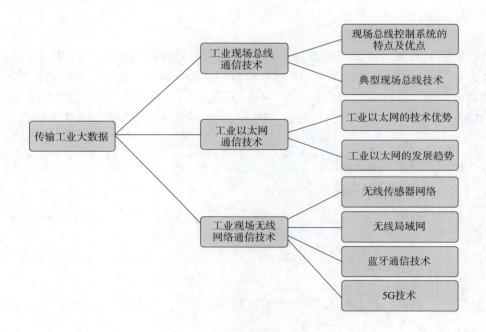

相关知识

工业大数据传输技术是指数据源与数据宿之间通过一个或多个数据信道或链路、共同遵循一个通信协议而进行的数据传输技术。它主要是按照适当的规则,经过一条或多条链路,在数据源和数据宿之间进行多元数据汇集与传输的过程。大数据在科学及商业应用领域都具有很大价值。传统的电路交换具有稳定的特点,但其要求足够可用的线宽;而大数据的特点是对时延的不敏感性,但其占用网络资源却很大,因而保证数据传输的实时性是数据传输过程中的核心要务。

1. 工业现场总线通信技术

现场总线的一般定义为:一种用于智能化现场设备和自动化系统的开放式、数字化、双向串行、多节点的通信总线。现场总线作为工厂数字通信网络的基础,沟通了生产过程现场及控制设备之间及其与更高控制管理层次之间的联系。它不仅是一个基层网络,而且还是一种开放式、新型全分布控制系统,这项以智能传感、控制、计算机、数字通信等技术为主要内容的综合技术已经在世界范围内受到关注,成为自动化技术发展的热点,并将导致自动化系统结构与设备的深刻变革。

(1) 现场总线控制系统的特点及优点

现场总线控制系统具有可操作性与互用性、现场设备的智能化与功能自治性、系统的开放性、系统结构的高度分散性和对现场环境的适应性5个特点。现场总线控制系统使自控设备与系统步入了信息网络的行列,为其应用开拓了更为广阔的领域,其具有以下优点:节省维护开销,节省安装费用,节省硬件数量与投资,用户具有高度的系统集成主动权,提高了系统的准确性与可靠性。

(2) 典型现场总线技术

目前国际上有40多种现场总线技术,但没有任何一种能覆盖所有的应用面,按其传输数据的大小可分为3类:传感器总线,属于位传输;设备总线,属于字节传输;现场总线,属于数据流传输。目前主要的总线有 Profibus 现场总线、LonWorks 现场总线、基金会现场总线、CAN 现场总线等。常见的现场总线技术特点与应用情况介绍如表4.1所示。

表4.1 常见的现场总线技术特点与应用情况介绍

总线类型	技术特点	主要应用场合	价格	支持公司
FF	功能强大,本安,实时性好,总线供电;但协议复杂,实际应用少	流程控制	较贵	Honeywell、Rosemount、ABB、Foxboro、横河等
WorldFIP	有较强的抗干扰能力,实时性好,稳定性好	工业过程控制	一般	Alstone
Profibus – PA	本安,总线供电,实际应用较多;但支持的传输介质较少,传输方式单一	过程自动化	较贵	Siemens

续表

总线类型	技术特点	主要应用场合	价格	支持公司
Profibus-DP/FMS	速度较快，组态配置灵活	车间级通信、工业、楼宇自动化	一般	Siemens
CAN	采用短帧，抗干扰能力强，速度较慢，协议芯片内核由国外厂商垄断	汽车检测、控制	较便宜	Philips、Siemens、Honeyell 等
LonWorks	支持 OSI 七层协议，实际应用较多，开发平台完善，协议芯片内核由国外厂商垄断	楼宇自动化、工业、能源	较便宜	Echelon

2. 工业以太网通信技术

由于以太网技术标准开放性好，应用广泛，使用透明、统一的通信协议，因此成为工业控制领域唯一的统一通信标准。工业以太网与商业以太网都符合 OSI 模型，但针对工业控制实时性、高可靠性的要求，工业以太网在链路层、网络层增加了不同的功能模块，在物理层增加了电磁兼容性设计，解决了通信实时性、网络安全性、抗强电磁干扰等技术问题。

（1）工业以太网的技术优势

工业以太网技术具有价格低廉、稳定可靠、通信速率高、软硬件产品丰富、应用广泛以及支持技术成熟等优点，已成为最受欢迎的通信网络之一。近些年来，随着网络技术的发展，以太网进入控制领域，形成新型的以太网控制网络技术。这主要是由于工业自动化系统向分布化、智能化控制方面发展，开放的、透明的通信协议是必然的要求。

以太网技术引入工业控制领域，其技术优势主要有以下 5 点：①软硬件成本低廉；②以太网能实现工业控制网络与企业信息网络的无缝连接，形成企业级管控一体化的全开放网络；③它是全开放、全数字化的网络，遵照网络协议，不同厂商的设备可以很容易地实现互联；④通信速率高；⑤可持续发展潜力大。

（2）工业以太网的发展趋势

工业以太网在工业设备领域的可持续性和可拓展性是工业互联网中的重点。在大数据时代下，云计算、分布式数据存储和处理的需求使工业互联网接入因特网成为日益迫切的需求，在目前的工业以太网框架中，所使用的第二代互联网 IPv4 技术面临着网络地址资源有限的挑战。在这样的环境下，IPv6 应运而生。这不但解决了网络地址资源数量的问题，也为车间底层的通信设备互联互通，车间底层终端（智能设备、人员、控制系统）和云端服务器、控制终端之间的通信数量限制扫清了障碍。

3. 工业现场无线网络通信技术

无线网络技术在工业控制中的应用，主要包括数据采集、视频监控等，可以帮助用户实现移动设备与固定网络的通信或移动设备之间的通信,且坚固、可靠、安全。它适用于各种工业环境,即使在极恶劣的情况下也能够保证网络的可靠性和安全性。目前,在工业自动化领域中的无线通信技术协议主要是:对于可用于现场设备层的无线短程网,采用的主流协议是 IEEE 802.15.4;对于适应较大传输覆盖面和较大信息传输量的无线局域网,采用的是 IEEE 802.11 系列;对于较大数据容量的短程无线通信,工业界广泛采用的是蓝牙标准。

(1) 无线传感器网络

ZigBee 通信技术具有功耗低、数据传输可靠性高、网络容量大、时延小、兼容性、安全性以及实现成本低 7 大特点。ZigBee 网络拓扑结构可根据应用的需要组织成星形网络,也可以组织成点对点网络。在星形结构中,所有设备都与中心设备 PAN 网络协调器通信。典型星形网络拓扑结构如图 4.19 所示。

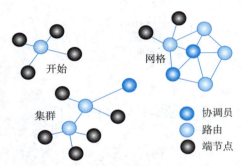

图 4.19 典型星形网络拓扑结构

与星形网络不同,点对点网络中,只要其中的设备彼此都在对方的无线辐射范围内,任何两个设备之间都可以直接通信。点对点网络中也需要网络协调器,负责实现管理链路状态信息、认证设备身份等功能。点对点网络模式可以支持 adhoc 网络,允许通过多跳路由的方式在网络中传输数据。不过一般认为自组织问题由网络层来解决,不在 IEEE 802.15.4 标准讨论范围内。点对点网络可以构造更复杂的网络结构,适合于设备分布范围广的应用。

(2) 无线局域网

利用无线局域网组建自动化工业网络,相比之下具有有线固定网络无法比拟的优势:①无线网络拓扑更适合工业网络应用;②无须布线,省去了施工的麻烦;③覆盖范围广。

无线局域网现主要应用在远程视频传输、门禁/考勤管理系统、安防管理系统、生产设备联网自动化、电信/光纤网络监控、医疗/实验仪器联网自动化、工业/流程联网控管等领域。

(3) 蓝牙通信技术

蓝牙是取代数据电缆的短距离无线通信技术,可以支持物体与物体之间的通信,工作频段是全球开放的 2.4 GHz 频段,可以同时进行数据和语音传输,传输速率可达到 10 Mbit/s,使在其范围内的各种信息化设备都能实现无缝资源共享。蓝牙技术的应用非常广泛而且极具潜力。它可以应用于无线设备、图像处理设备、安全产品、消费娱乐、汽车产品、家用电器、医疗健身、建筑、玩具等领域。

(4) 5G 技术

目前,工业互联网的网络化特征主要是:互联网使工厂机器、控制平台及制造业下游之间保持互联、互通、互动,并借助网络中的云计算、大数据资源,对整个产业制造环节进行分析、设计和动态调整等智能化控制,打造一个开放与智能的工业生态体系,最终达到使整个工业生产零库存、低能耗、个性化与大规模定制共存,以及可对工业系统进行远程维护和优化等目的。显然,此时的工业互联网利用网络化产生的功能,仍局限于工业制造自身领域。

 任务拓展

传输工业大数据——实现工业智能化转型的关键技术之一

传输工业大数据是实现工业智能化转型的关键技术之一。通过传输工业大数据,可以对工业生产过程进行实时监测和数据采集,及时获取生产环节的各项指标和参数。这些数据可用于分析和预测生产趋势、故障预警等,帮助企业及时调整生产计划和资源配置,提高生产效率,推动工业智能化转型升级。

在建设现代化产业体系中,传输工业大数据在国家发展战略中具有重要的科技创新引领作用,可以促进产业升级、推动创新驱动发展、优化资源配置和促进科技成果转化,为国家经济发展和社会进步提供有力支撑,实现高质量发展的目标。

作业:通过网络查询资料,掌握工业物联网的传输技术是如何实现的。

Task 13 Apprehend Transmission of Industrial Big Data

Learning Objective

①Master industrial fieldbus communication technology.
②Master industrial Ethernet communication technology.
③Master wireless network communication technology for industrial sites.

Suggested Hours

2 hours

Work Situations

In the Industrial Internet, the main role of the communication system is to transmit information securely and reliably to its destination. The heterogeneous nature of the Industrial Internet means that the communication methods and systems used within it are also heterogeneous and complex.

Knowledge Map

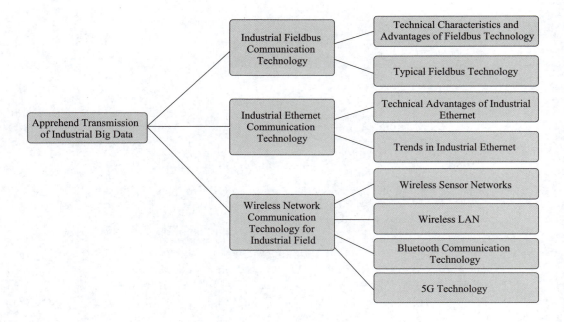

Project 4 Network Transmission of Industrial Internet

Relevant Knowledge

Industrial big data transmission technology involves the transmission of data between a data source and a data host. This transmission occurs over one or more data channels or links, which collectively adhere to a communication protocol. It is primarily a process of aggregating multiple data streams and transmitting them between a data source and a data host across one or more links, according to appropriate rules. Big data is of great value in both scientific and commercial applications. Traditional circuit switching is known for its stability but requires ample available bandwidth. In contrast, big data applications are less sensitive to latency but consume significant network resources. Therefore, ensuring real-time data transmission is a fundamental priority in the data transmission process.

1. Industrial Fieldbus Communication Technology

A fieldbus is generally defined as an open, digital, bidirectional, serial, multi-node communication bus for intelligent field devices and automation systems. It serves as the foundation of a factory's digital communication network, facilitating communication between the production process site and control equipment. Additionally, it establishes connections with higher control and management levels. It serves not only as a grassroots network but also as an open, new type of fully distributed control system. This integrated technology encompasses intelligent sensing, control, computers, digital communications, and other technologies as its primary components. It has attracted worldwide attention as a focal point in the development of automation technology. Moreover, it is poised to bring about profound changes in the structure of automation systems and equipment.

(1) Technical Characteristics and Advantages of Fieldbus Technology

The fieldbus control system possesses five key characteristics: interoperability and compatibility, intelligence and autonomy of field devices, system openness, a highly decentralized system structure, and adaptability to the field environment. It integrates automatic control equipment and systems into the realm of information networks at the site. This extension of application offers several advantages: reduced maintenance costs, decreased installation costs, minimized hardware quantities and investment, and enhanced user initiative in system integration, resulting in improved accuracy and reliability.

(2) Typical Fieldbus Technology

At present, there are over 40 types of fieldbuses in the international arena, but none can cover all application domains. Based on the amount of data they transmit, buses can be categorized into three types: sensorbuses, which transmit bits; device buses, which transmit bytes; and fieldbuses, which transmit data streams. Currently, the main field buses include Profibus, LonWorks, Foundation fieldbus, CAN bus, and others. The characteristics and applications of common fieldbus technologies are described in Table 4.1.

Table 4.1 Introduction to the Characteristics and Applications of Common Fieldbus Technologies

Bus Type	Technical characteristics	Main applications	prices	Supporting Companies
FF	Powerful, intrinsically safe, good real time, bus-powered; but complex protocols, few practical applications	Process control	More expensive	Honey、Rosemount、ABB、Foxboro、YOKOGAWA, etc.
WorldFIP	Strong anti interference ability, good realtime, good stability	Industrial process control	Average	Alstone
Profibus-PA	Intrinsically safe, bus powered, more practical applications; however, fewer transmission media are supported, and the transmission method is singular	Process automation	More expensive	Siemens
Profibus-DP/FMS	Higher speed and flexible configuration	Shop floor level communications、Industrial、Building automation	Average	Siemens
CAN	Adopt short frame, strong anti-interference ability, slow speed, protocol chip kernel monopolized by foreign manufacturers	Automotive testing、Control	Cheaper	Philips、Siemens、Honeywell, etc.
LonWorks	Support OSI seven-layer protocol, more practical applications, the development platform is perfect, the protocol chip kernnel monopoly by foreign manufacturers.	Building automation、Industry、Energy	Cheaper	Echelon

2. Industrial Ethernet Communication Technology

Due to the openness of the Ethernet technology standard, its widespread application, and the use of transparent and unified communication protocols, it has become the sole unified communication standard in the field of industrial control. Both Industrial Ethernet and Commercial Ethernet adhere to the OSI model. However, Industrial Ethernet addresses the specific demands of real-time communication and high reliability in industrial control by incorporating distinct functional modules in the link layer and network layer. It also incorporates electromagnetic compatibility design in the physical layer to address technical challenges related to real-time communication, network security, and resistance to strong electromagnetic interference.

(1) Technical Advantages of Industrial Ethernet

Industrial Ethernet technology has gained widespread popularity due to several advantages, including its low cost, stability, and reliability, as well as its high communication rates. Additionally, there is a rich array of hardware and software products available for Industrial

Ethernet, and it has a broad range of applications. Moreover, mature support technology is in place for this technology. In recent years, with the development of network technology, Ethernet has entered the control field, forming a new type of Ethernet control network technology. This development is mainly due to the trend towards distributed and intelligent control in industrial automation systems, where open and transparent communication protocols are an inevitable requirement.

When Ethernet technology is introduced into the field of industrial control, its technical advantages mainly include the following five points: the low cost of hardware and software; the ability to achieve seamless integration between the industrial control network and the enterprise information network, forming an all-encompassing network for enterprise-level management and control; it is an all-digital network that complies with network protocols, allowing equipment from different vendors to easily interoperate; its high communication rate; and its large potential for sustainable development.

(2) Trends in Industrial Ethernet

The sustainability and scalability of Industrial Ethernet within the field of industrial equipment are key focuses in the Industrial Internet. In the era of big data, the demand for cloud computing, distributed data storage, and processing make Internet access for the Industrial Internet an increasingly urgent need. Within the current industrial Ethernet framework, the second-generation Internet IPv4 technology used faces the challenge of limited network address resources. In this environment, IPv6 was developed. This solution addresses the issue of limited network address resources and paves the way for interconnection and interoperability among communication devices in the workshop. It also alleviates restrictions on the number of communications between the bottom workshop terminals—such as intelligent devices, personnel, and control systems—and the servers and control terminals in the cloud.

3. Wireless Network Communication Technology for Industrial Field

Wireless network technology finds application in industrial control, primarily for data acquisition and video monitoring. It facilitates communication between mobile devices and fixed networks, as well as between mobile devices themselves. This technology is known for its robustness, reliability, and safety. It is suitable for a variety of industrial environments and can ensure the reliability and security of the network even in extremely harsh conditions. Currently, the primary wireless communication technology protocols in industrial automation include several options. For short-range network usage in field equipment layers, the dominant protocol is IEEE 802.15.4. Meanwhile, for wireless LANs that require broader transmission coverage and handle larger amounts of information, the IEEE 802.11 series is preferred. Additionally, for short-range wireless communication requiring substantial data capacity, the Bluetooth standard is extensively utilized by the industry.

(1) Wireless Sensor Networks

ZigBee communication technology has seven main features: low power consumption, high reliability of data transmission, large network capacity, low latency, compatibility, security, and a low cost of implementation. The ZigBee network topology can be organized into a star network (e.g., Figure 4.19) or a point-to-point network, according to the needs of the application. In a star structure, all devices communicate with a central device, known as the PAN (Personal Area Network) coordinator.

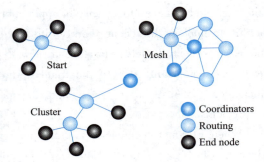

Figure 4.19　Typical Star Network Topology

Unlike a star network, in a point-to-point network, any two devices can communicate directly with each other as long as they are within each other's wireless radiation range. A network coordinator is also required in a point-to-point network and is responsible for implementing functions such as managing link status information and authenticating devices. The point-to-point network model can support ad hoc networks, allowing data to be transmitted across the network via multi-hop routing. However, it is generally accepted that self-organization is addressed by the network layer and is outside the scope of the IEEE 802.15.4 standard. Peer-to-peer networks allow for more complex network structures to be constructed and are suitable for applications where devices are widely distributed.

(2) Wireless LAN

The use of wireless LAN to set up automated industrial networks offers advantages that wired, fixed networks cannot match: the wireless network topology is more suitable for industrial network applications; there is no need for wiring, which eliminates the hassle of construction; and it provides wide coverage.

Wireless LAN is now predominantly used in several areas, including remote video transmission, access control and attendance management systems, security management systems, networking automation for production equipment, monitoring of telecommunication and fiber optic networks, networking automation for medical and laboratory equipment, and industrial or process networking control.

(3) Bluetooth Communication Technology

Bluetooth is a short-range wireless communication technology that can replace data cables and support object-to-object communication. It operates in the globally open 2.4 GHz band, which allows for simultaneous data and voice transmission at rates up to 10 Mbit/s. This makes it possible for all kinds of information technology devices within its range to share resources seamlessly. Bluetooth technology has a wide range of applications and great potential. It can be utilized in various fields, including wireless devices, image processing equipment, security products, consumer electronics, automotive products, home appliances, medical fitness, construction, toys, and more.

(4) 5G Technology

At present, the networked characteristics of the Industrial Internet are primarily as follows: The Internet enables interconnectedness, interoperability, and interaction among factory machines, control platforms, and downstream manufacturing processes. Leveraging cloud computing and big data resources, it facilitates intelligent control over the entire industrial manufacturing chain, including analysis, design, and dynamic adjustment. This approach fosters an open and intelligent industrial ecosystem, ultimately aiming for zero inventory, low energy consumption, and the coexistence of individualized and mass customization in industrial production. Additionally, it supports remote maintenance and optimization of industrial systems. It is evident that, at this time, the functions enabled by the networking of the Industrial Internet are still predominantly confined to the field of industrial manufacturing itself.

Mission Expansion

Transmission of Industrial Big Data—One of the Key Technologies for Realizing Industrial Intelligence Transformation

Transferring industrial big data is one of the key technologies for achieving industrial intelligence transformation. By transmitting industrial big data, real-time monitoring and data collection of industrial production processes can be carried out, and various indicators and parameters of the production process can be obtained in a timely manner. These data can be used to analyze and predict production trends, fault warnings, etc., helping enterprises adjust production plans and resource allocation in a timely manner, improve production efficiency, and promote industrial intelligence transformation and upgrading.

In the construction of a modern industrial system, the transmission of industrial big data plays an important role in leading scientific and technological innovation in the national development strategy. It can promote industrial upgrading, drive innovation driven development, optimize resource allocation, and promote the transformation of scientific and technological achievements, providing strong support for national economic development and social progress, and achieving the goal of high-quality development.

Assignment: Master how the transmission technology of industrial Internet of Things is implemented by searching for information through the internet.

项目 5

工业大数据集成与融合

任务 14 集成工业大数据

集成工业大数据

🌀 学习目标

①掌握工业大数据集成框架。
②掌握基于 CPS 的工业大数据集成。
③理解基于云平台的工业大数据集成。

🌀 建议学时

2 课时

🌀 工作情境

工业制造数据具有规模海量、多源异构、多时空尺度、多维度等特点,具备大数据特征。通过工业大数据建立生产过程和运行决策间的关系,能对制造运行状态进行统计和分析,有助于提升生产效率和产品质量、降低能耗、保障设备健康等。

知识导图

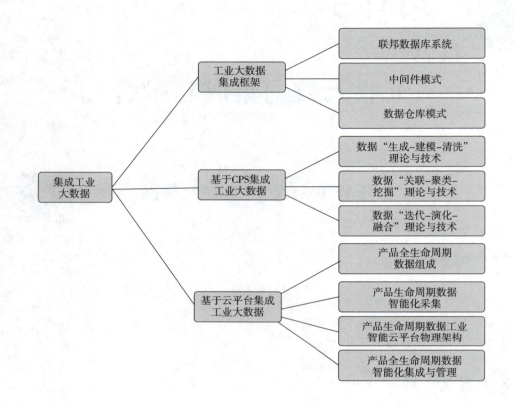

相关知识

数据集成是将不同来源、格式、特点及性质的数据在逻辑上或物理上有机地集中，从而为企业提供全面的数据共享。在企业数据集成领域，已经有很多成熟的框架可以利用。数据集成通常采用联邦式、基于中间件模型和数据仓库等方法来构造集成的系统，这些技术在不同的着重点和应用上解决数据共享和为企业提供决策支持。

1. 工业大数据集成框架

（1）联邦数据库系统

联邦数据库系统由半自治数据库系统构成，相互之间分享数据，联盟各数据源之间相互提供访问接口。联邦数据库系统可以是集中数据库系统或分布式数据库系统及其他联邦式系统。这种模型又分为紧耦合和松耦合两种情况，紧耦合提供统一的访问模式，一般是静态的，在增加数据源上比较困难；而松耦合则不提供统一的接口，但可以通过统一的语言访问数据源，其中的核心是必须解决所有数据源语义上的问题。

（2）中间件模式

通过统一的全局数据模型来访问异构的数据库、遗留系统、Web 资源等。这是比较流行的数据集成方法，它通过在中间层提供一个统一的数据逻辑视图来隐藏底层的数据细节，使用户可以把集成数据源作为一个统一的整体。

（3）数据仓库模式

数据仓库是在企业管理和决策中面向主题的、集成的、与时间相关的和不可修改的数据集合。其中，数据被归类为广义的、功能上独立的、没有重叠的主题。

上述几种方法在一定程度上解决了应用之间的数据共享和互通的问题，但也存在以下异同：联邦数据库系统主要面向多个数据库系统的集成，其中数据源有可能要映射到每一个数据模式，当集成的系统很大时，对实际开发将带来巨大的困难。数据仓库技术则在另外一个层面上表达数据之间的共享，它主要是为了针对企业某个应用领域提出的一种数据集成方法，即面向主题并为企业提供数据挖掘和决策支持的系统。

2. 基于 CPS 集成工业大数据

信息物理系统（Cyber-Physical Systems，CPS）的概念最早在 2006 年由美国自然基金委提出。根据《中国信息物理系统白皮书（2017）》，CPS 通过集成先进的感知、计算、通信、控制等信息技术和自动控制技术，构建了物理空间与信息空间中人、机、物、环境、信息等要素相互映射、适时交互、高效协同的复杂系统，实现系统内资源配置和运行的按需响应、快速迭代、动态优化。它通过人机交互接口实现和物理进程的交互，使用网络化空间以远程的、可靠的、实时的、安全的、协作的方式操控一个物理实体。国际上较为认可的 CPS 架构是一个 5C 的结构，如图 5.1 所示。

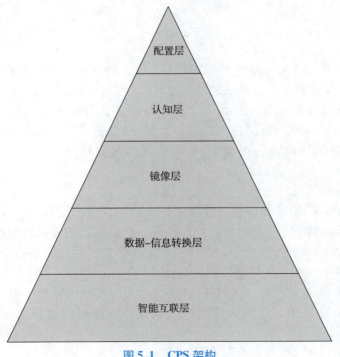

图 5.1　CPS 架构

基于 CPS 的制造集成系统是指借助先进的传感、通信、计算和控制技术实现生产过程中信息单元和物理实体在网络环境下的高度集成和交互，实时传输动态网络环境下海量感知数据至信息层，集成规约多源多模态异构数据，并精准控制混杂动态环境下车间异构制造资源的行为协同，从而实现车间内"人-机-物-环境"全要素的智能感知互联、高效数据传输与集成、实时交互与控制、智能协作与共融，如图 5.2 所示。最终达到自主协调、效率提升、性能优化和安全保障的智能制造目标。

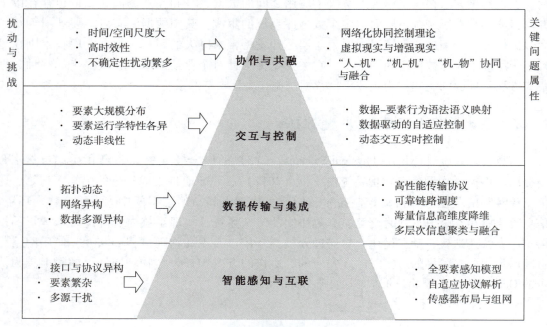

图 5.2　基于 CPS 的制造集成系统

根据《中国信息物理系统白皮书（2017）》，基于 CPS 的制造集成系统包含三个层次的内容，①单元级；②系统级；③系统之系统级（SoS 级），如图 5.3 所示。

基于 CPS 的工业大数据集成是指基于一致性原理，对覆盖全要素、全流程、全业务的相关数据进行生成—建模—清洗—关联—聚类—挖掘—迭代—演化—融合等操作，有效真实刻画和反映运行状态、要素行为等各类动态演化过程、演化规律、统计学特性等。

（1）数据"生成-建模-清洗"理论与技术

包括多源/多维/异构/多模态复杂数据分类与建模，非完备信息系统的空值属性估算与特征约简技术，数据溯源方法和源数据特征提取，数据级同质多源数据准确性/完整性/一致性理论与验证。

（2）数据"关联-聚类-挖掘"理论与技术

包括多学科/多物理量/多尺度信息融合的数据实时生成机制产生机理，数据与制造运行映射关系，特征级异构对象行为性能模式识别，数据模态更新与模态衍生动态增长规则。

（3）数据"迭代-演化-融合"理论与技术

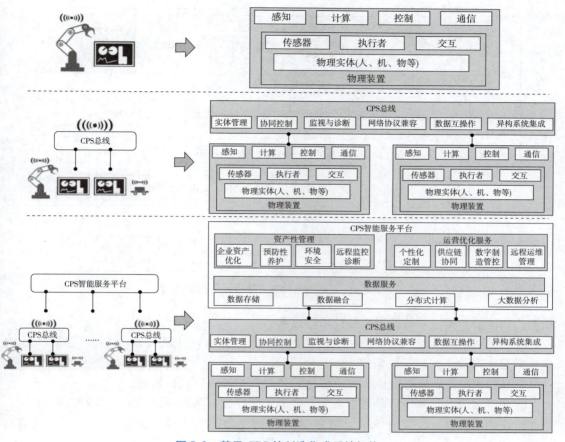

图 5.3　基于 CPS 的制造集成系统机构

包括实时数据及历史数据的关联、比对和整合方法，基于数据与物理对象映射关系的交互融合与优化，针对相似或不同特征模式多源数据的相关性动态演化，决策级全要素数据演化规律与统计特性分析。

3. 基于云平台集成工业大数据

面向制造的工业智能云平台由三部分组成，即由信息技术企业主导建设的基础架构层，由工业企业主导建设的服务层，由工业企业、众多开发者与用户等多主体参与应用开发的应用层，如图 5.4 所示。

（1）产品全生命周期数据组成

①在产品概念阶段，利用用户需求、市场信息、投资规划等数据形成新的产品概念或产品改进。

②在产品设计阶段，产品设计团队利用产品功能和外观描述数据、产品配置数据、设计参数和测试数据、相似产品的历史数据等进行产品设计。

③在原材料采购阶段，通过制造商数据，如类型、质量、原材料性能等，以及供应商

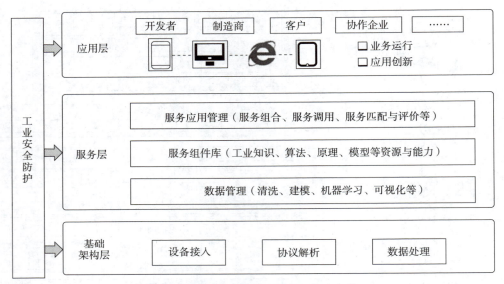

图5.4 面向制造的工业智能云平台架构

数据，如价格、距离等数据形成最佳采购方案。

④在制造阶段，对产品制造工艺的属性、性能、参数和生产要素（如人、机、物、环境）数据实时收集并记录以监控生产过程。

⑤在物流阶段，库存数据、订单数据、位置数据等用以优化物流。

⑥在售卖阶段，基于订单数据，客户数据，库存数据和供应商的数据等及时售出产品，且此阶段的用户偏好、偏好人群、订单分布等信息数据可用于产品设计、生产、物流等阶段。

⑦在使用阶段，将产品状态数据、运行环境数据、用户行为数据等用于产品维修和产品设计改进。

⑧在售后服务阶段，基于失败数据和案例、维修数据、元件质量和状态等数据，预测产品寿命和产品失效时间。

⑨在回收/废物处理阶段，基于产品状态数据和历史维修数据，分析和决策何时、何地、如何来回收产品或废物处理。

（2）产品生命周期数据智能化采集

为了保证数据的有效性，可以采用多种动、静态数据采集并行的方式，从而实现产品生命周期数据的多角度采集，为产品全生命周期的数据处理分析提供数据支撑。

①基于物联网的动态实时数据采集；

②基于BOM的评估系统与企业信息系统集成的数据采集；

③基于数据库的静态数据采集。

（3）产品生命周期数据工业智能云平台物理架构

基于物联网、云计算技术，借鉴工业智能云平台，构建产品全生命周期数据工业智能云平台物理架构，如图5.5所示。

（4）产品全生命周期数据智能化集成与管理

项目 5　工业大数据集成与融合

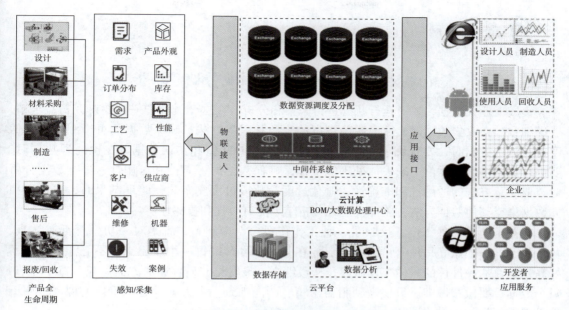

图 5.5　产品全生命周期数据工业智能云平台物理架构

针对产品全生命周期数据的集成问题，分析并设计基于工业云平台数据集成与管理架构，如图 5.6 所示。

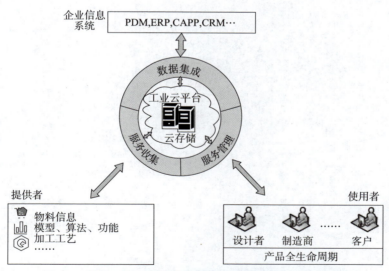

图 5.6　基于工业云平台的产品全生命周期数据集成与管理

249

 **任务拓展**

精益求精严谨细致——工业大数据的采集和分析

集成工业大数据,要对运行状态进行采集和分析,在这个过程中一定要讲究精益求精、严谨细致。在收集数据时,需要明确数据的来源和采集方法,确保数据的可追溯性和可信度;在清洗数据时,要仔细检查数据的质量,剔除异常值和错误数据。在预处理数据时,要进行数据平滑、插值、缺失值处理等操作,确保数据的可靠性和可用性;进行数据分析时,要注意方法的适用性和准确性,避免过度简化或过度复杂化;验证结果时,要使用独立数据集或其他验证方法,验证模型或分析结果的有效性和鲁棒性。

精益求精是一种态度,反映了一种工作作风;严谨细致,就是对一切事情都有认真、负责的态度。把做好每件事情的着力点放在每一个环节、每一个步骤上,不心浮气躁,不好高骛远,从一件件的具体工作做起,从最细小、最常见、最普通的方面做起,每个环节、每个数据都要做精做细。只要做到精益求精、严谨细致,今天就没有学不好的课程,明天就没有做不好的工作。

作业:结合工业大数据的特点,谈谈大数据分析的注意事项。

Project 5

Integration and Fusion of Industrial Big Data

Task 14   Integration of Industrial Big Data

Learning Objective

①Master industrial big data integration framework.
②Master industrial big data integration based on CPS.
③Understand industrial big data integration based on cloud platforms.

Suggested Hours

2 hours

Work Situations

Industrial manufacturing data is characterized by its massive scale, multi-source heterogeneity, multi-temporal and spatial scales, and multi-dimensionality, among other big data characteristics. Establishing relationships between the production process and operational decisions through industrial big data allows for the statistical analysis and evaluation of manufacturing operational status. This, in turn, helps to improve production efficiency and product quality, reduce energy consumption, and ensure the health and longevity of equipment.

Knowledge Map

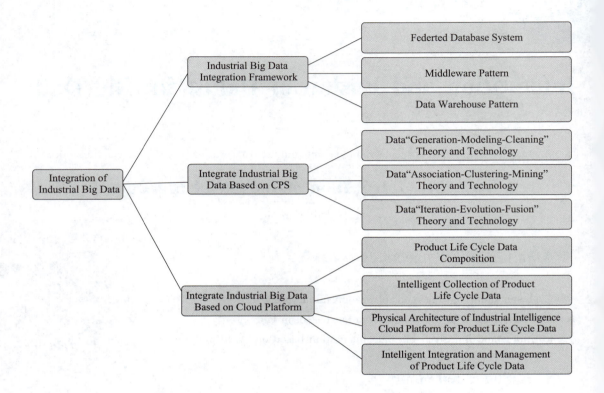

Relevant Knowledge

Data integration involves the logical or physical consolidation of data from different sources, formats, characteristics, and properties to provide comprehensive data sharing within an enterprise. In the field of enterprise data integration, there are already many mature frameworks that can be utilized. Approaches such as federated, middleware-based models, and data warehouses are commonly employed to structure integrated systems. These technologies address data sharing and decision support for the enterprise, each with a different focus and application.

1. Industrial Big Data Integration Framework

(1) Federated Database System

The Federated Database System (FDBS) is composed of semi-autonomous database systems that share data with each other and provide access interfaces to one another's data sources within the federation. The FDBS can be a centralized database system or a distributed database system, as well as other federated systems. This model is categorized into two types: tight coupling and loose coupling. Tight coupling offers a unified access mode, which is generally static and makes adding data sources difficult. In contrast, loose coupling does not offer a unified interface but can access data sources through a common language, with the core challenge being the need to address the semantic interoperability of all data sources.

(2) Middleware Pattern

Access to heterogeneous databases, legacy systems, web resources, etc., is facilitated through a unified global data model. This approach is more popular for data integration as it conceals the underlying data details by providing a unified logical view of the data at the middleware layer. It enables users to perceive the integrated data sources as a cohesive whole.

(3) Data Warehouse Pattern

A data warehouse is a subject-oriented, integrated, time-variant, and non-volatile collection of data used in enterprise management and decision-making. Within it, data are organized into broad, functionally independent, non-overlapping themes.

The aforementioned approaches have addressed the issues of data sharing and interoperability between applications to a certain extent. However, they also share the following similarities and differences: The Federated Database System is primarily aimed at integrating multiple database systems, where the data source may need to align with each data model. When the integrated system is extensive, it can pose significant challenges to actual development. Data warehouse technology represents another level of data sharing and is mainly a data integration method designed for specific application domains within an enterprise, that is, a system that is subject-oriented and provides data mining and decision support for the enterprise.

2. Integrate Industrial Big Data Based on CPS

The Concept of Cyber-Physical Systems (CPS) was first proposed by the National Natural Science Foundation of China in 2006. According to the "China Cyber-Physical System White Paper (2017)", CPS constructs a complex system by integrating advanced sensing, computing, communication, control, and other information technologies with automatic control technologies. This system achieves on-demand response, rapid iteration, and dynamic optimization of resource allocation and operations within the system. It does this by mapping the elements of people, machines, objects, environments, and information across physical and information spaces to each other, enabling them to interact at the right time and collaborate in a highly efficient manner. CPS realizes interaction with physical processes through human-computer interaction interfaces and uses networked space to manipulate physical entities in a remote, reliable, real-time, safe, and collaborative manner. The more internationally recognized CPS architecture follows a 5C structure, as depicted in Figure 5.1.

A manufacturing integrated system based on CPS utilizes advanced sensing, communication, computing, and control technologies to achieve a high degree of integration and interaction between information units and physical entities in the production process within a network environment. This

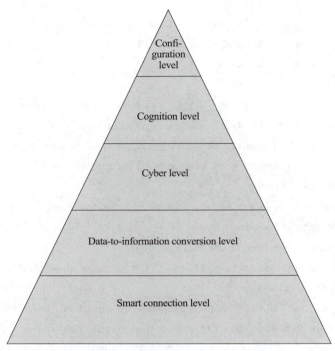

Figure 5.1 CPS architecture

system integrates multi-source, multi-modal heterogeneous data and accurately controls the behavioral synergy of heterogeneous manufacturing resources in the workshop under mixed dynamic conditions. It does this by transmitting massive sensory data in real-time to the information layer in dynamic network environments. Thus, it realizes the intelligent perception, interconnection, efficient data transmission and integration, real-time interaction and control, and intelligent collaboration and integration of all elements of 'human-machine-object-environment' in the workshop, as depicted in Figure 5.2. Ultimately, it aims to achieve the intelligent manufacturing goals of autonomous coordination, efficiency improvement, performance optimization, and safety assurance.

According to the China Cyber-Physical System White Paper (2017), the CPS-based manufacturing integrated system encompasses three levels of content, as depicted in Figure 5.3: ①unit level; ②system level; ③system of systems (SoS) level.

Industrial big data integration based on CPS involves operations such as generation, modeling, cleaning, association, clustering, mining, iteration, evolution, and fusion of relevant data that covers all elements, processes, and businesses, based on the principle of consistency. It effectively and accurately depicts and reflects various dynamic evolution processes, evolution rules, statistical characteristics, and such as operating status and element behavior.

(1) Data "Generation-Modeling-Cleaning" Theory and Technology

It includes the classification and modeling of multi-source, multi-dimensional, heterogeneous, and multi-modal complex data, as well as the estimation of null attributes and technology for feature

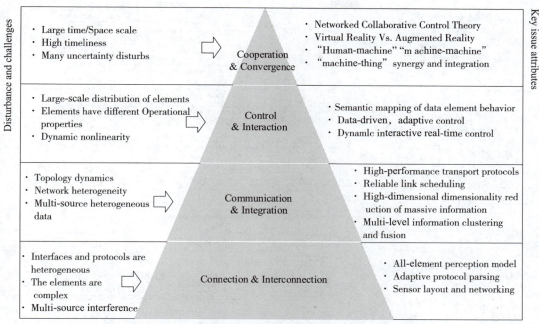

Figure 5.2 Manufacturing Integrated System Based on CPS

reduction in incomplete information systems. It also encompasses methods for data traceability and the extraction of features from source data, along with theories and verification for data-level homogeneity, multi-source data accuracy, integrity, and consistency.

(2) Data "Association-Clustering-Mining" Theory and Technology

It includes the real-time data generation mechanism for the fusion of multi-disciplinary, multi-physical quantity, and multi-scale information. This involves the mapping relationship between data and manufacturing operations, the identification of feature-level heterogeneous object behavior and performance patterns, and the update and derivation of dynamic growth rules for data modalities.

(3) Data "Iteration-Evolution-Fusion" Theory and Technology

It includes methods for the correlation, comparison, and integration of real-time and historical data, interactive fusion and optimization based on the mapping relationship between data and physical objects. It also involves the correlation and dynamic evolution of multi-source data across similar or different feature modalities, and comprehensive data evolution and statistical characterization analysis at the decision-making level.

3. Integrate Industrial Big Data Based on Cloud Platform

The manufacturing-oriented industrial intelligent cloud platform consists of three parts: the infrastructure layer, led by information technology enterprises; the service layer, led by industrial enterprises; and the application development layer, which is contributed to by multiple entities such as industrial companies, developers, and users, as depicted in Figure 5.4.

(1) Product Life Cycle Data Composition

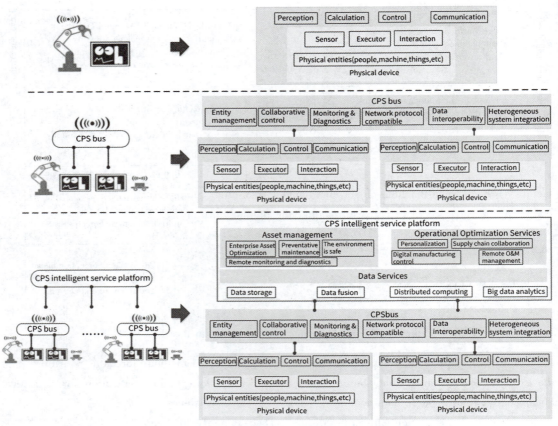

Figure 5.3　Manufacturing Integrated System Organization Based on CPS

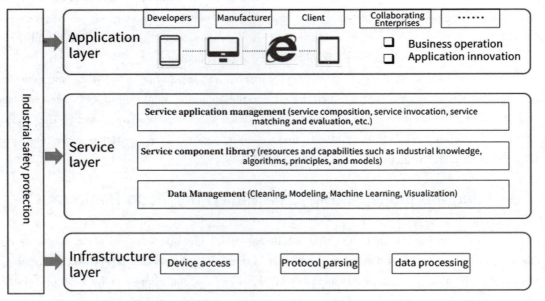

Figure 5.4　Manufacturing-oriented Industrial Intelligent Cloud Platform Architecture

①In the product concept stage, data such as user needs, market information, and investment planning are used to develop new product concepts or product improvements.

②In the product design stage, the product design team uses data on product function and appearance descriptions, product configuration, design parameters, and test data, as well as historical data from similar products, to design the product.

③In the raw material procurement phase, the optimal procurement plan is formulated by considering manufacturer data, such as material type and quality, and supplier data, such as price and distance.

④During the manufacturing phase, attributes, performance, parameters, and production factors (e.g., man-machine-object-environment) of the product manufacturing process are collected and recorded in real-time to monitor the production process.

⑤In the logistics stage, inventory data, order data, and location data are utilized to optimize logistics operations.

⑥In the sales stage, products are sold promptly based on order data, customer data, inventory data, and supplier data. Additionally, information such as user preferences, preference groups, and order distribution can be leveraged in product design, production, and logistics.

⑦During the use phase, data on product status, operating environment, and user behavior are collected for product maintenance and to inform design improvements.

⑧In the after-sales service stage, predictions about product lifespan and potential failures can be made using failure data, case histories, maintenance records, and component quality and status data.

⑨In the recycling/waste disposal stage, decisions on when, where, and how to recycle products or perform waste disposal are made based on product status data and historical maintenance data.

(2) Intelligent Collection of Product Life Cycle Data

To ensure data validity, a combination of dynamic and static data collection methods can be employed for multi-angle data acquisition throughout the product life cycle, providing support for data processing and analysis.

①Dynamic, real-time data collection based on the Internet of Things (IoT);

②Data collection through the integration of the Bill of Materials (BOM) evaluation system and the enterprise information system;

③Static data collection based on databases.

(3) Physical Architecture of Industrial Intelligence Cloud Platform for Product Life Cycle Data

Leveraging the Internet of Things and cloud computing technologies, and utilizing the industrial intelligent cloud platform as a reference, the physical architecture for the product life cycle data industrial intelligent cloud platform is constructed, as depicted in Figure 5.5.

(4) Intelligent Integration and Management of Product Life Cycle Data

Addressing the integration challenges of product full life cycle data, the data integration and management architecture is analyzed and designed based on the industrial cloud platform, as depicted in Figure 5.6.

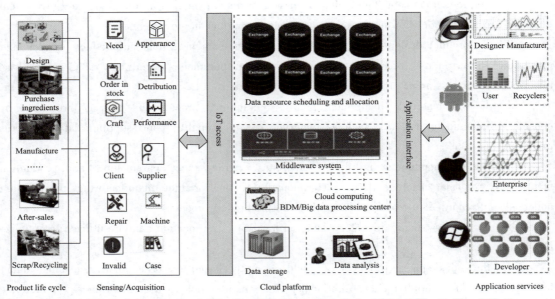

Figure 5.5 Physical Architecture of Product Life Cycle Data Industrial Intelligent Cloud Platform

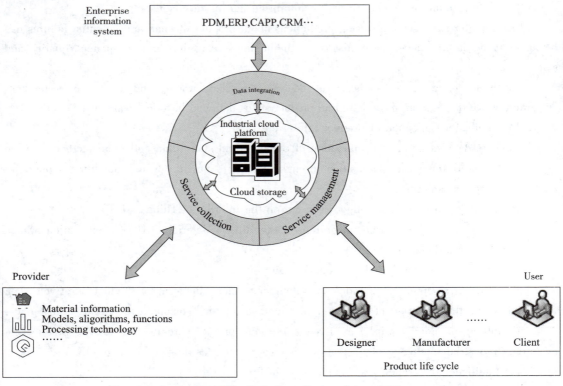

Figure 5.6 Product Life Cycle Data Integration and Management Based on Industrial Cloud Platform

Project 5 Integration and Fusion of Industrial Big Data

 **Mission Expansion**

Strive for Excellence, be Rigorous and Meticulous—Collection and Analysis of Industrial Big Data

Integrating industrial big data requires collection and analysis of operating status. In this process, we must pay attention to excellence, rigor and meticulousness. When collecting data, we need to clarify the source and collection method of the data to ensure the traceability and credibility of the data; when cleaning the data, we must carefully check the quality of the data and remove outliers and erroneous data. When preprocessing data, we need to perform data smoothing, interpolation, missing value processing and other operations to ensure the reliability and availability of the data; when performing data analysis, we must pay attention to the applicability and accuracy of the method to avoid oversimplification or over complication; when verifying the results, we must use independent data sets or other verification methods to verify the validity and robustness of the model or analysis results.

Striving for excellence is an attitude that reflects a work style; being rigorous and meticulous means having a serious and responsible attitude towards everything. Focus on every link and every step to do everything well. Don't be impatient or aim too high. Start with specific work, from the smallest, most common and most ordinary aspects. Every link and every data should be refined and detailed. As long as you strive for excellence, rigor and meticulousness, there will be no bad courses today and no bad work tomorrow.

Assignment: Combined with the characteristics of industrial big data, talk about the precautions for big data analysis.

任务 15　融合工业大数据

融合工业大数据

学习目标

①理解基于服务的工业大数据融合技术。
②理解基于数字孪生的工业大数据融合技术。

建议学时

2 课时

工作情境

制造业全球化、产品个性化、绿色低碳制造等对制造业企业构成了巨大挑战。在这种背景下，制造企业有效利用全球制造资源并与业务合作伙伴进行有效协作变得越来越重要。这需要建立协作和灵活的制造模式，以促进内部和外部制造资源的有效整合、无缝合作以及不同企业之间的资源共享。

知识导图

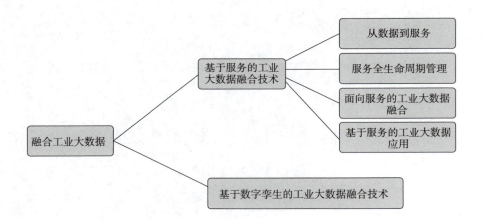

相关知识

1. 基于服务的工业大数据融合技术

在面向服务的智能制造中,产品生命周期中的所有制造资源和能力都被虚拟化,然后封装为服务,用户可以根据他们的需求访问这些服务。考虑产品全生命周期中各个阶段的不同应用,可以将制造服务大致分为两类:①面向过程和操作的生产相关的服务;②面向市场和消费的产品相关的服务,如图 5.7 所示。

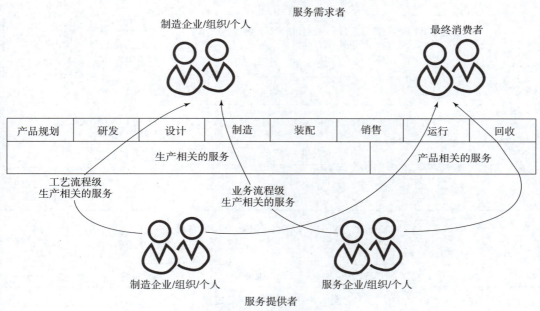

图 5.7 制造服务分类

(1) 从数据到服务

如图 5.8 所示,制造服务封装是从制造现场的"人-机-物-环境"采集它们的状态及参数信息,将这些多源异构的数据进行归一化处理,形成统一的数据描述,并采用统一的通信接口和协议进行传输,从而为"人-机-物-环境"各种对象的服务化封装和智能监测提供数据基础。

(2) 服务全生命周期管理

服务的流通、交易和共享依赖于对服务的高效管理。参照产品生命周期管理的划分,服务全生命周期如图 5.9 所示,包括制造服务的生命周期开始,生命中期和生命周期结束。因此服务全生命周期管理可以分为:①服务生成阶段;②服务预申请阶段;③服务应用阶段;④服务应用后阶段。

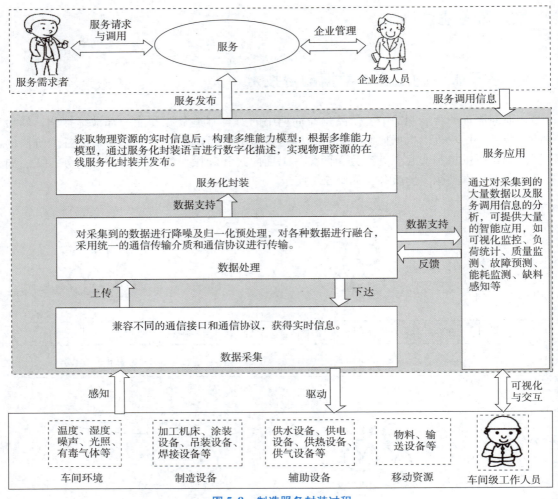

图 5.8 制造服务封装过程

(3) 面向服务的工业大数据融合

如图 5.10 所示，面向服务的工业大数据融合分为：

① 车间内数据融合与集成：可以实现终端设备与企业信息管理系统之间的完整连接，以实现车间内制造执行的自动控制。

② 企业内数据融合与集成：促进生产相关数据、产品相关数据和其他业务管理数据的整合，以及车间与其他企业信息子系统中数据的融合与集成。

③ 企业间的数据融合与集成：主要针对大量不同企业间在泛在服务管理和应用过程中的数据集成、存储、检索、分析、使用、数据安全等问题。

(4) 基于服务的工业大数据应用

通过协调相关的制造设施、资源和活动，制造活动将原材料投入转化为成品产出和增值服务。在制造过程中可以实施的一些大数据应用包括：① 智能设计；② 物料配给和跟踪；③ 制造过程控制；④ 智能设备维护等。

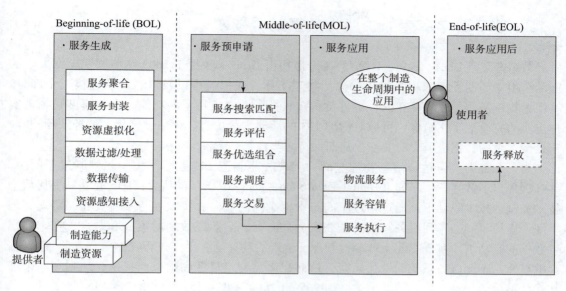

图 5.9 服务全生命周期

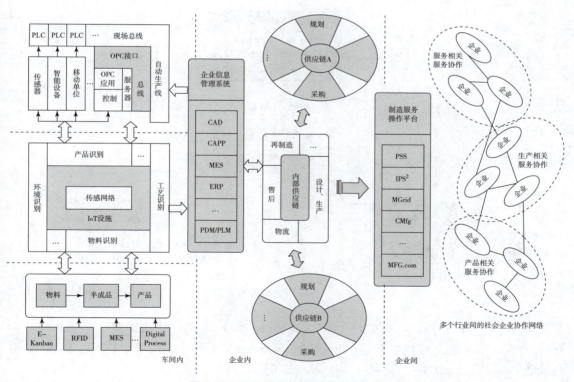

图 5.10 面向服务的工业大数据融合

2. 基于数字孪生的工业大数据融合技术

数字孪生（Digital Twin，DT）的概念最初由 Grieves 教授于 2003 在美国密歇根大学的产品全生命周期管理课程上提出，包括物理实体、虚拟模型以及二者间的连接三个部分。其中，物理实体是客观存在的，主要负责接收指令并完成特定的功能。虚拟模型是物理实体忠实的完全数字化镜像，可以对物理实体的活动进行仿真、评估、优化、调控及预测等。连接使二者的数据进行实时交互，从而保持同步性与一致性。

为了无缝集成与融合信息物理空间，实现智能制造，将数字孪生引入到制造车间中，并首次提出了数字孪生车间（Digital Twin Shop – floor，DTS）的概念：DTS 是在新一代信息技术和制造技术驱动下，通过物理车间与虚拟车间的双向真实映射与实时交互，实现物理车间、虚拟车间、车间服务系统的全要素、全流程、全业务数据的集成和融合，在车间孪生数据的驱动下，实现车间生产要素管理、生产活动计划、生产过程控制等，在物理车间、虚拟车间、车间服务系统间迭代运行，从而在满足特定目标和约束前提下，达到车间生产和管控最优的一种车间运行新模式。如图 5.11 所示是数字孪生车间概念模型。

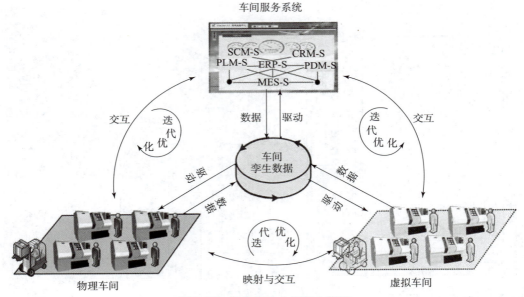

图 5.11 数字孪生车间概念模型

数字孪生车间包括：物理车间（Physical Shop – floor，PS）、虚拟车间（Virtual Shop – floor，VS）、车间服务系统（Shop – floor Service System，SSS）、车间孪生数据（Shop – floor Digital Twin Data，SDTD）、连接（Connection，CN）。

PS 是车间客观存在的生产设备、人员、产品、物料等实体的集合，主要负责接收 SSS 下达的生产任务，并严格按照 VS 仿真优化后的预定义生产指令，执行生产活动并完成生产任务。PS 的设备、人员、产品、物料等生产要素的实时状态数据可通过各类传感器进行有效采集。由于这些数据来自不同数据源，存在数据结构不同、接口不同、语义各异等问题，因此，为了实现对多源异构数据的统一接入，需要一套标准的接口与协议转换装置。

VS 是 PS 的忠实完全数字化镜像，从几何、物理、行为、规则多个层面对 PS 进行描述与刻画，主要负责对 PS 的生产资源与生产活动进行仿真、评估及优化，并对实际生产过程进行实时监测、预测与调控等。VS 本质上是由多个几何、物理、行为及规则模型构成的模型集合，能够对 PS 进行全面的多维度描述与刻画。根据数字孪生三层结构，VS 中包括人员、设备、工具等单个生产要素的单元级模型，由多个生产要素单元级模型构成的系统级产线模型，以及包括多个系统级产线模型及模型间交互与耦合关系的复杂系统级车间模型。

SDTD 是 PS、VS、SSS 相关数据、领域知识以及通过数据融合产生的衍生数据的集合，是 PS、VS、SSS 运行交互与迭代优化的驱动。融合数据是 SDTD 的重要组成部分，是通过特定的规则将来自物理和信息空间的数据聚合在一起得到的。其中，物理空间的数据主要指 PS 相关数据，这些数据是物理实体产生的真实数据；信息空间的数据主要指 VS 相关数据和 SSS 相关数据，这些数据不是从物理空间直接采集得到的，而是在物理数据的基础上，利用信息空间模型仿真、算法推演、系统衍生等过程得到的，是对物理数据的补充。

SSS 是数据驱动的各类服务功能的集合或总称，它将 DTS 运行过程中所需数据、模型、算法、仿真、结果进行服务化封装，形成支持 DTS 管控与优化的功能性与业务性服务。SSS 的运行过程包括子服务封装、需求解析、服务组合及服务应用。

CN 实现 DTS 各部分的互联互通，包括 PS 和 SDTD 的连接（CN_PD）、PS 和 VS 的连接（CN_PV）、PS 和 SSS 的连接（CN_PS）、VS 和 SDTD 的连接（CN_VD）、VS 和 SSS 的连接（CN_VS）、SSS 和 SDTD 的连接（CN_SD）。

如图 5.12 所示，为实现对车间数据的集成与融合，需要对 PS、VS 及 SSS 中的数据进行生成、建模、清洗、关联、聚类、挖掘、迭代、演化、融合等一系列操作。

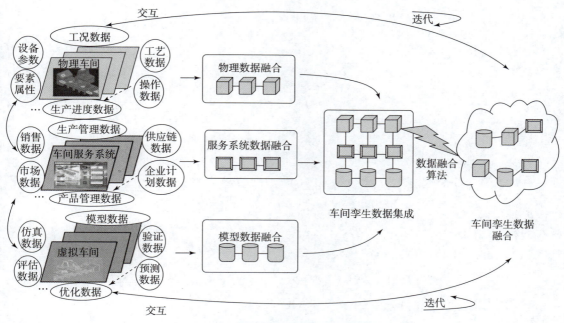

图 5.12　基于数字孪生的工业大数据融合

任务拓展

金山银山不如绿水青山——工业发展的同时也要兼顾环境保护

在工业互联网建设的工业领域需要注意生态文明建设。生态文明是人类文明发展的一个新的阶段，即工业文明之后的文明形态，是实现人与自然和谐发展的新要求。从历史来看，生态兴则文明兴，生态衰则文明衰。

保护生态环境就是保护生产力，改善生态环境就是发展生产力。对人类来说，金山银山固然重要，但是绿水青山才是我们幸福生活的重要内容，是金钱代替不了的。你挣到了钱，但是空气、饮用水都不合格，哪有什么幸福可言？

作业：通过网络查询相关资料，了解已经建设工业互联网的领域的生态文明建设情况。

Task 15 Fusion of Industrial Big Data

 Learning Objective

①Understand service – based industrial big data fusion technology.
②Understand industrial big data fusion technology based on digital twins.

 Suggested Hours

2 hours

 Work Situations

Manufacturing globalization, product personalization, and green, low-carbon manufacturing have posed significant challenges to manufacturing companies. Against this backdrop, it has become increasingly important for manufacturing enterprises to effectively utilize global manufacturing resources and to collaborate effectively with business partners. This necessitates the establishment of a collaborative and flexible manufacturing model that facilitates the effective integration of internal and external manufacturing resources, seamless cooperation, and resource sharing among different enterprises.

 knowledge map

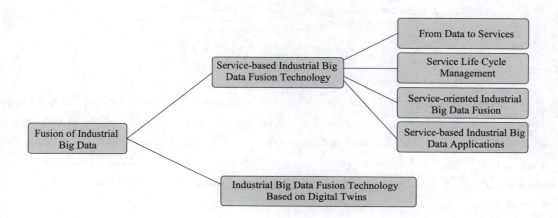

Relevant Knowledge

1. Service-based Industrial Big Data Fusion Technology

In service-oriented smart manufacturing, all manufacturing resources and capabilities throughout the product life cycle are virtualized and then encapsulated as services. Users can access these resource services based on their needs. Taking into account the different applications at each stage of the product life cycle, manufacturing services can be broadly categorized into two types: ①Production-related services that are oriented toward processes and operations; ②Product-related services that are oriented toward the market and consumption, as depicted in Figure 5.7.

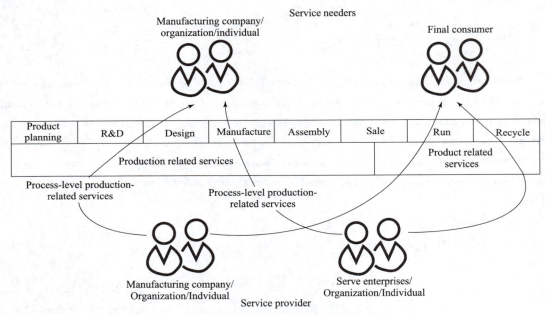

Figure 5.7　Manufacturing Service Classification

(1) From Data to Services

As depicted in Figure 5.8, manufacturing service encapsulation involves collecting status and parameter information from the "man-machine-object-environment" elements of the manufacturing site. It normalizes these multi-source heterogeneous data to form a unified data description. The encapsulation process utilizes unified communication interfaces and protocols for transmission. This approach provides a data foundation for service-oriented encapsulation and intelligent monitoring of various "human-machine-object-environment" entities.

(2) Service Life Cycle Management

The circulation, transaction, and sharing of services rely on efficient service management.

Project 5 Integration and Fusion of Industrial Big Data

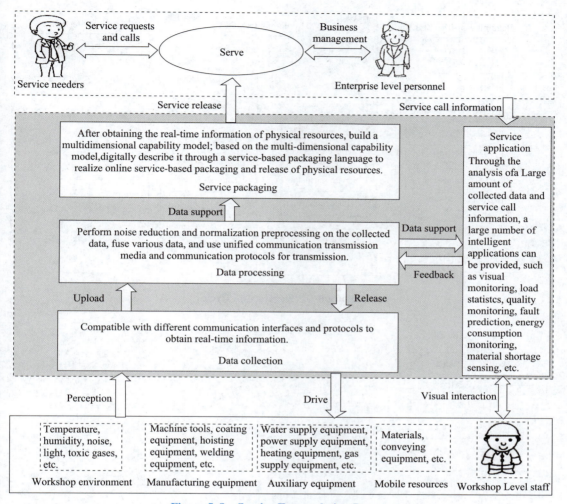

Figure 5.8 Service Encapsulation Process

Referring to the division of product life cycle management, the service life cycle encompassed by service life cycle management is depicted in Figure 5.9. This includes the beginning, middle, and end stages of the manufacturing services life cycle. Consequently, service life cycle management can be divided into: ①the service generation stage; ②the service pre-application stage; ③the service application stage; ④the service post-application stage.

(3) Service-oriented Industrial Big Data Fusion

As depicted in Figure 5.10, service-oriented industrial big data fusion is categorized into:

①Data fusion and integration within the workshop: The complete connection between terminal equipment and the enterprise information management system can be realized, enabling the automatic control of manufacturing execution within the workshop.

②Data fusion and integration within the enterprise: This promotes the integration of production-related data, product-related data, and other business management data. It also

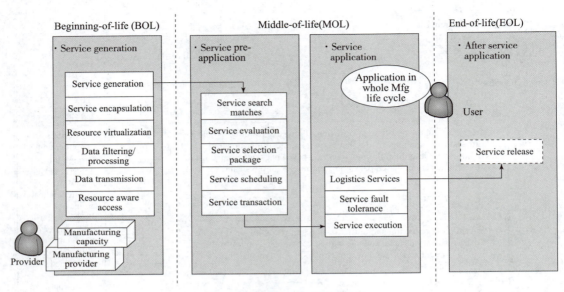

Figure 5.9　Service Life Cycle

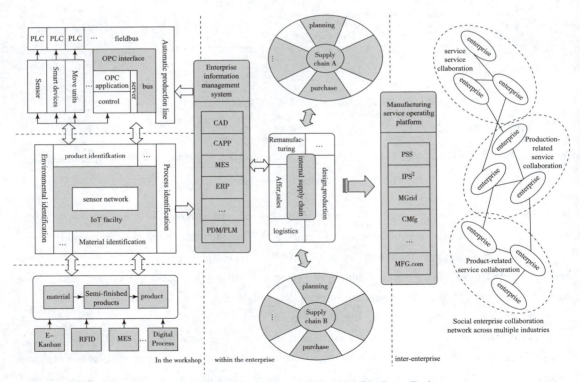

Figure 5.10　Service-Oriented Industrial Big Data Fusion

facilitates the fusion and integration of data from the workshop and other enterprise information subsystems.

③Data fusion and integration between enterprises: This primarily focuses on issues such as data integration, storage, retrieval, analysis, utilization, and data security during the process of ubiquitous service management and application among a multitude of different enterprises.

(4) Service-based Industrial Big Data Applications

Manufacturing activities transform raw material inputs into finished product outputs and value-added services by coordinating the related manufacturing facilities, resources, and activities. Some big data applications that can be implemented in the manufacturing process include: ①intelligent design; ② material distribution and tracking; ③ manufacturing process control; ④ intelligent equipment maintenance, among others.

2. Industrial Big Data Fusion Technology Based on Digital Twins

The concept of the digital twin was first proposed by Professor Grieves in the product life cycle management course at the University of Michigan in 2003 and consists of three parts: the physical entity, the virtual model, and the connection between the two. The physical entity exists objectively and is primarily responsible for receiving instructions and performing specific functions. The virtual model is a faithful and complete digital replica of the physical entity, capable of simulating, evaluating, optimizing, controlling, and predicting the activities of the physical entity.

The connection facilitates real-time interaction of data between the two, ensuring synchronization and consistency.

To seamlessly integrate and converge the information-physical space and achieve intelligent manufacturing, digital twins are introduced into the manufacturing workshop. The concept of the digital twin workshop (DTS) is introduced: DTS, which is powered by the new generation of information and manufacturing technologies, aims to integrate and converge all elements, processes, and business data of physical workshops, virtual workshops, and workshop service systems through bidirectional real mapping and real-time interaction between physical and virtual workshops. Driven by workshop twin data, DTS executes and iteratively operates workshop production factor management, production activity planning, production process control, and so on, within physical workshops, virtual workshops, and workshop service systems. DTS represents a novel workshop operation model that can achieve optimal workshop production and control while adhering to specific goals and constraints, as depicted in Figure 5.11.

The digital twin workshops comprise the following elements: physical shop-floor (PS), virtual shop-floor (VS), shop-floor service system (SSS), and shop-floor digital twin data (SDTD), as well as the connection mechanisms (CN).

PS consists of production equipment, personnel, products, materials, and other entities that exist objectively within the workshop. It is primarily responsible for receiving production tasks issued by the SSS, executing production activities, and completing production tasks in strict accordance with the predefined production instructions optimized by VS. Real-time status data for PS equipment, personnel, products, materials, and other production factors can be effectively collected through

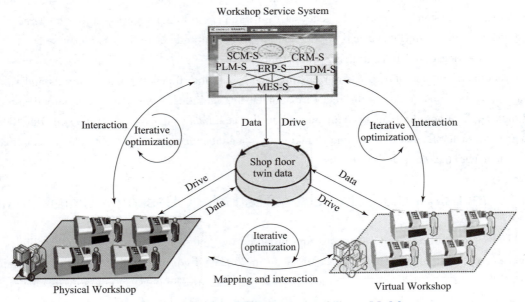

Figure 5.11　Digital Twin Workshop Concept Model

various sensors. Since these data originate from different sources with varying data structures, interfaces, and semantics, a set of standard interface and protocol conversion devices is necessary to unify the reception of heterogeneous data from multiple sources.

VS serves as a faithful and fully digitalized replica of PS, describing and portraying PS across geometric, physical, behavioral, and rule dimensions. It is mainly responsible for simulating, evaluating, and optimizing the production resources and activities of PS. VS enables real-time monitoring, prediction, and regulation of the actual production process. Essentially, VS is a collection of models composed of multiple geometric, physical, behavioral, and rule models, providing a comprehensive multi-dimensional description and characterization of PS. Following the three-layer structure of the digital twin, VS includes unit-level models for individual production factors such as personnel, equipment, tools, etc., and a system-level production line model made up of multiple unit-level models of production factors. It also encompasses complex system-level shop floor models with multiple system-level production line models and their inter-model interactions and coupling relationships.

SDTD represents a collection of data related to PS, VS, and SSS, domain knowledge, and derived data generated through data fusion. It acts as the primary driving force for the interaction and iterative optimization of operations among PS, VS, and SSS. Fusion data, an integral part of SDTD, is obtained by aggregating data from both physical and informational spaces using specific rules. The data in the physical space mainly pertain to PS-related data, which are actual data generated by physical entities. In contrast, the data in the informational space pertain to VS-related data and SSS-related data, which are not directly collected from the physical space. These data, supplementing the physical data, are derived from physical data through processes such as model simulation, algorithmic deduction, and system derivation within the informational space.

SSS refers to a suite of data-driven service functions that encapsulate data, models, algorithms, simulations, and results required in the DTS operation process in a service-oriented manner. This encapsulation forms functional and business services that support the control and optimization of DTS. The operational process of SSS includes sub-service encapsulation, requirement analysis, service composition, and service application.

CN facilitates the interconnection and interoperability of various components within the DTS, encompassing connections between PS and SDTD (CN_PD), PS and VS (CN_PV), PS and SSS (CN_PS), VS and SDTD (CN_VD), VS and SSS (CN_VS), and SSS and SDTD (CN_SD).

As depicted in Figure 5.12, to achieve the integration and fusion of workshop data, a series of operations must be conducted on data within PS, VS, and SSS. These operations include generation, modeling, cleaning, correlation, clustering, mining, iteration, evolution, and fusion.

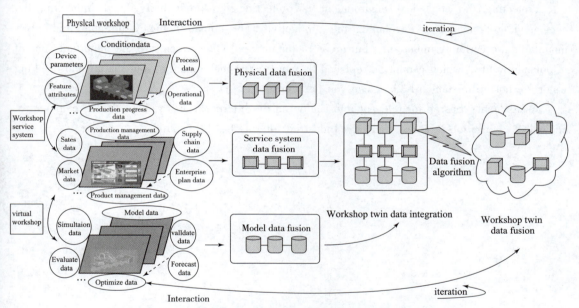

Figure 5.12　Industrial Big Data Integration Based on Digital Twins

Mission Expansion

Gold and Silver Mountains Are Not as Good as Green Mountains and Clear Waters— Industrial Development Should Also Take Environmental Protection Into Consideration

In the industrial field of industrial Internet construction, attention should be paid to the construction of ecological civilization. Ecological civilization is a new stage in the development of human civilization, that is, the form of civilization after industrial civilization, and it is also a new requirement for achieving harmonious development between man and nature. From a historical perspective, civilization prospers when ecology thrives, and civilization declines when ecology declines.

Protecting the ecological environment is protecting the productivity, and improving the ecological environment is developing the productivity. For human beings, the gold and silver mountains are certainly important, but green mountains and clear waters are the important content of our happy life, which cannot be replaced by money. You make money, but the air and drinking water are not up to standard, how can you be happy?

Assignment: Search for relevant information on the Internet to learn about the development of ecological civilization in areas where the Industrial Internet has been built.

项目 6

工业互联网安全实践

任务 16　认知工业互联网安全框架

认知工业互联网
安全框架

学习目标

①了解工业互联网安全框架内容与范围。
②了解工业互联网相关安全框架。
③了解工业互联网安全框架设计方法。
④了解工业互联网安全防护基本思路。

建议学时

3 课时

工作情境

　　安全体系是工业互联网系统稳定运行的保障。公司在完成工业互联网建设前，针对所有员工开展一次关于工业互联网安全的培训。你作为培训项目负责人，需要提前了解，进行技术储备，确保培训工作的顺利开展，为后续工业互联网系统的安全运营提供保障。

知识导图

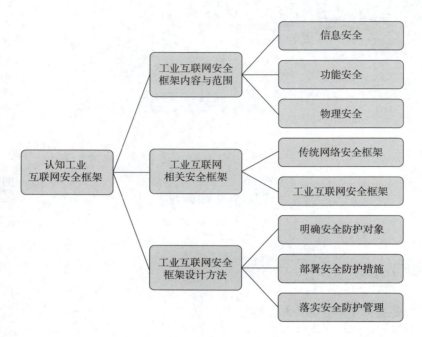

相关知识

工业互联网满足了工业智能化发展的需求。它是具有低时延、高可靠、广覆盖特点的关键网络基础设施，是新一代信息通信技术与先进制造业深度融合所形成的新兴业态和应用模式。工业互联网深刻变革传统工业的创新、生产、管理、服务方式，催生新技术、新模式、新业态、新产业，正成为繁荣数字经济的新基石、创新网络国际治理的新途径和统筹两个强国建设的新引擎。

工业互联网包括网络、平台、安全三大体系。其中，网络体系是基础。工业互联网将连接对象延伸到工业全系统、全产业链、全价值链，可实现人、物品、机器、车间、企业等全要素，以及设计、研发、生产、管理、服务等各环节的泛在深度互联。平台体系是核心。工业互联网平台作为工业智能化发展的核心载体，实现海量异构数据汇聚与建模分析、工业制造能力标准化与服务化、工业经验知识软件化与模块化以及各类创新应用开发与运行，支撑生产智能决策、业务模式创新、资源优化配置和产业生态培育。安全体系是保障。建设满足工业需求的安全技术体系和管理体系，增强设备、网络、控制、应用和数据的安全保障能力，识别和抵御安全威胁，化解各种安全风险，构建工业智能化发展的安全可信环境。

1. 工业互联网安全框架内容与范围

工业领域的安全一般分为三类：信息安全（Information Security）、功能安全（Functional Safety）和物理安全（Physical Safety）。传统工业控制系统安全最初多关注功能安全与物理安全,即防止工业安全相关系统或设备的功能失效;当失效或故障发生时,保证工业设备或系统仍能保持安全条件或进入安全状态。近年来,随着工业控制系统信息化程度的不断加深,针对工业控制系统的信息安全问题不断凸显,业界对信息安全的重视程度逐步提高。

与传统的工控系统安全和互联网安全相比,工业互联网的安全挑战更为艰巨:一方面,工业互联网安全打破了以往相对明晰的责任边界,其范围、复杂度、风险度产生的影响要大得多,其中工业互联网平台安全、数据安全、联网智能设备安全等问题越发突出;另一方面,工业互联网安全工作需要从制度建设、国家能力、产业支持等更全局的视野来统筹安排,目前很多企业还没有意识到安全部署的必要性与紧迫性,安全管理与风险防范控制工作亟须加强。

因此,工业互联网安全框架需要统筹考虑信息安全、功能安全与物理安全,聚焦信息安全,主要解决工业互联网面临的网络攻击等新型风险,并考虑其信息安全防护措施的部署可能对功能安全和物理安全带来的影响。由于物理安全相关防护措施较为通用,故在本项目不作重要考虑,主要对工业互联网的信息安全与功能安全进行讨论。

2. 工业互联网相关安全框架

(1) 传统网络安全框架

1) OSI 安全体系结构

OSI 安全体系结构是国际标准化组织(ISO)在对 OSI 开放系统互联环境的安全性深入研究的基础上提出的。它定义了为保证 OSI 参考模型的安全应具备的 5 类安全服务,包括鉴别服务、访问控制、数据完整性、数据保密性和不可抵赖性,以及为实现这 5 类安全服务所应具备的 8 种安全机制,包括加密、数字签名、访问控制、数据完整性、鉴别交换、业务流填充、路由控制以及公证。OSI 安全体系结构如图 6.1 所示。安全体系结构中的 5 类安全服务及 8 种安全机制可根据所防护网络的具体要求适当地配置于 OSI 参考模型的 7 个层次中。

OSI 安全体系结构针对 OSI 参考模型中层次的不同,部署不同的安全服务与安全机制,体现出分层防护的思想,具有很好的灵活性。然而,OSI 安全体系结构专注于网络通信系统,其应用范围具有一定的局限性。同时,OSI 安全体系结构实现的是对网络的静态安全防护,而网络的安全防护具有动态性,该体系结构对于持续变化的内外部安全威胁缺乏足够的监测与应对能力。此外,OSI 安全体系结构主要从技术层面出发对网络的安全防护问题进行讨论,未考虑管理在安全防护中的地位和作用,面对更复杂、更全面的安全保障要求,仅依靠 OSI 安全体系结构是远远不够的。

2) P2DR 模型

P2DR (Policy Protection Detection Response) 模型是美国 ISS 公司提出的动态网络安全体系模型。

P2DR 模型建立在基于时间的安全理论基础上,将网络安全的实施分为防护、检测和响应三个阶段。在整体安全策略的指导下部署安全防护措施,实时检测网络中出现的风险,对风险及时进行处置,并对处置过程中的经验进行总结,以便对防护措施进行调整和完善,使防护、检测和响应组成了如图 6.2 所示的动态安全循环,从而保障网络的安全。

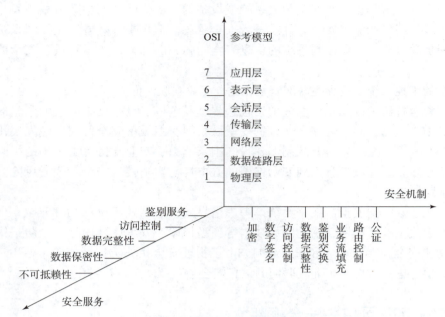

图 6.1　OSI 安全体系结构

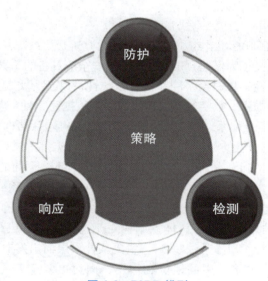

图 6.2　P2DR 模型

P2DR 模型是一种基于闭环控制的动态安全模型,适用于需要长期持续安全防护的网络系统。从总体上来讲,该模型与 OSI 安全体系结构一样,都局限于从技术上考虑网络的安全问题,忽视了管理对于安全防护的重要性,在模型的具体实施过程中极有可能因安全策略执行的不当而影响安全防护效果。

3）信息保障技术框架

信息保障技术框架（Information Assurance Technical Framework, IATF）是美国国家安全

局于 1998 年提出的,该框架提出保障信息系统安全应具备的三个核心要素,即人、技术和操作。其中,人这一要素包括保障人身安全、对人员进行培训、制定安全管理制度等,强调了人作为防护措施的具体实施者在安全防护中的重要地位。技术这一要素强调要在正确的安全策略指导下采取措施来为信息系统提供安全保障服务并对入侵行为进行检测。操作这一要素则明确了要保证信息系统的日常安全应采取的具体防护手段。此外,该框架将网络系统的安全防护分为网络和基础设施防御、网络边界防御、局域计算环境防御和支撑性基础设施防御四部分。在每个部分中,IATF 都描述了其特有的安全需求和相应的可供选择的技术措施,为更好地理解网络安全的不同方面、分析网络系统的安全需求以及选取恰当的安全防御机制提供了依据。信息保障技术框架如图 6.3 所示。

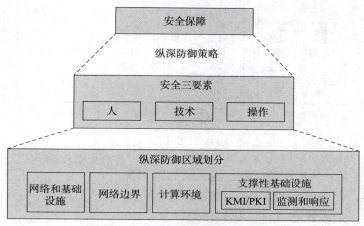

图 6.3　信息保障技术框架

IATF 通过对上述四个部分分别部署安全保障机制,形成对网络系统的纵深防御,从而降低安全风险,保障网络系统的安全性。但 IATF 与 OSI 安全体系结构一样,实现的都是对网络系统的静态安全防护,并未对网络系统部署动态持续的安全防护措施。

4) IEC 62443

IEC 62443 是国际电工委员会工业过程测量、控制与自动化/网络与系统信息安全工作组与国际自动化协会共同制定的工业控制系统安全防护系列标准。该标准将工业控制系统按照控制和管理的等级划分成相对封闭的区域,区域之间的数据通信通过管道进行,通过在管道上安装信息安全管理设备来实现分级保护,进而实现控制系统的网络安全纵深防御。IEC 62443 实施案例如图 6.4 所示。

IEC 62443 系列标准中,对安全技术与安全管理的实施均提出了要求,但从总体上来看,与 OSI 安全体系结构和 IATF 一样,实现的都是静态安全防护。而工业互联网的安全防护是一个动态过程,需要根据外部环境的变化不断进行调整。在工业互联网安全框架的设计中,需要将动态防护的理念纳入其中。

(2) 工业互联网安全框架

1) 美国工业互联网联盟 (IIC) 的 IISF

2016 年 9 月 19 日,美国工业互联网联盟 (Industrial Internet Consortium,IIC) 正式发布工业互联网安全框架 (Industrial Internet Security Framework,IISF) 1.0 版本,拟通过该框

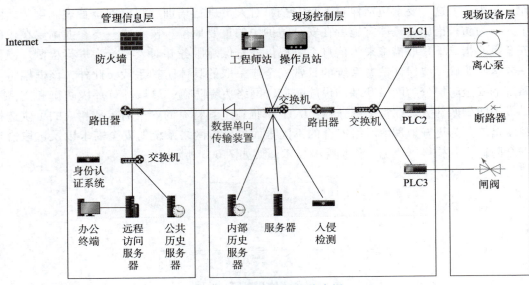

图 6.4 IEC 62443 实施案例

架的发布为工业互联网安全研究与实施提供理论指导。

IISF 的实现主要从功能视角出发，定义了如图 6.5 所示的 6 个功能，即端点保护、通信和连接保护、安全监测和分析、安全配置和管理、数据保护以及安全模型和策略，并将这 6 个功能分为 3 个层次。其中，顶层包括端点保护、通信和连接保护、安全监测和分析以及安全配置和管理 4 个功能，为工业互联网中的终端设备及设备之间的通信提供保护，对用于这些设备与通信的安全防护机制进行配置，并监测工业互联网运行过程中出现的安全风险。在 4 个功能之下是一个通用的数据保护层，对这 4 个功能中产生的数据提供保护。在最下层是覆盖整个工业互联网的安全模型与策略，它将上述 5 个功能紧密结合起来，实现端到端的安全防护。

图 6.5 工业互联网安全框架

总的来看，美国 IISF 聚焦于 IT 安全，侧重于安全实施，明确了具体的安全措施，对于工业互联网安全框架的设计具有很好的借鉴意义。

2) 德国工业 4.0 安全框架

德国工业 4.0 注重安全实施，由网络安全组牵头出版了《工业 4.0 安全指南》《跨企业安全通信》《安全身份标识》等一系列指导性文件，指导企业加强安全防护。德国虽然从多个角度对安全提出了要求，但是并未形成成熟的安全体系框架。但安全作为新的商业模式的推动者，在工业 4.0 参考架构（RAMI 4.0）中起到了承载和连接所有结构元素的骨架作用。

德国 RAMI 4.0 从 CPS 功能视角、全生命周期价值链视角和全层级工业系统视角 3 个视角构建了如图 6.6 所示的工业 4.0 参考架构。从 CPS 功能视角看，安全应用于所有不同层次，因此，安全风险必须作整体考虑；从全生命周期价值链视角看，对象的所有者必须考虑全生命周期的安全性；从全层级工业系统视角看，需要对所有资产进行安全风险分析，并对资产所有者提供实时保护措施。

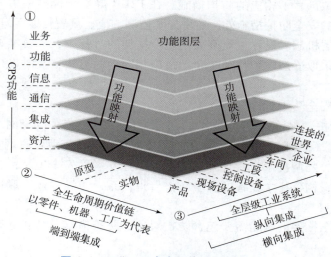

图 6.6　工业 4.0 参考架构（RAMI 4.0）

德国 RAMI 4.0 采用了分层的基本安全管理思路，侧重于防护对象的管理。在工业互联网安全框架的设计过程中可借鉴这一思路，并且从实施的角度将管理与技术相结合，以便更好地指导工业互联网企业部署安全实施。

通过对以上相关网络安全框架的分析，总结出以下 3 个方面的共性特征，在工业互联网安全框架的设计中值得思考并充分借鉴：一是分类别部署安全防护措施，二是构建动态安全模型成为主流，三是技术手段与管理手段相结合。

3. 工业互联网安全框架设计方法

工业互联网安全框架是在充分借鉴传统网络安全框架和国外相关工业互联网安全框架的基础上，并结合我国工业互联网的特点提出的，旨在指导工业互联网相关企业开展安全防护体系建设，提升安全防护能力。对于工业互联网安全框架的构建，本书从以下 3 方面进行阐述。

首先，要明确安全防护对象是前提。

安全防护对象的确定是一个根本问题，是明确工业互联网安全防护工作范畴的基础，并为防护工作的实施指明方向。在传统网络安全框架与国外相关工业互联网安全框架中，都明确界定了防护对象。2016 年 8 月工业互联网产业联盟（AII）发布的《工业互联网体系架构（版本 1.0）》中的安全体系部分也从防护对象角度提出了工业互联网安全的 5 大重点方向，即设备安全、控制安全、网络安全、应用安全和数据安全。因此，本框架充分借鉴这一思路,将设备、控制、网络、应用、数据作为工业互联网安全防护的研究对象。

其次,要明确部署安全防护措施。

工业互联网安全框架的实施离不开安全防护措施的部署。在诸多传统网络安全框架中,都将安全防护措施作为框架的重要组成部分。OSI 安全框架中阐述的安全服务与安全机制即是针对不同防护对象部署了相应的防护措施。在 P2DR 等安全模型中引入了动态安全的理念,除了部署静态的安全防护措施外,还增加了监测响应、处置恢复等环节,形成了动态、闭环的安全防护部署机制。设计工业互联网安全框架的过程中,需要结合工业互联网安全防护的特殊要求,采取静态防护与动态防护措施相结合的方式,及时发现并加以有效处置安全事件。

最后,要落实安全防护管理。

在网络安全防护领域有"三分技术、七分管理"的传统。传统网络安全框架 IATF、IEC 62443 等均强调了管理对于网络安全防护的重要性。国外工业互联网安全相关框架也将管理与技术相结合,强调技术与管理并重。设计工业互联网安全框架的过程中,需要将技术与管理有效结合,构建科学完备的安全防护管理体系,指导工业互联网相关企业提升安全防护管理水平。

工业互联网安全框架的构建需要包含防护对象、防护措施及防护管理 3 个方面,如图 6.7 所示。

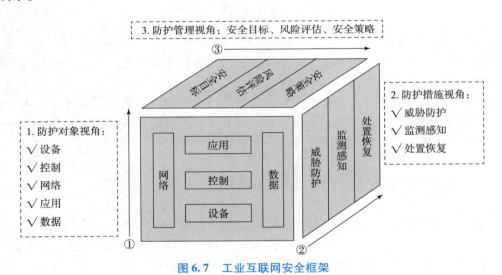

图 6.7 工业互联网安全框架

其中,防护对象视角涵盖设备、控制、网络、应用和数据 5 大安全重点;防护措施视角包括威胁防护、监测感知和处置恢复 3 大环节,威胁防护环节针对 5 大防护对象部署主被动安全防护措施,监测感知和处置恢复环节通过信息共享、监测预警、应急响应等一系列安全措施、机制的部署来增强动态安全防护能力;防护管理视角根据工业互联网安全目标对其面临的安全风险进行安全评估,并选择适当的安全策略作为指导,实现防护措施的有效部署。

工业互联网安全框架的 3 个防护视角之间相对独立,但彼此之间又相互关联。从防护对象视角来看，安全框架中的每个防护对象都需要采用一系列合理的防护措施并依据完备的防护管理流程对其进行安全防护；从防护措施视角来看，每一类防护措施都有其适用的防护对象，并在具体防护管理流程指导下发挥作用；从防护管理视角来看，防护管理流程的实现离不开对防护对象的界定，并需要各类防护措施的有机结合使其能够顺利运转。工业互联网安全框架的3个防护视角相辅相成，互为补充，形成一个完整、动态、持续的防护体系。

 任务拓展

发展和安全并重——工业互联网安全发展实践

近年来，中国工业互联网平台数量快速增长，平台应用服务已延伸到企业设计、生产、管理、运营等多个环节和供应链、产业链全链条。工业互联网平台汇集核心工艺、控制参数、工业机理模型等大量重要数据，大规模的数据接入导致安全威胁逐渐向跨行业跨领域甚至产业链范围渗透。工业互联网平台安全防护和保障刻不容缓。工业企业依赖供应链管理、资源配置等重要业务系统，来实现和供应链上下游企业的采购、生产等环节的实时业务协同。但供应链上下游企业安全能力参差不齐，部分安全能力"短板"使企业一旦遭受网络攻击，影响可能层层传导，引发涟漪效应，轻则导致上下游企业信息交互中断、生产计划紊乱，重则造成生产供应中断，上下游多家企业停工停产。

从我国工业互联网安全发展实践来看，我国必须坚持发展和安全并重，把安全发展贯彻国家发展各个领域全过程，在工业互联网系列政策中同步强化安全设计，不断完善工业互联网安全体系化布局。

作业：分组调研我国工业互联网面临的安全威胁，设计解决方案。

Project 6

Industrial Internet Security Practices

Task 16 Understanding the Industrial Internet Security Framework

 Learning Objective

①Understand the content and scope of the industrial Internet security framework.
②Understand Industrial Internet security frameworks.
③Understand the design method of Industrial Internet security framework.
④Understand the basic concepts of Industrial Internet security protection.

 Suggested Hours

3 hours

 Working Context

The security system is essential for the stable operation of the Industrial Internet system. Before the company completes the construction of the Industrial Internet, it conducts a training program on Industrial Internet security for all employees. As the person in charge of the training program, you need to understand the requirements in advance, make technical preparations, ensure the smooth implementation of the training, and provide a safeguard for the safe operation of the subsequent Industrial Internet system.

Knowledge Map

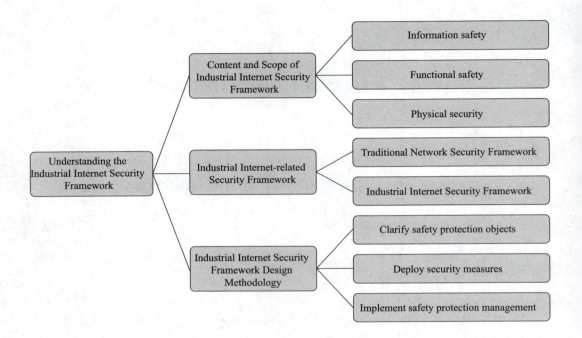

Relevant Knowledge

The Industrial Internet meets the needs of the intelligent development of industry. It is a key network infrastructure characterized by low latency, high reliability, and wide coverage, and represents an emerging industry and application model formed by the deep integration of new-generation information and communication technologies with advanced manufacturing industries. The Industrial Internet has profoundly changed the innovation, production, management, and service methods of traditional industries, giving rise to new technologies, modes, business forms, and industries. It is becoming a new cornerstone of a thriving digital economy, a new approach to innovating the international governance of the network, and a new engine for coordinating the construction of two robust countries.

The Industrial Internet encompasses three systems: network, platform, and security. Among these, the network system serves as the foundation. The Industrial Internet extends the connection object to the entire industrial system, the entire industrial chain, and the entire value chain, enabling the ubiquitous and deep interconnection of all elements, such as people, goods, machines, workshops, enterprises, as well as the various stages of design, research and development, production, management, and service. The platform system is the core, acting as the central carrier for the development of industrial intelligence. The Industrial Internet platform facilitates the aggregation and modeling analysis of massive heterogeneous data, the standardization and servitization of industrial manufacturing capabilities, the softwareization and modularization of industrial knowledge, and the development and operation of various innovative applications. It supports intelligent decision-making in production, business model innovation, optimal resource allocation, and the cultivation of an industrial ecosystem. The security system is a guarantee, establishing a security technology and management system tailored to industrial needs. It enhances the security capabilities of equipment, networks, controls, applications, and data, identifies and defends against security threats, resolves various security risks, and creates a secure and trustworthy environment for the development of industrial intelligence.

1. Content and Scope of Industrial Internet Security Framework

Security in the industrial field is generally categorized into three types: information security, functional safety, and physical security. Traditional industrial control system security initially focuses on functional safety and physical safety, which involves preventing functional failures in industrial safety-related systems or equipment, and ensuring that industrial equipment or systems can maintain safe conditions or enter a safe state upon failure or malfunction. In recent years, as the degree of informatization of industrial control systems has deepened, issues of information security for these systems have increasingly come to the fore, and the industry's attention to information security has been growing.

Compared with traditional industrial control system security and Internet security, the security challenges facing the Industrial Internet are even more significant. On one hand, Industrial Internet security disrupts the previously clear boundaries of responsibility. Its scope, complexity, and risk level create a much broader impact, where the security of the Industrial Internet platform, data, and networked intelligent devices become increasingly prominent. On the other hand, Industrial Internet security efforts need to be coordinated from a more global perspective, considering aspects such as system construction, national capacity, and industrial support. Currently, many enterprises have not yet recognized the necessity and urgency of security measures. There is an urgent need to strengthen security management and risk prevention and control.

Therefore, the Industrial Internet security framework must consider information security, functional safety, and physical security in an integrated manner, with a focus on information security. It should primarily address new types of risks faced by the Industrial Internet, such as cyberattacks, and consider the impact that the deployment of its information security protection measures may have on functional safety and physical security. While physical security-related protective measures are more general, they are less critical to address in this context. The main discussion will focus on the information security and functional safety aspects of the Industrial Internet.

2. Industrial Internet-related Security Framework

(1) Traditional Network Security Framework

1) OSI Security Architecture

The OSI security architecture was proposed by the International Organization for Standardization (ISO) following in-depth research on the security of the OSI open systems interconnection environment. It defines that the security of the OSI reference model should encompass five types of security services, including authentication, access control, data integrity, data confidentiality, and non-repudiation. Additionally, it outlines that there should be eight kinds of security mechanisms to realize these five types of security services. These mechanisms include encryption, digital signatures, access control, data integrity verification, authentication exchanges, traffic padding, routing control, and notarization. The OSI security architecture as depicted in Figure 6.1. The five types of security services and eight types of security mechanisms within the security architecture can be appropriately configured across the seven layers of the OSI reference model, according to the specific requirements of the network being protected.

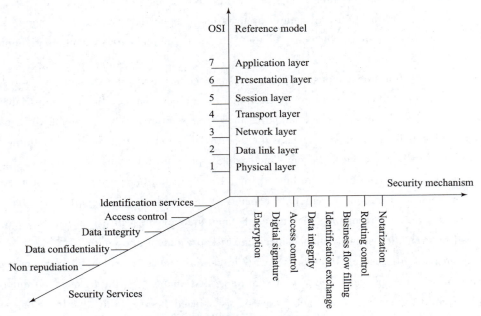

Figure 6.1 OSI Security Architecture

The OSI security architecture deploys different security services and mechanisms across various levels of the OSI reference model, embodying the concept of layered protection and offering good flexibility. However, the OSI security architecture is primarily focused on network communication systems, which imposes certain limitations on its scope of application. At the same time, while the OSI security architecture provides static security protection for networks, network security itself is dynamic. The architecture lacks robust monitoring and responsive capabilities to address the continuously evolving internal and external security threats. Additionally, the OSI security architecture predominantly addresses the technical aspects of network security protection, without fully considering the status and role of management within the security framework. Faced with more complex and comprehensive security demands, relying solely on the OSI security architecture is insufficient.

2) P2DR Model

The P2DR (Policy Protection Detection Response) model is a dynamic network security system model proposed by ISS. The P2DR model is constructed on the foundation of time-based security theory, and the implementation of network security is divided into three stages: protection, detection, and response. Guided by an overarching security strategy, security measures are deployed, risks within the network are detected in real time, and these risks are addressed promptly. The experiences gained during the disposal process are then summarized, allowing for the adjustment and enhancement of protective measures. This process creates a dynamic security cycle that integrates protection, detection, and response, as depicted in Figure 6.2, ensuring the ongoing security of the network.

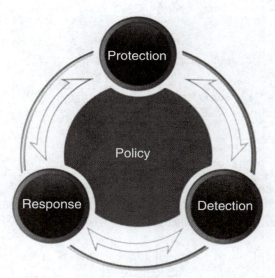

Figure 6.2 P2DR Model

The P2DR model is a dynamic security framework based on closed-loop control, which is suitable for network systems that require long-term, continuous security protection. Generally, like the OSI security architecture, this model is limited to the technical aspects of network security and often overlooks the importance of management in security protection. In the specific implementation of the model, there is a significant risk that improper execution of security policies may negatively impact the effectiveness of security protection.

3) Information Assurance Technology Framework

The Information Assurance Technical Framework (IATF) was proposed by the U.S. National

Security Agency in 1998. The framework suggests that safeguarding information systems security should involve three core elements: people, technology, and operations. Among these, the human element encompasses the protection of personal safety, training of personnel, and the development of security management systems, emphasizing the importance of people as the specific implementers of protective measures within security protection. The technology element underscores the need to implement measures under the guidance of correct security policies to provide security services for information systems and detect intrusions. The operational element delineates the specific actions that should be taken to ensure the ongoing security of the information system. Additionally, the framework categorizes the security protection of network systems into four components: network and infrastructure defense, network boundary defense, local computing environment defense, and supporting infrastructure defense. In each of these components, the IATF outlines specific security requirements and corresponding alternative technical measures, providing a foundation for a better understanding of various aspects of network security, analyzing the security needs of network systems, and selecting appropriate security defense mechanisms. The specific content of the IATF is depicted in Figure 6.3.

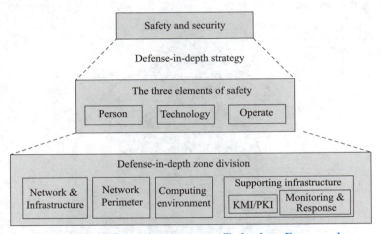

Figure 6.3 Information Assurance Technology Framework

By the deployment of the aforementioned four components of the security mechanism, IATF aims to establish a depth of defense for the network system, thereby reducing security risks and protecting the network system's security. However, like the OSI security architecture, the IATF provides static security protection for the network system and does not implement dynamic, continuous security protection measures.

4) IEC 62443

IEC 62443 is a series of standards for industrial control system security protection jointly developed by the International Electrotechnical Commission's Industrial Process Measurement, Control and Automation/Network and System Information Security Working Group (IEC/TC65/WG10) and the International Society of Automation (ISA99). This standard categorizes the industrial control system into relatively isolated zones based on the level of control and management. Data communication between these zones is facilitated through secured channels, and hierarchical protection is achieved by installing information security management equipment at these junctions. This setup, in turn, realizes a depth defense for the network security of the control system, as depicted in Figure 6.4.

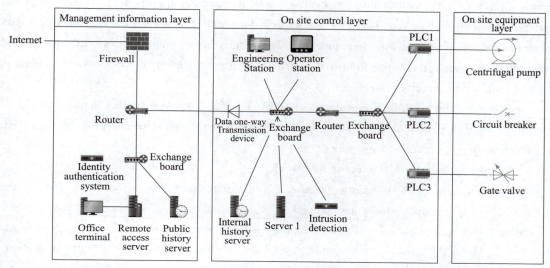

Figure 6.4 IEC 62443 Implementation Case

The IEC 62443 series of standards have set forth requirements for the implementation of security technologies and security management. However, like the OSI security architecture and IATF, they generally provide for static security protection. The security protection for the Industrial Internet is a dynamic process that necessitates continuous adjustment in response to changes in the external environment. Therefore, the design of the Industrial Internet security framework should incorporate the concept of dynamic protection.

(2) Industrial Internet Security Framework

1) IISF of the U.S. Industrial Internet Consortium (IIC)

On September 19, 2016, the U.S. Industrial Internet Consortium (IIC) officially released version 1.0 of the Industrial Internet Security Framework (IISF), which is intended to provide theoretical guidance for Industrial Internet security research and implementation.

The implementation of IISF primarily focuses on the functional perspective, defining six functions as depicted in Figure 6.5: endpoint protection, communication and connection protection, security monitoring and analysis, security configuration management, data protection, and security model and policy. These six functions are divided

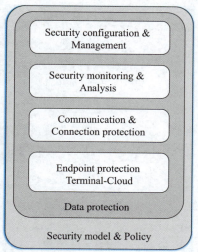

Figure 6.5 Industrial Internet Security Implementation Framework

into three layers. The top layer consists of four functions—endpoint protection, communication and connection protection, security monitoring and analysis, and security configuration management—which provide protection for end devices and the communication between devices within the Industrial Internet. They also configure the security protection mechanisms for these devices and communications, and monitor the security risks that arise during the operation of the Industrial Internet. Below these four functions is a generalized data protection layer that safeguards the data generated by the aforementioned four functions. The bottom layer comprises a security model and policy that encompass the entire Industrial Internet, tightly integrating the above five functions to achieve end-to-end security protection.

In general, the U. S. IISF concentrates on IT security, emphasizes the implementation of security, specifies particular security measures, and holds significant reference value for the design of Industrial Internet security frameworks.

2) Germany Industry 4.0 Security framework

Germany's Industry 4.0 initiative focuses on the implementation of security, led by the Network Security Group, which has published a series of guiding documents, such as the 'Industry 4.0 Security Guide,' 'Cross-Enterprise Secure Communications,' and 'Secure Identity Marking.' These documents aim to guide enterprises in strengthening their security protection. Although Germany has not yet formed a mature security system framework, it has put forward requirements for security from multiple perspectives. Security, as an enabler of new business models, plays a crucial role in the Industry 4.0 Reference Architecture (RAMI 4.0), acting as a framework that carries and connects all structural elements.

The German RAMI 4.0 model constructs the Industry 4.0 Reference Architecture, as depicted in Figure 6.6, from three perspectives: the Cyber-Physical Systems (CPS) functional perspective, the full lifecycle value chain perspective, and the full-tier industrial system perspective. From the

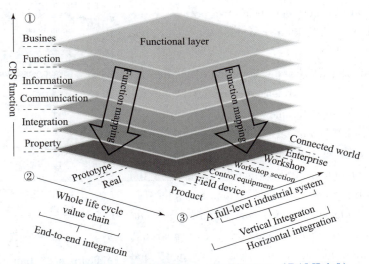

Figure 6.6 Industry 4.0 Reference Architecture (RAMI 4.0)

CPS functional perspective, safety is applied at all different levels, necessitating a holistic consideration of safety risks. From the full lifecycle value chain perspective, the owner of the object must consider the safety across the entire lifecycle. From the full-tier industrial system perspective, all assets need to be analyzed for safety risks, and real-time protection measures should be provided to the asset owner.

3. Industrial Internet Security Framework Design Methodology

The Industrial Internet security framework is proposed based on fully leveraging traditional network security frameworks and relevant foreign Industrial Internet security frameworks, combined with the characteristics of China's Industrial Internet. It aims to guide Industrial Internet-related enterprises in constructing a security protection system and enhancing their security protection capabilities. In constructing the Industrial Internet security framework, this book approaches from the following three aspects:

Firstly, it is a prerequisite to clarify the security protection object. The determination of the security protection object is a fundamental issue and forms the basis for clarifying the scope of Industrial Internet security protection work and indicating the direction for implementing the protection work. In traditional network security frameworks and relevant foreign Industrial Internet security frameworks, the protection object is clearly defined. The security system part of the Industrial Internet Architecture (Version 1.0) released by the Industrial Internet Industry Alliance (AII) in August 2016 also puts forward five key directions of Industrial Internet security from the perspective of the protection object: device security, control security, network security, application security, and data security. Therefore, this framework fully adopts this concept and takes equipment, control, network, application, and data as the research objects of Industrial Internet security protection.

Secondly, security protection measures should be clearly deployed. The implementation of the Industrial Internet security framework is inseparable from the deployment of security protection measures. In many traditional network security frameworks, security protection measures are an important part of the framework. The OSI security framework elaborates on security services and security mechanisms that correspond to different protection objects with corresponding protection measures. P2DR and other security models introduce the concept of dynamic security, adding monitoring, response, and recovery links to the deployment of static security measures, forming a dynamic, closed-loop security deployment mechanism. In the process of designing the Industrial Internet security framework, it is necessary to combine the special requirements of Industrial Internet security protection and adopt a combination of static and dynamic protection measures to detect and effectively address security incidents in a timely manner.

Lastly, security protection management should be implemented. In the field of network security protection, there is a saying, "three parts technology, seven parts management." Traditional network security frameworks like IATF and IEC62443 emphasize the importance of management in network security protection. Foreign Industrial Internet security-related frameworks also integrate management and technology, emphasizing both aspects. In the process of designing the Industrial Internet security framework, it is necessary to effectively combine technology and management, establish a scientific and comprehensive security protection management system, and guide Industrial Internet-related enterprises to improve their level of security protection management.

The construction of the Industrial Internet security framework encompasses three aspects: protection objects, protection measures and protection management. As depicted in Figure 6.7.

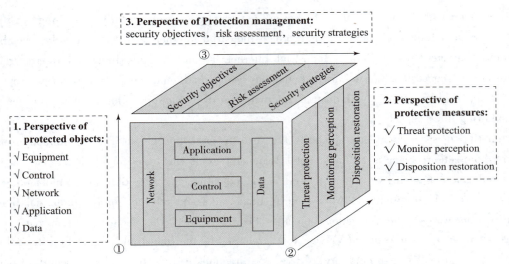

Figure 6.7　Industrial Internet Security Framework

Among them, the protection object perspective covers five major security priorities: equipment, control, network, application, and data. The protection measure perspective includes three major links: threat protection, monitoring and sensing, and response and recovery. The threat protection link deploys active and passive security measures for the five major protection objects. The monitoring and sensing and response and recovery links enhance dynamic security protection capabilities through the deployment of a series of security measures and mechanisms, such as information sharing, monitoring and early warning, and emergency response. From the perspective of protection management, a security risk assessment is conducted based on the security objectives of the Industrial Internet security framework, and appropriate security policies are selected as a guide to achieve the effective deployment of protective measures.

The three protection perspectives of the Industrial Internet security framework are relatively independent yet interrelated. From the perspective of the protection object, each protection object in the security framework requires a series of reasonable protection measures and a complete protection management process for security protection. From the perspective of protection measures, each type of protection measure has its applicable protection object and functions under the guidance of a specific protection management process. From the perspective of protection management, the realization of the protection management process is inseparable from the definition of the protection object and requires the organic integration of various types of protection measures to ensure its smooth operation. The three protection perspectives of the Industrial Internet security framework complement and support each other, forming a complete, dynamic, and continuous protection system.

Mission Expansion

Equal Emphasis on Development and Security—the Development Practice of Industrial Internet Security

In recent years, the number of Industrial Internet platforms in China has been growing rapidly, and platform application services have extended to multiple stages, including enterprise design, production, management, operation, and the entire supply chain. The Industrial Internet platform aggregates a vast amount of critical data, such as core processes, control parameters, and industrial mechanism models. Large-scale data access can lead to the gradual infiltration of security threats across industries, fields, and even the entire industrial chain. The security protection and assurance of the Industrial Internet platform cannot be delayed. Industrial enterprises rely on supply chain management and resource allocation for real-time business collaboration with upstream and downstream enterprises in procurement and production. However, the security capabilities of these supply chain partners vary. If a company with weaker security is attacked, the impact may ripple through the chain, potentially causing disruptions in information exchange, production planning, and even halting the production and supply processes of the affected enterprises.

Without network security, there is no national security. From the perspective of China's Industrial Internet security development practices, China must maintain a balanced approach to development and security. It should integrate security development across all areas and throughout the entire process of national development. In the series of policies related to the Industrial Internet, there should be a synchronized effort to strengthen security design and continuously enhance the systematic layout of the Industrial Internet security framework.

Assignment: Conduct research on the security threats faced by China's Industrial Internet in groups, and design solutions to address them.

任务 17　在网络安全等级保护 2.0 框架下保障工业控制系统安全

学习目标

①了解网络安全等级保护 2.0 的基本要求。
②掌握保障工业互联网安全的维度及措施。

在等保 2.0 框架下
保障工业控制系统安全

建议学时

3 课时

工作情境

公司要求根据国家网络安全法律规定,对工业互联网络进行等级保护测评。现要求你了解网络安全等级保护 2.0 相关要求,并制定公司工业互联网安全保障措施。

知识导图

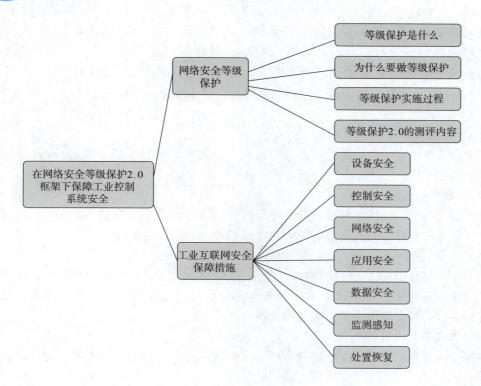

相关知识

1. 网络安全等级保护

（1）等级保护是什么

网络安全等级保护是国家信息安全保障的基本制度、基本策略、基本方法。网络安全等级保护工作是对信息和信息载体按照重要性等级分级别进行保护的一种工作。信息系统运营、使用单位应当选择符合国家要求的测评机构，依据《信息安全技术网络安全等级保护基本要求》等技术标准，定期对信息系统开展测评工作。

（2）为什么要做等级保护

1）法律规章要求

《中华人民共和国网络安全法》明确规定信息系统运营、使用单位应当按照网络安全等级保护制度要求，履行安全保护义务，如果拒不履行，将会受到相应处罚。

第二十一条规定：网络运营者应当按照网络安全等级保护制度的要求，履行下列安全保护义务，保障网络免受干扰、破坏或者未经授权的访问，防止网络数据泄露或者被窃取、篡改。

第三十八条规定：关键信息基础设施的运营者应当自行或者委托网络安全服务机构对其网络的安全性和可能存在的风险每年至少进行一次检测评估，并将检测评估情况和改进措施报送相关负责关键信息基础设施安全保护工作的部门。

第五十九条规定：网络运营者不履行义务的，由有关主管部门责令改正，给予警告；拒不改正或者导致危害网络安全等后果的，处一万元以上十万元以下罚款，对直接负责的主管人员处五千元以上五万元以下罚款。关键信息基础设施的运营者不履行义务的，由有关主管部门责令改正，给予警告；拒不改正或者导致危害网络安全等后果的，处十万元以上一百万元以下罚款，对直接负责的主管人员处一万元以上十万元以下罚款。

2）行业要求

在金融、电力、广电、医疗、教育等行业，主管单位明确要求从业机构的信息系统要开展等级保护工作。

3）企业系统安全的需求

信息系统运营、使用单位通过开展等级保护工作可以发现系统内部的安全隐患与不足之处，可通过安全整改来提升系统的安全防护能力，降低被攻击的风险。

（3）等级保护实施过程

网络安全等级保护工作包括定级、备案、建设整改、等级测评、监督检查五个阶段。在等级保护全流程中，涉及四个不同的角色，分别是运营使用单位、公安机关、深信服、测评机构。网络安全等级保护实施过程如图6.8所示。

（4）等级保护2.0的测评内容

等级保护2.0测评分为安全物理环境、安全通信网络、安全区域边界、安全计算环境、

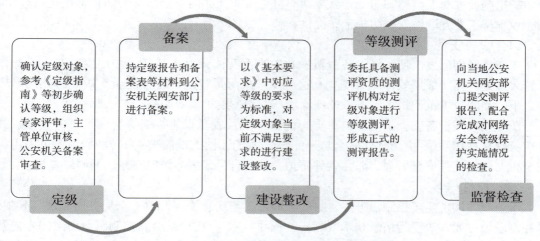

图 6.8　网络安全等级保护实施过程

安全管理中心、安全管理制度、安全管理机构、安全人员管理、安全建设管理、安全运维管理十个层面，如图 6.9 所示。

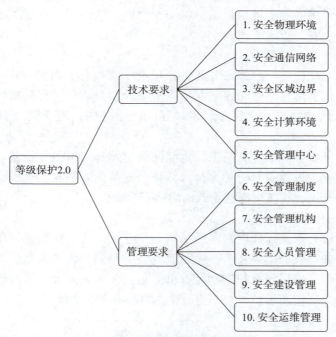

图 6.9　等级保护 2.0 测评

2. 工业互联网安全保障措施

工业互联网安全框架在实施过程中的重点是针对防护对象采取行之有效的防护措施。为此，本书针对工业互联网安全的五大防护对象面临的安全威胁，分别介绍其可采取的安全防护措施，并对监测感知与处置恢复两类贯穿工业互联网安全系统的防护措施进行介绍，为企业部署工业互联网安全防护工作提供参考。

（1）设备安全

工业互联网的发展使现场设备由机械化向高度智能化发生转变，并产生了嵌入式操作系统+微处理器+应用软件的新模式，这就使未来海量智能设备可能会直接暴露在网络攻击之下，面临攻击范围扩大、扩散速度增加、漏洞影响扩大等威胁。

工业互联网设备安全指工厂内单点智能器件以及成套智能终端等智能设备的安全，具体应分别从操作系统/应用软件安全与硬件安全两方面出发来部署安全防护措施，可采用的安全机制包括固件安全增强、恶意软件防护、设备身份鉴别与访问控制、漏洞修复等。

（2）控制安全

工业互联网使生产控制由分层、封闭、局部逐步向扁平、开放、全局方向发展。其中，在控制环境方面，表现为信息技术（IT）与操作技术（OT）融合，控制网络由封闭走向开放；在控制布局方面表现为控制范围从局部扩展至全局，并伴随着控制监测上移与实时控制下移。上述变化改变了传统生产控制过程封闭、可信的特点，造成安全事件危害范围扩大、危害程度加深、信息安全与功能安全问题交织等后果。

对于工业互联网控制安全防护，主要从控制协议安全、控制软件安全及控制功能安全三个方面考虑，可采用的安全机制包括协议安全加固、软件安全加固、恶意软件防护、补丁升级、漏洞修复、安全监测审计等。

（3）网络安全

工业互联网的发展使工厂内部网络呈现出IP化、无线化、组网方式灵活化与全局化的特点，工厂外网呈现出信息网络与控制网络逐渐融合、企业专网与互联网逐渐融合以及产品服务日益互联网化的特点。这就造成传统互联网中的网络安全问题开始向工业互联网蔓延。

工业互联网网络安全防护应面向工厂内部网络、外部网络及标识解析系统等方面，具体包括网络结构优化、边界安全防护、接入认证、通信内容防护、通信设备防护、安全监测审计等多种防护措施，构筑全面、高效的网络安全防护体系。

1）优化网络结构设计

在网络规划阶段，需设计合理的网络结构。一方面，通过在关键网络节点和标识解析节点采用双机热备和负载均衡等技术，应对业务高峰时期突发的大数据流量和意外故障引发的业务连续性问题，确保网络长期稳定、可靠运行。另一方面，通过合理的网络结构和设置来提高网络的灵活性和可扩展性，为后续网络扩容做好准备。

2）网络边界安全

根据工业互联网中网络设备和业务系统的重要程度，将整个网络划分成不同的安全域，形成纵深防御体系。安全域是一个逻辑区域，同一安全域中的设备资产具有相同或相近的安全属性，如安全级别、安全威胁、安全脆弱性等，同一安全域内的系统相互信任。在安全域之间采用网络边界控制设备，以逻辑串接的方式进行部署，对安全域边界进行监视，识别边界上的入侵行为并进行有效阻断。

3）网络接入认证

接入网络的设备与标识解析节点应该具有唯一性标识，网络应对接入的设备与标识解析节点进行身份认证,保证合法接入和合法连接,对非法设备与标识解析节点的接入行为进行阻断与告警,形成网络可信接入机制。网络接入认证可采用基于数字证书的身份认证等机制来实现。

4)通信和传输保护

通信和传输保护是指采用相关技术手段来保证通信过程中的机密性、完整性和有效性,防止数据在网络传输过程中被窃取或篡改,并保证合法用户对信息和资源的有效使用。同时,在标识解析体系的建设过程中,需要对解析节点中存储以及在解析过程中传输的数据进行安全保护。

5)网络设备安全防护

为了提高网络设备与标识解析节点自身的安全性,保障其正常运行,网络设备与标识解析节点需要采取一系列安全防护措施。

6)安全监测审计

网络安全监测指通过漏洞扫描工具等方式探测网络设备与标识解析节点的漏洞情况,并及时提供预警信息。网络安全审计指通过镜像或代理等方式分析网络与标识解析系统中的流量,并记录网络与标识解析系统中的系统活动和用户活动等各类操作行为以及设备运行信息,发现系统中现有的和潜在的安全威胁,实时分析网络与标识解析系统中发生的安全事件并告警。同时,记录内部人员的错误操作和越权操作,并进行及时告警,减少内部非恶意操作导致的安全隐患。

(4)应用安全

工业互联网应用主要包括工业互联网平台与工业应用程序两大类,其范围覆盖智能化生产、网络化协同、个性化定制、服务化延伸等方面。目前工业互联网平台面临的安全风险主要包括数据泄露、篡改、丢失、权限控制异常、系统漏洞利用、账户劫持、设备接入安全等。对工业应用程序而言,最大的风险来自安全漏洞,包括开发过程中编码不符合安全规范而导致的软件本身的漏洞,以及由于使用不安全的第三方库而出现的漏洞等。

相应地,工业互联网应用安全也应从工业互联网平台安全与工业应用程序安全两方面进行防护。对于工业互联网平台,可采取的安全措施包括安全审计、认证授权、分布式拒绝服务(Distributed Denial of Service,DDoS)攻击防护等。对于工业应用程序,建议采用全生命周期的安全防护,在应用程序的开发过程中进行代码审核并对开发人员进行培训,以减少漏洞的引入;对运行中的应用程序定期进行漏洞排查,对应用程序的内部流程进行审核和测试,并对公开的漏洞和后门加以修补;对应用程序的行为进行实时监测以发现可疑行为并进行阻止,从而减少未公开漏洞带来的危害。

(5)数据安全

工业互联网相关的数据按照其属性或特征,可以分为四大类:设备数据、业务系统数据、知识库数据、用户个人数据。根据数据敏感程度的不同,可将工业互联网数据分为一般数据、重要数据和敏感数据三种。工业互联网数据涉及数据采集、传输、存储、处理等各个环节。随着工厂数据由少量、单一、单向向大量、多维、双向转变,工业互联网数据体量不断增大、种类不断增多、结构日趋复杂,并出现数据在工厂内部与外部网络之间的双向流动共享。由此带来的安全风险主要包括数据泄露、非授权分析、用户个人信息泄露等。

对于工业互联网的数据安全防护，应采取明示用途、数据加密、访问控制、业务隔离、接入认证、数据脱敏等多种防护措施，覆盖包括数据收集、传输、存储、处理等在内的全生命周期的各个环节。

(6) 监测感知

监测感知是指部署相应的监测措施，主动发现来自系统内外部的安全风险，具体措施包括数据采集、收集汇聚、特征提取、关联分析、状态感知等。

1) 数据采集

数据采集指对工业现场网络及工业互联网平台中各类数据进行采集，为网络异常分析、设备预测性维护等提供数据来源。

2) 收集汇聚

对数据的收集汇聚主要分为两个方面：一是对 SCADA、MES、ERP 等工业控制系统及应用系统所产生的关键工业互联网数据进行汇聚，包括产品全生命周期的各类数据的同步采集、管理、存储及查询，为后续过程提供数据来源；二是对全网流量进行监听，并将监听过程中采集到的数据进行汇聚。

3) 特征提取

特征提取是指对数据特征进行提取、筛选、分类、优先级排序、可读等处理，从而实现从数据到信息的转化过程，该过程主要是针对单个设备或单个网络的纵向数据分析。信息主要包括内容和情景两方面，内容指工业互联网中的设备信号处理结果、监控传输特性、性能曲线、健康状况、报警信息、DNC 及 SCADA 网络流量等；情景指设备的运行工况、维护保养记录、人员操作指令、人员访问状态、生产任务目标、行业销售机理等。

4) 关联分析

关联分析基于大数据进行横向大数据分析和多维分析，通过将运行机理、运行环境、操作内容、外部威胁情报等有机结合，利用群体经验预测单个设备的安全情况，或根据历史状况和当前状态的差异进行关联分析，进而发现网络及系统的异常状态。

5) 状态感知

状态感知基于关联分析过程，实现对工业互联网相关企业网络运行规律、异常情况、安全目标、安全态势、业务背景等的监测感知，确定安全基线，结合大数据分析等相关技术，发现潜在安全威胁，预测黑客攻击行为。

(7) 处置恢复

处置恢复机制是确保落实工业互联网信息安全管理，支撑工业互联网系统与服务持续运行的保障。通过处置恢复机制，在风险发生时，灾备恢复组织能根据预案及时采取措施进行应对，及时恢复现场设备、工业控制系统、网络、工业互联网平台、工业应用程序等的正常运行，防止重要数据丢失，并通过数据收集与分析机制，及时更新优化防护措施，形成持续改进的防御闭环。处置恢复机制主要包括响应决策、备份恢复、分析评估等。

任务拓展

《中华人民共和国网络安全法》——网络空间健康发展的法律保障

《中华人民共和国网络安全法》是我国于2016年11月7日颁布的法律，旨在维护国家网络安全，保护公民、法人和其他组织的合法权益，促进网络安全事业的发展。该法律明确了网络安全的基本要求和原则，包括网络主权、网络平等、法律遵守、安全保障等。它规定了网络运营者的责任和义务，要求网络运营者采取必要的技术措施和管理措施，保障网络的安全运行，并及时采取措施应对网络安全事件。

其还规定了网络安全的监管机制和责任分工，明确了相关政府部门的职责和权力，加强了对网络基础设施的保护和管理，加强了网络信息的安全保护，防止网络攻击、网络犯罪和网络数据泄露等问题。此外，网络安全法还涉及个人信息保护、网络安全检测和应急响应等方面的内容，要求网络运营者和个人用户保护个人信息的安全，并配合相关部门进行网络安全检测和应急响应工作。

《中华人民共和国网络安全法》的实施对于保护国家网络安全、维护社会稳定和促进经济发展具有重要意义。它为网络安全工作提供了法律依据和指导，推动了网络安全技术和管理的发展，维护了国家和人民的利益和安全。

作业：研读国家工业信息安全发展研究中心发布的《2022年工业信息安全态势报告》，撰写报告分享启发。

Task 17 Securing Industrial Control Systems in the Framework of Equal Assurance 2.0

Learning Objective

①Understand the basic requirements of network security level protection 2.0.
②Master the dimensions and measures to ensure the security of the Industrial Internet.

Suggested Hours

3 hours

Work Situations

The company is required to conduct a level protection assessment of industrial interconnection networks in compliance with national network security laws and regulations. You are now tasked with understanding the requirements related to Equal Protection 2.0 and formulating the company's Industrial Internet security measures.

Knowledge Map

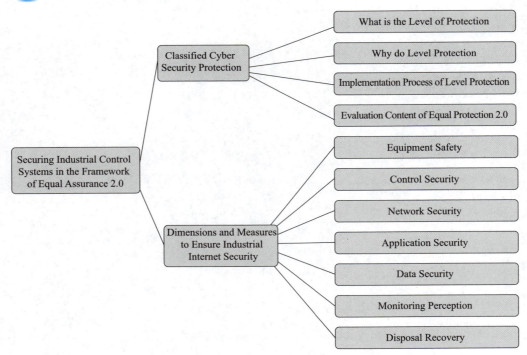

Project 6 Industrial Internet Security Practices

 Relevant Knowledge

1. Classified Cyber Security Protection

(1) What is the Level of Protection

Network security level protection is a fundamental system, strategy, and method for ensuring national information security. The work of network security level protection involves safeguarding information and its carriers according to their importance, in a tiered manner. Information system operators and users should select assessment organizations that meet national requirements to protect information and its carriers. They must adhere to the 'Basic Requirements for the Network Security Level Protection of Information Security Technology' and other relevant technical standards. Additionally, they should regularly conduct evaluation work on information systems.

(2) Why do Level Protection

1) Requirements of Laws and Regulations

The Network Security Law clearly stipulates that information system operators and users must fulfill their security protection obligations in accordance with the requirements of the network security level protection system, and those who refuse to do so will be punished accordingly.

Article 21 states that network operators shall, in accordance with the requirements of the network security level protection system, perform the following security protection obligations: to protect the network from interference, damage, or unauthorized access, and to prevent network data leakage, theft, or tampering.

Article 38 stipulates that operators of critical information infrastructure must, either on their own or by commissioning a network security service organization, conduct at least one test and assessment of their network's security and potential risks each year. They must also report the test and assessment results, along with improvement measures, to the relevant departments responsible for the security protection of critical information infrastructures.

Article 59 stipulates that if a network operator fails to fulfill its obligations, the relevant competent department shall order corrections and issue a warning. If the operator refuses to make corrections or if this failure leads to jeopardizing network security or other consequences, a fine of not less than 10,000 yuan but not more than 100,000 yuan will be imposed on the operator. Additionally, the person directly responsible for the matter, as well as the person in charge, will be fined not less than 5,000 yuan but not more than 50,000 yuan. If operators of critical information infrastructure do not fulfill their obligations, the relevant competent department shall order correction and issue a warning. Refusal to make corrections or actions that lead to jeopardizing network security or related consequences will result in a fine of more than 100,000 yuan but less than one million yuan for the operator, and a fine of more than 10,000 yuan but less than 100,000 yuan for the directly responsible person in charge.

2) Industry Requirements

In industries such as finance, electric power, broadcasting, television, healthcare, and education, the responsible authorities explicitly require organizations to implement level protection for their information systems.

3) Demand for Enterprise System Security

By conducting level protection work, operators and users of information systems can identify hidden security issues and deficiencies within the system. They can enhance the system's security protection capabilities through security rectification, thereby reducing the risk of attacks.

(3) Implementation Process of Level Protection

The network security level protection process encompasses five stages: grading, filing, construction and rectification, level assessment, supervision and inspection. Throughout the entire level protection process, four distinct roles are involved: operational units, public security organs, security certification bodies (SZSS), measurement and evaluation organizations. The workflow for each stage of graded protection is depicted in Figure 6.8.

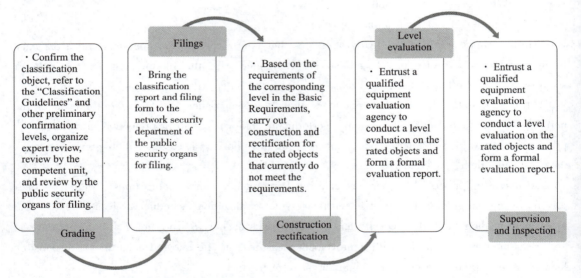

Figure 6.8　Implementation Process of Network Security Level Protection

(4) Evaluation Content of Equal Protection 2.0

Grade protection evaluation is divided into ten levels: security physical environment, security communication network, security area boundary, security computing environment, security management center, security management system, security management organization, security personnel management, security construction management, security operation and maintenance management, as depicted in Figure 6.9.

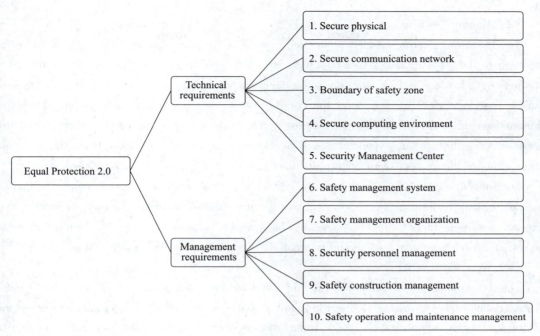

Figure 6.9 MLPS 2.0 Assessment

2. Dimensions and Measures to Ensure Industrial Internet Security

The focus in the process of implementing the Industrial Internet security framework is to take effective protective measures for the protected objects. To this end, this book introduces security measures for the five protection objects facing security threats in Industrial Internet security. It respectively introduces the security protection measures that can be taken and presents two types of Industrial Internet system protection measures: monitoring, perception, and disposal, providing enterprises with reference for deploying Industrial Internet security protection work.

(1) Equipment Safety

The development of the Industrial Internet has transformed field equipment from mechanization to high intelligence, producing a new model of embedded operating system + microprocessor + application software. This makes future masses of intelligent devices susceptible to network attacks, facing the extension of the scope of attacks, the increase in diffusion speed, and the extension of the impact of vulnerabilities and other threats.

Industrial Internet device security refers to the security of intelligent devices such as single-point intelligent devices and complete sets of intelligent terminals in the factory. Security protection measures should be deployed from two aspects: operating system/application software security and hardware security. The security mechanisms that can be adopted include firmware security enhancement, malware protection, device identification and access control, and vulnerability repair.

(2) Control Security

The Industrial Internet has led production control to gradually develop from layered, closed, and local to flat, open, and global direction. Among these changes, in the control environment, information technology (IT) and operation technology (OT) integrate, the control network transitions from closed to open, and the control layout extends from local to global. The above changes have altered the closed and trustworthy characteristics of traditional production control processes, resulting in an expanded scope of security incidents, increased harm degree, and interweaving of information security and functional safety issues.

For Industrial Internet control security protection, consideration is given mainly to control protocol security, control software security, and control function security. The security mechanisms that can be used include protocol security hardening, software security hardening, malware protection, patch upgrades, vulnerability repairs, security monitoring, and auditing.

(3) Network Security

The development of the Industrial Internet has made the internal network of the factory exhibit characteristics of being wireless, flexible, and globally connected. The external network of the factory shows gradual integration of the information network and the control network, enterprise private network, and the Internet, as well as increasing Internet products and services. Consequently, network security problems from the traditional Internet have begun to spread to the Industrial Internet.

Industrial Internet network security protection should focus on the internal network of the factory, the external network, and the identification analysis system. This includes network structure optimization, border security protection, access authentication, communication content protection, communication equipment protection, security monitoring, auditing, and other protective measures, to build a comprehensive and efficient network security protection system.

1) Optimize Network Structure Design

In the stage of network planning, it is necessary to design a reasonable network structure. On one hand, technologies such as dual-system hot backup and load balancing are employed on key network nodes and identity resolution nodes to address business continuity issues caused by sudden large data traffic and unexpected faults during peak hours, ensuring long-term stable and reliable network operation. On the other hand, a reasonable network structure and settings can enhance the flexibility and scalability of the network and prepare for subsequent network extension.

2) Network Boundary Security

According to the importance of network equipment and business systems in the Industrial Internet, the entire network is divided into different security domains to establish a defense system in depth. A security zone constitutes a logical division. Device assets within the same security zone share similar security attributes, such as security levels, threats, and vulnerabilities. Systems within the same security zone trust each other. A network boundary control device is deployed between security domains in a logical series mode to monitor security domain boundaries, identify intrusions, and effectively block them.

3) Network Access Authentication

Devices and ID resolution nodes accessing the network should possess unique IDs. The network must authenticate these devices and ID resolution nodes to ensure legitimate access and connection, while also blocking and raising alarms for the access behaviors of unauthorized devices and ID resolution nodes, thereby establishing a trusted network access mechanism. Network access authentication can be achieved through an identity authentication mechanism based on digital certificates.

4) Communication and Transmission Protection

Communication and transmission protection involve employing relevant technical measures to guarantee the confidentiality, integrity, and efficacy of the communication process. This prevents data theft or tampering during network transmission, ensuring legitimate users can effectively utilize information and resources. Simultaneously, when constructing the identity parsing system, it's essential to safeguard the data stored in parsing nodes and transmitted during the parsing process.

5) Network Device Security Protection

To enhance the security of network devices and identity resolution nodes and ensure their normal operation, a series of security protection measures should be implemented.

6) Safety Monitoring Audit

Network security monitoring involves detecting vulnerabilities in network devices and identification and analysis nodes using vulnerability scanning tools and providing timely warning information. Network security auditing entails analyzing network traffic and the identity resolution system through mirroring or proxy, recording system activities, user activities, and device operation information in the network and identity resolution system. This helps discover existing and potential security threats, analyze security events, and generate real-time alarms. Additionally, the system records incorrect and unauthorized operations by internal personnel, generating alarms promptly to mitigate security risks stemming from non-malicious operations.

(4) Application Security

Industrial Internet applications mainly comprise Industrial Internet platforms and industrial applications, encompassing intelligent production, network collaboration, personalized customization, service extension, and other aspects. Presently, Industrial Internet platforms primarily face security risks such as data leakage, tampering, loss, abnormal permission control, system vulnerability exploitation, account hijacking, and device access security. As for industrial applications, the primary risk stems from security vulnerabilities, including those within the software itself due to non-compliant coding with security specifications during development, as well as vulnerabilities arising from the utilization of insecure third-party libraries.

Consequently, Industrial Internet application security should be safeguarded from two angles: Industrial Internet platform security and industrial application security. For Industrial Internet platforms, security measures should include security audits, authentication and authorization mechanisms, and defense against DDoS attacks. Regarding industrial applications, it is recommended to implement full life cycle security protection, conduct code audits during application development, and provide training for developers to mitigate the introduction of vulnerabilities. Additionally, regular vulnerability assessments should be performed on operational applications, internal application processes audited and tested, and any identified vulnerabilities and backdoors patched promptly. Real-time monitoring of application behavior should also be employed to detect suspicious activities and block them, thus minimizing the impact of undisclosed vulnerabilities.

(5) Data Security

The data related to the Industrial Internet can be categorized into four types based on their attributes or characteristics: equipment data, business system data, knowledge base data, and user personal data. Depending on the sensitivity level, Industrial Internet data can be classified as general data, important data, and sensitive data. Industrial Internet data encompasses various stages, including collection, transmission, storage, and processing. As factory data transitions from small-scale, one-way transmission to large-scale, multidimensional, two-way communication, the volume, variety, and complexity of Industrial Internet data continue to increase. Additionally, there is bidirectional data flow and sharing between the factory and the external network, leading to security risks such as data leakage, unauthorized analysis, and the exposure of user personal information.

To protect the data security of the Industrial Internet comprehensively, various protective measures should be implemented across the entire data lifecycle, including collection, transmission, storage, and processing. These measures may include defining explicit purposes, employing data encryption, implementing access control, isolating services, conducting access authentication, and desensitizing data.

(6) Monitoring Perception

Monitoring and perception refers to the deployment of appropriate monitoring measures to proactively detect security risks from the system, including data collection, collection and aggregation, feature extraction, association analysis, and status awareness.

1) Data Collection

Data collection refers to the collection of all kinds of data in the industrial field network and Industrial Internet platform, for network anomaly analysis, equipment predictive maintenance, and other data sources.

2) Collect and Converge

The collection and aggregation of data is mainly divided into two aspects:

The first is the industrial control system such as SCADA, MES, and ERP. The key Industrial Internet data generated by the application system is aggregated, including the synchronization of various types of data throughout the product lifecycle, collection, management, storage, and query to provide data sources for subsequent processes.

The second is to monitor the whole network traffic and monitor it. The data collected during the listening process is aggregated.

3) Feature Extraction

Feature extraction refers to the processing of data features such as extraction, screening, classification, priority ordering, and readability. It realizes the transformation process from data to information, which mainly involves longitudinal data analysis for a single device or a single network. Information mainly includes content and scenario aspects. The content refers to the Industrial Internet equipment signal processing results, monitoring transmission features, performance curves, health status, alarm information, DNC and SCADA network traffic, etc. Scenario refers to equipment line operating conditions, maintenance records, personnel operation instructions, personnel visit status, production task objectives, industry sales machines, etc.

4) Association Analysis

Horizontal big data analysis and multi-dimensional analysis based on big data, through the operation mechanism, operation environment, organic combination of operation content, and external threat intelligence, using group experience to predict the security situation of a single device, or analyzing the difference between history and the current state according to the calendar, and then discovering the abnormal state of the network and system.

5) Status Awareness

State perception is based on the association analysis process to realize the network operation rules, abnormal situations, monitoring and perception of security objectives, security situation, business background, etc., determining security baseline, combined with big data analysis and other related technologies to detect potential security threats and predict hacker attacks.

(7) Disposal Recovery

The disposal and recovery mechanism aim to ensure the implementation of Industrial Internet information security management and support guarantees for the continuous operation of Industrial Internet systems and services. Through this mechanism, disaster recovery organizations can take timely measures based on plans when risks occur, respond effectively, and restore field equipment, industrial control systems, networks, Industrial Internet platforms, and industrial applications to normal operation. This helps prevent the loss of important data. Additionally, through the data collection and analysis mechanism, protective measures are updated and optimized in a timely manner, forming a closed loop of continuous improvement. The disposal and recovery mechanism mainly includes response decision-making, backup and recovery, analysis, and evaluation.

 Mission Expansion

Cybersecurity Law—Legal Guarantees for the Healthy Development of Cyberspace

The Cybersecurity Law of the People's Republic of China is a law enacted in China on November 7, 2016, aiming to maintain national cybersecurity, protect the legitimate rights and interests of citizens, legal persons, and other organizations, and promote the development of cybersecurity. The law specifies the basic requirements and principles of cybersecurity, including cyber sovereignty, cyber equality, legal compliance, security, etc. It stipulates the responsibilities and obligations of network operators, requiring them to take necessary technical and management measures to safeguard the safe operation of the network and respond to network security incidents promptly. It also stipulates the regulatory mechanism and division of responsibilities for network security, clarifying the duties and powers of relevant government departments and strengthening the protection and management of network infrastructure. Furthermore, it enhances the security protection of network information to prevent cyberattacks, cybercrimes, and network data leakage. Additionally, the cybersecurity law covers the protection of personal information, cybersecurity detection, and emergency response. It requires network operators and individual users to protect personal information and cooperate with relevant authorities in network security testing and emergency response. The implementation of the Cybersecurity Law of the People's Republic of China is of great significance in protecting national network security, maintaining social stability, and promoting economic development. It provides a legal basis and guidance for network security work, promotes the development of network security technology and management, and safeguards the interests and security of the state and the people.

Assignment: Study the "2022 Industrial Information Security Situation Report" issued by the National Industrial Information Security Development Research Center, write a report and share inspiration.

任务 18　部署防火墙保障网络安全

部署防火墙保障
网络安全

学习目标

①了解防火墙的功能和应用场景。
②掌握防火墙在工业互联网中的部署。

建议学时

4 课时

工作情境

当前，随着网络技术的不断发展，计算机网络为人们的生活带来了极大便利，也促进了工业互联网的发展和提速，然而，利用计算机网络进行的各种违法犯罪活动也在迅速增长，计算机犯罪、黑客、有害程序和后门等问题严重威胁着网络安全。作为工业互联网内部网络与外部公共网络之间的第一道屏障，防火墙是最先受到人们重视的网络安全产品之一。为了增强工业互联网的安全性，需要安装部署防火墙。

知识导图

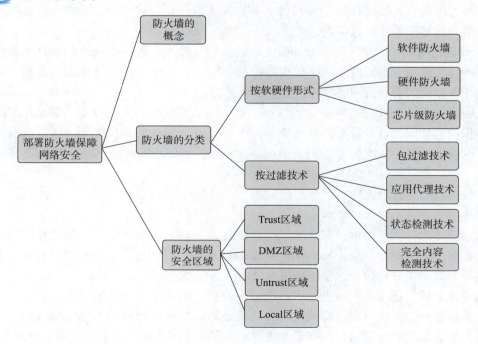

相关知识

1. 防火墙的概念

防火墙也称防护墙，它是一种位于内部网络与外部网络之间的网络安全系统，是一项信息安全的防护系统，依照特定的规则，允许或是限制传输的数据通过。

防火墙起源于建筑领域，原本是指房屋之间修建的一道墙，用以防止火灾发生时火势蔓延，阻止火势从一个区域蔓延到另一个区域。在网络中，防火墙是一种位于内部网络与外部网络之间的网络安全系统，可将内部网和外部网（如互联网）分开的方法，它实际上是一种隔离技术。防火墙是在两个网络通信时执行的一种访问控制尺度，它能允许你"同意"的人和数据进入你的网络，同时将你"不同意"的人和数据拒之门外，最大限度地阻止网络中的黑客来访问你的网络。同时，防火墙可依照特定的规则，允许或是限制传输的数据通过。与路由器相比，防火墙提供了更丰富的安全防御策略，提高了安全策略下数据报转发效率，由于防火墙用于边界安全，因此往往兼备 NAT、VPN 功能。

2. 防火墙的分类

①按软、硬件形式的不同，防火墙可分为软件防火墙、硬件防火墙、芯片级防火墙。

a. 软件防火墙：安装在操作系统上的软件，软件防火墙通过软件去实现隔离内部网与外部网之间的一种保护屏障。由于它安装在系统主机上，因此需要依赖计算机硬件资源来工作，需要消耗系统的内存和 CPU 资源。软件防火墙像其他软件产品一样需要在每台计算机上安装并做好配置才可以使用。

b. 硬件防火墙：本质上是把软件防火墙嵌入在硬件中，硬件防火墙的硬件和软件都需要单独设计，使用专用网络芯片来处理数据包，同时，采用专门的操作系统平台，从而避免通用操作系统的安全漏洞导致内网安全受到威胁。

c. 芯片级防火墙：芯片级防火墙以专用的硬件作为基础，不需要专门的操作系统的支持。专用的芯片因为自身特点，具有更快的工作速度，更高的处理能力，以及更有效率的性能。专有的 ASIC 芯片促使它们比其他种类的防火墙速度更快，处理能力更强，性能更高。

②按过滤技术区分，防火墙分为包过滤、应用级网关和代理服务器等几大类型。

a. 包过滤技术。

包过滤技术是一种简单、有效的安全控制技术，它工作在网络层，通过在网络间相互连接的设备上加载允许、禁止来自某些特定的源地址、目的地址、TCP 端口号等规则，对通过设备的数据包进行检查，限制数据包进出内部网络。

包过滤的最大优点是对用户透明，传输性能高。但由于安全控制层次在网络层、传输层，安全控制的力度也只限于源地址、目的地址和端口号，因而只能进行较为初步的安全控制，对于恶意的拥塞攻击、内存覆盖攻击或病毒等高层次的攻击手段，则无能为力。

b. 应用代理技术。

应用代理防火墙工作在 OSI 的第七层,它通过检查所有应用层的信息包,并将检查的内容信息放入决策过程,从而提高网络的安全性。

应用网关防火墙是通过打破客户机/服务器模式实现的。每个客户机/服务器通信需要两个连接:一个是从客户端到防火墙,另一个是从防火墙到服务器。另外,每个代理需要一个不同的应用进程或一个后台运行的服务程序,对每个新的应用必须添加针对此应用的服务程序,否则不能使用该服务。所以,应用网关防火墙具有可伸缩性差的缺点。

c. 状态检测技术。

状态检测防火墙工作在 OSI 的第二至四层,采用状态检测包过滤的技术,是传统包过滤功能扩展而来。状态检测防火墙在网络层有一个检查引擎截获数据包并抽取出与应用层状态有关的信息,并以此为依据决定对该连接是接受还是拒绝。这种技术提供了高度安全的解决方案,同时具有较好的适应性和扩展性。状态检测防火墙一般也包括一些代理级的服务,它们提供附加的对特定应用程序数据内容的支持。

状态检测防火墙基本保持了简单包过滤防火墙的优点,性能比较好,同时对应用是透明的,在此基础上,对于安全性有了大幅提升。这种防火墙摒弃了简单包过滤防火墙仅仅考查进出网络的数据包,不关心数据包状态的缺点,在防火墙的核心部分建立状态连接表,维护了连接,将进出网络的数据当成一个个的事件来处理。主要特点是由于缺乏对应用层协议的深度检测功能,无法彻底地识别数据包中大量的垃圾邮件、广告以及木马程序等。

d. 完全内容检测技术。

完全内容检测技术防火墙综合状态检测与应用代理技术,并在此基础上进一步基于多层检测架构,把防病毒、内容过滤、应用识别等功能整合到防火墙里,其中还包括 IPS 功能,多单元融为一体,在网络界面对应用层扫描,把防病毒、内容过滤与防火墙结合起来,这体现了网络与信息安全的新思路,(因此也被称为"下一代防火墙技术")。它在网络边界实施 OSI 第七层的内容扫描,实现了实时在网络边缘部署病毒防护、内容过滤等应用层服务措施。完全内容检测技术防火墙可以检查整个数据包内容,根据需要建立连接状态表,具有网络层保护强,应用层控制细等优点,但由于功能集成度高,对产品硬件的要求比较高。

3. 防火墙的安全区域

安全区域(Security Zone),简称为区域(Zone)。安全区域是一个或多个接口的集合,防火墙通过安全区域来划分网络,标识报文流动的"路线"。默认情况下,报文在同一个安全区域内流动时不受控制,报文在不同的安全区域之间流动时受到控制。

华为防火墙上默认提供了四个安全区域,分别是 Trust、DMZ、Untrust 和 Local,每个安全区域都有一个唯一的安全级别,用 1~100 的数字表示,数字越大,则代表该区域内的网络越可信,通过把防火墙的不同接口划分到不同的安全区域中,就可以在防火墙上划分出不同的安全区域网络。

①Trust 区域:Trust 区域的默认安全级别是 85,该区域内网络的受信任程度高,通常用来定义内部用户所在的网络。

②DMZ 区域：DMZ（Demilitarized Zone）区域的默认安全级别是 50，该区域内网络的受信任程度中等，通常用于定义内网服务器所在区域。因为这种设备虽然部署在内网，但是经常需要被外网访问，存在较大安全隐患，同时一般又不允许其主动访问外网，所以将其部署在一个优先级比 Trust 低，但是比 Untrust 高的安全区域中。DMZ 起源于军方，是介于严格的军事管制区和松散的公共区域之间的一种有着部分管制的区域。防火墙设备引用了这一术语，指的是介于内部网络和外部网络之间的安全区域。

③Untrust 区域：Untrust 区域的默认安全级别是 5，该区域代表的是不受信任的网络，通常用来定义 Internet 等不安全的网络。

④Local 区域：Local 区域的默认安全级别是 100，代表防火墙本身。Local 区域中不能添加任何接口，但防火墙上所有接口本身都隐含属于 Local 区域。

如图 6.10 所示为防火墙部署在企业内部的真实环境组网图。从图中我们可以看出，企业内部网络中的用户、服务器，以及位于外部的 Internet，都被划分到不同的安全区域中，防火墙对各个安全区域之间流动的报文进行安全检查。

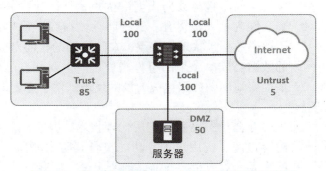

图 6.10　防火墙部署在企业内部的真实环境组网图

4. 课堂实践

某防火墙组网网络拓扑图如图 6.11 所示，以华为虚拟仿真软件 eNSP 为例，安装部署一台防火墙，实现工业互联网内网用户能访问互联网，外网用户能访问服务器区的 Web 服务，内网用户能访问服务器区的 ICMP、Web 服务。

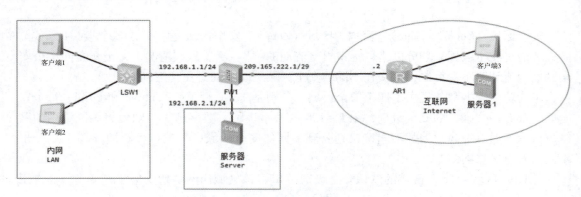

图 6.11　某防火墙组网网络拓扑图

步骤 1：初始化防火墙，允许管理员通过 Web 管理防火墙。

启动防火墙，通过配置线登录防火墙的 CLI 界面后，进行防火墙的初始化。首先输入默认用户名 admin，密码 Admin@123，登录防火墙。其次出现是否需要修改密码的提示，选择 y。最后输入旧密码 Admin@123，最后输入新密码，再重复输入一遍新密码，即可登录防火墙。新密码要求满足密码复杂性要求，即最低 8 位字符，包含大写字母、小写字母、数字、特殊字符的 3 种，如图 6.12 所示。

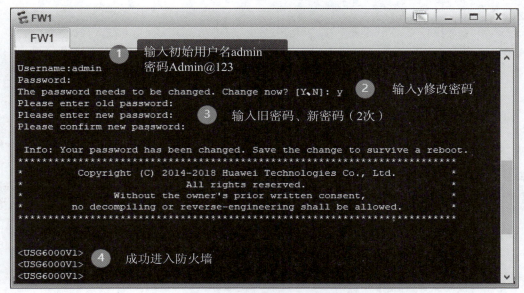

图 6.12　通过 CLI 登录防火墙后修改密码

进入防火墙的管理端口，修改管理端口的 IP 地址，允许使用 Web 方式管理防火墙。命令如下：

```
<USG6000V1>system-view
[USG6000V1]interface GigabitEthernet 0/0/0
[USG6000V1-GigabitEthernet0/0/0]ip address 192.168.100.100 24/* 修改防火墙的管理地址为192.168.100.100,具体的 IP 地址需要根据现场的管理 PC 确定*/
[USG6000V1-GigabitEthernet0/0/0]service-manage https permit/* 允许管理员使用Web方式管理防火墙*/
```

步骤 2：连接防火墙的 G0/0/0 口，打开浏览器，通过 Web 方式管理防火墙。

首先，在现场部署安装防火墙时，需要使用双绞线把管理 PC 和防火墙的 G0/0/0 口连接。

其次，为了在实验环境中学习的需要，我们给防火墙 eNSP 添加一朵云，然后修改云的参数配置，把云连接到防火墙 G0/0/0 口，使之能连接防火墙，如图 6.13、图 6.14 所示。

最后，在浏览器中输入 https://192.168.100.100：8443，使用 Web 方式登录防火墙，如图 6.15 所示。

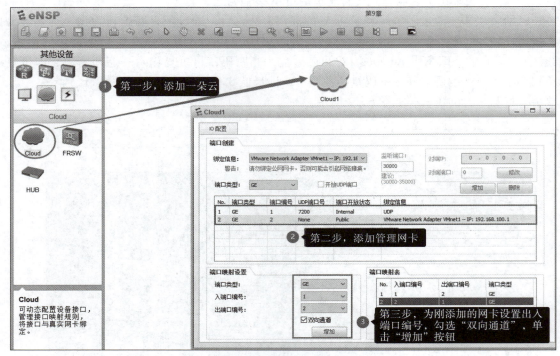

图 6.13　在 eNSP 中添加管理防火墙的网卡

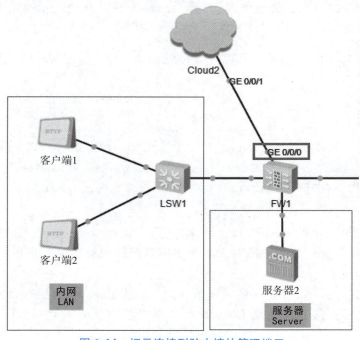

图 6.14　把云连接到防火墙的管理端口

项目6　工业互联网安全实践

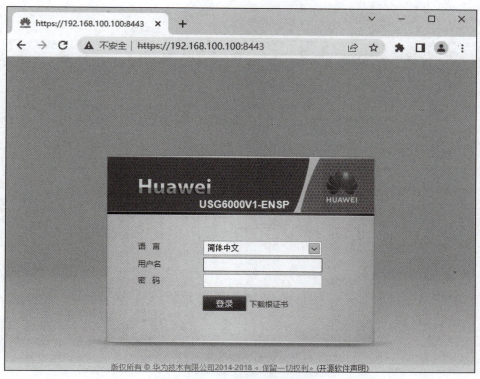

图 6.15　通过网页登录防火墙

步骤 3：配置防火墙各接口地址及所属的安全区域。

首先，配置防火墙外网口 IP 地址和安全区域。

详细步骤：输入用户名和密码登录防火墙后，单击"网络—接口—GE1/0/1"，选择外网口 GE1/0/1 归属的安全区域"untrust"，然后输入外网口 IP 地址和网关，单击"确定"按钮，如图 6.16 所示。

其次，配置防火墙内网口 IP 地址和安全区域。

步骤：输入用户名和密码登录防火墙后，单击"网络—接口—GE1/0/2"，选择内网口 GE1/0/2 归属的安全区域"trust"，然后输入内网口 IP 地址，单击"确定"按钮，如图 6.17 所示。

最后，配置防火墙 DMZ 口 IP 地址和安全区域。

步骤：单击"网络—接口—GE1/0/3"，选择 DMZ 口 GE1/0/3 归属的安全区域"dmz"，然后输入 dmz 口 IP 地址，单击"确定"按钮，如图 6.18 所示。

步骤 4：配置安全策略，满足数据流向要求。

首先，添加允许内网访问外网的安全策略。

详细步骤：单击"策略—安全策略—新建安全策略"，策略名称输入"允许内网访问外网"，源安全区域选择"trust"，目的安全区域选择"untrust"，动作选择"允许"，单击"确定"按钮，如图 6.19 所示。

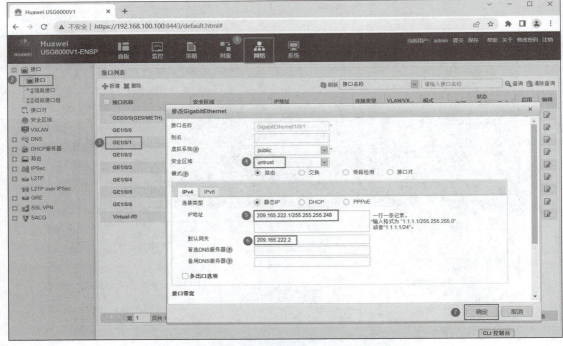

图 6.16　设置防火墙外网口 IP 地址及安全区域

图 6.17　设置防火墙内网口 IP 地址及安全区域

项目 6　工业互联网安全实践

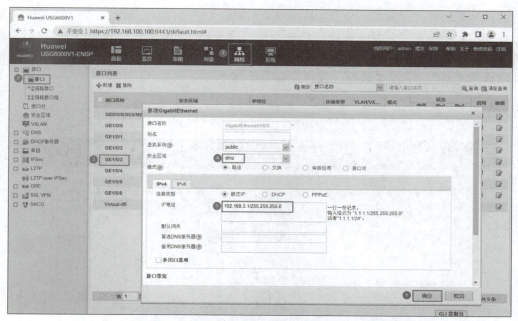

图 6.18　设置防火墙 DMZ 口 IP 地址及安全区域

图 6.19　添加允许内网访问外网的安全策略

其次，添加允许内网访问服务器区的安全策略。

详细步骤：单击"策略—安全策略—新建安全策略"，策略名称输入"允许内网访问服务器区"，源安全区域选择"trust"，目的安全区域选择"dmz"，服务选择"icmp"，http 动作选择"允许"，单击"确定"按钮，如图 6.20 所示。

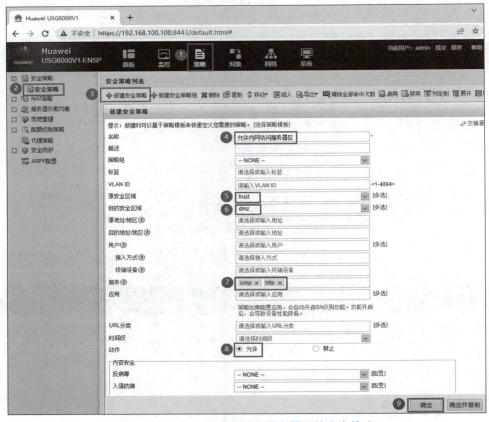

图 6.20　添加允许内网访问服务器区的安全策略

最后，添加允许外网访问服务器区的安全策略。

详细步骤：单击"策略—安全策略—新建安全策略"，策略名称输入"允许外网访问服务器区"，源安全区域选择"untrust"，目的安全区域选择"dmz"，服务选择"http"，动作选择"允许"，单击"确定"按钮，如图 6.21 所示。

步骤 5：配置 NAT，满足内网访问外网需求。

由于内网使用的都是私有 IP 地址，要访问外网，必须经过网络地址转换，把私有地址转换为公有地址才能访问互联网。

详细步骤：单击"策略—NAT 策略—新建"，名称输入"允许内网私有地址转换"，源安全区域选择"trust"，目的类型选择"目的安全区域"和"untrust"，转换后的数据包选择"出接口地址"，单击"确定"按钮，如图 6.22 所示。

步骤 6：配置服务器映射，满足外网用户访问服务器区 Web 服务需求。

由于服务器区的服务器使用的都是私有 IP 地址，外网用户要访问服务器区资源，必须

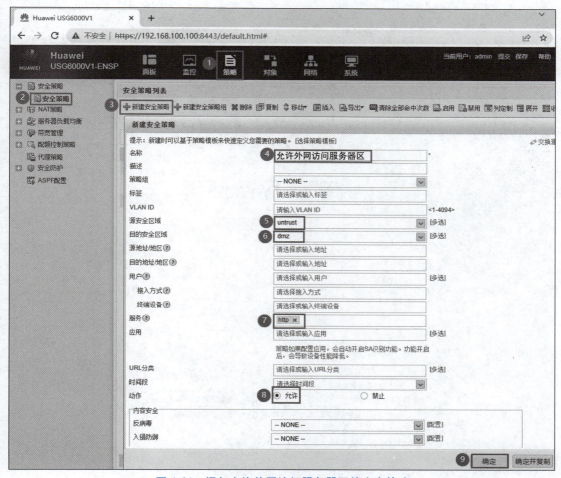

图 6.21　添加允许外网访问服务器区的安全策略

经过服务器地址映射，把私有地址映射为公有地址后，才能被访问。

详细步骤：单击"策略—NAT 策略—服务器映射—新建"，名称输入"允许外网用户访问 WEB 服务"，公网地址输入"209.165.222.10"，私网地址输入"192.168.3.2"，指定协议中，公网端口 80，私网端口 80，单击"确定"按钮，如图 6.23 所示。

步骤 7：给其他设备配置 IP 地址。

首先，配置互联网路由器 IP 地址（在虚拟仿真实验中为了测试方便需要配置，在实践工程项目中，互联网区域不需要进行配置）。

```
<Huawei>system-view
Enter system view,return user view with Ctrl+Z.
[Huawei]interface GigabitEthernet 0/0/0
[Huawei-GigabitEthernet0/0/0]ip address 209.165.222.2 24
[Huawei-GigabitEthernet0/0/0]quit
```

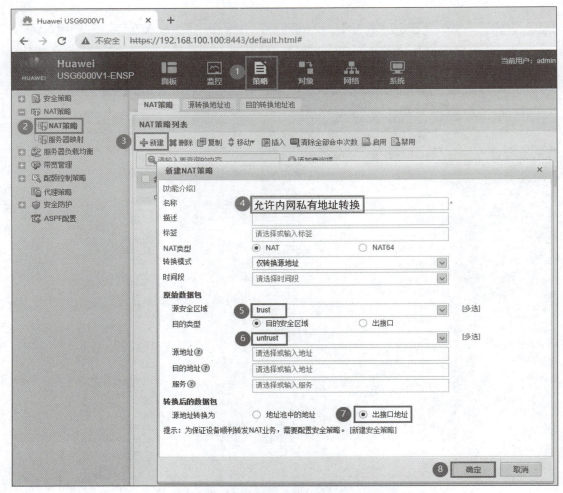

图 6.22　配置 NAT 满足内网访问外网需求

```
[Huawei]interface GigabitEthernet 0/0/1
[Huawei-GigabitEthernet0/0/1]ip address 8.8.8.1 24
[Huawei-GigabitEthernet0/0/1]quit
[Huawei]interface GigabitEthernet 0/0/2
[Huawei-GigabitEthernet0/0/2]ip address 9.9.9.2 24
[Huawei-GigabitEthernet0/0/2]quit
```

其次，终端设备配置 IP 地址。

步骤：双击终端设备，输入 IP 地址、子网掩码、网关等参数，单击"保存"按钮，如图 6.24 所示。

最后，启动服务器区 Web 服务。

详细步骤：双击服务器设备—单击"服务器信息"选项卡—单击"HttpServer"—选择文件根目录（建议在文件根目录中创建一个 aa.txt 文本文件，便于测试），单击"启动"按钮，如图 6.25 所示。

项目 6　工业互联网安全实践

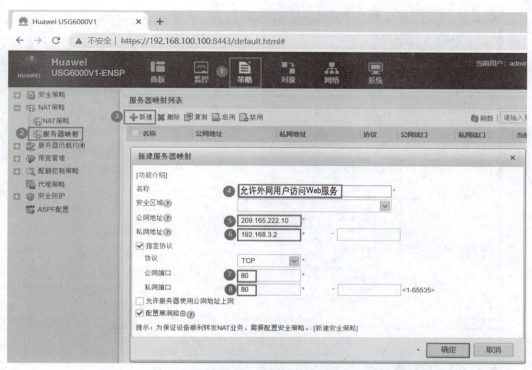

图 6.23　配置服务器映射满足外网用户访问服务器区 Web 服务需求

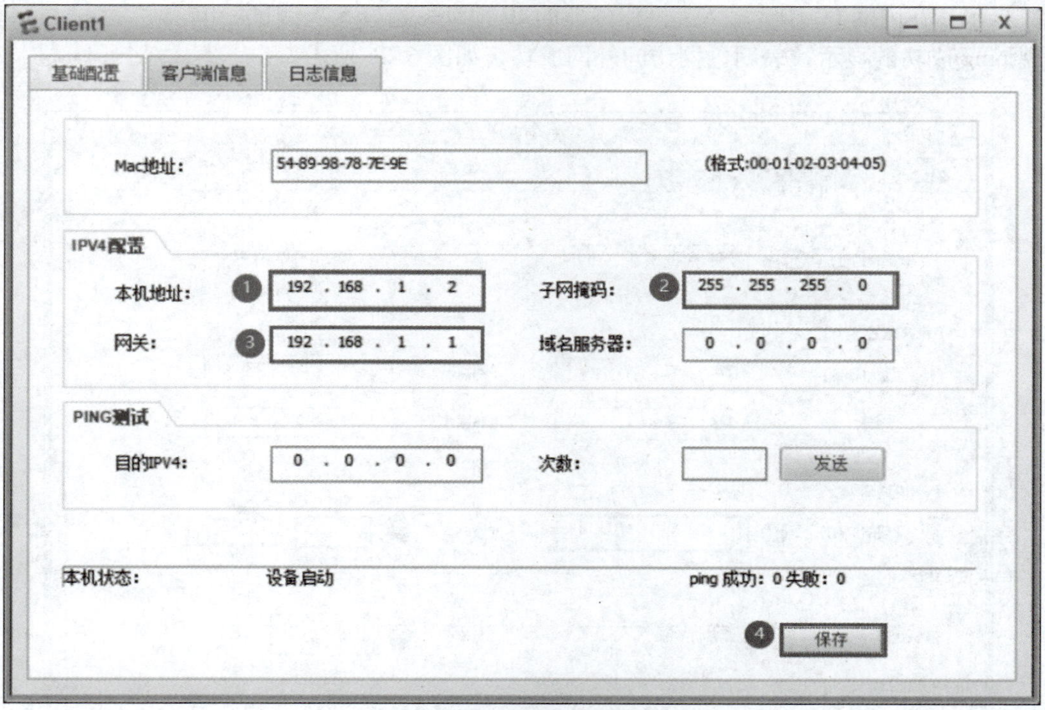

图 6.24　终端设备配置 IP 地址

325

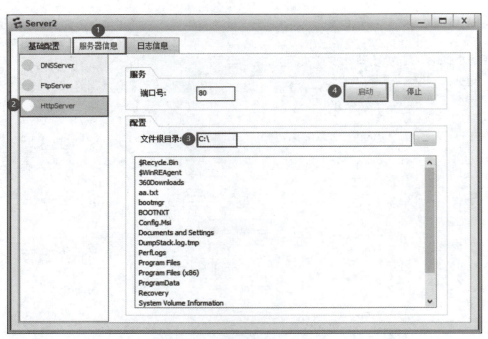

图 6.25 启动服务器区 Web 服务

步骤 8：测试网络连通性。

首先，内网访问外网测试。

步骤：在内网 PC 中，输入外网服务器的 IP 地址—选择 5 次测试—单击"发送"按钮—出现 ping 成功的显示，表明内网访问外网成功，如图 6.26 所示。

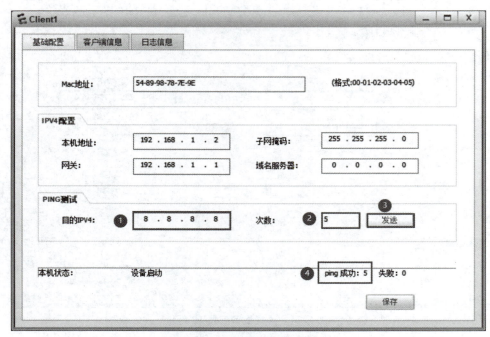

图 6.26 内网访问外网测试

其次，进行内网访问服务器区服务器测试。

步骤1：在内网 PC 中，输入服务器的 IP 地址—选择 5 次测试—单击"发送"按钮—出现 ping 成功的显示，表明内网访问服务器区 ICMP 服务成功，如图 6.27 所示。

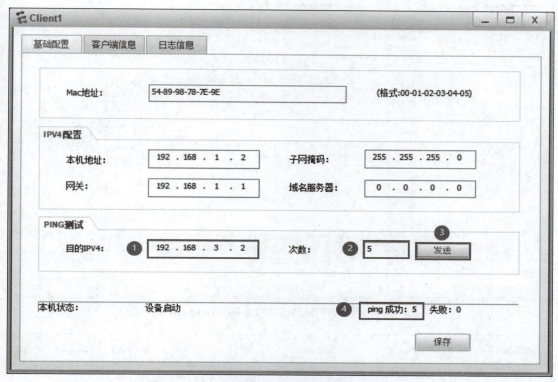

图 6.27　内网访问服务器区服务器 ICMP 服务测试

步骤2：在内网 PC 中，选择"客户端信息"选项卡—选择"HttpClient"—输入访问的地址"http://192.168.3.2/aa.txt"—单击"获取"按钮—出现访问成功的显示，表明内网访问服务器区 Web 服务成功，如图 6.28 所示。

最后，外网用户访问服务器区 Web 服务测试。

步骤1：在外网 PC 中，选择"客户端信息"选项卡—选择"HttpClient"—输入访问的地址"http://209.165.222.10/aa.txt"—单击"获取"按钮—出现访问成功的显示，表明内网访问服务器区 Web 服务成功，如图 6.29 所示。

步骤2：保存防火墙配置。

详细步骤：在防火墙的右上角，单击"保存"按钮—单击"确定"按钮，保存防火墙的配置信息，如图 6.30 所示。

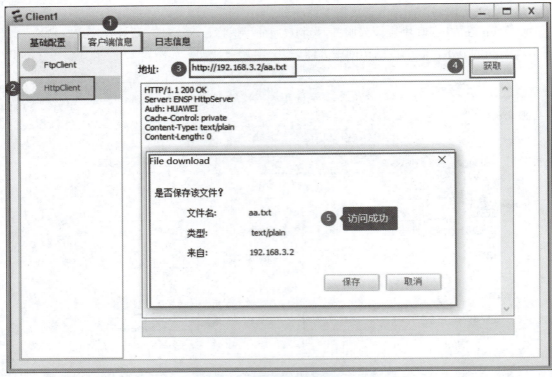

图 6.28　内网访问服务器区服务器 Web 服务测试

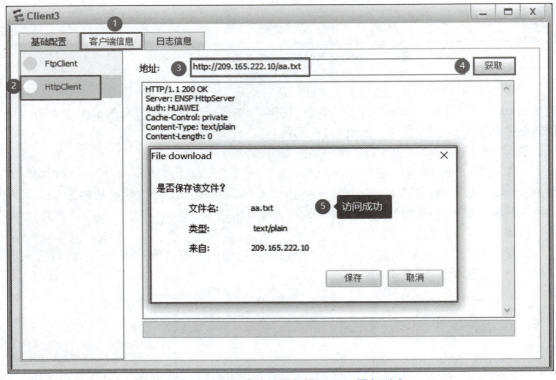

图 6.29　外网用户访问服务器区 Web 服务测试

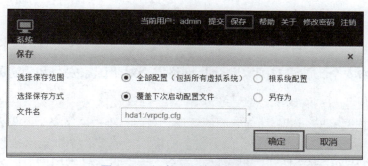

图 6.30　保存防火墙的配置信息

任务拓展

【没有网络安全，就没有国家安全】网络安全对于国家安全和稳定的重要性

"没有网络安全就没有国家安全，就没有经济社会稳定运行，广大人民群众利益也难以得到保障。"维护网络安全是全社会共同的责任。当前，维护网络安全不仅仅是防范网络病毒，它已涉及经济安全、社会安全、国家安全的层面，因此，全社会必须以高度的责任感和历史使命感构筑网络安全防线，捍卫网络安全。大学生在日常用网时，要提高自身的责任感，安全使用网络，时刻注意规范自身的网络行为。

作业：在工业互联网网络安全加固防范中，请收集国产信创安全设备都有哪些，这些设备分别是哪些国内品牌企业生产的，在网络安全中，起着什么样的角色？

Task 18 Deploy a Firewall to Secure Your Network

Learning Objective

①Master firewall features and application scenarios.
②Master firewall deployment in the Industrial Internet.

Suggested Hours

2 hours

Work Situations

Currently, with the advancement of network technology, computer networks have greatly facilitated people's lives. Network technology has played a significant role in the development of the Industrial Internet. However, various illegal and criminal activities exploiting computer networks are also proliferating rapidly. Examples include computer crimes, hacking, harmful programs, and backdoors, which pose serious threats to network security. Firewalls serve as the primary barrier between the internal network and the external public network of the Industrial Internet. They are among the earliest network security products to receive attention. To bolster the security of the Industrial Internet, it is essential to install and deploy firewalls.

⦿ Knowledge Map

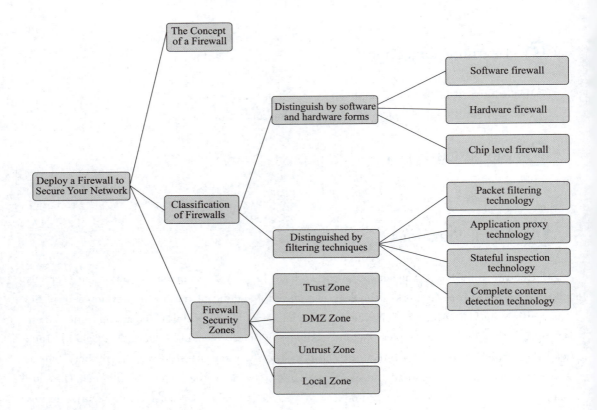

⦿ Relevant Knowledge

1. The Concept of a Firewall

Firewall also known as a protective wall, is a network security system situated between an internal network and an external network. It serves as an information security protection system, allowing or restricting the passage of transmitted data based on specific rules.

Originated from the construction field, firewalls were initially referred to as walls built between houses to prevent the spread of fire in case of a fire outbreak, thereby containing it within a designated area. In networking, a firewall functions similarly by separating the internal network from the external network, serving as an isolation technique. A firewall acts as an access control measure enforced when two networks communicate. It permits the entry of people and data that are authorized while blocking unauthorized access attempts. By doing so, it maximizes the prevention of hackers from infiltrating the network.

Firewalls facilitate the passage or restriction of transmitted data in accordance with predefined rules. Compared to routers, firewalls offer more comprehensive security defense policies, enhancing datagram forwarding efficiency under security policies. Additionally, firewalls include NAT (Network Address Translation) and VPN (Virtual Private Network) functionalities, further bolstering network security.

2. Classification of Firewalls

①According to the different forms of software and hardware, firewalls can be categorized into software firewalls, hardware firewalls, and chip-level firewalls.

a. A software firewall is installed as software on the operating system. It acts as a protective barrier that separates the intranet from the extranet through software means. Since it operates on the system host, it relies on the computer's hardware resources to function. This may result in the consumption of system memory and CPU resources. Like other software products, software firewalls need to be installed and configured on each computer before they can be utilized.

b. A hardware firewall is essentially a software firewall integrated into hardware. Hardware firewalls necessitate separate designs for both hardware and software components. They utilize specialized network chips to process packets and operate on a specialized operating system platform. As a result, they circumvent the security vulnerabilities present in general-purpose operating systems, thereby mitigating potential threats to intranet security.

c. A chip-level firewall is a firewall built on dedicated hardware. It operates independently of a specialized operating system and utilizes proprietary chips with faster operating speeds, higher processing power, and more efficient performance. These proprietary ASIC (Application-Specific Integrated Circuit) chips enable chip-level firewalls to outperform other types of firewalls in terms of speed, processing power, and performance.

②Distinguished by filtering technology, firewalls are divided into several major types, such as packet filtering, application-level gateways, and proxy servers.

a. Packet filtering technology.

Packet filtering technology operates at the network layer and is a straightforward and effective security control method. Rules are configured on devices interconnected between networks to allow or prohibit packets based on specific source address, destination address, and TCP port number. It inspects packets passing through the devices and restricts packets from entering and leaving the internal network.

The primary advantage of packet filtering is its transparency to users and high transmission performance. It provides security control at the network and transport layers, limiting security control to source address, destination address, and port number. However, it lacks defense against advanced attacks such as malicious congestion attacks, memory overwrite attacks, or viruses.

b. Application proxy technology.

Application proxy firewall operates at the seventh layer of the OSI model and inspects all application layer packets. It enhances network security by incorporating information about packet contents into the decision-making process. However, it breaks the client-server model, requiring two connections for each client-server communication—one from the client to the firewall and the other from the firewall to the server. This approach may result in poor scalability due to the need for additional application processes or services running in the background.

c. Stateful inspection technology.

Stateful inspection firewalls operate at layers two to four of the OSI model and utilize stateful inspection packet filtering. They intercept packets and extract information about the application layer's state, which is used to determine whether to accept or reject connections. This technology offers a highly secure solution, adaptability, and scalability. While maintaining the benefits of simple packet filtering firewalls, stateful inspection firewalls improve security and performance by maintaining a stateful connection table. However, they may lack deep inspection capabilities for application layer protocols, limiting their ability to identify spam, advertisements, Trojan horses, etc, in packets.

d. Complete content detection technology.

The Complete content detection technology firewall integrates stateful detection with application proxy technology and incorporates anti-virus, content filtering, application identification, and IPS functions into one unit. By scanning the application layer at the network interface, it offers comprehensive network and information security. This next-generation firewall technology performs OSI Layer 7 content scanning at the network edge in real-time, providing strong network layer protection and fine application layer control. However, due to its high level of functional integration, it may require relatively high hardware specifications.

3. Firewall Security Zones

A security zone is essentially a designated area within a network. It consists of one or more interfaces and is utilized by firewalls to segment the network and regulate the flow of messages. By default, messages exchanged within the same security zone are unrestricted, whereas those traversing between different security zones are subject to control.

By default, Huawei Firewall provides four security zones: Trust, DMZ, Untrust, and Local. Each of these zones is assigned a unique security level, denoted by a numerical value ranging from 1 to 100. A higher security level indicates a higher degree of trustworthiness within the network zone. Segmenting the firewall's interfaces into distinct security zones enables the segregation of various network segments, thereby enhancing network security.

①Trust zone: The default security level of the Trust zone is 85, indicating a high level of trust. This zone typically encompasses the network where internal users reside.

②DMZ zone: The default security level of the DMZ zone is 50, representing a moderate degree of trust. It is commonly used to host intranet servers. While deployed within the intranet, these servers often require external network access, posing a security risk. To mitigate this risk,

DMZ devices are placed in a security zone with a lower priority than Trust but higher than Untrust. The concept of DMZ originated in the military as a partially regulated zone between a strictly regulated military zone and a loosely regulated public zone, hence the term used by firewall devices to refer to the security zone between internal and external networks.

③Untrust zone: The default security level for the Untrust zone is 5, indicating an untrusted network such as the Internet.

④Local zone: The default security level of the Local zone is 100, representing the firewall itself. Interfaces cannot be added to the Local zone, as all firewall interfaces inherently belong to it.

In a real-world deployment as depicted in Figure 6.10, users, servers, and the Internet are segregated into different security zones within an enterprise network. The firewall conducts security inspections on messages traversing between these security zones.

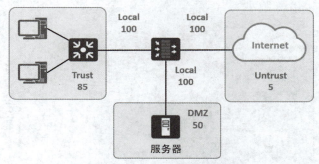

Figure 6.10 Firewall Networking Topology

4. Classroom Practice

A network structure is depicted in Figure 6.11. Take Huawei virtual simulation software eNSP as an example, it installs and deploys a firewall. It implements Industrial Internet intranet users can access the Internet. Extranet users can access Web services in the server area. Intranet users can access ICMP and Web services in the server area.

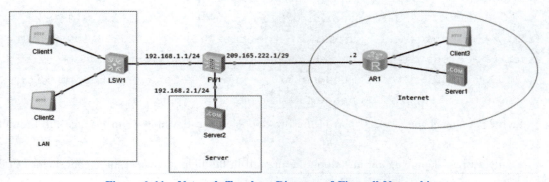

Figure 6.11 Network Topology Diagram of Firewall Networking

Step 1: Initialise the firewall and allow administrators to manage the firewall via Web.

Start the firewall and initialise it after logging into the firewall's CLI interface via the configuration line. First, enter the default user name "admin" and password "Admin@123" to log in the firewall. Then you will be prompted to change the password, selecty. Finally, enter the old password Admin@123, and then enter the new password. Repeat the new password again to log in to the firewall. The new password is required to meet the password complexity requirements. That is, a minimum of 8 characters, containing 3 types of upper case letters, lower case letters, numbers, and special characters. As depicted in Figure 6.12.

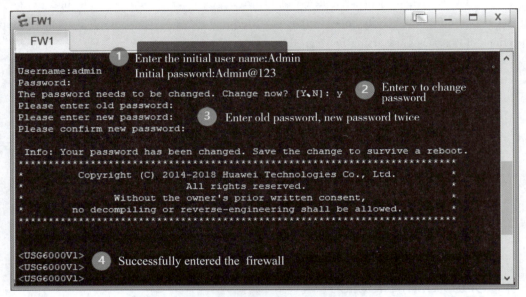

Figure 6.12　Modifying the Password After Logging In to the Firewall Through CLI

Enter the management port of the firewall and update the IP address of the management port to enable firewall management via the Web method using the following commands:

```
<USG6000V1>system-view
[USG6000V1]interface GigabitEthernet 0/0/0
[USG6000V1-GigabitEthernet0/0/0]ip address 192.168.100.100 24/*
Modify the management address of the firewall to 192.168.100.100. The exact IP address needs to be determined by the management PC at the site*/
[USG6000V1-GigabitEthernet0/0/0]service-manage https permit/*
Allow administrators to manage the firewall using Web*/
```

Step 2: Connect the G0/0/0 port of the firewall. We open the browser to manage the firewall via Web.

Firstly, when deploying and installing the firewall in the field, connect the management PC to the G0/0/0 port of the firewall using a twisted pair cable.

Secondly, for experimental purposes in the eNSP environment, add a cloud to the firewall eNSP and modify the parameter configuration of the cloud. Connect the cloud to the firewall's G0/0/0 port to establish connectivity with the firewall, as depicted in Figures 6.13 and 6.14.

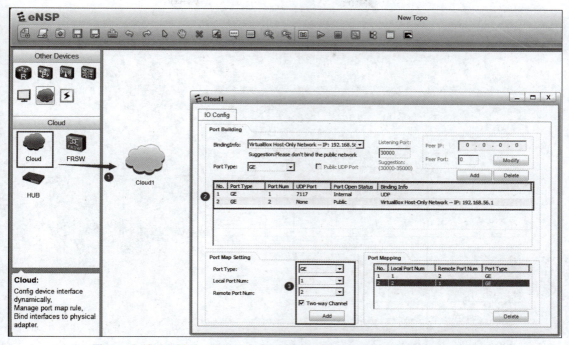

Figure 6.13 Add the Network Card of the Management Firewall in eNSP

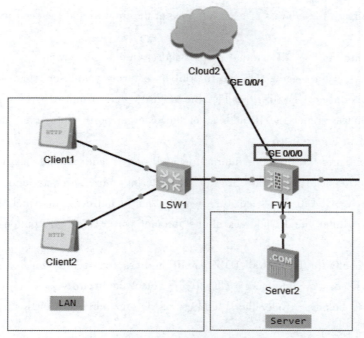

Figure 6.14 Management Port for Connecting Cloud to Firewall

Finally, we type https://192.168.100.100:8443 into our browser. Use the Web method to log into the firewall, as depicted in Figure 6.15.

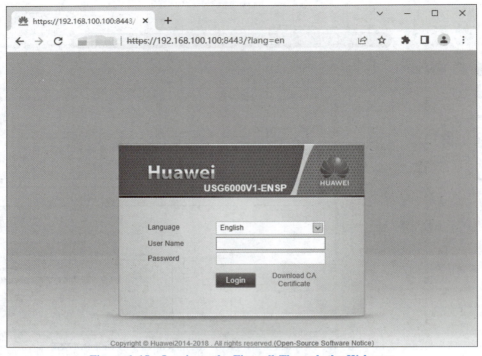

Figure 6.15　Log in to the Firewall Through the Webpage

Step 3: Configure the address of each interface of the firewall and the security zone to which it belongs.

First, configure the firewall external port IP address and security zone.

Detailed steps: After logging into the firewall by entering your user name and password. We click Network—Interface—GE1/0/1—Select the security zone (untrust) to which the external port GE1/0/1 belongs—Enter the IP address of the external port—Enter the gateway—Click OK button as depicted in Figure 6.16.

Then, we configure the firewall's internal network port IP address and security zone.

Steps: After we log in to the firewall by entering our username and password, click Network—Interfaces—GE1/0/2—Select the security zone (untrust) to which the intranet port GE1/0/2 belongs—Enter the IP address of the intranet port—Click OK button, as depicted in Figure 6.17.

Finally, we configure the firewall DMZ port IP address and security zone.

Steps: Click Network—Interfaces—GE1/0/3—Select the security zone (dmz) to which the DMZ port GE1/0/3 belongs—Enter the IP address of the dmz port—Click OK button, as depicted in Figure 6.18.

Step 4: We configure the security policy to meet the data flow requirements.

Project 6 Industrial Internet Security Practices

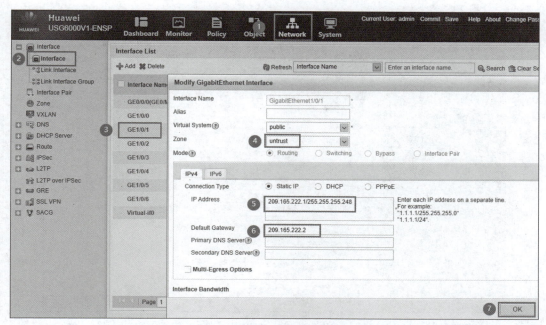

Figure 6.16 Setting the IP Address and Security Area of the External Network Port of the Firewall

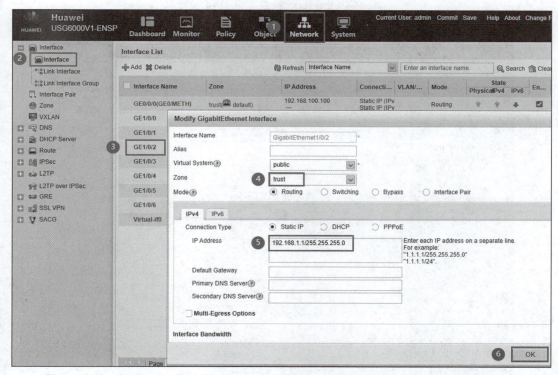

Figure 6.17 Setting the IP Address and Security Area of the Network Port in the Firewall

First, we add a security policy that allows intranet access to the extranet.

Detailed steps: Click Policy—Security Policy—Add Security Policy—Enter Policy Name: Allow LAN access to WAN—Source Zone Selection: trust—Destination Zone Selection: untrust—

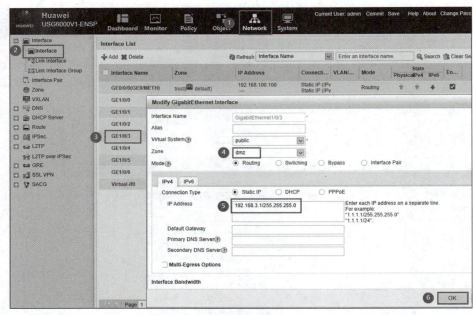

Figure 6.18 Setting the IP Address and Security Area of the Firewall DMZ Port

Action Selection：Permit—Click OK button，as depicted in Figure 6.19.

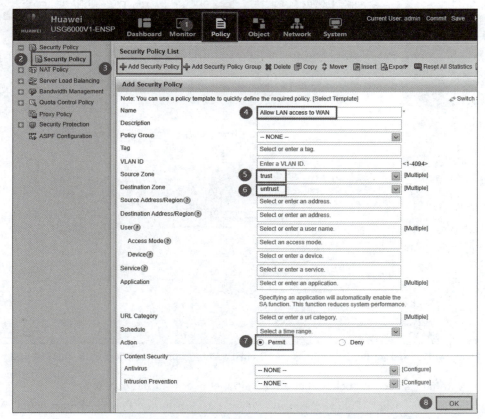

Figure 6.19 Add a Security Policy That Allows Intranet Access to the Extranet

Next, we add the security policy that allows intranet access to the server zone. Detailed steps: Click Policy—Security Policy—Add Security Policy—Enter Policy Name: Allow LAN access to DMZ—Source Zone Selection: trust—Destination Zone Selection: dmz—Service Selection: http, icmp—Action Selection: Permit—Click OK button, as depicted in Figure 6.20.

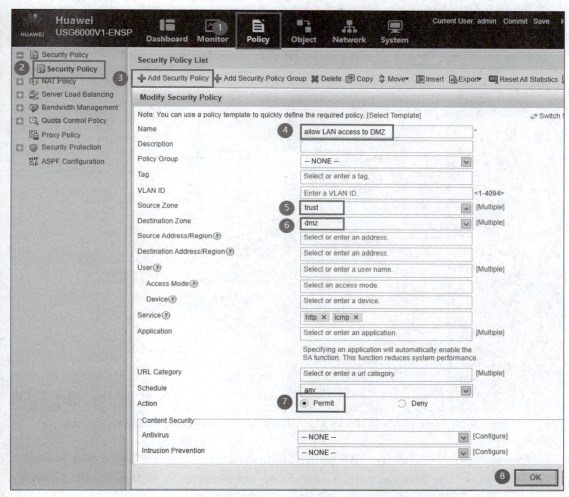

Figure 6.20 Add a Security Policy That Allows Intranet Access to the Server Area

Finally, we add the security policy that allows external access to the server zone.

Detailed steps: Click Policy—Security Policy—Add Security Policy—Enter Policy Name: Allow WAN access to DMZ—Source Zone Selection: untrust—Destination Zone Selection: dmz—Service Selection: http—Action Selection: Permit—Click OK button, as depicted in Figure 6.21.

Step 5: We configure NAT for internal network access to external network requirements.

Since the intranet employs private IP addresses, accessing the extranet necessitates network address translation (NAT). We must convert the private address to a public address to enable internet access.

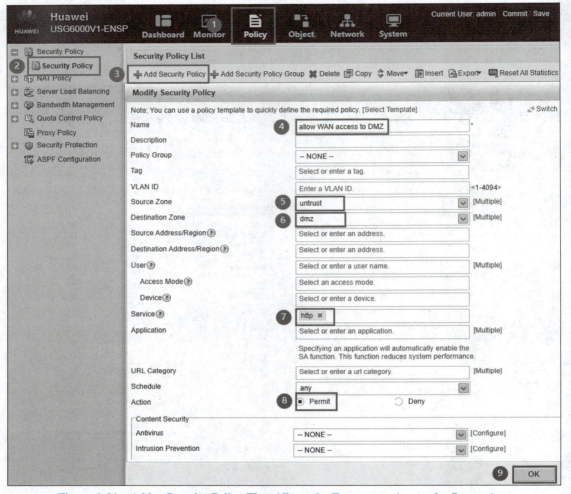

Figure 6.21   Add a Security Policy That Allows the Extranet to Access the Server Area

Detailed steps: Click Policy—NAT Policy—Add—Name input: NAT—Source Zone Selection: trust—Destination Type Selection: Destination Zone, untrust—Translated Data Packet Selection: Outbound interface—Click OK button, as depicted in Figure 6.22.

Step 6: We configure the server mapping to meet the needs of users from outside the network to access the server area Web services.

This is because the servers in the server zone use private IP addresses. To access the resources in the server zone, users from outside the network must go through server address mapping. That is, private addresses are mapped to public addresses before they can be accessed.

Detailed steps: Click Policy—NAT Policy—Server Mapping—Add—Name input: WEB—Public IP Address input: 209.165.222.10—Private IP Address input: 192.168.3.2—Check Specify protocol, the Public Port 80, the Private Port 80—Click OK button, as depicted in Figure 6.23.

Project 6 Industrial Internet Security Practices

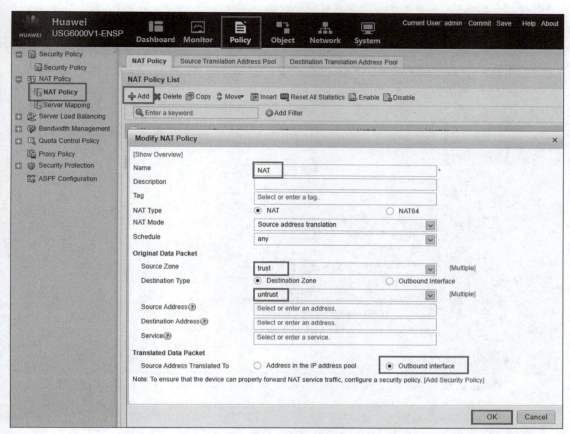

Figure 6.22 Configuring NAT to Meet the Requirements of Intranet Access to the Extranet

Step 7: We configure IP addresses for the other devices.

First, we configure the Internet router IP address. It needs to be configured for testing convenience in virtual simulation experiments. However, in the practical engineering project, the Internet area does not need to be configured.

```
<Huawei>system-view
Enter system view,return user view with Ctrl+Z.
[Huawei]interface GigabitEthernet 0/0/0
[Huawei-GigabitEthernet0/0/0]ip address 209.165.222.2 24
[Huawei-GigabitEthernet0/0/0]quit
[Huawei]interface GigabitEthernet 0/0/1
[Huawei-GigabitEthernet0/0/1]ip address 8.8.8.1 24
[Huawei-GigabitEthernet0/0/1]quit
[Huawei]interface GigabitEthernet 0/0/2
[Huawei-GigabitEthernet0/0/2]ip address 9.9.9.2 24
[Huawei-GigabitEthernet0/0/2]quit
```

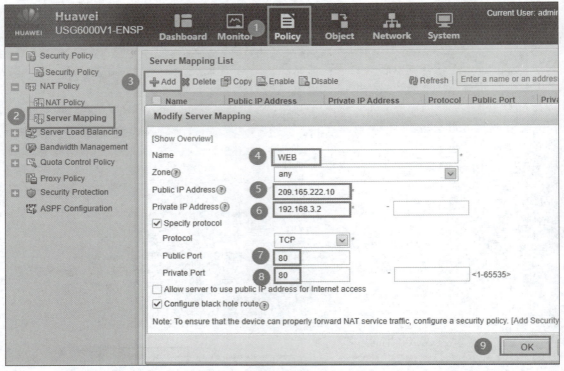

Figure 6.23 Configure the Server Mapping to Meet the Needs of Extranet Users to Access the Web Services in the Server Area

Next, the end device is configured with an IP address.

Detailed steps: Double click the terminal device—Enter IP address, Subnet Mask, Gateway and other parameters. Click the Save button, as depicted in Figure 6.24.

Finally, we start the server zone Web service.

Detailed steps: Double-click the server device—Click Server Info—Click HttpServer—Select the root directory of the file (it is recommended to create an aa.txt text file in the root directory of the file to facilitate the test) —Click Start button, as depicted in Figure 6.25.

Step 8: We test network connectivity.

First, the intranet access to the extranet test.

Detailed steps: In our intranet PC, we enter the IP address of the extranet server—select 5 test times—Click Send button—the display of ping success appears. This indicates that the intranet access to the extranet is successful, as depicted in Figure 6.26.

Next, we conduct an intranet access to the server zone server test.

Step 1: In the intranet PC, enter the IP address of the server—select 5 test times—Click Send button—the display of ping success appears, indicating that the intranet access to the server zone ICMP service is successful. As depicted in Figure 6.27.

Project 6 Industrial Internet Security Practices

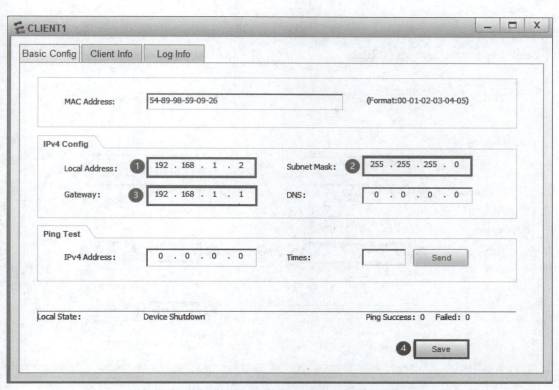

Figure 6.24 Configuring IP Address of Terminal Equipment

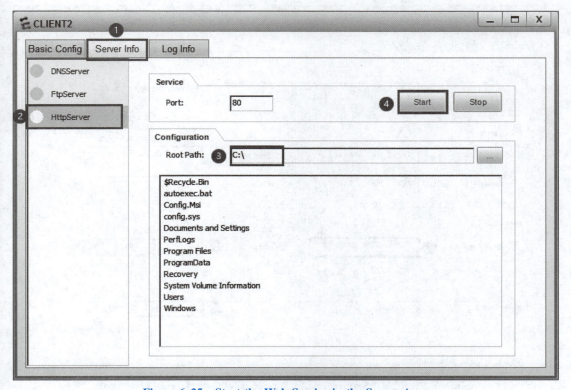

Figure 6.25 Start the Web Service in the Server Area

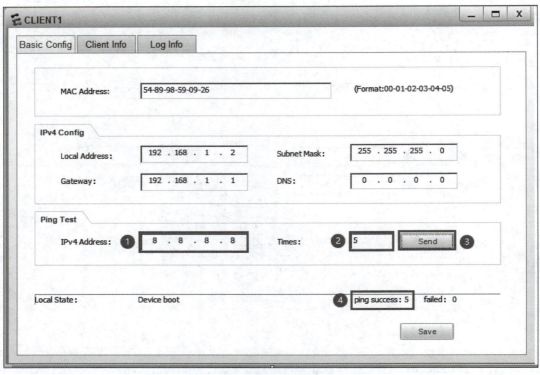

Figure 6.26　Test of Intranet Access to Internet

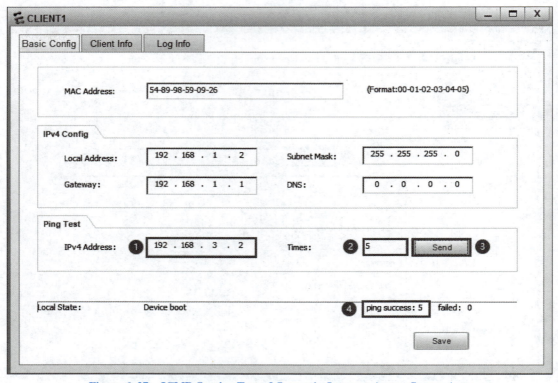

Figure 6.27　ICMP Service Test of Server in Intranet Access Server Area

Step 2: In the intranet PC, select Client Info—Select HttpClient—Enter the address of the access: http://192.168.3.2/aa.txt—Click Go button—The display of access success appears, indicating that the intranet accesses the server zone WEB service successfully. As depicted in Figure 6.28.

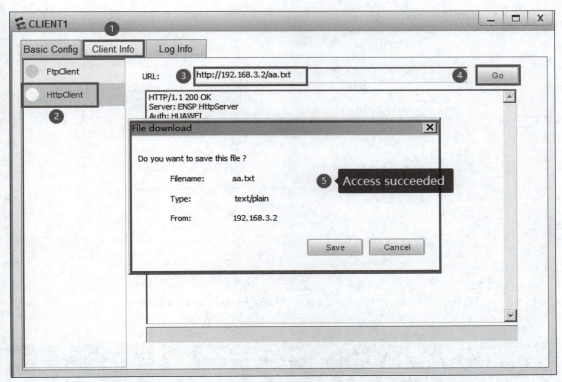

Figure 6.28 Web Service Test of Server Area Server for Intranet Access

Finally, the WEB service is tested by an external user accessing the server area.

Steps 1: In the extranet PC, select Client Info—select HttpClient—enter the address of the access: http://209.165.222.10/aa.txt—Click Go button—the display of access success appears, indicating that the intranet access to the server area Web service is successful. As depicted in Figure 6.29.

Step 2: Save the Firewall Configuration.

Detailed steps: In the upper right corner of the firewall, click Save button—Click OK button to save the firewall configuration information. As depicted in Figure 6.30.

工业互联网工程实践（双语版）

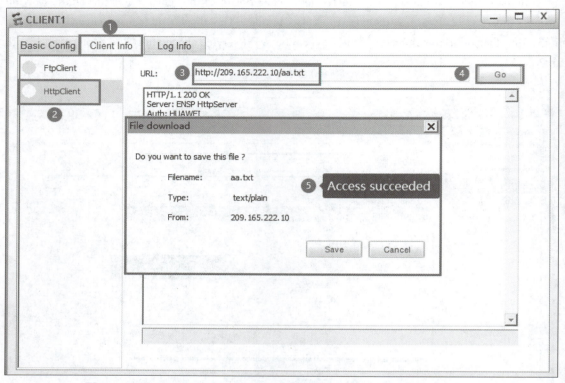

Figure 6.29　Test of Internet Users' Access to Web Services in Server Area

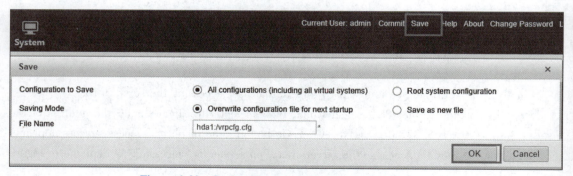

Figure 6.30　Saving Firewall Configuration Information

 **Mission Expansion**

[No Cybersecurity, No National Security] The Importance of Cybersecurity for National Security and Stability

"Without cybersecurity, there is no national security, stable economic and social operation, and the interests of the general public can hardly be safeguarded." Maintaining cybersecurity is the shared responsibility of society as a whole. Currently, cybersecurity maintenance encompasses more than just preventing cyber viruses; it also involves economic, social, and national security. Therefore, society as a whole must construct a network security defense line and protect network security with a strong sense of responsibility and historical mission. College students should utilize the Internet safely and regulate their online behavior in their daily internet usage.

Assignment: What are the security devices in the cybersecurity hardening and prevention of the Industrial Internet? What role do these play in cyber security?

参考文献
References

［1］张洁，吕佑龙，张朋，等．数据技术基础［M］．北京：清华大学出版社，2023．
［2］朱海平．数字化与智能化车间［M］．北京：清华大学出版社，2021．
［3］尹周平，陶波．工业物联网技术及应用［M］．北京：清华大学出版社，2022．
［4］张洁，吕佑龙，汪俊亮，等．智能车间的大数据应用［M］．北京：清华大学出版社，2020．
［5］陶飞，戚庆林，张萌，等．数字孪生及车间实践［M］．北京：清华大学出版社，2021．
［6］钟文基．网络工程实践［M］．北京：中国水利水电出版社，2022．
［7］Chun H, Shudan L. Securing the future of industrial operations: a blockchain-enhanced trust mechanism for digital twins in the Industrial Internet of Things［J］．International Journal of Computers and Applications，2024，46（5）．
［8］Feng P, Wei D, Li Q, et al. GlareShell: Graph learning-based PHP webshell detection for web server of Industrial Internet［J］．Computer Networks，2024，245．
［9］Kumar S, Kumar A. Image-based malware detection based on convolution neural network with autoencoder in Industrial Internet of Things using Software Defined Networking Honeypot［J］．Engineering Applications of Artificial Intelligence，2024，133（PD）．
［10］Hajlaoui R, Moulahi T, Zidi S, et al. Towards smarter cyberthreats detection model for Industrial Internet of things（IIoT）4.0［J］．Journal of Industrial Information Integration，2024，39．
［11］Bao Y, Zhang X, Wang C, et al. Further extension from smart manufacturing system （SMS）to social smart manufacturing system（SSMS）based on Industrial Internet［J］．Computers & Industrial Engineering，2024，191．
［12］Hakiri A, Gokhale A, Yahia B S, et al. A comprehensive survey on digital twin for future networks and emerging Internet of Things industry［J］．Computer Networks，2024，244．
［13］Santos E S D L, Filho R F C R P, Macêdo N E. Belt rotation in pipe conveyors: Development of an overlap monitoring system using digital twins, Industrial Internet of things, and autoregressive language models［J］．Measurement，2024，230．
［14］Feng J, Yan R, Han G, et al. BDPM: A secure batch dynamic password management scheme in Industrial Internet environments［J］．Future Generation Computer Systems，2024，157．